Advanced Digital, Modeling and Control Applies into Various Processes

Advanced Digital, Modeling and Control Applies into Various Processes

Editors

Rudolf Kawalla
Beloglazov Ilya

Basel • Beijing • Wuhan • Barcelona • Belgrade • Novi Sad • Cluj • Manchester

Rudolf Kawalla
Institute of Metal Forming
TU Bergakademie Freiberg
Freiberg
Germany

Beloglazov Ilya
Mineral Processing
St. Petersburg Mining University
St. Petersburg
Russia

Editorial Office
MDPI AG
Grosspeteranlage 5
4052 Basel, Switzerland

This is a reprint of the Special Issue, published open access by the journal *Symmetry* (ISSN 2073-8994), freely accessible at: www.mdpi.com/journal/symmetry/special_issues/Advanced_Digital_Modeling_Control_Various_Processes.

For citation purposes, cite each article independently as indicated on the article page online and using the guide below:

Lastname, A.A.; Lastname, B.B. Article Title. *Journal Name* **Year**, *Volume Number*, Page Range.

ISBN 978-3-7258-1426-8 (Hbk)
ISBN 978-3-7258-1425-1 (PDF)
https://doi.org/10.3390/books978-3-7258-1425-1

© 2024 by the authors. Articles in this book are Open Access and distributed under the Creative Commons Attribution (CC BY) license. The book as a whole is distributed by MDPI under the terms and conditions of the Creative Commons Attribution-NonCommercial-NoDerivs (CC BY-NC-ND) license (https://creativecommons.org/licenses/by-nc-nd/4.0/).

Contents

About the Editors vii

Preface ix

Ilia Beloglazov
Review of Advanced Digital Technologies, Modeling and Control Applied in Various Processes
Reprinted from: *Symmetry* **2024**, *16*, 536, doi:10.3390/sym16050536 1

Shamil Islamov, Alexey Grigoriev, Ilia Beloglazov, Sergey Savchenkov and Ove Tobias Gudmestad
Research Risk Factors in Monitoring Well Drilling—A Case Study Using Machine Learning Methods
Reprinted from: *Symmetry* **2021**, *13*, 1293, doi:10.3390/sym13071293 5

Aleksandr Kulchitskiy
Optical Inspection Systems for Axisymmetric Parts with Spatial 2D Resolution
Reprinted from: *Symmetry* **2021**, *13*, 1218, doi:10.3390/sym13071218 24

Aleksei Boikov, Roman Savelev, Vladimir Payor and Alexander Potapov
Universal Approach for DEM Parameters Calibration of Bulk Materials
Reprinted from: *Symmetry* **2021**, *13*, 1088, doi:10.3390/sym13061088 39

Aleksei Boikov, Vladimir Payor, Roman Savelev and Alexandr Kolesnikov
Synthetic Data Generation for Steel Defect Detection and Classification Using Deep Learning
Reprinted from: *Symmetry* **2021**, *13*, 1176, doi:10.3390/sym13071176 52

Sergei Kryltcov, Aleksei Makhovikov and Mariia Korobitcyna
Novel Approach to Collect and Process Power Quality Data in Medium-Voltage Distribution Grids
Reprinted from: *Symmetry* **2021**, *13*, 460, doi:10.3390/sym13030460 62

Natalia Koteleva and Ilya Tkachev
Virtual Soft Sensor of the Feedstock Composition of the Catalytic Reforming Unit
Reprinted from: *Symmetry* **2021**, *13*, 1233, doi:10.3390/sym13071233 80

Natalia Vasilyeva, Elmira Fedorova and Alexandr Kolesnikov
Big Data as a Tool for Building a Predictive Model of Mill Roll Wear
Reprinted from: *Symmetry* **2021**, *13*, 859, doi:10.3390/sym13050859 97

Anna Turysheva, Irina Voytyuk and Daniel Guerra
Estimation of Electricity Generation by an Electro-Technical Complex with Photoelectric Panels Using Statistical Methods
Reprinted from: *Symmetry* **2021**, *13*, 1278, doi:10.3390/sym13071278 108

Vladimir Bazhin and Olga Masko
Monitoring of the Behaviour and State of Nanoscale Particles in a Gas Cleaning System of an Ore-Thermal Furnace
Reprinted from: *Symmetry* **2022**, *14*, 923, doi:10.3390/sym14050923 122

Zhulong Wu, Yingqi Li, Shaohan Cui, Xiao Li, Zhihong Zhou and Xiaobao Tian
A Study of the Critical Velocity of the Droplet Transition from the Cassie to Wenzel State on the Symmetric Pillared Surface
Reprinted from: *Symmetry* **2022**, *14*, 1891, doi:10.3390/sym14091891 135

Jichang Ma, Hui Xie, Kang Song and Hao Liu
Self-Optimizing Path Tracking Controller for Intelligent Vehicles Based on Reinforcement Learning
Reprinted from: *Symmetry* **2021**, *14*, 31, doi:10.3390/sym14010031 . . . . **147**

Tieyu Zhao and Yingying Chi
Key Validity Using the Multiple-Parameter Fractional Fourier Transform for Image Encryption
Reprinted from: *Symmetry* **2021**, *13*, 1803, doi:10.3390/sym13101803 . . . . **184**

About the Editors

Rudolf Kawalla

Professor Rudolf Kawalla is the director of the Metal Forming Institute, Freiberg University of Mining and Technology, Freiberg, Germany. Professor Kawalla's interests lie in materials and metal-forming technologies, modelling of materials and hot and cold rolling processes, thin slabs and strips, and the physical and numerical simulation of steel and nonferrous metals production processes. He is the author of more than 250 papers and 30 patents. He has been awarded the title of honorary professor by the National University of Science and Technology "MISiS", Moscow, Russia and by Silesian University of Technology, Katowice, Poland.

Beloglazov Ilya

Dr. Beloglazov is an associate professor of the Department of Automation of Technological Processes and Productions in St. Petersburg Mining University, Saint-Petersburg, Russia.

Dr. Beloglazov specializes in digital technologies and has experience with application software packages and equipment in the field of process automation. He is a specialist in modelling physicochemical and high-temperature processes. He is the author of more than 100 scientific papers and 17 patents.

Preface

Dear Readers,

We are pleased to introduce this Special Issue dedicated to cutting-edge digital technologies. It presents advanced challenges, including process control strategies, and studies of various technological and physical systems that are simultaneously affected by various disturbances. Digital transformation brings together leading research addressing the global challenges of transitioning to a resource-efficient, process-safe, and sustainable future. By analysing the flow symmetry of liquids and gases, the distribution of bulk materials, mechanical damage, temperature drops, and electromagnetic radiation, it is possible to study the operation of technological processes and control systems. If the task is limited to only one discipline, or several disciplines in control and design, then there is a high probability that the forecast of the system's behaviour will be insufficiently accurate or completely incorrect. Interdisciplinary analysis solutions can help engineers investigate the individual and collective effects of symmetric or asymmetric actions, thereby identifying the most detailed solution, as needed.

In this Special Issue on symmetry, we mainly discuss the application of symmetry to process modelling and control systems, such as when modelling a process by obtaining the static or dynamic characteristics of an object via methods of numerical modelling, artificial intelligence, or neural networks. These process modelling techniques can also be effectively applied to control system design, Big Data collection and synthesis, data processing, and problem identification. For this reason, it is necessary to consider many parameters and knowledge of the dynamics of transient processes, which will contribute to the rapid development of advanced control systems.

Rudolf Kawalla and Beloglazov Ilya
Editors

Editorial

Review of Advanced Digital Technologies, Modeling and Control Applied in Various Processes

Ilia Beloglazov

Department of Mineral Processing, Automation of Technological Processes and Production, St. Petersburg Mining University, 199106 St. Petersburg, Russia; beloglazovii@pers.spmi.ru

Citation: Beloglazov, I. Review of Advanced Digital Technologies, Modeling and Control Applied in Various Processes. *Symmetry* **2024**, *16*, 536. https://doi.org/10.3390/sym16050536

Received: 19 February 2024
Accepted: 15 April 2024
Published: 30 April 2024

Copyright: © 2024 by the author. Licensee MDPI, Basel, Switzerland. This article is an open access article distributed under the terms and conditions of the Creative Commons Attribution (CC BY) license (https://creativecommons.org/licenses/by/4.0/).

This special issue reviews advanced digital technologies in modeling and control of technological processes. Methods of numerical modeling, artificial intelligence, machine learning, automatic control and optimization theory were considered in the published manuscripts of the special issue. It is especially noteworthy that this special issue is devoted to solving specific applied problems based on international standards, which has recently become of paramount importance for the scientific and professional community [1].

Conducting applied research by international scientific teams is of great importance for the development of science and the unification of scientific teams, especially given the current tensions in the world. The presented special issue includes a number of studies carried out by international teams. Collaboration between scientists from different countries allows the sharing of knowledge, experience and resources, which contributes to a better understanding of complex problems and the development of innovative solutions. Such research leads to new discoveries and technological breakthroughs that can have important implications for critical areas of science and technology.

Considering the impact of advanced digital technologies in artificial intelligence and big data, the authors presented their research manuscripts in various fields such as mining and mineral processing, mineral processing, vision and image processing systems. Invited editors and reviewers conducted a comprehensive review process for each manuscript in accordance with the journal's policies and guidelines. Twenty-seven papers were submitted to this special issue, and after comprehensive review, 12 high-quality papers were accepted for publication. It should be noted that this special issue is one of the most viewed (Viewed by 32,481), over the past 2 years, the total number of citations, at the time of writing this review is 231, and the average citation per article is more than 19. The contributions are listed in List of Contributions.

The challenge of energy efficiency in medium and high voltage networks is of great importance to reduce energy losses and improve overall energy efficiency. Some of the key aspects of this challenge include the development of more efficient transmission and distribution methods, the use of intelligent control and monitoring systems, and improved power transformation and switching technologies. In addition, introducing renewable energy sources into the grid can also help increase energy efficiency. Overall, these measures can significantly reduce energy losses and improve the sustainability and reliability of energy supply. Thus, contribution 1 focuses on developing the structure of a fast and flexible data acquisition system based on the proposed approach for measuring power quality indicators in three-phase distribution networks. contribution 2 presents a computational tool for evaluating the energy produced by low-power photovoltaic systems based on the specific conditions of the region under study. The approach presented in this work will allow to determine the relationship between climatic factors affecting energy production in PV systems operating in any region, as well as to evaluate the most favorable geographical location of PV panels, which contributes to improving the efficiency of solar-to-electric energy conversion.

Another relevant challenge is the use of predictive models for fault detection. This is of great importance in various fields including mineral processing, equipment maintenance, aviation and many others. Predictive models based on data analytics and machine learning can help predict possible malfunctions and failures of equipment based on historical performance data. In contribution 3, the authors review an approach to study metallurgical processes using analysis of a large array of operational control data. Using steel rolling production as an example, they consider the development of a predictive model based on the processing of a large array of operational control data. The purpose of the work is to implement a predictive model of roll wear of rolling mill rolls based on a large array of operational control data. The predictive model of mill roll wear will allow rational use of rolls in terms of minimizing the total roll wear.

Another example of control of process parameters is the approach to create a virtual soft sensor, which allows to establish a correct relationship between the fractional composition and individual composition of hydrocarbons (contribution 4). The virtual soft sensor is based on chemical and mathematical principles. The paper shows the application of this technique on data from a real refinery. Obtaining accurate data on the individual composition of the feedstock using the virtual soft sensor will optimize the catalytic reforming process and thus indirectly improve its environmental friendliness and enrichment efficiency.

An important direction is the development of autonomous transportation control systems, where artificial intelligence, machine learning, sensor and automation technologies play a key role. These systems can be applied to various modes of transportation, including cars, buses, trains, unmanned aerial vehicles (drones), and even marine vessels. In this regard, the authors of contribution 5 propose the use of a self-optimizing controller structure with trajectory tracking based on reinforcement learning. For lateral vehicle control, a steering method based on combining reinforcement learning methods and traditional PID controllers is developed to adapt to different tracking scenarios. The interactive learning mechanism based on advanced control structures can realize online optimization of PID controller parameters to better handle tracking error under complex trajectories and dynamic changes of vehicle model parameters.

A similarly excellent example is the manuscript: contribution 6 on machine learning for the oil and gas industry. This work is devoted to the most relevant issues of machine learning and artificial intelligence. One of the goals of this research was to build a model for predicting possible risks arising in the process of well drilling. Drilling wells for oil and gas production is a very complex and expensive part of reservoir development. Therefore, along with preventing injuries, the task of saving the cost of downtime and repair of drilling equipment is worthwhile. Nowadays, companies have started looking for ways to improve drilling efficiency and minimize downtime using digital technologies.

The author of contribution 7 devotes a large dissertation research to solving the problem of improving the accuracy of determining the main shape-forming dimensions of axisymmetric parts using an inspection system that implements the optical method of spatial resolution. This work shows the influence of the projection error of a passive optical system for controlling the geometric parameters of bodies of rotation by the image of its sections obtained by a digital camera with non-telecentric optics on the accuracy of measurements. In the field of image processing, the authors of contribution 8 proposed an algorithm for symmetric encryption using multi-parameter fractional Fourier transform. The presented algorithm with two vector parameters has enhanced security, which becomes the main technical means to protect information security.

In the field of molecular dynamics modeling, the authors of contribution 9 proposed a cross-scale critical velocity prediction model for superhydrophobic surfaces with symmetric structure based on mechanical equilibrium system. The study of the critical velocity of a droplet at transition is very important for many applications such as windshield glass fogging protection, medical cooling spray, anti-icing of aircraft surfaces and circuits, and fouling protection of photovoltaic panels. Another example of the use of numerical modeling methods is the work contribution 10 where the authors determined stable zones in the gas duct of an ore-heat furnace on the basis of computational fluid dynamics methods. This approach is necessary to improve the efficiency of control of the composition of waste gases in the production of metallurgical silicon. This work allowed solving the practical problem of determining the place for installation of measuring equipment.

Another important direction of the presented special issue was a series of scientific papers by Boykov et al. devoted to modeling of various processes. The contribution 11 describes the development of a universal calibration approach for modeling using the discrete element method (DEM). The discrete element method is the most popular approach for computer simulation of the behavior of bulk materials. The corresponding software implementing DEM in a graphical user interface is a highly efficient tool for mining equipment optimization. Recently, DEM is often used in combination with CFD and other methods, which opens up the possibility of calculating complex multiphase processes. contribution 12, which deserves special attention, presents a methodology for training neural networks for vision tasks on synthesized data using the example of steel defect recognition in automated production control systems. The process of procedural generation of a dataset of steel slab defects with symmetric distribution is described. The results of training two neural networks Unet and Xception on the generated data grid and their testing on real data are presented.

Acknowledgments: I dedicate this manuscript to the memory of a remarkable scientist, friend and colleague of Boikov Alexey, author of two relevant scientific articles in this special issue, who left a great scientific contribution to the development of modern digital technologies. His ideas and approaches have already been further developed and are a reminder of his good deeds for us.

Conflicts of Interest: The author declares no conflict of interest.

List of Contributions

1. Kryltcov, S.; Makhovikov, A.; Korobitcyna, M. Novel approach to collect and process power quality data in medium-voltage distribution grids. *Symmetry* **2021**, *13*, 460, https://doi.org/10.3390/sym13030460.
2. Turysheva, A.; Voytyuk, I.; Guerra, D. Estimation of electricity generation by an electro-technical complex with photoelectric panels using statistical methods. *Symmetry* **2021**, *13*, 1278. https://doi.org/10.3390/sym13071278.
3. Vasilyeva, N.; Fedorova, E.; Kolesnikov, A. Big data as a tool for building a predictive model of mill roll wear. *Symmetry* **2021**, *13*, 859. https://doi.org/10.3390/sym13050859.
4. Koteleva, N.; Tkachev, I. Virtual soft sensor of the feedstock composition of the catalytic reforming unit. *Symmetry* **2021**, *13*, doi:10.3390/sym13071233.
5. Ma, J.; Xie, H.; Song, K.; Liu, H. Self-optimizing path tracking controller for intelligent vehicles based on reinforcement learning. *Symmetry* **2022**, *14*, 31. https://doi.org/10.3390/sym14010031.
6. Islamov, S.; Grigoriev, A.; Beloglazov, I.; Savchenkov, S.; Gudmestad, O.T. Research risk factors in monitoring well drilling—a case study using machine learning methods. *Symmetry* **2021**, *13*, 1293. https://doi.org/10.3390/sym13071293.
7. Kulchitskiy, A. Optical inspection systems for axisymmetric parts with spatial 2d resolution. *Symmetry* **2021**, *13*, 1218. https://doi.org/10.3390/sym13071218.
8. Zhao, T.; Chi, Y. Key validity using the multiple-parameter fractional fourier transform for image encryption. *Symmetry* **2021**, *13*, 1803. https://doi.org/10.3390/sym13101803.
9. Wu, Z.; Li, Y.; Cui, S.; Li, X.; Zhou, Z.; Tian, X. A Study of the Critical Velocity of the Droplet Transition from the Cassie to Wenzel State on the Symmetric Pillared Surface. *Symmetry* **2022**, *14*, 1891. https://doi.org/10.3390/sym14091891.
10. Bazhin, V.; Masko, O. Monitoring of the Behaviour and State of Nanoscale Particles in a Gas Cleaning System of an Ore-Thermal Furnace. *Symmetry* **2022**, *14*, 923. https://doi.org/10.3390/sym14050923.
11. Boikov, A.; Savelev, R.; Payor, V.; Potapov, A. Universal approach for dem parameters calibration of bulk materials. *Symmetry* **2021**, *13*, 1088. https://doi.org/10.3390/sym13061088.

12. Boikov, A.; Payor, V.; Savelev, R.; Kolesnikov, A. Synthetic data generation for steel defect detection and classification using deep learning. *Symmetry* **2021**, *13*, 1176. https://doi.org/10.3390/sym13071176.

Reference

1. Litvinenko, V.; Bowbrick, I.; Naumov, I.; Zaitseva, Z. Global guidelines and requirements for professional competencies of natural resource extraction engineers: Implications for ESG principles and sustainable development goals. *J. Clean. Prod.* **2022**, *338*, 130530. [CrossRef]

Disclaimer/Publisher's Note: The statements, opinions and data contained in all publications are solely those of the individual author(s) and contributor(s) and not of MDPI and/or the editor(s). MDPI and/or the editor(s) disclaim responsibility for any injury to people or property resulting from any ideas, methods, instructions or products referred to in the content.

Article

Research Risk Factors in Monitoring Well Drilling—A Case Study Using Machine Learning Methods

Shamil Islamov [1], Alexey Grigoriev [2], Ilia Beloglazov [3,*], Sergey Savchenkov [4] and Ove Tobias Gudmestad [5]

[1] Department of Development and Operation of Oil and Gas Fields, Saint Petersburg Mining University, 199106 Saint Petersburg, Russia; Islamov_ShR@pers.spmi.ru
[2] Well Placement Department, SevKomNeftegaz LLC, 629830 Gubkinsky, Russia; AS_Grigorev6@skn.rosneft.ru
[3] The Automation of Technological Processes and Production Department, Saint Petersburg Mining University, 199106 Saint Petersburg, Russia
[4] Patent and Licensing Department, Saint Petersburg Mining University, 199106 Saint Petersburg, Russia; Savchenkov_SA@pers.spmi.ru
[5] Faculty of Science and Technology, University of Stavanger, N-4036 Stavanger, Norway; ove.t.gudmestad@uis.no
* Correspondence: Beloglazov_II@pers.spmi.ru

Citation: Islamov, S.; Grigoriev, A.; Beloglazov, I.; Savchenkov, S.; Gudmestad, O.T. Research Risk Factors in Monitoring Well Drilling—A Case Study Using Machine Learning Methods. *Symmetry* 2021, 13, 1293. https://doi.org/10.3390/sym13071293

Academic Editor: Xin Luo

Received: 26 May 2021
Accepted: 15 July 2021
Published: 18 July 2021

Publisher's Note: MDPI stays neutral with regard to jurisdictional claims in published maps and institutional affiliations.

Copyright: © 2021 by the authors. Licensee MDPI, Basel, Switzerland. This article is an open access article distributed under the terms and conditions of the Creative Commons Attribution (CC BY) license (https://creativecommons.org/licenses/by/4.0/).

Abstract: This article takes an approach to creating a machine learning model for the oil and gas industry. This task is dedicated to the most up-to-date issues of machine learning and artificial intelligence. One of the goals of this research was to build a model to predict the possible risks arising in the process of drilling wells. Drilling of wells for oil and gas production is a highly complex and expensive part of reservoir development. Thus, together with injury prevention, there is a goal to save cost expenditures on downtime and repair of drilling equipment. Nowadays, companies have begun to look for ways to improve the efficiency of drilling and minimize non-production time with the help of new technologies. To support decisions in a narrow time frame, it is valuable to have an early warning system. Such a decision support system will help an engineer to intervene in the drilling process and prevent high expenses of unproductive time and equipment repair due to a problem. This work describes a comparison of machine learning algorithms for anomaly detection during well drilling. In particular, machine learning algorithms will make it possible to make decisions when determining the geometry of the grid of wells—the nature of the relative position of production and injection wells at the production facility. Development systems are most often subdivided into the following: placement of wells along a symmetric grid, and placement of wells along a non-symmetric grid (mainly in rows). The tested models classify drilling problems based on historical data from previously drilled wells. To validate anomaly detection algorithms, we used historical logs of drilling problems for 67 wells at a large brownfield in Siberia, Russia. Wells with problems were selected and analyzed. It should be noted that out of the 67 wells, 20 wells were drilled without expenses for unproductive time. The experiential results illustrate that a model based on gradient boosting can classify the complications in the drilling process better than other models.

Keywords: machine learning; drilling problems; artificial intelligence; risk factor evaluation; gradient boosting

1. Introduction

Today, the use of machine learning (ML) capabilities in the oil and gas industry is becoming a central topic in various research centers and universities in the modern world. ML algorithms can provide practical solutions for analyzing and leveraging big historical data. ML technology has long been successfully used in computer science, engineering, mathematics, physics and astronomy, neuroscience, and medicine [1–10].

However, for the oil and gas industry, the use of such technologies has significantly increased in recent years [11–18]. An important task in the development of the oil and gas industry in the coming years is to increase the efficiency of producing oil and gas and drilling wells, and the main impetus to the introduction of methods of ML was the fall in oil prices. Oil and gas companies have concentrated on resource efficiency, optimizing their production processes [19–30].

This challenge should be solved at the expense of the overall development of fundamental and applied research and the rapid introduction of the results obtained. In drilling, one of the main issues in improving the quality of well construction is a reduction in the number and severity of problems, which is closely related to the use of modern computer–mathematical methods and computer technology. The use of such tools will help to identify wells with problems during drilling and further determine the symmetry or asymmetry of the well placement. The use of a symmetrical arrangement is advisable when operating a reservoir with fixed oil-bearing contours, i.e., with an equal distribution of the reservoir energy. The placement of wells on an asymmetric grid is distinguished according to the density of the grid, according to the rate of well commissioning, and according to the order in which wells are commissioned.

It is worth noting that the use of high-performance data analysis software is not a novelty for the oil industry. Since the 1990s, technologies for the collection and analysis of well data have been widely used. However, large capital expenditures on the implementation of these tools scared off many companies since their implementation could not be financially justified.

Currently, one of the main challenges facing the oil and gas industry is to improve the efficiency of well drilling.

The requirements of the practice of drilling deep oil and gas wells require a wide range of requirements for the theory of machine learning. In this case, the theory should be defined as a normal process at the time of origin, and during development, considering any problem as an integral part of the drilling processes. It is desirable that a theoretical description of drilling problems (DPs) allows not only judging them at a qualitative level but also quantifying the interrelation of their essential variables. Several years ago, these tasks seemed laborious.

Existing works were aimed at improving the drilling process using methods of artificial intelligence (AI).

Zhan and colleagues [31], in their work, used a nonparametric system of fuzzy inferences to predict the state of the rotary steerable system (RSS) by forecasting the state of the RSS in real time based on the operating mode and drilling parameters. This method allows reducing the cost of repair and maintenance of the drilling equipment.

Wang [32] presented an approach that uses multilayer neural network modeling to predict nonlinear optimization of DPs. The proposed model can not only predict the pump pressure, as the desired parameter, but can also ensure the impact of each input parameter in this model.

The mechanism of damage to drilling equipment is usually accompanied by several successive incidents that contribute to the loss of efficiency. Consequently, recognition, classification, elimination of breakdowns, and calculation of the remaining useful life are impossible without constant monitoring of the health of the system. Therefore, Camci and colleagues [33], with the help of the hidden Markov model, created a model capable of monitoring the current state of the mechanism, through signals sent by sensors. In particular, this model has shown excellent results for diagnosing the condition of drill bits.

At present, methods of programming neural networks for solving problems in various fields have been widely used. An artificial neural network is an interconnected group of nodes, similar to our brain system [34]. For example, Lind and Kabirova [35] used the neural programming method to predict possible problems that may arise when drilling wells, based on information about the oil field reserves. The results obtained showed the effectiveness of the neural network application for solving this problem.

A Bayesian neural network was used in the work by Al-yami and Schubert [36]. The method used allowed creating a system for making expert decisions in drilling. This method can be used to train young engineers. The system can also provide advice during all stages of well construction. This advice can be on well completion, monitoring of drilling and cementing of wells, selection of drilling fluids, etc.

Drilling engineers are always looking for methods to predict unexpected drilling situations and to improve the associated parameters accordingly. The prediction of the drilling rate is given high priority because of its impact on the optimization of various parameters, which directly reduces costs. Jahanbakhshi and colleagues used a neural network to predict the rate of penetration (ROP) [37]. The type of rock, mechanical properties of the formation, hydraulics, the type of bit and its features, and rotor speed were chosen as input parameters. Monazami and colleagues [38], in their article, also used a neural network to estimate the ROP. The authors considered this method as the most useful tool in forecasting in comparison with the currently available procedures. The model allows the drilling crew to assess the ROP not only at the planning stage but also during drilling. The results of this work showed that neural programming for the quality of ROP prediction is superior to conventional methods. Amer and colleagues [39] used the method of backpropagation to predict the ROP, which showed its success in their work.

Gidh and colleagues [40] also used an artificial neural network to develop a program to optimize drilling parameters. The result of this work was a model capable of choosing the optimal ROP and weight on the bit to extend the life of the bit. This model selects the necessary drilling parameters based on the expected characteristics of the rock on which the drilling will take place. Further, all parameters were adjusted for the relevant conditions.

In another publication, the ROP, together with the specific mechanical energy found by Rashidi and colleagues [41], was used to calculate the bit wear in real time. Between the specific mechanical energy and the weight on the bit, a linear relationship was obtained. Based on the analysis of a vast number of experiments, the authors believe that this model can become a valuable tool in the analysis of bit wear in real time.

Valisevich and colleagues [42], using an artificial neural network, created a model optimizing the development of bits in real time. All this led to an increase in the drilling speed, and a decrease in bit wear during drilling.

Another application of neural networks was presented by Dashevskiy and colleagues [43]. This work allowed simulating a nonlinear drilling system with a minimal error share by monitoring its dynamic behavior. The authors achieved the primary aim of the work—the use of neural networks for the intelligent control of drilling in dynamics.

GirirajKumar and colleagues [44], for an improvement in drilling, suggested using an optimally tuned proportional–integral–differential (PID) controller in high-performance drilling systems. The primary aim of their work was to obtain a stable, reliable, and controlled system by tuning the PID controller, using the optimization algorithm for swarm intelligence. The results of their work showed that tuning the PID controller using RI (swarm intelligence) provides a smaller overshoot.

Using a neural network, Lind and colleagues created an algorithm for predicting the loss of drilling fluids [45]. This system allows one to receive a recommendation for the selection of drilling fluids.

Static training methods for predicting torque and friction in real time were applied by Hegde and colleagues [46]. They considered algorithms such as regression, random forest, and the support vector method. These methods can be used to predict DPs and take appropriate measures to eliminate them. For example, an unexpected change in the value of torque may be a sign of a complication.

Another common complication—the instability of the walls of the well—with the help of a neural network, was predicted by Okpo and colleagues [47]. The program developed by the authors was used to predict the geomechanical parameters of the formation. The model was developed in a Neuroph Studio, and the platform of the neural network was Java and Netbeans IDE. The main advantage of this model is its simplicity and open-source code.

Unrau and colleagues [48], using an ML method, improved the existing alarm system on a drilling rig. The standard alarm systems used for drilling can register too many false alarms that significantly affect the drilling process. The ML algorithm proposed by the authors can be used to reduce false alarms while maintaining the efficiency of the alarm system. The model successfully detects kicks and loss.

As noted above, the integration of AI methods in a drilling process has great practical importance.

A DP is a violation of the continuity of the technological process of the construction of a well, requiring, for its liquidation, carrying out special works not planned in the project. In the process of drilling oil and gas wells, due to phenomena of a geological nature, there are, from time to time, problems in the technological process. This could be loss of drilling mud and fluid, kicks, or a stuck drill and casing columns [49].

Drilling crews constantly face a lot of difficult situations, the exits from which can be very expensive, and even impossible. A drill string may be stuck, by pressing against the wall of the well during a draw-down, or as a result of key seating. To eliminate these problems, additional efforts will be required to free the drill string. Sometimes, these efforts can fail. Then, drilling a side track is required [50].

Making a decision to eliminate these problems is a complex process. The damage from complications consists of the time spent for the elimination of DPs, and costs for materials and energy. To minimize the risks of drilling problems, work is being carried out to minimize vibrations of the bottom of the drilling assembly [51]; a mathematical model of a screw downhole motor (SDM)–drilling string (DS) system is being developed, which allows predicting the range of DS self-oscillations and boundaries of rotational and translational wave disturbances for the case of string modeling as a heterogeneous rod when drilling directionally straight sections of a well [52]. Thus, preventing problems and accordingly minimizing the risks of their occurrence are an actual problem today.

The aim of this work was to find a learning algorithm to recognize and classify DPs while drilling wells. Of the eight methods of ML, gradient boosting (GB) was chosen. This algorithm showed a high-performance precision, recall, and F-score (see below). This learning algorithm, based on historical data from previously drilled wells, classifies the DPs better than other algorithms. Such a decision support system will help engineers to intervene in the drilling process and prevent high expenses due to unproductive time and equipment repair. Another significant plus is worth noting. That is, the algorithm, in addition to the classification of DPs, accurately determines the standard drilling mode. This minimizes the possibility of triggering false alarms, which will also save drilling time. False alarms are also one of the problems when drilling wells which take up a significant amount of time and money.

2. Existing Methodologies

In order to create a program that classifies the problems in the drilling process, the main methods of ML with which the calculation was performed were considered. These methods have shown successful applicability in solving problems in various industries.

2.1. Logistic Regression

Logistic regression is a statistical technique for analyzing a dataset that has one or more independent variables that determine the outcome. The outcome is measured using a dichotomous variable (which has only two possible outcomes). It is used to predict the binary outcome (1/0, Yes/No, True/False) given a set of explanatory variables [53].

It is worth noting that this method is based on fairly strong probabilistic assumptions, which have several interesting consequences. First, the linear classification algorithm turns out to be the optimal Bayesian classifier. Secondly, the forms of the activation function (it is the sigmoid function) and the loss function are uniquely determined. Thirdly, an interesting additional possibility arises, along with the classification of the object, to obtain numerical estimates of the probability of problems belonging to each of the classes [54].

2.2. Naive Bayesian Classifier

A naive Bayesian classifier is a simple probabilistic classifier based on the application of Bayes' theorem with strict (naive) assumptions about independence.

In other words, a naive Bayesian classifier assumes that the presence of a particular feature in a class is not related to the presence of any other feature. For example, circulation loss can be detected by the following signs: the fluid flow from the well decreases, the level in the tanks decreases, and the outlet pressure decreases. Even if these parameters are dependent on each other or on the presence of other parameters, a naive Bayesian classifier will consider all of these properties independently of each other to create the likelihood that well loss is occurring [55].

Depending on the exact nature of the probabilistic model, naive Bayesian classifiers can be trained very effectively. In many practical applications, the maximum likelihood method is used to estimate the parameters for naive Bayesian models. In other words, one can work with a naive Bayesian model not believing in Bayesian probability and not using Bayesian methods [56].

2.3. Method K-Nearest Neighbors

The method of k-nearest neighbors is a metric algorithm for automatic classification of objects. The main principle of the method of nearest neighbors is that the object is assigned to the class that is the most common among the neighbors of this element.

Neighbors are taken based on a set of objects whose classes are already known, and, based on the key value for this method, the value of k is calculated, in order to find which class is the most numerous among them. Each object has a finite number of attributes.

It is assumed that there is a certain set of objects with an already existing classification [57].

In the learning process, the algorithm simply remembers all the feature vectors and the corresponding class labels. When working with real data, i.e., observations whose class labels are unknown, the algorithm calculates the distance between the new observation vector and the ones previously stored. Then, k-nearest vectors are selected, and the new object belongs to the class that owns most of them.

2.4. Decision Tree

Decision trees are a simple and widely used classification method. This method applies a simple idea to solve a problem. Decision trees ask thoughtful questions about the attributes of a test record. Each time the tree receives a response, the next question is asked until a conclusion is drawn about the class label of the record [58].

A decision tree is a graphical method that describes solutions and their possible outcomes. Decision trees consist of three types (Figure 1):

1. Decision node: This is often represented by squares that show what can be conducted. The lines coming out of the square show all the available options available on the node.
2. Probability knot: This is often represented by circles showing random results. Exodus odds are events that can occur but are beyond the control of the manager.
3. Closing node: This is represented by triangles or lines that do not have additional solution nodes or random nodes. Terminal nodes represent the final outcomes of the decision process.

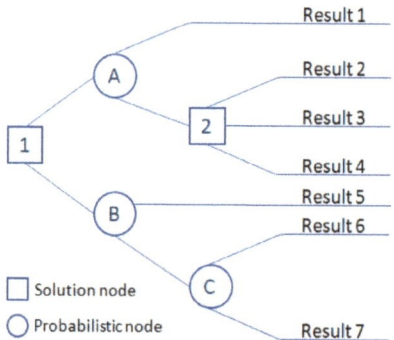

Figure 1. Decision tree diagram.

2.5. Support Vector Machine

The support vector method is a set of similar algorithms of the form "learning with the teacher", used for classification problems and regression analysis. This method belongs to the family of linear classifiers. A special property of the support vector method is a continuous decrease in the empirical classification error and an increase in the gap. Therefore, this method is also known as the classifier method with the maximum gap.

The basic idea of the method of support vectors is the translation of the original vectors into a space of higher dimension, and the search for a separating hyperplane with the maximum gap in this space. Two parallel hyperplanes are constructed on both sides of the hyperplane that separates the classes. The separating hyperplane is a hyperplane that maximizes the distance to two parallel hyperplanes. The algorithm works under the assumption that the greater the difference or the distance between these parallel hyperplanes, the smaller the average classifier error [59].

2.6. Random Forest

A random forest is a set of decision trees. In regression problems, their answers are averaged, and in classification problems, a decision is made by voting on the majority.

The method is based on the construction of a large number (assembly) of decision trees, each of which is constructed from a sample obtained from the initial training sample using a sample with a return. In contrast to the classical algorithms for constructing decision trees, in the method of random forests, when building each tree in the stages of vertex splitting, only a fixed number of randomly selected attributes of the training sample are used, and a complete tree is built, i.e., each sheet. The tree contains observations of only one class. Classification is carried out by voting classifiers, defined by individual trees, and regression estimation by averaging the regression estimates of all trees. It is known that the accuracy of ensembles of classifiers essentially depends on the variety of classifiers that make up the ensemble, or, in other words, on how correlated their decisions are. That is, the more diverse the classifiers of an ensemble, the higher the probability of a correct classification [60].

2.7. Gradient Boosting

Boosting is a procedure for the sequential construction of a composition of ML algorithms, where each subsequent algorithm seeks to compensate for the shortcomings of the composition of all previous algorithms. Boosting is a «greedy» algorithm for composing the final algorithms (Figure 2).

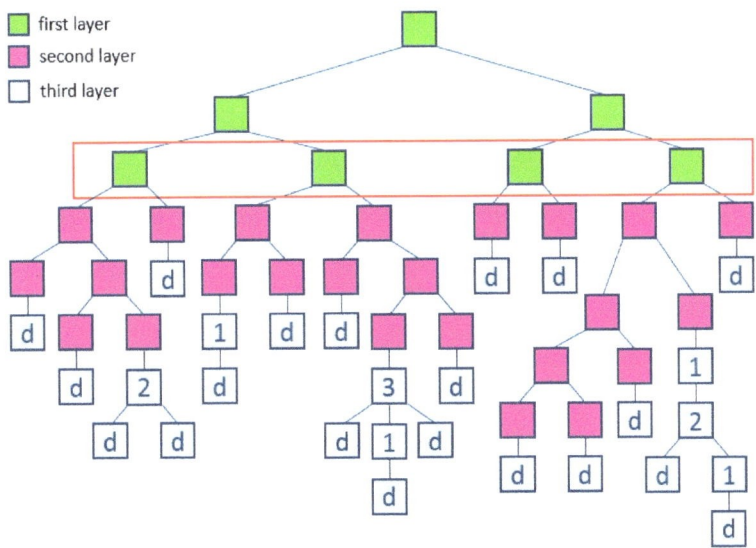

Figure 2. Example of gradient boosting.

Boosting over decision trees is considered one of the most effective methods in terms of the quality of classification. In many experiments, there was an almost unlimited reduction in the error rate on an independent test sample, as the composition was increased. Moreover, the quality of the test sample often continued to improve even after achieving an unmistakable recognition of the entire training sample. This overturned the ideas that existed for a sufficiently long time that it is necessary to limit the complexity of the algorithms in order to increase the generalizing ability. With the example of boosting, it became clear that a good quality can have arbitrarily complex compositions, if properly tuned.

Subsequently, the booster phenomenon received a theoretical justification. It turned out that weighted voting does not increase the effective complexity of the algorithm but only smooths out the answers of the basic algorithms. Quantitative estimates of the generalization of the boosting capacity are formulated in terms of indentation. The effectiveness of the boost is explained by the fact that as the basic algorithms are added, the indentation of the learning objects increases. Additionally, the booster continues to expand classes, even after achieving an unmistakable classification of the training sample (Figure 2) [61,62].

2.8. Neural Network

An artificial neural network is a mathematical model, as well as a software or hardware implementation, built on the principle of the organization and functioning of biological neural networks—the nerve cell networks of a living organism. This concept arose when studying the processes occurring in the brain, and when trying to simulate these processes. The first such attempt was the neural networks of McCulloch and Pitts [63]. After the development of learning algorithms, the resulting models began to be used for practical purposes: in forecasting problems, for pattern recognition, in control tasks, etc.

A neural network is a system capable of changing its structure under the influence of external factors. An artificial network is trained on input data. During the training, the internal parameters of the artificial neural network are adjusted to the input data, which makes it possible to isolate patterns in the data or to solve problems of prediction, classification, and clustering. When using an artificial neural network for data analysis, the researcher solves several problems: what learning algorithm to use, what is the network configuration, etc. The required internal parameters are found automatically, according to the chosen algorithm and configuration [63].

2.9. Evaluation of the Quality of Machine Learning Methods

Metrics are used to evaluate model quality and compare algorithms. Before moving to the metrics, we need to introduce an important concept for describing these metrics in terms of classification errors—the confusion matrix.

Having two classes and an algorithm that predicts the belonging of each object to one of the classes, the classification error matrix will look similar to that shown in Table 1.

Table 1. Metrics by model.

	y = 1	y = 0
y' = 1	True Positive (TP)	False Positive (FP)
y' = 0	False Negative (FN)	True Negative (TN)

In Table 1, "y'" is the answer of the algorithm on the object, and "y" is the true label of the class on this object.

Thus, classification errors are of two types: false negative (FN) and false positive (FP).

2.10. Precision, Recall, and F-Score

Recall demonstrates the ability of the algorithm to detect a given class, and precision demonstrates the ability to distinguish this class from other classes.

To assess the quality of the models used to classify the complications in the drilling process, the widely used precision, recall, and F-score metrics were used.

$$precision = \frac{TP}{TP + FP} \quad (1)$$

$$recall = \frac{TP}{TP + FN} \quad (2)$$

where *TP*—positive observation which was expected to be positive; *FN*—observation is positive, but it was predicted negatively; *FP*—observation is negative, but it was predicted positively.

There are several different ways to combine precision and recall in an aggregated quality criterion. The F-score is an average harmonic of precision and recall:

$$F_\beta = \left(1 + \beta^2\right) \cdot \frac{precision \cdot recall}{(\beta^2 \cdot precision) + recall} \quad (3)$$

where β, in this case, determines the weight of accuracy in the metric, and for $\beta = 1$, this is the average harmonic (with a factor of 2, meaning that in the case of precision = 1 and recall = 1, we have $F_\beta = 1$); the F-score reaches a maximum for completeness and accuracy of one, and is close to zero if one of the arguments is close to zero.

The sklearn library in Python has a convenient function metric, classification_report, which returns the recall, precision, and F-score for each of the classes, as well as the number of instances of each class [64].

3. Given Data

As initial data, reports on drilling 67 wells were assessed. Many of the wells have had DPs that have led to rig downtime and loss of productive drilling time. The analysis of the total time spent on drilling all wells showed that about 10.33% of this time was unproductive operating time.

It is worth noting that 10.33% is an important value, considering that the average cost per hour of drilling varies from RUB 15,000 to 55,000. Additionally, in this database, there is a well in which the unproductive time was 50% of the total operating time.

The main causes of unproductive drilling time at one specific field are shown in Figure 3. The greatest losses of time were due to rig downtime in waiting for contractors and equipment. Then, there is unproductive time due to the liquidation of penalties (unscheduled work, redrilling due to the fault of the contractor, etc.). In this project, we are interested in the trouble (DPs) that arises during the drilling process. This includes kicks, loss of circulation, and borehole instability.

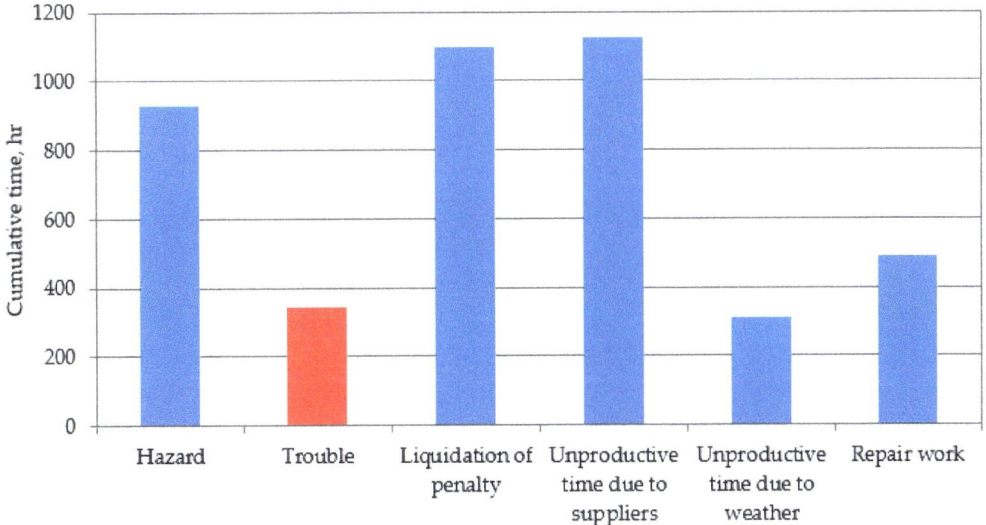

Figure 3. Distribution of non-productive time in field.

Wells with problems were identified and analyzed. It should be noted that out of 67 wells, 20 wells were drilled without expenses for unproductive time. The most common problem is related to the seizure that occurs when the casing runs down. It is worth noting that in this project, calculations were made for complications arising directly during drilling. For three wells, trouble arose during drilling, and detailed records are available.

For further analysis, all drilling parameters that were recorded for each well were considered. The analysis of the data showed that not all the wells from the sample have the same number of corresponding recorded drilling parameters. Some wells recorded the minimum number of parameters. We would like to note that drilling reports were provided for 67 wells, but the files with the recorded drilling parameters were provided for 78 wells. Therefore, data representing 78 wells were analyzed. For a wide analysis of the drilling parameters recorded on the wells, reports from 78 wells were taken into account. It can be seen from Figure 4 that only eight parameters are the most commonly reported for all wells; these are highlighted in red. Additionally, these parameters will be used as input parameters for the classification of complications.

After the work was conducted, for the three wells in which the DPs were plotted, the recorded drilling parameters were plotted. The graphs were constructed using the Python programming language, Figures 5–7.

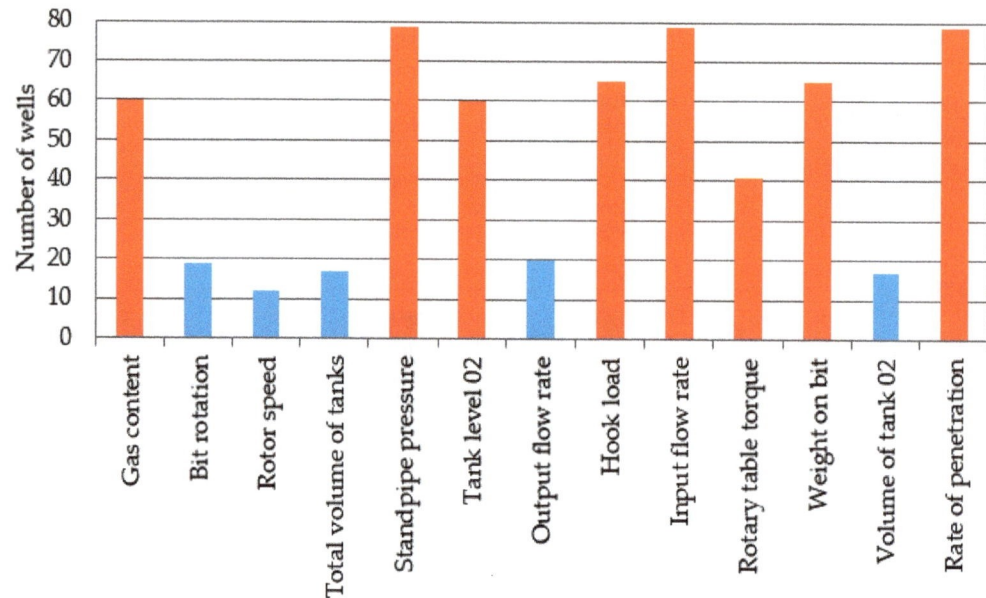

Figure 4. Drilling parameters analyzed for wells.

Well 1. The DP was associated with borehole instability due to technical water entering at a depth of 2882 m (Figure 5). It can be noted that this problem was accompanied by steep changes in drilling parameters. In particular, the value of the hook load, rotary table torque, etc., steeply increased. To eliminate this problem, the drilling crew spent 231 hours working on it.

Well 2. During well drilling, in the interval 239–263 m, the drilling fluid was lost at a volume of 40 m^3 (Figure 6). A total of 7.1 hours of unproductive time were spent on solving this problem. It is worth noting that the graph clearly shows that during the loss, circulation significantly decreased the level of the fluid capacity to mud tank № 2. A mud tank is an open-top container, typically made of square steel tubes and steel plates, to store drilling fluid on a drilling rig. They are also called mud pits, as they were once simple pits in the ground.

Well 3. When drilling to 2493 m, the drilling fluid was lost. The total loss was 55 m^3 (Figure 7). To eliminate the complication, colmatage fluid was injected. The total time taken to combat the DP was 27.9 hours. This well is one of those that did not record the complete list of required drilling parameters.

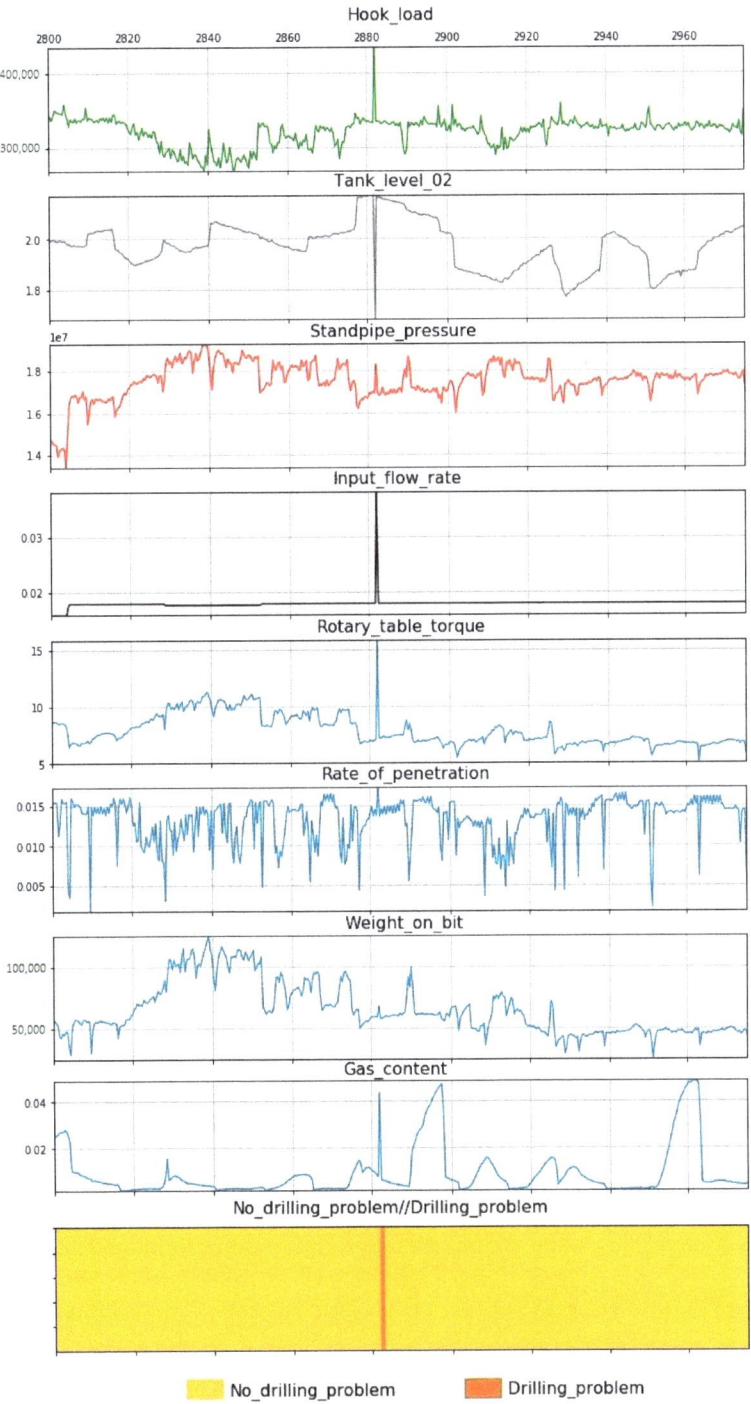

Figure 5. Drilling problem at well 1—borehole instability, drilling parameters versus time.

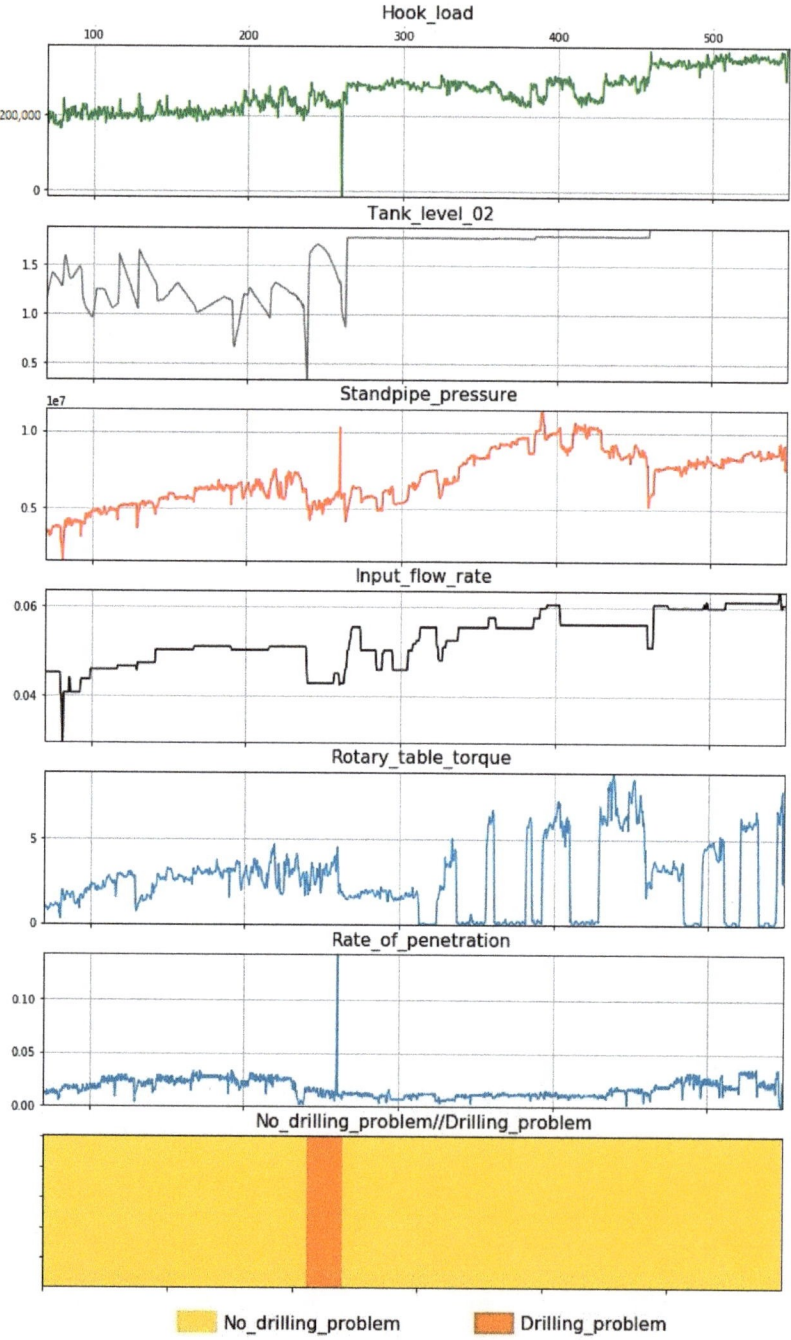

Figure 6. Drilling problem at well 2—circulation loss, drilling parameters versus time.

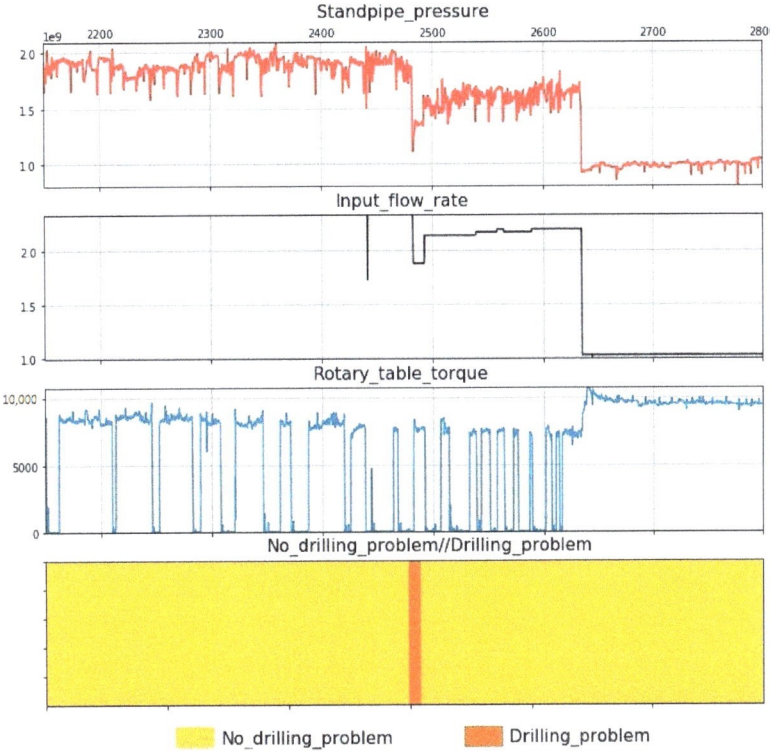

Figure 7. Drilling problem at well 3—circulation loss, drilling parameters versus time.

4. Results

According to the algorithms of machine training given in the previous chapter, calculations were performed to classify (forecast) the problems in the drilling process. For calculations, the Python programming language and the scikit-learn library were used.

The percentage of training and test samples among the data was set as 65/35%, respectively. The training sample is a sample based on which the chosen algorithm adjusts the dependency model. The test sample is the sample by which the accuracy of the model used is checked. The following drilling parameters were used as input parameters:

- Standpipe pressure;
- Tank level 02;
- Input flow rate;
- Hook load;
- Rotary table torque;
- Rate of penetration;
- Weight on bit;
- Gas content.

As a result of the calculations, the following metrics were obtained, for the subsequent detection of the most accurate model.

Table 2 shows that the following algorithms of machine learning (ML) have the highest values of the metrics: decision tree; random forest; gradient boosting (GB).

Table 2. Metrics by model.

Algorithm	Metrics (Determination of Drilling Problems)		
	Precision	Recall	F-Score
Logistic regression	0.00	0.00	0.00
Naive Bayesian classifier	0.03	1.00	0.06
Method of k-nearest neighbors	0.83	0.64	0.73
Decision tree	0.97	0.87	0.92
Support vector method	0.00	0.00	0.00
Random forest	0.98	0.93	0.95
Gradient boosting	1.00	0.93	0.97
Neural network	1.00	0.53	0.70

Next, we considered the number of correct and incorrect assumptions in the calculation of algorithms. Table 3 presents the case for situations where there are no problems while drilling, and in Table 4, the classification of problems while drilling is shown. The goal is to see how the algorithm can misclassify the drilling process. "Right" is the number of correctly predicted values; "False" is the number of misplaced predictions when drilling without a problem being recognized. From the data presented, it can be seen that the greatest number of correct and accurate classifications of situations is obtained using the ML method of gradient boosting (GB). GB allowed, with the lowest number of errors, classifying the complication from the available dataset.

Table 3. Accuracy of prediction of a normal situation.

Algorithm	Situation	Right	False
Logistic regression	Normal	3916	1
Naive Bayesian classifier	Normal	2484	1433
Method of k-nearest neighbors	Normal	3911	6
Decision tree	Normal	3916	1
Support vector method	Normal	3917	0
Random forest	Normal	3915	2
Gradient boosting	Normal	3917	0
Neural network	Normal	3917	0

Table 4. Accuracy of prediction of a problem situation.

Algorithm	Situation	Right	False
Logistic regression	Problem	0	45
Naive Bayesian classifier	Problem	45	0
Method of k-nearest neighbors	Problem	29	16
Decision tree	Problem	39	6
Support vector method	Problem	0	45
Random forest	Problem	39	6
Gradient boosting	Problem	42	3
Neural network	Problem	27	18

Then, a sensitivity analysis was performed (Figure 8), when the drilling parameters were removed from the gradient boosting, in turn, by their weight coefficients from the smallest to the largest. This allowed understanding how many parameters at the input are needed in this situation for the correct operation of gradient boosting. It was established that when the parameters such as "Gas content", "Weight on bit", and "Rate of penetration" are removed from the model, the system classifies the drilling problems with the same accuracy. Accordingly, it can be concluded that this algorithm, in the event of an emergency situation, can classify drilling problems according to the five available parameters without a loss of accuracy: "Rotary table torque", "Standpipe pressure", "Hook load", "Tank level 02", and "Input flow rate".

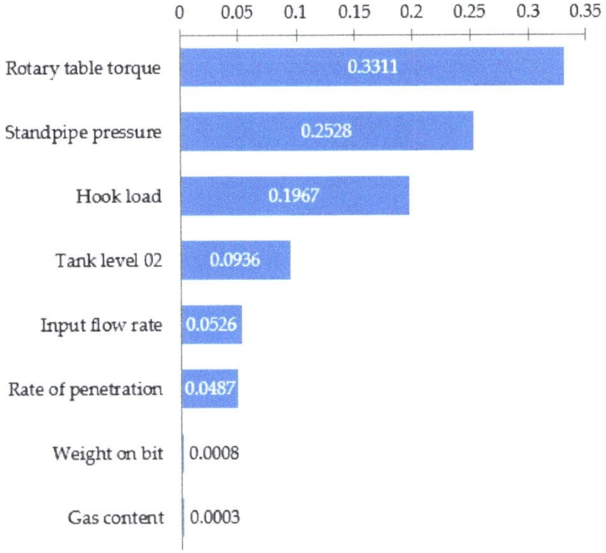

Feature	Importance
Rotary table torque	0.3311
Standpipe pressure	0.2528
Hook load	0.1967
Tank level 02	0.0936
Input flow rate	0.0526
Rate of penetration	0.0487
Weight on bit	0.0008
Gas content	0.0003

Figure 8. Feature importance for gradient boosting.

5. Discussion

Based on the results of this work, an algorithm of gradient boosting is capable of recognizing and classifying complications in the process of drilling wells better than other algorithms. This algorithm has the highest value of the test metrics and the greatest number of correct and accurate classifications. The algorithm returned the correct prediction of a normal situation 3917 times out of 3917, and the correct prediction of a problem situation 42 times out of 45. It can be argued that using the gradient boosting algorithm while drilling wells will help, in terms of time, in assisting with the drilling process and prevent high expenses for rig downtime and equipment repair. The program will signal a possible problem. It is worth noting that in this work, we did not use too much initial data. Therefore, it is recommended to increase the efficiency of the model, in order to test it on a higher number of initial data.

Worth noting is another significant plus. The algorithm, in addition to the classification of DPs, accurately determines the standard drilling mode (without problem). This minimizes the possibility of triggering false alarms, which will also save drilling time. False alarms are also one of the problems when drilling wells, which take up a significant amount of time and money. Additionally, if new technologies are introduced by companies in oil and gas production, this will allow businesses to save their costs. For example, in the construction of a drilling rig that reaches hundreds of millions of dollars, even a 5% reduction in planning time can have a significant positive impact on the company's profits [65].

Nybø [66,67] solved a similar problem. In this work, a hybrid system was developed that includes a physical model and AI. Together, they allow one to recognize the problems when drilling much better than individually. Additionally, in this paper, the problem of the small number of studies on the introduction of methods of ML in the drilling sector was addressed. The authors of this work are also convinced that this integration of machines and people will significantly increase the efficiency of drilling wells.

Based on the results of the analysis using eight algorithms, it can be seen that the logistic regression and support vector method show metrics equal to zero for the recognition of complications. Perhaps these values are associated with the small number of initial data of complications. Therefore, these algorithms show such poor results. As noted above, for further work, it is recommended to experiment with a much larger number of initial data.

6. Conclusions

In trying to avoid the problems in the drilling process, their classification and timely elimination remain an urgent problem to date. The aim of this work was to create a program capable of recognizing and classifying drilling problems (DPs). Following the results of this work, the following achievements were made:

1. Based on the literature review, a wide application of AI in drilling was shown, from the creation of training programs to the prediction of the rate of penetration.
2. During the analysis of the initial data, wells with problems that were encountered during drilling were identified. To model the presented DPs, a computer model was set up.
3. During the analysis of the drilling reports, a list of the main parameters was compiled, which participated as input for the model: standpipe pressure; tank level; input flow rate; hook load; rotary table torque; rate of penetration; weight on bit; gas content.
4. Of the eight methods of machine learning (ML), the GB method was chosen. This algorithm showed a high-performance precision, recall, and F-score.
5. For the GB method, the parameters that make the greatest contribution to the operation of the algorithm were established using the feature importation parameter. These are the rotary table torque, standpipe pressure, and hook load.
6. During the GB analysis, it was established that in the case of removing parameters such as gas content, the model continued to work without changing the accuracy of the classification of the DPs.
7. Although the ultimate goal of this work was to teach the program to classify the problems in the drilling process, in the future, it is necessary to consider the possibility of predicting the drilling problems in real time, for example, using time series. Such a model will avoid problems, preventing high costs.
8. In the future, it is necessary to train the algorithm on a larger number of data on wells with problems. This will expand the application of the program and elucidate how to classify various types of drilling problems.
9. It will be useful to test the model by specifying not only drilling parameters but also geophysical logging data, on the input. This will allow models to take into account such a parameter as lithology. Depending on the different rocks, the log data will show the different behaviors of the curves.
10. It is also recommended to use geomechanical parameters of the formation as input data. These data will allow predicting possible problem areas of the well in advance that are prone to collapse.

Author Contributions: Conceptualization, A.G. and I.B.; formal analysis, S.S.; investigation, A.G.; methodology, A.G. and S.I.; project administration, A.G. and S.I.; resources, I.B. and O.T.G.; software, A.G.; supervision, O.T.G.; validation, A.G.; visualization, S.S.; writing—original draft, S.I.; writing—review and editing, I.B. and O.T.G. All authors have read and agreed to the published version of the manuscript.

Funding: This research received no external funding.

Institutional Review Board Statement: Not applicable.

Informed Consent Statement: Not applicable.

Data Availability Statement: The data presented in this study are available on request from the corresponding author. The data are not publicly available due to their storage in private networks.

Conflicts of Interest: The authors declare no conflict of interest.

Abbreviations

AI	Artificial intelligence
DPs	Drilling problems
GB	Gradient boosting
ML	Machine learning
PID	Proportional–integral–differential
ROP	Process rate of penetration
RSS	Rotary steerable system

References

1. Hochreiter, S.; Schmidhuber, J. Long short-term memory. *Neural Comput.* **1997**, *9*, 1735–1780. [CrossRef] [PubMed]
2. Jones, D.T. Protein secondary structure prediction based on position-specific scoring matrices. *J. Mol. Biol.* **1999**, *292*, 195–202. [CrossRef]
3. LeCun, Y.; Bengio, Y.; Hinton, G. Deep learning. *Nature* **2015**, *521*, 436–444. [CrossRef]
4. Milo, R.; Shen-Orr, S.S.; Itzkovitz, S.; Kashtan, N.; Chklovskii, D.M.; Alon, U. Network motifs: Simple building blocks of complex networks. *Science* **2002**, *298*, 824–827. [CrossRef]
5. Nielsen, H.; Engelbrecht, J.; Brunak, S.; Heijne, G.V. Identification of prokaryotic and eukaryotic signal peptides and prediction of their cleavage sites. *Protein Eng.* **1997**, *10*, 1–6. [CrossRef]
6. Olden, J.D.; Jackson, D.A. Illuminating the "black box": A randomization approach for understanding variable contributions in artificial neural networks. *Ecol. Model.* **2002**, *154*, 135–150. [CrossRef]
7. Reichstein, M.; Camps-Valls, G.; Stevens, B.; Jung, M.; Denzler, J.; Carvalhais, N. Deep learning and process understanding for data-driven Earth system science. *Nature* **2019**, *566*, 195–204. [CrossRef]
8. Rubinov, M.; Sporns, O. Complex network measures of brain connectivity: Uses and interpretations. *NeuroImage* **2010**, *52*, 1059–1069. [CrossRef] [PubMed]
9. Tu, J.V. Advantages and disadvantages of using artificial neural networks versus logistic regression for predicting medical outcomes. *J. Clin. Epidemiol.* **1996**, *49*, 1225–1231. [CrossRef]
10. Voyant, C.; Notton, G.; Kalogirou, S.; Nivet, M.-L.; Paoli, C.; Motte, F.; Fouilloy, A. Machine learning methods for solar radiation forecasting: A review. *Renew. Engergy* **2017**, *105*, 569–582. [CrossRef]
11. Almeida, T.L.P.; Passos, B.A.F.; Costa, J.L.S.; Andrade, A.J.N. Identifying clay mineral using angular competitive neural network: A machine learning application for porosity estimative. *J. Pet. Sci. Eng.* **2021**, *200*, 108303. [CrossRef]
12. Hajizadeh, Y. Machine learning in oil and gas; a SWOT analysis approach. *J. Pet. Sci. Eng.* **2019**, *176*, 661–663. [CrossRef]
13. Hanga, K.M.; Kovalchuk, Y. Machine learning and multi-agent systems in oil and gas industry applications: A survey. *Comput. Sci. Rev.* **2019**, *34*, 100191. [CrossRef]
14. Nima, M.; Hamzeh, G.; David, A.W.; Mohammad, M.; Shadfar, D.; Sina, R.; Alireza, S.; Amirafzal, K.S. A geomechanical approach to casing collapse prediction in oil and gas wells aided by machine learning. *J. Pet. Sci. Eng.* **2021**, *196*, 107811.
15. Mohamed, L.; Mohamed, S.; Sofiène, T. Detection and sizing of metal-loss defects in oil and gas pipelines using pattern-adapted wavelets and machine learning. *Appl. Soft Comput.* **2017**, *52*, 247–261.
16. Sina, R.; Mohammad, M.; Hamzeh, G.; David, A.W.; Nima, M.; Jamshid, M.; Shadfar, D. Determination of bubble point pressure & oil formation volume factor of crude oils applying multiple hidden layers extreme learning machine algorithms. *J. Pet. Sci. Eng.* **2021**, *202*, 108425.
17. Hao, C.; Chao, Z.; Ninghong, J.; Ian, D.; Shenglai, Y.; Yong, Z.Y. A machine learning model for predicting the minimum miscibility pressure of CO2 and crude oil system based on a support vector machine algorithm approach. *Fuel* **2021**, *290*, 120048.
18. Boikov, A.V.; Savelev, R.V.; Payor, V.A.; Potapov, A.V. Evaluation of bulk material behavior control method in technological units using dem. *CIS Iron Steel Rev.* **2020**, *20*, 3–6. [CrossRef]
19. Litvinenko, V.S.; Tsvetkov, P.S.; Molodtsov, K.V. The social and market mechanism of sustainable development of public companies in the mineral resource sector. *Eurasian Min.* **2020**, *2020*, 36–41. [CrossRef]
20. Kamatov, K.A.; Buslaev, G.V. Solutions for drilling efficiency improvement in extreme geological conditions of Timano-Pechora region. In Proceedings of the SPE Russian Petroleum Technology Conference, Moscow, Russia, 26 October 2015; pp. 1–10.
21. Charfeddine, L.; Barkat, K. Short-and long-run asymmetric effect of oil prices and oil and gas revenues on the real GDP and economic diversification in oil-dependent economy. *Energy Econ.* **2020**, *86*, 104680. [CrossRef]
22. Aleksandrova, T.; Aleksandrov, A.; Nikolaeva, N. An investigation of the possibility of extraction of metals from heavy oil. *Miner. Process. Extr. Metall. Rev.* **2017**, *38*, 92–95. [CrossRef]
23. Nevskaya, M.A.; Seleznev, S.G.; Masloboev, V.A.; Klyuchnikova, E.M.; Makarov, D.V. Environmental and business challenges presented by mining and mineral processing waste in the Russian Federation. *Minerals* **2019**, *7*, 445. [CrossRef]
24. Liu, T.; Leusheva, E.; Morenov, V.; Li, L.; Jiang, G.; Fang, C.; Zhang, L.; Zheng, S.; Yu, Y. Influence of polymer reagents in the drilling fluids on the efficiency of deviated and horizontal wells drilling. *Energies* **2020**, *13*, 4704. [CrossRef]
25. Gang, H.; Zhaoqiang, X.; Guorong, W.; Bin, Z.; Yubing, L.; Ye, L. Forecasting energy consumption of long-distance oil products pipeline based on improved fruit fly optimization algorithm and support vector regression. *Energy* **2021**, *224*, 120153.

26. Yurak, V.V.; Dushin, A.V.; Mochalova, L.A. Vs sustainable development: Scenarios for the future. *J. Min. Inst.* **2020**, *242*, 242–247. [CrossRef]
27. Kondrasheva, N.K.; Rudko, V.A.; Kondrashev, D.O.; Gabdulkhakov, R.R.; Derkunskii, I.O.; Konoplin, R.R. Effect of delayed coking pressure on the yield and quality of middle and heavy distillates used as components of environmentally friendly marine fuels. *Energy Fuels* **2019**, *33*, 636–644. [CrossRef]
28. Kondrasheva, N.K.; Rudko, V.A.; Ancheyta, J. thermogravimetric determination of the kinetics of petroleum needle coke formation by decantoil thermolysis. *ACS Omega* **2020**, *5*, 29570–29576. [CrossRef] [PubMed]
29. Seçkin, K.; Aytaç, S.; Stelios, B.; Wasim, A. A new forecasting model with wrapper-based feature selection approach using multi-objective optimization technique for chaotic crude oil time series. *Energy* **2020**, *212*, 118750.
30. Hebert, D.; Misiti, A. The Growing Role of Artificial Intelligence in Oil and Gas. Available online: https://insights.globalspec.com/article/2772/the-growing-role-of-artificial-intelligence-in-oil-and-gas (accessed on 23 April 2021).
31. Zhan, S.; Rodiek, J.; Heuermann-Kuehn, L.E.; Baumann, J. Prognostics health management for a directional drilling system. In Proceedings of the Prognostics and System Health Management Conference, Shenzhen, China, 24–25 May 2011; pp. 1–7.
32. Wang, Y. *Drilling Hydraulics Optimization Using Neural Networks*; University of Louisiana at Lafayette Press: Lafayette, LA, USA, 2015.
33. Camci, F.; Chinnam, R.B. Dynamic bayesian networks for machine diagnostics: Hierarchical hidden Markov models vs. competitive learning. In Proceedings of the International Joint Conference on Neural Networks, Montreal, QC, Canada, 31 July–4 August 2005; pp. 1–6.
34. Yang, Z.R.; Yang, Z. *Comprehensive Biomedical Physics*, 1st ed.; Elsevier Science & Technology: Stockholm, Sweden, 2004.
35. Lind, Y.B.; Kabirova, A.R. Artificial neural networks in drilling troubles prediction. In Proceedings of the SPE Russian Oil and Gas Exploration & Production Technical Conference and Exhibition, Moscow, Russia, 14–16 October 2014; pp. 1–7.
36. Al-yami, A.S.H.; Schubert, J. Systems and Methods for Expert Systems for Well Completion using Bayesian Decision Models (BDNs), Drilling Fluids Types, and Well Types. Available online: https://hdl.handle.net/1969.1/177120 (accessed on 23 April 2021).
37. Jahanbakhshi, R.; Keshavarzi, R.; Jafarnezhad, A. Real-time prediction of rate of penetration during drilling operation in oil and gas wells. In Proceedings of the Rock Mechanics/Geomechanics Symposium, Chicago, IL, USA, 24–27 June 2012; pp. 1–9.
38. Monazami, M.; Hashemi, A.; Shahbazian, M. Drilling rate of penetration prediction using artificial neural network: A case study of one of Iranian southern oil fields. *J. Oil. Gas. Bus.* **2012**, *6*, 21–31.
39. Amer, M.M.; Dahab, A.S.; El-Sayed, A.H. An ROP predictive model in nile delta area using artificial neural networks. In Proceedings of the SPE Kingdom of Saudi Arabia Annual Technical Symposium and Exhibition, Dammam, Saudi Arabia, 24–27 April 2017; pp. 1–11.
40. Gidh, Y.; Purwanto, A.; Bits, S. Artificial neural network drilling parameter optimization system improves ROP by predicting/managing bit wear. In Proceedings of the SPE Intelligent Energy International, Utrecht, The Netherlands, 27–29 March 2012; pp. 1–13.
41. Rashidi, B.; Hareland, G.; Nygaard, R. Real-time drill bit wear prediction by combining rock energy and drilling strength concepts. In Proceedings of the Abu Dhabi International Petroleum Exhibition and Conference, Abu Dhabi, United Arab Emirates, 3–6 November 2008; pp. 1–9.
42. Valisevich, A.; Ruzhnikov, A.; Bebeshko, I.; Moreno, R.; Zhentichka, M.; Bits, S. Drillbit optimization system: Real-time approach to enhance rate of penetration and bit wear monitoring. In Proceedings of the SPE Russian Petroleum Technology Conference, Moscow, Russia, 26–28 October 2015; pp. 1–14.
43. Dashevskiy, D.; Dubinsky, V.; Macpherson, J.D. Application of neural networks for predictive control in drilling dynamics. In Proceedings of the SPE Annual Technical Conference and Exhibition, Houston, TX, USA, 3–6 October 1999; pp. 1–9.
44. GirirajKumar, S.M.; Jayaraj, D.; Kishan, A.R. PSO based tuning of a PID controller for a high-performance drilling machine. *Int. J. Comput. Appl.* **2010**, *1*, 12–18. [CrossRef]
45. Lind, Y.B.; Samsykin, A.V.; Galeev, S.R. Information and analytical system for prevention of drilling fluid loss. In Proceedings of the SPE Russian Petroleum Technology Conference, Moscow, Russia, 26–28 October 2015; pp. 1–12.
46. Hegde, C.; Wallace, S.; Gray, K. Real Time prediction and classification of torque and drag during drilling using statistical learning methods. In Proceedings of the SPE Eastern Regional Meeting, Morgantown, VA, USA, 13–15 October 2015; pp. 1–13.
47. Okpo, E.E.; Dosunmu, A.; Odagme, B.S. Artificial neural network model for predicting wellbore instability. In Proceedings of the SPE Nigeria Annual International Conference and Exhibition, Lagos, Nigeria, 2–4 August 2016; pp. 1–10.
48. Unrau, S.; Torrione, P.; Hibbard, M.; Smith, R.; Olesen, L.; Watson, J. Machine learning algorithms applied to detection of well control events. In Proceedings of the SPE Kingdom of Saudi Arabia Annual Technical Symposium and Exhibition, Dammam, Saudi Arabia, 24–27 April 2017; pp. 1–10.
49. Shchepetov, O.A. System classification of failures in drilling. *Vestn. Astrakhan State Tech. Univ. Ser. Manag. Comput. Sci. Inform.* **2009**, *2*, 36–42.
50. Aldred, W.; Plumb, D.; Bradford, I.; Cook, J.; Gholkar, V.; Cousins, L.; Minton, R.; Fuller, J.; Goraya, S.; Tucker, D. Managing drilling risk. *Oilfield Rev.* **1999**, *11*, 2–19.
51. Dvoynikov, M.V. Research on technical and technological parameters of inclined drilling. *J. Min. Inst.* **2017**, *223*, 86–92.

52. Litvinenko, V.S.; Dvoynikov, M.V. Methodology for determining the parameters of drilling mode for directional straight sections of well using screw downhole motors. *J. Min. Inst.* **2020**, *41*, 105–112. [CrossRef]
53. Logistical Regression for Kettles: Detailed Explanation. Available online: https://www.machinelearningmastery.ru/logistic-regression-for-dummies-a-detailed-explanation-9597f76edf46/ (accessed on 2 July 2021).
54. Vorontsov, K.V. *Lectures on Linear Classification Algorithms*; Moscow Institute of Physics and Technology Press: Moscow, Russia, 2009.
55. Commonly Used Machine Learning Algorithms (with Python and R Codes). Available online: https://www.analyticsvidhya.com/blog/2017/09/common-machine-learning-algorithms/ (accessed on 2 July 2021).
56. Ray, S. Easy Steps to Learn Naive Bayes Algorithm with Codes in Python and R. Available online: https://www.analyticsvidhya.com/blog/2017/09/naive-bayes-explained/ (accessed on 23 April 2021).
57. Piryonesi, S.M.; Tamer, E.E. Role of data analytics in infrastructure asset management: Overcoming data size and quality problems. *J. Transp. Eng. Part B Pavements* **2020**, *146*, 1–7. [CrossRef]
58. Decision Tree Classifier. Available online: http://mines.humanoriented.com/classes/2010/fall/csci568/portfolio_exports/lguo/decisionTree.html (accessed on 2 July 2021).
59. Vorontsov, K.V. *Lectures on the Support Vector Machine*; Moscow Institute of Physics and Technology Press: Moscow, Russia, 2007.
60. Chistyakov, S.P. Random forest. *Proc. Karelian Res. Cent. Russ. Acad. Sci.* **2013**, *1*, 117–136.
61. Vorontsov, K.V. *Mathematical Methods of Learning by Precedents: A Course of Lectures*; Moscow Institute of Physics and Technology Press: Moscow, Russia, 2009.
62. Matthew, M. More Steps to Mastering Machine Learning with Python. Available online: http://www.kdnuggets.com/2017/03/seven-more-steps-machine-learning-python.html (accessed on 23 April 2021).
63. McCulloch, U.S.; Pitts, V. *Logical Calculus of Ideas Relating to Nervous Activity*; Foreign Literature Publishing House: Moscow, Russia, 1956.
64. Labintcev, E. Metrics in the Problems of Machine Learning. Available online: https://habrahabr.ru/company/ods/blog/328372/ (accessed on 23 April 2021).
65. Nelson, A. Driving Efficiency in the Oil and Gas Industry. Available online: https://biarri.com/driving-efficiency-oil-gas-industry/ (accessed on 23 April 2021).
66. Nybø, R. *Efficient Drilling Problem Detection*; Norwegian University of Science and Technology Press: Trondheim, Norway, 2009.
67. Nybø, R.; Sui, D. Closing the integration gap for the next generation of drilling decision support systems. In Proceedings of the SPE Intelligent Energy Conference & Exhibition, Utrecht, The Netherlands, 1–3 April 2014; pp. 1–10.

Article
Optical Inspection Systems for Axisymmetric Parts with Spatial 2D Resolution

Aleksandr Kulchitskiy

Department of Automation of Technological Processes and Production, Saint Petersburg Mining University, 119106 Saint Petersburg, Russia; kulchitskiy_aa@pers.spmi.ru

Abstract: The article proposes a solution to the problem of increasing the accuracy of determining the main shaping dimensions of axisymmetric parts through a control system that implements the optical method of spatial resolution. The influence of the projection error of a passive optical system for controlling the geometric parameters of bodies of revolution from the image of its sections, obtained by a digital camera with non-telecentric optics, on the measurement accuracy is shown. Analytical dependencies are derived that describe the features of the transmission of measuring information of a system with non-telecentric optics in order to estimate the projection error. On the basis of the obtained dependences, a method for compensating the projection error of the systems for controlling the geometry of the main shaping surfaces of bodies of revolution has been developed, which makes it possible to increase the accuracy of determining dimensions when using digital cameras with a resolution of 5 megapixels or more, equipped with short-focus lenses. The possibility of implementing the proposed technique is confirmed by the results of experimental studies.

Keywords: axisymmetric parts; optical control; control of geometric parameters; method with spatial resolution; projection method; error compensation

1. Introduction

Currently, production efficiency depends on the ability to control the quality of the processed workpieces in a timely manner, the condition of technological equipment and the progress of technological processes at all stages of production. To solve these problems, it is proposed to use optoelectronic devices (including machine vision systems), which make it possible to create automated control systems for various industries [1].

As examples of the use of tools that implement the optical method of control, one can cite the tasks of assessing the cryolite ratio [2], determining the position of the electrodes of ore-thermal furnaces [3] in the metallurgical industry, assessing the efficiency of flotation [4] at obage fabrics, monitoring of self-oscillations in the process of cutting materials based on the registration of the light field [5] and roughness measurement [6,7] in mechanical engineering. Technical vision systems are also used in studies of the mechanical properties of bulk materials [8,9].

The problem of automated control of geometric parameters is an urgent one [10]. Currently, optoelectronic measuring systems have been implemented that implement the projection method [11] and use telecentric optical systems with a collimator illumination system [12]. The main advantage of telecentric optics is a constant magnification factor over the entire operating range and, therefore, the absence of perspective distortions for extended objects, but at the same time, its use greatly increases the cost of the system, limits layout solutions (product inspection only in transmitted light) and the control area to 340 mm, determined by the field of view of existing lenses. The use of digital cameras with non-telecentric optics makes it possible to remove these restrictions. As examples, we can consider the control of the geometry of the current-carrying rods of electrolyzers [13] in metallurgy and the nature of chip formation [14] in the machine-building industry.

The use of active control systems with structured illumination is known [15]; however, an example of a significant drawback of the presented system is the determination of the size of the product in only one section. Comprehensive control of spatial geometry is provided by active optical 3D scanning systems, individual samples of which are certified as measuring instruments [16,17]; however, problems with the control of products with a surface with a pronounced indicatrix of reflection (typical for mechanical engineering products) increase digitization errors [18].

Thus, it can be noted that the use of passive projection systems that implement the spatial resolution method for solving problems of controlling the main shaping dimensions of axisymmetric objects is a promising direction of development. The use of digital cameras with entocentric optics in such systems makes it possible to reduce the cost of control systems and expand their functionality by increasing the variety of possible layout solutions that allow working in both transmitted and reflected light. The latter is an important condition for their use in conjunction with mirror converters, [19] the use of which meaning it is possible to solve the problem of compensating for the positioning error without increasing the number of cameras.

2. Statement of Research Objectives

The main problem of using control systems with entocentric optics for solving problems of controlling the geometric parameters of products is the dependence of the results on many external factors. These include aberrations of the optical system, errors in determining coordinates, positioning of the control object, extraneous illumination, refraction of the medium etc. with the relative position of the control object and the digital camera, and taking into account the imperfection of the optical system, the calibration procedure of the control systems is used [20,21]. Calibration techniques are constantly being improved [22–24] and allow for a reduction in systematic error in determining the size of products from their images to a value equivalent to 1–2 px for digital cameras with a resolution of up to 5 Mp, equipped with long-focus lenses. Together with the method of complex error compensation [25], which compensates for background illumination errors and noise components, they provide the ability to control flat products with an error of up to 0.1%.

If until recently digital cameras with a resolution of 0.3–2 Mp were used (in 2017—85% [26]), then the current trend is to increase the resolution of cameras to 5 . . . 10 Mp [27], and, in the near future, up to 16 . . . 25MP. The use of high-resolution cameras makes it possible to expand the application of machine vision systems to the tasks of controlling geometric parameters, providing the ability to control with a relative error of less than 0.1%.

However, an increase in resolution leads to the fact that when measuring the dimensions of bodies of revolution, previously imperceptible components of systematic errors appear in the projection, in which the visible image is not located in the plane of symmetry of the part (Figure 1). In this regard, the analysis of the sources of such errors and methods of their compensation becomes an urgent task of the study.

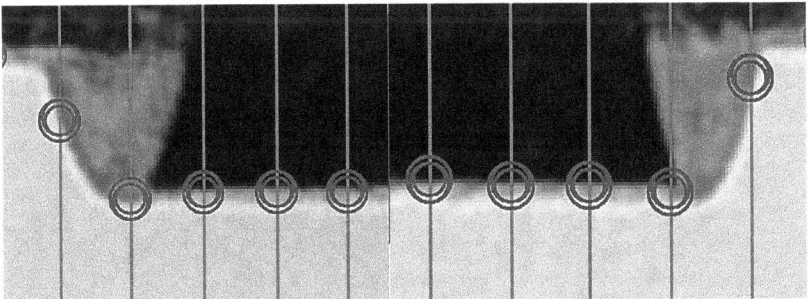

Figure 1. Fragments of the part image in the object edge search window.

A feature of the formation of an image of bodies of revolution in reflected light by an entocentric system (Figure 2) is that the observed image is not located in the plane of symmetry but is displaced by a distance of l along the optical axis towards the camera. This leads to the fact that, on the one hand, the observed size d is less than the controlled size of the section D, but it is located closer to the calibration plane (coinciding with the axis of symmetry), which leads to a change in the linear increase in V for the observed size d upward. In addition, the displacement of the body of revolution relative to the optical axis by a distance y leads to the rotation of the image by an angle α. Figure 2 shows a geometric model of the formation of an image of an axisymmetric part by entocentric optics for f = 7 mm, L = 200 mm and D = 100 mm. For clarity of presentation of changes in the main parameters, they are shown in Figure 2 next to their corresponding designations.

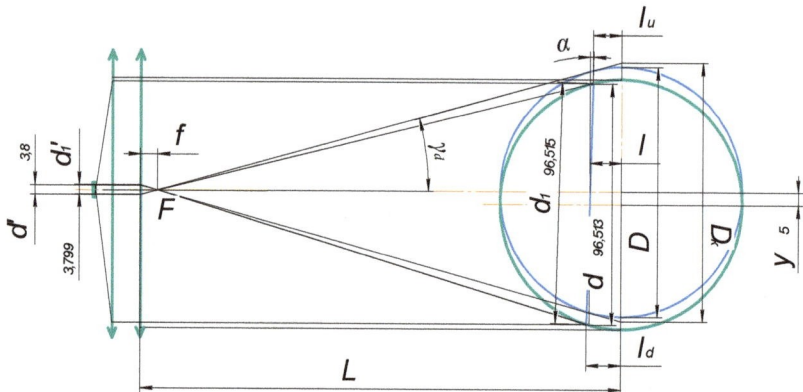

Figure 2. Formation of an image of an axisymmetric part by an entocentric optical system.

To assess the influence of these factors on the error in determining the dimensions, we determine the values of these parameters.

Figure 2 shows the fixed inverse image of the section of the body of revolution D has an apparent size d

$$d = D \cdot \sqrt{1 - \left(\frac{\frac{D}{2}}{L-f}\right)^2} \qquad (1)$$

where: L—working distance, f—focal length.

The visible image is smaller than the object, and this difference only grows with decreasing focal length. In this case, the image is displaced along the optical axis by

$$l = \frac{D^2}{4 \cdot (L-f)}. \qquad (2)$$

Observation angle γ_D of controlled size D.

$$\gamma_D = a\sin\left(\frac{\frac{D}{2}}{L-f}\right) \qquad (3)$$

All this leads to errors in estimating the size of products. The dependences of the calibration errors δv, the projection error δd and the total error δΣ on the ratio of the determined dimensions D to the width of the field of view B are shown in Figure 3 for 12 and 25 mm lenses.

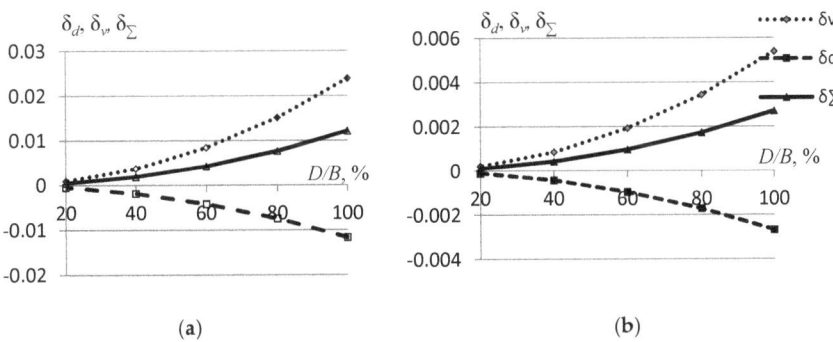

Figure 3. Calibration error and projection error in determining the dimensions of the body of revolution, for systems with focal length: (**a**) 12 mm and (**b**) 25 mm.

It can be seen from the graphs that when the size of the test object almost completely coincides with the field of view, the error for a 12 mm objective can reach 1%, and for a 25 mm objective—0.25%. Thus, when measuring the dimensions of parts that occupy most of the field of view of a digital camera, the influence of these errors can be considered significant for the control of products according to 8–9 qualities. With product sizes less than 50% of the field of view, the considered error for a 25 mm lens is ~0.07% and becomes insignificant for cameras with a resolution of up to 5 Mp.

3. Materials and Methods

Numerical simulation and experimental research was carried out based on the use of cameras for image registration: Basler Pilot piA2400-17 (sensor: CCD 2/3 "; resolution 2456 × 2058), with Ricoh FL-CC2514-2M lenses (f = 25 mm), Ricoh FL- HC0612A-VG with f = 12 mm; ACE acA640-120gm (sensor: CCD 1/4 "; resolution 659 × 494) and 5,0 МпUSB camera (sensor: CMOS 1/2.5", resolution 2592 × 1944) with Computar M1214-MP2 lens with f = 6 mm.

The software implementation was carried out in the LabVIEW environment using the Vision library (technical vision module) [28]. The built-in calibration function was used based on the image obtained using the Calibration Training utility against a standard point pattern with a step of 10 × 10 mm, made by laser graphing with an error of no more than 0.01 mm (Figure 4a).

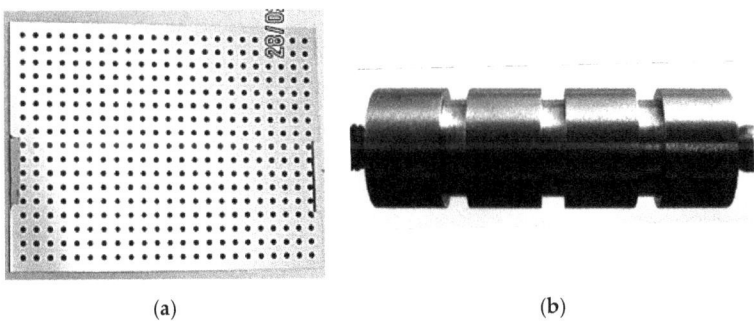

Figure 4. Point pattern (**a**) and sample parts Ø 25 mm (**b**).

For control, 3 samples of parts were made, which were shafts 75 mm long with four separated grooved surfaces Ø 15, 20, 25 mm (Figure 4b). The actual dimensions of the samples were estimated using a digital micrometer CDWAS 0–25 Δ = ±0.002 mm and a linear displacement transducer with a rod LIR14-20-01 of the 2nd accuracy class with a digital display device LIR-510A-00 using plane-parallel gauge blocks.

The position of the test object, which affects the accuracy of the calibration procedure, was estimated using the developed software in the LabVIEW environment [29], the operation algorithm of which is described in [30].

The study of the error compensation technique was carried out in reflected light. Figure 5 shows fragments of experimental studies, illustrating the comparative results of the evaluation of the sample sizes with calibration—Distortion Model: Polynomial (K1, K2, K3), using the developed compensation algorithms and without these same algorithms.

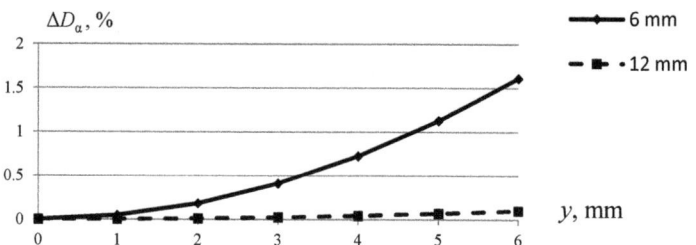

Figure 5. The value of the error in determining the diametrical dimensions of the body of revolution when the optical axis does not intersect with the axis of rotation of the controlled part.

4. Results

To determine the amount of compensation, you need to derive the inverse relationship. The initial data are the parameters f, D_k—the calculated size, based on the calibration data in the symmetry plane n_d—the number of pixels that make up the image of the visible size d'.

The following dependencies can be used to compensate for the perspective error:

$$D = D_K \cdot \cos\left(\tan^{-1}\left(\frac{d'}{2f}\right)\right) \tag{4}$$

or

$$D = D_K \cdot \cos\left(\tan^{-1}\left(\frac{D_{HK}}{2(L-f)}\right)\right) \tag{5}$$

where D_{HK} is the diameter obtained as a result of measurements from the image.

To compensate for the manifestation of a perspective error in the horizontal plane, it is necessary to take into account the change in the linear magnification factor when mixing the visible image along the x axis by l, which can be determined by formula (3).

The cross section is observed at an angle ν, which can be determined from the dependence

$$\nu = \sin^{-1}\frac{z}{L-f} \tag{6}$$

where z is the displacement relative to the optical axis along the axis of symmetry of the body of revolution.

The change in Δl can be determined from the dependence

$$\Delta l = \frac{D^2(1-\cos\nu)}{4\cdot(L-f)}. \tag{7}$$

To take into account the displacements of the shaft axis in the vertical plane relative to the axis of symmetry of the body of revolution by y, we define the rotation of the observed section by the angle α

$$\alpha = \tan^{-1}\left(\frac{y}{L-l}\right).$$

This will displace the image horizontally and resize the image by

$$\Delta_\alpha = D \cdot \cos \alpha. \tag{8}$$

Figure 5 shows a graph of the dependence of the relative error in determining the dimensions of bodies of revolution in case of violation of the condition of crossing the axis of symmetry of the body of rotation of the optical axis of a digital camera, presented in a relative form of dependence for lenses: with f = 6 mm L = 39 mm and f = 12 mm and L = 145 mm.

Notes for algorithm for complex compensation of errors:

1. correction of the horizontal component, takes into account the rotation of the test object relative to the vertical axis by changing the parameter z of expression (7).

2. correction, takes into account the violation with respect to the condition of perpendicularity of the test object of the optical axis of the digital camera and can be determined by the expression $\Delta_\alpha = D \cdot \cos \beta$, where β is the angle of inclination of the test object.

3. correction, taking into account the position of the test object, can be performed based on the linear magnification measurement dependence, which can be calculated by the formula $\delta V_P = \frac{X_{P1}-f}{X_P-f} = \frac{X_P \pm \Delta X - f}{X_P - f}$, where: ΔX—displacement of the controlled rod

Based on the obtained regularities, an algorithm for image processing and correction of the calculated values was developed for the complex compensation of errors in the control system of axisymmetric products, which is shown in Figure 6.

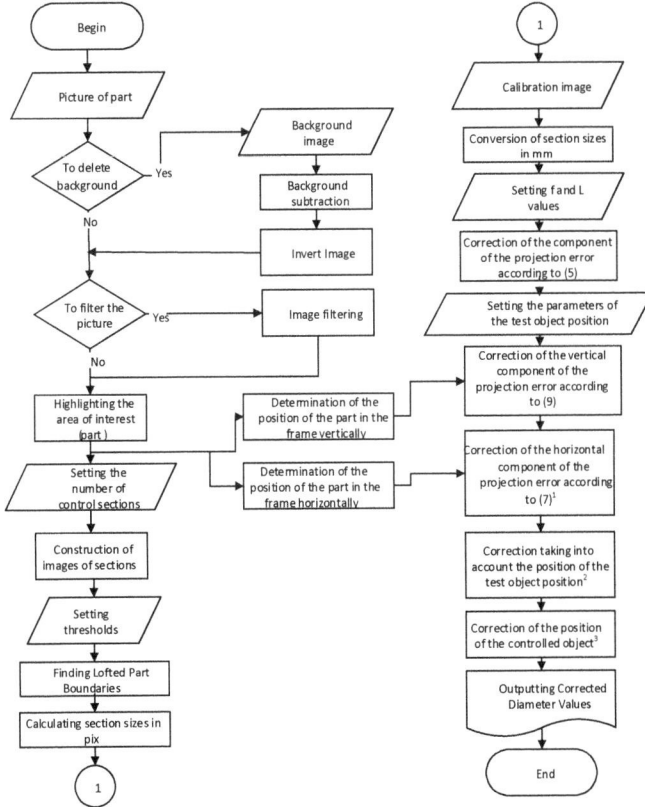

Figure 6. Algorithm for complex compensation of errors of the control system of axisymmetric products.

To assess the developed compensation technique, we calculate the main parameters shown in Figure 2. The results of modelling the error compensation process are presented in Table 1. Its results show the possibility of full compensation of the considered errors for an ideal optical system.

Table 1. Results of numerical simulation of compensation of projection error of the system for controlling the dimensions of axisymmetric objects.

f, mm	D, mm	L, mm	γ, °	V	l, mm	D, mm	d', mm	D_k, mm	$\gamma_{p'}$ °	$D_{p'}$ mm
6	49.27	72	21,916	0.0909	9.1952	45.709	4828	53,108	21,916	49.27
6	30.77	72	13,480	0.0909	3.5863	29.922	2876	31,642	13,480	30.77
6	25.38	72	11,085	0.0909	2.4399	24.906	2351	25,863	11,085	25.38
6	15.43	72	6712	0.0909	0.9018	15.324	1412	15.5363	6712	15.43
f, mm	D, mm	L, mm	γ, °	V	l, mm	m	d', mm	D_k, mm	$\gamma_{p'}$ °	$D_{p'}$ mm
f	D	L	α	V	l	d		D_k	α_p	D_p
12	49.27	153	10,062	0.0851	4.3041	48.512	4258	50,040	10,062	49.27
12	30.77	153	6264	0.0851	1.6787	30.586	2634	30,955	6264	30.77
12	25.38	153	5163	0.0851	1.1421	25.277	2168	25,483	5163	25.38
12	15.43	153	3136	0.0851	0.4221	15.406	1315	15,453	3136	15.43

In Figure 7—graphs of errors in determining the dimensions of a sample with a nominal Ø 25 mm: using only the calibration procedure (Cal.), using the projection error compensation algorithm (CA) and complex compensation (CC) errors for digital cameras whith f = 25 mm and f = 12 mm entocentric optics. The error graph for a camera with an f = 12 mm lens additionally shows a constant factor calibration (Const.) to clearly demonstrate lens distortion. Examples of measurement results with 60 sampling points are given.

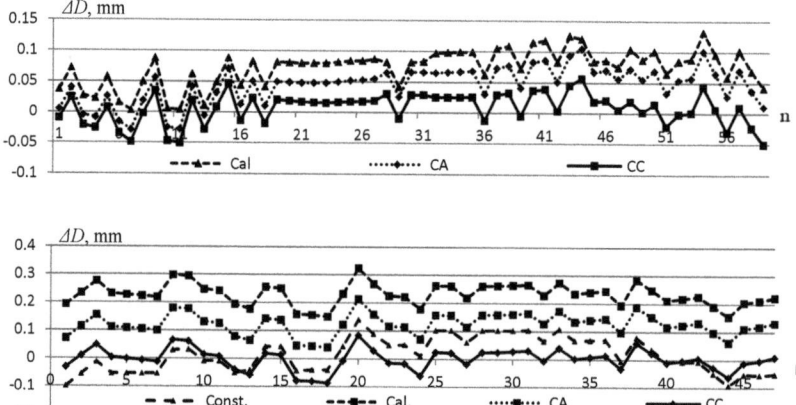

Figure 7. Errors in determining the dimensions of the bead in the absence and use of compensation algorithms for f = 25 and f = 12 mm—60 measurement points.

The results of a quantitative assessment of the results of the correction are presented in Table 2. A column was added showing correction results, combining projection error compensation and test object position error.

Table 2. Evaluation of methods for correction of dimensions for f = 25 mm.

Parameters	Calibration (Cal.)		Compensation of Projection Error (CA)			Compensation of Projection Error + Position of Test-Object			Complex Compensation (CC)	
f, mm	25	12	25	12		25	12		25	12
m	20	48	48	20	48	48	20	48	48	48	48
$\overline{M}$, mm	0.079	0.073	0.224	0.042	0.042	0.118	0.034	0.033	0.098	−0.004	0.006
$\overline{S}$,	0.079	0.081	0.237	0.048	0.053	0.135	0.041	0.046	0.118	0.026	0.057
δ *, mm	0.174	0.171	0.489	0.107	0.112	0.285	0.090	0.098	0.242	0.055	0.11

* $t_{0,04;48}$ = 2112; $t_{0,04;20}$ = 2204.

While analyzing the obtained values, it can be concluded during the use of cameras with a resolution of 5 Mp with long-focus lenses (with f = 25 mm and more) that the projection error is comparable to the positioning error, and the dominant error is the binarization error. For a 5-megapixel camera with a short-focus lens f = 12 mm, the projection error and displacement errors of the body of revolution have a significant effect on the accuracy of determining the dimensions of the bodies of revolution. Their compensation practically eliminates the systematic component, which decreases from approximately 1% to 0.024%, which is less than $\frac{1}{2}$ pix for the camera under consideration. It can be seen from the graphs that, as before, the dominant random component is the image binarization error equal to ±1.5 pix.

Figure 8 shows an example of comparing different calibration algorithms for a camera with lenses f = 25 mm and f = 25 mm. The object position error for 23 control points has not been corrected for clarity. The results of a quantitative assessment of the results of the correction are presented in Table 3.

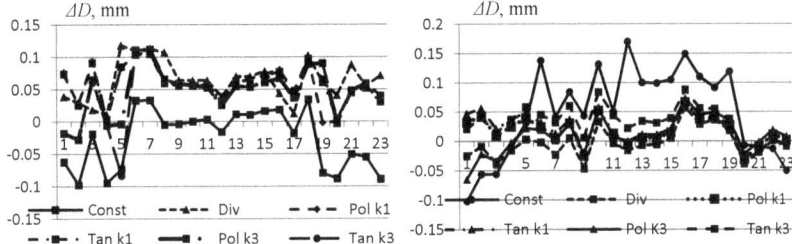

Figure 8. Errors in determining the roller diameter D_{nom} = 25 mm when using standard NI calibrations for f = 25 and 12 mm.

Comparison of the results of image correction for a lens with f = 25 mm shows that the use of standard calibrations of optical distortions NI with three coefficients makes it possible to almost completely eliminate the systematic component determined by distortions of the optical system ^{-}M = 0.001 ... 0.002 mm. The random component is mainly determined by the image binarization errors. The division of the field of view into two binarization areas (top and bottom) is insufficient. For a lens with f = 12 mm, due to the absence of image rotation, *the Divison* calibration provided a lower systematic error, with practically equal values of the random error, the spread of the values of which is within the statistical error of the estimate.

The effect of threshold binarization values can be clearly represented in Figure 9, from which it can be seen—when the threshold values are changed by 3 ... 4 units at the top of the image from 180/255 to 183/255 and from 140/255 to 136/254 at the bottom, results in a change in ± 1–2 pxs.

Table 3. Errors in determining the dimensions of a 25 mm diameter roller at different calibrations with a lens with f = 25 and 12 mm at m = 20.

Parameters	Sim.	Div.	Pol. k1	Tan. k1	Pol. k3	Tan. K3
			f = 25 mm			
$\overline{M}$, mm	−0.002	0.014	0.008	0.009	−0.002	−0.001
$\overline{S}$, mm	0.049	0.035	0.036	0.033	0.036	0.035
δ*, mm	0.109	0.078	0.080	0.072	0.080	0.078
			f = 12 mm			
$\overline{M}$, mm	0.05	−0.003	0.018	0.020	0.010	0.034
$\overline{S}$, mm	0.092	0.025	0.030	0.034	0.033	0.044
δ *, mm	0.203	0.056	0.066	0.075	0.072	0.097

* $t_{0,04;20}$ = 2204.

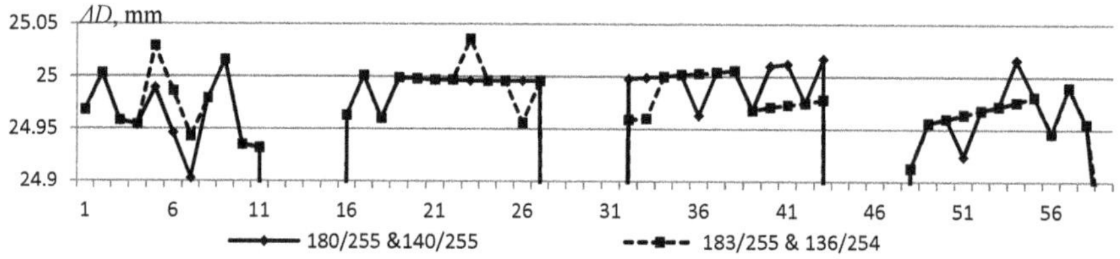

Figure 9. Sample dimensions Ø 25 mm, obtained in reflected light for two threshold binarization values for f = 25 mm.

A numerical estimate of the influence of the binarization threshold values during measurement of the dimensions of a detail for a 5MP camera with a long-focus lens f = 25 mm is given in Table 4.

Table 4. Evaluation of the effect of binarization threshold values for a long-focus lens with f = 25 mm.

Parameters	180/255 &140/255		183/255 & 136/254	
Bias Compensation	No	Yes	No	Yes
$\overline{M}$, mm	0.036	0.006	0.035	0.005
$\overline{S}$, mm	0.049	0.033	0.044	0.027
δ *, mm	0.108	0.073	0.098	0.059

* $t_{0,04;46}$ = 2114.

Due to the irregularity of illumination at the edges of the image, an error arises in determining the dimensions according to a fixed threshold binarization value, which affects the accuracy of determining the dimensions. The operation of subtracting the background does not always compensate for this component due to the appearance of a shadow when installing a part, which is absent when fixing the background.

The filtering procedure eliminates the noise component. Figure 10 and Table 5 demonstrate the application of Gausian and Smoothing filters with kernel sizes 3, 5, 7. Slight blurring of the image smoothed out the random noise component and surface flare.

The results of the study show that the use of filters can reduce the confidence interval by up to one and a half times. The values obtained show the preferred use of a 5-kernel smoothing filter.

The results of studying the compensation of systematic errors of a 0.3 Mp camera with an f = 6 mm lens at L = 275.5 mm are shown in Figure 11 and in Table 6. The developed distortion compensation (DDC) model based on the use of the image space sampling algorithm [31] has been added to the previously considered algorithms with standard NI calibrations.

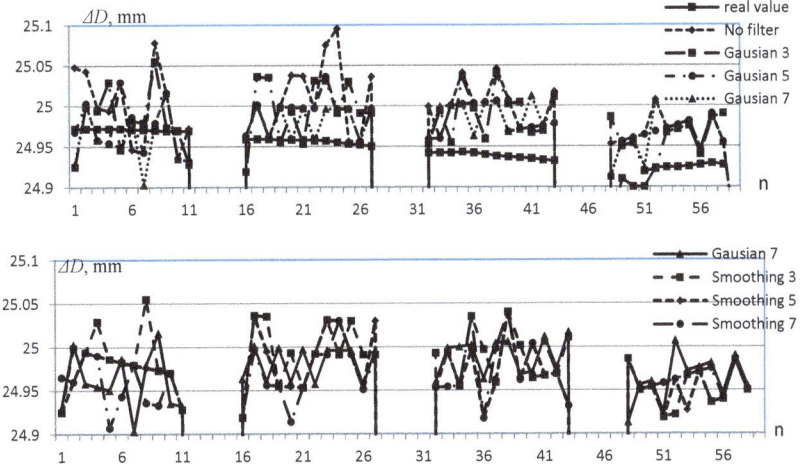

Figure 10. Dimensions of a specimen Ø 25 mm obtained in reflected light without the use of a filter and with a Gaussian and Smoothing filter for f = 25 mm.

Table 5. Evaluation of filtration calibration methods for a telephoto lens f = 25 mm.

Parameters	No Filter	Filter					
		Gausian			Smoothing		
Kernel		3	5	7	3	5	7
$\overline{M}$, mm	0.050	0.041	0.035	0.037	0.039	0.028	0.023
$\overline{S}$, mm	0.063	0.051	0.045	0.048	0.049	0.041	0.043
$\delta *$, mm	0.140	0.114	0.098	0.107	0.107	0.089	0.096

* $t_{0,04;46} = 2114$.

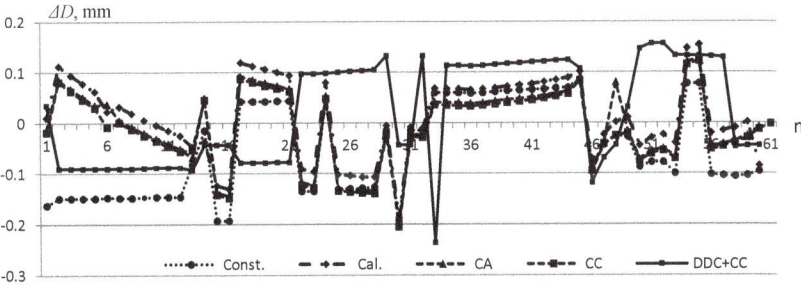

Figure 11. Errors in determining the dimensions of the bead in the absence and use of compensation algorithms for 0.3 Mp camera with a lens with f = 6 mm.

The results of comparison use the standard calibration Distortion Model: Polynomial (Kl, K2, KZ) and the developed one are shown in Figure 12 and Table 7.

Analyzing the obtained values, it can be concluded during the use of cameras with low resolution that the projection error is comparable to the positioning error, and the dominant error is the binarization error.

Table 6. Errors in determining the dimensions of a 25 mm diameter roller in the absence and use of compensation algorithms for a 0.3 Mp camera with a lens f = 6 mm.

Parameters	Constant Koefficient (Const.)	No Compensation (Cal.)	Compensation of Projection Error (CA)	Complex Compensation (CC)	Complex Compensation + Developer Cal. (DDC+CC)
$\overline{M}$, MM	−0.052	0.026	0.005	0.004	0.031
$\overline{S}$, MM	0.118	0.080	0.075	0.075	0.012
δ *, MM	0.249	0.169	0.158	0.158	0.110

* $t_{0,04;46}$ = 2114.

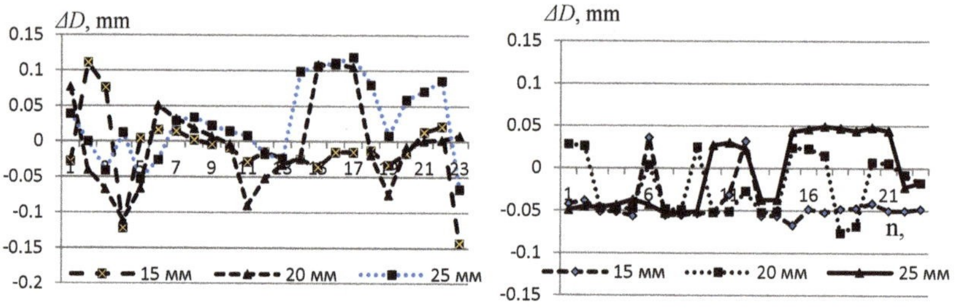

Figure 12. Errors in determining the dimensions of 15, 20 and 25 mm by a 0.3 Mp camera with a lens f = 6 mm by standard calibrations and a developed.

Table 7. Measurement errors of 15, 20 and 25 mm with a 0.3 Mp camera with an f = 6 mm lens using standard calibration and developed.

Parameters	15 mm		20 mm		25 mm	
Distortion Correction Methods	Standard	Developed	Standard	Developed	Standard	Developed
$\overline{M}$, mm	−0.012	0.042	−0.003	−0.021	0.029	−0.005
$\overline{S}$, mm	0.052	0.050	0.062	0.041	0.062	0.042
δ *, mm	0.118	0.112	0.139	0.092	0.139	0.095

* $t_{0,04;20}$ = 2204.

Investigation of algorithms for compensation of systematic errors for cameras with a resolution of 5.0 Mp was carried out using a USB camera with a 1/2.5″ sensor camera with a Ricoh FL-HC0612A-VG f = 6 mm lens at L = 114.8 mm.

The research results are shown in Figure 13 and in Table 8.

To assess the repeatability of measurement results by a control system with a 5-megapixel camera and f = 6 mm lens, the measurement errors of parts of different sizes were estimated. The results of measuring the diameters of parts with nominal Ø 15, 20 and 25 mm were compared using the developed calibration of the PDI. The results are shown in Figure 14 and Table 9.

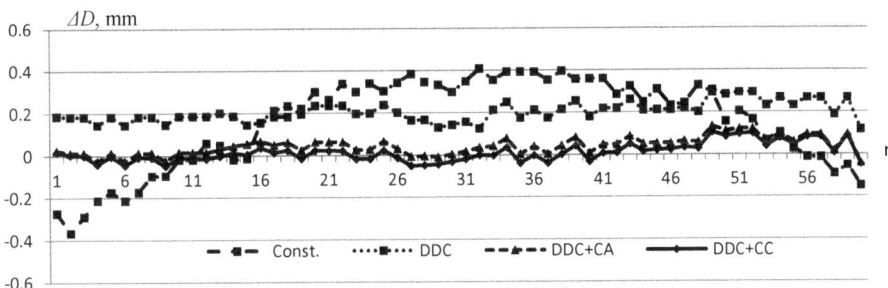

Figure 13. Errors in determining the dimensions of the bead $D_{nom}=25$ mm with a 5 Mp camera with f = 6 mm in the absence and use of compensation algorithms.

Table 8. Errors in determining the dimensions of the roller $D_{nom} = 25$ mm in the absence and use of compensation algorithms for a 5 Mp camera with f = 6 mm.

Parameters	Constant Coefficient (Const.)	No Compensation (DDC)	Compensation of Projection Error (DDC+CA)	Complex Compensation (DDC+CC)
$\overline{M}$, MM	0.154	0.205	0.042	0.011
$\overline{S}$,	0.264	0.211	0.057	0.042
$\delta *$, MM	0.559	0.448	0.122	0.089

* $t_{0,04;46} = 2114$.

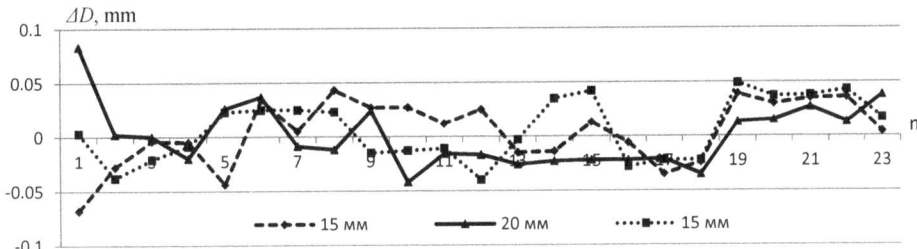

Figure 14. Uncertainties of determination of D_{nom} = 15, 20 and 25 mm with a 5 Mp camera with f = 6 mm lens when using the DTR calibration.

Table 9. Errors in determining the dimensions of the rollers during usage of compensation algorithms with a 5 Mp camera (f = 6 mm).

Parameters	D_{nom}		
	15 mm	20 mm	25 mm
$\overline{M}$, mm	0.003	0.001	0.001
$\overline{S}$,	0.033	0.032	0.035
$\delta *$, mm	0.072	0.070	0.077

* $t_{0,04;20} = 2204$.

5. Discussion

Compensation for systematic projection errors in the control of the main shaping dimensions of axisymmetric parts by the spatial method of optical radiation with 2D resolution from the images of their sections, when using digital cameras with lenses with a fixed focal length in transmitted light, is possible based on the obtained analytical dependences, taking into account the position of the test object and projection component errors. This allows for an increase in the accuracy of determining the main shaping dimensions in reflected light with non-collimated illumination for digital cameras with a resolution of 5 Mp or more, with lenses where the focal length is approximately 1.5 or more of the frame diagonal (short-focus optics).

During analyzation of the results obtained, it can be concluded that with a significant distortion of the Ricoh FL-HC0612A-VG lens, the developed calibration method, based on the use of the image space sampling algorithm, can reduce the confidence interval by more than four times.

Reduction of the error to 0.05% is possible with the use of more advanced image binarization techniques [32,33].

6. Conclusions

The works were carried out to compensate the projection error in the control of axisymmetric parts, solving the problem of increasing the accuracy of determining the main shaping dimensions by optical control systems by the geometric method, using digital cameras with a fixed focal length and receiving measurement information from the image of sections.

Experimental studies have shown the possibility of increasing the accuracy of measuring the diameters of bodies of revolution through control systems equipped with digital cameras with a resolution of 5 Mp or more, with short-focus optics, by an algorithmic method based on taking into account the peculiarities of transferring measurement information about the geometry of bodies of revolution by entocentric optics.

The developed method and software for complex compensation of errors in determining the main shaping geometry of axisymmetric objects allows for a reduction in error in determining dimensions in reflected light with non-colimated illumination for short-focus optics to $\Delta = \pm 0.1$ mm, corresponding to 9–10 accuracy grades for the investigated ranges of sizes of the test object, with a confidence level of 96%.

The problems of compensation of random components of errors should be solved in the future. It will make a full realization of the resolution of modern digital cameras possible, and determination of the position of objects under control in space for their non-fixed position.

Funding: This research received no external funding.

Conflicts of Interest: The author declares no conflict of interest.

References

1. Computer Vision: Technologies, Market Prospects. Available online: https://www.tadviser.ru/index.php/Article:_Computer_vision_:_technologies_,_market_,_prospects/ (accessed on 14 March 2021).
2. Bazhin, V.Y.; Boikov, A.V.; Ivanov, P.V. Optoelectronic method for monitoring the state of the cryolite melt in aluminum electrolyzers. *Russ. J. Non-Ferr. Met.* **2015**, *56*, 6–9. [CrossRef]
3. Martynov, S.A.; Bazhin, V.Y. Improving the control efficiency of metallurgical silicon production technology. *J. Phys. Conf. Ser.* **2019**, *1399*. [CrossRef]
4. Romachev, A.; Kuznetsov, V.; Ivanov, E.; Jörg, B. Flotation froth feature analysis using computer vision technology. In *E3S Web of Conferences*; EDP Sciences: Les Ulis, France, 2020; p. 192. [CrossRef]
5. Maksarov, V.V.; Makhov, V.E. Reduction of defects in the process of formation of preci-sion surfaces of titanium alloy products. *J. Phys. Conf. Ser.* **2020**, *1661*. [CrossRef]
6. Zmarzły, P. Influence of bearing raceway surface topography on the level of generated vibration as an example of operational heredity. *Indian J. Eng. Mater. Sci.* **2020**, *27*, 356–364.
7. Fuqin, D.; Liu, C.; Sze, W.; Deng, J.; Fung, K.; Leung, W.; Lam, E. An illumination-invariant phase-shifting algorithm for three-dimensional profilometry. In *Image Processing: Machine Vision Applications V*; International Society for Optics and Photonics: Bellingham, DC, USA, 2021; Volume 8300. [CrossRef]
8. Boikov, A.V.; Payor, V.A.; Savelev, R.V. Technicalvisionsystem for analysing the mechan-ical characteristics of bulk materials. *J. Phys. Conf. Ser.* **2018**, *944*. [CrossRef]

9. Beloglazov, I.I.; Boikov, A.V.; Petrov, P.A. Discrete element simulation of powder sintering for spherical particles. *Key Eng. Mater.* **2020**, *854*, 164–171. [CrossRef]
10. Maksarov, V.V.; Olt, J. Dynamic stabilization of machining process based on local metastability in controlled robotic systems of CNC machines. *Zap. Gorn. Inst.* **2017**, *226*, 446–451. [CrossRef]
11. The Opticline CS Measurement Systems [Electronic Resource]. Available online: https://www.jenoptik.com/products/metrology/opticline-optical-shaft-metrology/opticline%20cs-serie (accessed on 28 March 2020).
12. Makhov, V.E. Control of linear dimensions of products based on technologies from "National Instruments". Izvestiya vysshikh uchebnykh zavedeniy. *Priborostroenie* **2010**, *7*, 54–60.
13. Bazhin, V.Y.; Kulchitskiy, A.A.; Kadrov, D.N. Complex control of the state of steel pins in soderberg electrolytic cells by using computer vision systems. *Tsvetnye Met.* **2018**, 27–32. [CrossRef]
14. Maksarov, V.V.; Makhov, V.E. Intelligent systems for monitoring and controlling chip for-mation when cutting difficult-to-machine materials. *IOP Conf. Ser. Mater. Sci. Eng.* **2019**, *560*. [CrossRef]
15. Tan, Q.; Kou, Y.; Miao, J.; Liu, S.; Chai, B.A. Model of diameter measurement based on the machine vision. *Symmetry* **2021**, *13*, 187. [CrossRef]
16. Certificate of Type Approval of Measuring Instruments DE.C.27.004.A No. 52362, Optical Coordinate-Measuring Topometric Systems ATOS, Manufacturer GOMmbH, Germany Registration No. 54916-13, Type of Measuring Instruments Approved by Order of the Federal Agency for Technical Regulation and Metrology from September 23, 2013, No. 1110. Available online: https://www.ktopoverit.ru/prof/opisanie/54916-13.pdf (accessed on 14 March 2021).
17. Certificate of Approval of Measuring Instruments OS.C.27.004.A No. 75179 Optical Three-Dimensional Scanners RangeVisionPRO, Manufacturer RangeVision Limited Liability Company (Range Vision LLC). Moscow Region, Krasnogorsk, Registration No. 76251-19, the Type of Measuring Instruments Approved by Order of the Federal Agency for Technical Regulation and Metrology Dated September 27, 2019, No. 2316. Available online: https://rangevision.com/company/news/rangevision-pro-ofitsialno-zanesen-v-gosudarstvennyy-reestr-sredstv-izmereniy/ (accessed on 6 June 2021).
18. Eldib, I.S.A. Development of a Methodology for Improving the Technological Process of Cold Stamping of Products Based on Optical 3d-Scanning and Numerical Modeling, Dissertation for the Degree of Candidate of Technical Sciences-Specialty 05.16.05 Processing of Metals by Pressure, Moscow, Moscow Polytechnic University, 2020. Available online: https://viewer.rusneb.ru/ru/rsl01010248295?page=1&rotate=0&theme=white (accessed on 6 June 2021).
19. Kulchitsky, A.A.; Potapov, A.I.; Smirnov, A.G.; Boykov, V.I. The control system of the geometry of axisymmetric products with an angular mirror converter, Bulletin of higher educational institutions. *Instrumentation* **2020**, *63*, 720–726.
20. Brown, D.C. Close-range camera calibration. *Photogramm. Eng.* **1971**, *37*, 855–866.
21. Tsai, R.Y. A versatile camera calibration technique for high-accuracy 3D machine vision metrology using off-the-shelf TV cameras and lenses. *IEEE Int. J. Robot. Autom.* **1987**, *3*, 323–344. [CrossRef]
22. Zhang, Z. A flexible new technique for camera calibration. *IEEE Trans. Pattern Anal. Mach. Intell.* **2000**, *22*, 1330–1334. [CrossRef]
23. Fitzgibbon, A.W. Simultaneous linear estimation of multiple view geometry and lens distortion. In Proceedings of the 2001 IEEE Computer Society Conference on Computer Vision and Pattern Recognition (CVPR) 2001, Kauai, HI, USA, 8–14 December 2001. [CrossRef]
24. Antipov, I.T. *Mathematical Foundations of Spatial Analytical Phototriangulation*; Kartgeocenter-Geodezizdat: Moscow, Russia, 2003; 296p.
25. Abakumov, I.I.; Kulchitsky, A.A. Compensation of errors of passive optoelectronic monitoring system of geometry. *Meas. Tech.* **2016**, *8*, 56.
26. Industrial Cameras, Technical Features, and Market [Electronic Resource]. Available online: https://industryeurope.com/industrial-cameras-technical-features-and-market/ (accessed on 14 March 2021).
27. Muller, R. FRAMOS Market Survey. Available online: https://www.framos.com/en/news/framos-launches-embedded-vision-ecosystem-of-sensor-modules-and-adapters/ (accessed on 5 February 2021).
28. Kulchitskiy, A.A.; Kashin, D.A.; Romanova, N.A. The Program for Determining the Position of the Test Object during the Calibration of the Optical Projection System for the Control of Axisymmetric Products. Application No. 2020664591, Date of Receipt November 20, 2020, the Date of State Registration in the Register of Computer Programs November 25. 2020 year. Available online: https://elibrary.ru/download/elibrary_44762850_17629678.PDF (accessed on 6 June 2021).
29. Kulchitskiy, A.A.; Kashin, D.A.; Smirnov, A.G. The Program for Control of the Dimensions of Axisymmetric Products with Compensation for the Perspective Error of a Single-Channel Optical System. Application No. 2020664591, Date of Receipt November 20, 2020, the Date of State Registration in the Register of Programs for COMPUTER 25.11. February 2020. Available online: https://elibrary.ru/download/elibrary_44443086_50035226.PDF (accessed on 6 June 2021).
30. Kulchitskiy, A.; Zubareva, A. Reduction of measurement error of axisymmetric parts with an optical system. XIV international Scientific Conference "INTERAGROMASH 2021". *Precis. Agric. Agric. Mach. Ind.* **2021**, *1*, 1–11.
31. Abakumov, I.I.; Kulchitskiy, A.A. Algorithmic way to compensate for the errors of an automated electronic control system for geometric parameters of objects. In *Innovative Systems of Planning and Management in Transport and Mechanical Engineering: Collection of Works of the II International Scientific and Practical Conference Volume II*; National Mineral Resources University Mining: St. Petersburg, Russia, 2014; pp. 104–107.

32. Makhov, V.E.; Potapov, A.I.; Shaldaev, S.E. Investigation of the image boundaries by the contrast extraction method using an optoelectronic system Part 1. Scientific and methodological principles of image border control by the contrast extraction method. *Control. Diagn.* **2017**, *10*, 44–51.
33. Makhov, V.E.; Potapov, A.I.; Shaldaev, S.E. Investigation of the image boundaries by contrast extraction using an opto-electronic system Part 2. Experimental model studies of image boundaries based on wavelet transforms. *Kontrol. Diagn.* **2017**, *11*, 4–11. [CrossRef]

Article

Universal Approach for DEM Parameters Calibration of Bulk Materials

Aleksei Boikov [1,*], Roman Savelev [1], Vladimir Payor [1] and Alexander Potapov [2]

1. Department of Mineral Processing, Automation of Technological Processes and Production, St. Petersburg Mining University, 199106 St. Petersburg, Russia; s192088@stud.spmi.ru (R.S.); s192087@stud.spmi.ru (V.P.)
2. ESSS Rocky DEM, Florianopolis 88032-700, Brazil; potapov@esss.co
* Correspondence: boykov_av@pers.spmi.ru

Abstract: DEM parameters calibration is the most important step in preparing a DEM model. At the same time, the lack of a universal approach to DEM parameters calibration complicates this process. The paper presents the author's approach to creating a universal calibration approach based on the physical meaning of the friction coefficients and conducting symmetrical experiments at full scale and in a simulation, as well as the implementation of the approach in the form of a physical test rig. Several experiments were carried out to determine the DEM parameters of six material–boundary pairs. The resulting parameters were adjusted using a refinement experiment. The results confirmed the adequacy of the developed approach, as well as its applicability in various conditions. The limitations of both the approach itself and its specific implementation in the form of a test rig were identified.

Keywords: DEM; discrete element method; calibration; ore; universal approach; experiment; friction; friction coefficients; DEM parameters

1. Introduction

The discrete element method is the most popular approach for computer modeling of bulk materials' behavior. The corresponding software that implements DEM in the user graphic interface is a highly effective tool for optimizing mining equipment. Lately, DEM has often been used in conjunction with CFD and other methods, which opens up the possibility of calculating complex multiphase processes [1–5].

A number of input parameters in DEM software directly represent material properties (shape and size of particles, density, etc.). Friction coefficients (Table 1) have a direct physical representation; however, in DEM software these parameters are integrated into DEM codes of contact models and may affect the behavior of bulk materials in different ways, that is, they are code dependent [6,7]. Since the values of the friction coefficients (DEM parameters) significantly affect the behavior of bulk materials, in order to build an adequate model, they have to be calibrated [8–10].

Table 1. DEM parameters of bulk materials.

	Particle–Particle, PP	Particle–Boundary, PB
Dynamic Friction (DF)	DF_{PP}	DF_{PB}
Static Friction (SF)	SF_{PP}	SF_{PB}
Coefficient of Restitution (CoR)	CoR_{PP}	CoR_{PB}

Many researchers offer their approaches and solutions for the DEM parameters calibration. The whole set of existing calibration methods can be divided into two groups: the bulk calibration approach (BCA) and the direct measuring approach (DMA) [11]. A collaborative approach is also often used. In BCA, a laboratory experiment is performed first (for example, measuring the angle of repose and flow time from the funnel). For the material under study, the density, Young's modulus, Poisson's ratio, and particle-size distribution are measured in advance. The shape of the particles can be simplified (e.g., to a sphere) and the size increased to speed up the calculation. In this case, specific simplifications depend on the conditions for the further use of the obtained DEM parameters' value for modeling technological processes. Then, in the DEM software, the simulation parameters are set, and laboratory experiments are repeated in the model with varying DEM parameters. The parameters can be obtained both iteratively or using various optimization algorithms. The target is the minimum difference between the measured material properties (e.g., angle of repose) in the laboratory experiment and the simulation [12–15]. In the case of DMA, each parameter is measured separately using known techniques. Most often, BCA and DMA are combined to achieve the most adequate bulk material behavior in the model [16–20].

The main problems for creating a universal DEM parameters calibration approach are:

1. Code dependence (depending on DEM software and contact model).
2. A possibility for several sets of DEM parameters to provide similar bulk responses in the simulation.
3. The need to significantly simplify the model (including the shape and size of particles) to speed up the calculation. Thus, the use of calibrated values of DEM parameters is limited, as well as their dependence on a specific application (technological process).
4. Imperfection and inaccuracy of modern measuring tools (including visual estimation of the bulk material responses using machine vision).

Nevertheless, a number of researchers have proposed approaches that can be called universal with a number of limitations [21–23]. Many studies are aimed at reducing the number of simulations required to achieve the desired result using optimization algorithms or at obtaining a unique set of calibrated DEM parameters either by introducing special criteria or by estimating all the possible factors that affect the bulk responses [24,25]. In this case, BCA is applied, which indicates a possible loss of the physical meaning of the obtained DEM parameters. The question also arises whether the obtained set of parameters is unique, that is, the bulk responses values are achieved only with this set of DEM parameters values.

The article describes the developed author's approach and a test rig for the bulk materials' DEM parameters calibration. The approach is based on the transfer of the friction coefficients' physical meaning into the measurement of bulk materials macro parameters using a high-speed camera and the calibration of the obtained DEM parameters set based on a refinement experiment.

2. Materials and Methods

The developed approach is a result of the research conducted by the authors since 2017. Approaches to using the BCA method directly using the design of the experiment were considered [26]. One way or another, this approach did not solve the main problems given in the introduction. In the course of the research, the relationship between the physical meaning of the friction coefficients and DEM parameters was confirmed.

The physical meaning of these coefficients is as follows:

- For static friction (SF), this is the slope (tangent of the repose angle) at which the particle begins to slide over the surface (Figure 1a):

$$SF = \mathrm{tg}(\alpha) \tag{1}$$

where α—angle of shelf incline.

- For dynamic friction, the value is determined by the sliding time on a surface with a certain angle of repose (Figure 1a):

$$DF = \mathrm{tg}(\alpha) - \left(\frac{2S}{gt^2 \cos(\alpha)}\right) \tag{2}$$

where α—angle of shelf incline, S—distance of particle slide movement, t—time of sliding, g—gravity acceleration.

- For the coefficient of restitution, the value is determined by the angles and velocities of rupture and reflection (Figure 1b):

$$CoR = \frac{\cos(\beta_{reflection}) V_{reflection}}{\cos(\beta_{rupture}) V_{rupture}} \quad (3)$$

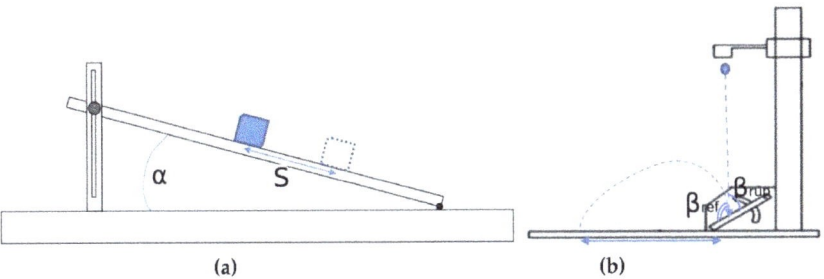

Figure 1. Coefficients measurement schemes; (**a**) measurement scheme for DF and SF; (**b**) measurement scheme for CoR.

The dynamic friction coefficient can be determined by the sliding time of the material along the inclined shelf. The coefficient of restitution can be determined by conducting experiments on the collision of particles with a vertical shelf [27–29]. Based on the physical meaning of the static friction coefficient, it can be determined by the angle of inclination of the shelf. A series of numerical experiments were carried out. In the first version, similar to [30], a box (without bottom) with particles was placed on a shelf, after which the shelf was slowly raised and the angle at which the box began to slide on the shelf was fixed. The second version involved the use of a counterweight for a box with particles standing on a horizontal plane. The counterweight force was slowly increased, and the force at which the box began to slide along the plane was recorded. However, the experiments carried out in the simulations did not show a correlation between SF_{PP}, SF_{PB}, and the angle of inclination of the shelf, as well as the force of the counterweight.

The approach was designed in such a way as to neutralize the main problems described in the introduction. For this, when developing, the authors started from the physical meaning of the coefficients, but transferring the meaning from a single particle to a portion of the investigated bulk material. It is possible to preserve the physical meaning of the calibrated DEM parameters, as well as reduce the number of possible parameter sets or even get a unique set. However, the approach has to include the determination of bulk material responses similar to the BCA method because of the problems with determining SF according to the physical meaning. This makes it possible to keep the methodology flexible and applicable to various DEM software and contact models.

The developed approach scheme is shown in Figure 2. For the investigated bulk material Young's modulus, Poisson's ratio, and particle size distribution are determined using well-known techniques [31–35]. A certain amount of material (portion) is poured into the developed test rig, and then its rheological properties are studied. The flow of the portion is recorded with a pre-installed high-speed camera. After that, the recording from the camera is sent to the computing device. A video processing algorithm developed using machine vision is used; values and parameters characterizing the rheology of the material are recorded. For DF coefficients, these parameters are flow times along the inclined shelves (Equation (1)); for CoR, these are angles and velocities of rupture and reflection (Equation (2)) [36]. Then, the experiments are repeated in the DEM software within the same conditions, but a series of numerical experiments are carried out, where the DEM parameters vary in a given range. For each experiment, an animation is recorded and then processed using similar machine vision algorithms. The experiments in the simulation are symmetrical to the full-scale experiments. A functional relationship is built between the parameters obtained from the simulations and DEM parameters. The obtained function depends on the particle size distribution and particle shape of the material, as well as on the applied contact model and its specific implementation in the DEM software. This means that the input data must be determined in advance. As a result, the obtained dependence is substituted with the values from a full-scale experiment, which makes it possible to obtain specific values of DEM parameters. In this case, the obtained values require clarification; therefore, the repose angle and the flow time are additionally measured. Then, in DEM software, DEM parameters are iteratively varied in a narrow range, which results in fairly accurate results of DEM parameters values.

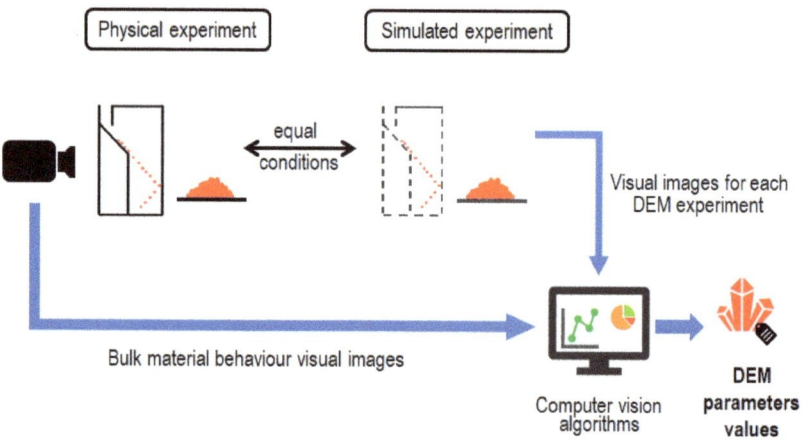

Figure 2. Scheme of the proposed DEM parameters calibration approach.

The test rig at the current stage of research is shown in Figure 3. The test rig has the shape of a rectangular parallelepiped measuring $1 \times 1.5 \times 0.13$ m with inclined shelves located inside, vertical partitions 1–2, bins for loading bulk material, and a funnel-shaped device for testing the angle of rupture and repose, as well as a system of dampers for controlling the flow of materials.

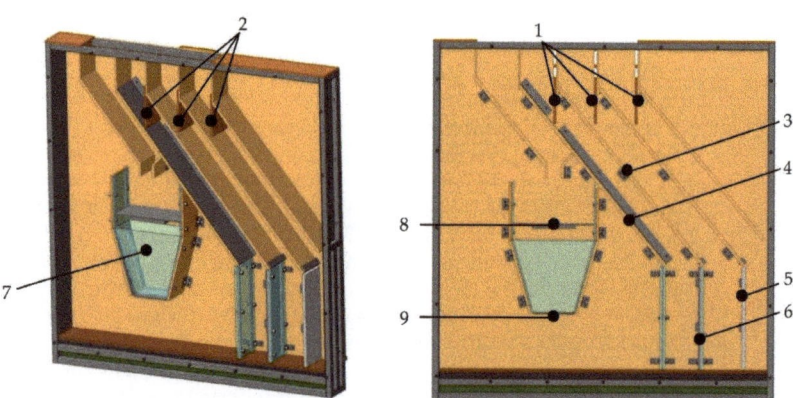

Figure 3. Design of the test rig (model). 1,2—vertical partitions, 3—shelf for DF$_{PP}$, 4—shelf for DF$_{PB}$, 5, 6—collision walls, 7—discharge hopper, 8—upper partition (for angle of rupture), 9—lower partition (for angle of repose).

The flow of the material portion in the test rig occurs under the gravity force and is regulated by mechanical extraction of the partitions 1–2. Determination of CoR$_{PP}$ and DF$_{PP}$ requires the preparation of shelf 3 with a uniformly poured bulk material under study. The bulk material is poured into an adhesive (for example, epoxy resin, liquid nails, ceramic glue). Particles of bulk material are mechanically embedded in the adhesive. After a while, the substance solidifies and, as a result, a shelf is formed of particles of the bulk material under study. The control of the uniformity of the formation of the shelf is carried out visually. Figure 4 shows an analogue of the shelf used in the simulations.

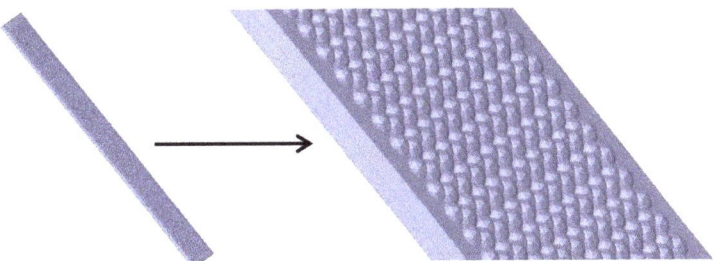

Figure 4. Shelf with particles used in the simulations.

After the completion of the preliminary preparation of the test rig, the material portions are divided into weighed portions for each type of testing. At the beginning of the experiment, portions of the investigated bulk material of the same mass are poured into the upper hoppers. The weight of the samples is determined using a laboratory balance and is about 700 g with an error of no more than 0.5 g. After mechanical removal (of the dampers 2), the bulk material begins to slide along shelves 3 and 4, which is fixed by the algorithm as the beginning of the experiment. Shelves are angled at 40 degrees with a sliding path of 800 mm. This makes it possible to visually distinguish bulk materials with different dynamic coefficients of friction. At the end of the flow of material from each shelf, the algorithm separately fixes the moment in time and calculates the flow time. The experiment is repeated several times. The results are converted to DF$_{PP}$ and DF$_{PB}$, respectively.

The full-scale experiment continues, but the shelf with particles 3 and 4 moves to position 5, as a result of which the flow from the shelf ends with the collision of particles with walls 5 and 6. CoR$_{PP}$ and CoR$_{PB}$ parameters are determined using equation:

$$CoR = k * \frac{\cos(\beta_{refl}) V_{refl}}{\cos(\beta_{rupt}) V_{rupt}} \tag{4}$$

where β_{refl}, β_{rupt} angles of reflection and rupture of bulk material flow, V_{refl}, V_{rupt} the speed of reflection and rupture at the point of impact, k—coefficient that depends on the specifics of the experiment and is taken into account at the stage of refinement of the initially obtained values (by default $k = 1$) [34].

As a refinement experiment for the investigated bulk material, the angles of repose and rupture are determined using device 7. Bulk material is poured into the upper part. After that, partition 8 is pulled out and the angle of rupture is fixed. Then, partition 9 is pulled out, and the material is poured onto the lower shelf of the test rig. As a result, the repose angle and time of flow from the funnel are recorded.

The computer vision system is implemented using LabVIEW software tools. The image from the camera is taken in perspective. Using the reference points on the test rig, the image is projected onto a vertical plane. The original image (Figure 5a) then goes through several stages. It is first filtered and binarized using image thresholding (Figure 5b), then reconstructed using morphological image processing (Figure 5c). Further, depending on the task, there is a search for geometric primitives, or the hit of particles in the region of interest (ROI) is recorded. For example, when determining the angle of the repose (Figure 5d), the boundaries of the object are determined, after which a geometric primitive is built—a triangle. The resulting left and right angles of the triangle are averaged. To determine the flow time, the first entry of particles into the ROI is recorded next to shelves 3 and 4. It is recommended to use a camera with a speed of at least 100 frames per second.

Figure 5. Image processing algorithm example for angle of repose; (**a**)–original image; (**b**)–binarized image; (**c**)–morphological processing applied; (**d**)–final result.

3. Results

As an example of the work of the developed approach, a series of experiments were carried out. For this, three different types of metal steels with different degrees of surface roughness were used as the boundary material. Iron ore and waste rock were used as bulk materials in the experiments. The task was to obtain DEM parameters for two bulk materials and three steels (six boundary–material pairs). Physical implementation of the developed test rig is shown in Figure 6.

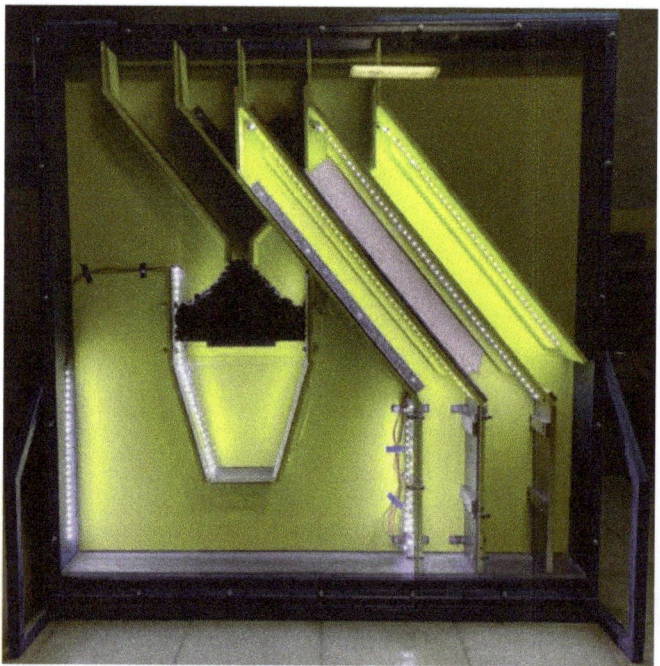

Figure 6. General view of the test rig physical implementation.

3.1. Experiment Setup

Before the start of the experiments, according to the developed methodology, shelves with particles fixed with glue were prepared for ore and waste rock (Figure 7).

Figure 7. Shelf with ore particles in a full-scale experiment.

In addition, a DEM model was prepared for simulations in Rocky DEM software. The parameters of bulk materials and model are presented in Table 2.

Table 2. DEM parameters of bulk materials.

Parameter	Ore	Waste Rock	Boundary (Steel)
Poisson's ratio	0.3		0.3
Young modulus, kPa	10^6		2.95×10^6
Density, kg/m^3	3120	2700	7700
Shape	10-sided polyhedron		-
Particle size, mm distribution	100% 9.5—12.5		-
Contact model	Nonlinear Hertz–Mindlin		
Gravity acceleration, m/s^2	9.81		

For simplicity, the particles are represented in the model as a 10-sided polyhedron (Figure 8).

Figure 8. Particles shape used in the simulations.

3.2. Determining DF_{PB} and DF_{PP}

The first step is to determine the dynamic coefficient of friction. For this, for each boundary–material pair, experiments were carried out to determine the time of sliding on an inclined shelf. Each experiment was performed three times. The measurement results are presented in the Table 3.

Table 3. Results of full-scale experiments to determine dynamic friction based on the flow time.

Ore		Flow Time, s		
Material/Experiment	I	II	III	Average
Steel 1	0.45	0.47	0.49	0.47
Steel 2	0.47	0.45	0.46	0.46
Steel 3	0.56	0.47	0.43	0.49
Particle–particle	0.54	0.6	0.57	0.57
Waste Rock		Flow Time, s		
Material/Experiment	I	II	III	Average
Steel 1	0.45	0.43	0.42	0.43
Steel 2	0.46	0.48	0.47	0.47
Steel 3	0.47	0.47	0.50	0.48
Particle–particle	0.59	0.56	0.52	0.56

Next, a series of simulations were carried out in Rocky DEM. The DF_{PB} and DF_{PP} coefficients varied from 0.1 to 0.9 with a step of 0.1. The flow time was recorded for each experiment. According to the data, functional dependence was built (Figure 9).

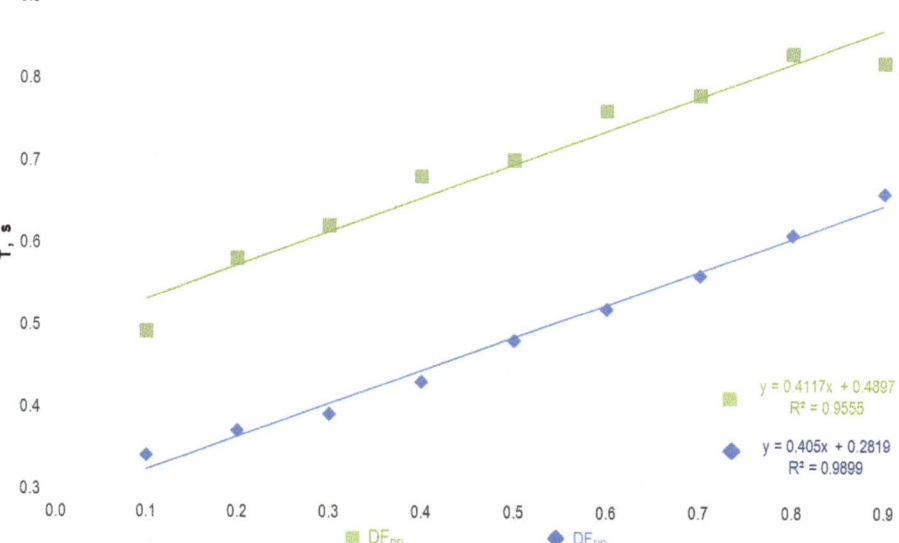

Figure 9. Dependence between flow time (T, s) and DF parameters in simulations.

From the obtained dependences, the DF coefficients were evaluated, presented in Table 4. Figure 10 shows an example of a visual comparison of a full-scale experiment with an ore–steel 1 pair and simulation with a DF_{PB} value of 0.3. Visually, it is noticeable that the flow time is almost identical. Moreover, according to the obtained dependence, the value of the coefficient for this pair is 0.29.

Table 4. Summary values of calculated friction coefficients.

	Ore	Steel 1	Steel 2	Steel 3
DF_{PB}	-	0.46	0.44	0.51
DF_{PP}	0.20	-	-	-
CoR_{PB}	-	0.29	0.31	0.35
CoR_{PP}	0.35	-	-	-
	Waste Rock	Steel 1	Steel 2	Steel 3
DF_{PB}	-	0.37	0.46	0.49
DF_{PP}	0.16	-	-	-
CoR_{PB}	-	0.27	0.28	0.31
CoR_{PP}	0.19	-	-	-

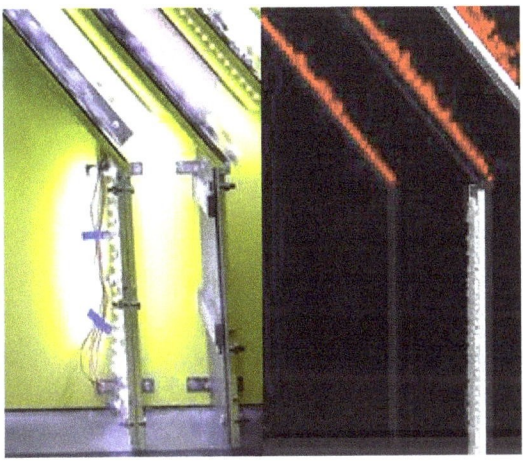

Figure 10. Comparison of simulation and full-scale experiment particles sliding at the same time.

3.3. Determining CoR_{PB} and CoR_{PP}

After the DF coefficients have been obtained for all pairs, it is possible to proceed with the CoR coefficient determination. For this, the shelves (steel) are mounted vertically. The angles of rupture and reflection, as well as the velocities before and after the collision of particles with the shelves, were determined by software algorithms of the computer vision system and recalculated into the values of the CoR_{PP} and CoR_{PB} coefficients according to Equation (4). Simultaneously, numerical experiments were carried out with varying CoR coefficients in the range from 0.1 to 0.9. Similarly, the values obtained by Equation (4) made it possible to refine the values of the coefficients obtained in full-scale experiments (coefficient k in formula 4). Figure 11 shows an example of a collision in a full-scale experiment.

Based on the results, four coefficients were obtained for all pairs. The results are presented in Table 4.

3.4. Determining SF_{PB} and SF_{PP}. Refinement of Results

The SF_{PB} and SF_{PP} coefficients are selected iteratively during the simulations of material flow from the funnel and the formation of rupture and repose angles using the bisection method. This takes into account the fact that SF < DF in most of the use cases. In addition, an error is included in the values of the coefficients in Table 4. Full-scale experiments were carried out to determine bulk responses for ore and waste rock. After that, a series of numerical experiments was launched, in which DF_{PB} and DF_{PP} were varied in the range of obtained value ± 0.05, SF_{PB} in [0.1; DF_{PB}], and SF_{PP} in [0.1; DF_{PP}].

The specified maximum tolerance was no more than four degrees or 10% of the obtained value in a full-scale experiment. The obtained values of the repose angles in full-scale experiments and in the model after calibration are presented in Table 5.

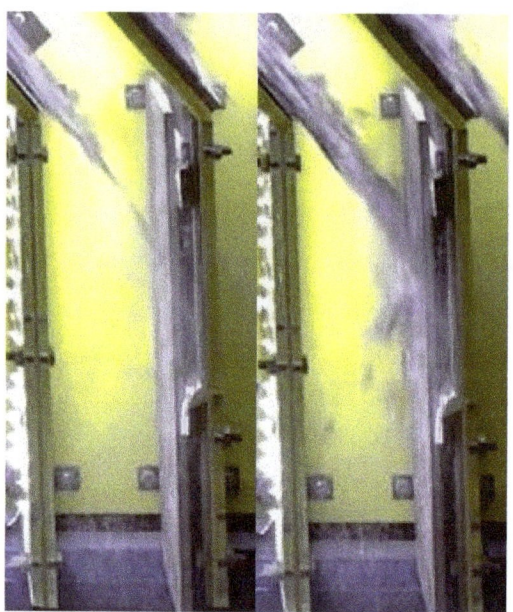

Figure 11. Collision in a full-scale experiment. Original image.

Table 5. Obtained values of the repose and rupture angles.

	Angle of Repose		Angle of Rupture	
	Simulation	Experiment	Simulation	Experiment
Ore	30	28	44	41
Waste Rock	34	35	42	38

Based on the results of the refinement experiment, the values of the DEM parameters were recalculated. The calibrated values are presented in Table 6.

Table 6. Calibrated DEM parameters.

	Ore	Steel 1	Steel 2	Steel 3
SF_{PB}	-	0.33	0.32	0.35
SF_{PP}	0.26	-	-	-
DF_{PB}	-	0.46	0.44	0.51
DF_{PP}	0.20	-	-	-
CoR_{PB}	-	0.29	0.31	0.35
CoR_{PP}	0.35	-	-	-
	Waste Rock	**Steel 1**	**Steel 2**	**Steel 3**
SF_{PB}	-	0.31	0.32	0.33
SF_{PP}	0.32	-	-	-
DF_{PB}	-	0.37	0.46	0.49
DF_{PP}	0.16	-	-	-
CoR_{PB}	-	0.27	0.28	0.31
CoR_{PP}	0.19	-	-	-

An example of an original image obtained from a video camera in a full-scale experiment, and the result obtained in a calibrated model, are presented in Figure 12.

Figure 12. An example of a full-scale experiment and a simulation. Refinement experiment. Original images.

4. Discussion

The developed approach was combined. Four coefficients (DF_{PB}, DF_{PP}, CoR_{PB}, and CoR_{PP}) were determined by methods based on their physical meanings. However, then, the SF coefficients were determined using a refinement test with the determination of the macro parameters of the bulk material, where the values of other coefficients vary within a narrow range. This made it possible to obtain a unique combination of DEM parameters that do not lose their physical meaning and adequately reproduce the behavior of bulk material in the DEM model.

The obtained results shown in Table 4 make it possible to judge that with different surface roughness, DF_{PB} parameters obtained using the developed approach have regular differences. Thus, steel 1 and steel 2 have almost the same roughness (steel 2 is slightly larger), and steel 3 has a much higher roughness. At the same time, DF_{PB} for steel 3–ore and steel 3–waste rock pairs is higher than for other pairs. The DF coefficients obtained after the refinement experiment (Table 5) did not change compared to the initial ones (Table 4). This was due to the fact that the regression algorithm in the refinement experiment achieved the desired result immediately after the selection of the SF parameters. With a higher required accuracy, the DF coefficients could change in the range of obtained value ± 0.05. In general, possible differences in the values of the parameters before and after the refinement experiment are associated with the inaccuracy of the motion measurement using a video camera, as well as the image processing algorithms.

Although the approach was developed for the study of absolutely any bulk materials, the specific implementation of the approach in the form of a physical test rig has a number of limitations. These limitations arise due to the specific design features and the capabilities and accuracy of the measuring devices. First, the test rig is designed for particles no larger than 15 mm. In the opposite case, material sticking can form in narrow places of the test rig, as well as possible errors in the representation of macro parameters (for example, the angle of rupture in the refinement tests). At the same time, materials with particles more than 15 mm can be crushed to the required size, and experiments can be carried out on a test rig. For this, it is necessary that the shape of the particles in the initial and final forms is the same. That is, for particles with specific shapes (ball, cube, etc.), this option is not suitable. It is also recommended to examine materials with particles of at least 1 mm in size. On the one hand, particles can seep through the slits in the structure; on the other hand, a low-resolution video camera may not detect their movement (in particular, this concerns image processing algorithms). Secondly, the image processing algorithms require refinement in order to improve the accuracy of the unambiguousness of the results obtained. It is planned to consider other algorithms for determining the repose angle of bulk material and improve the accuracy of determining the flow time.

In general, the calculation time for all simulations was about 4 h on 10 cores of the average processor in the Rocky DEM. With several GPUs, calculations can be significantly sped up. This means that the calibration of DEM parameters could be a relatively quick and easy process.

5. Conclusions

This paper describes the author's approach to determining and calibrating the DEM parameters of a wide range of bulk materials. Features of the approach are identification of each DEM parameter accordingly to its physical meaning and conducting symmetrical experiments in full-scale and simulation. The approach itself can be applied to any bulk material. The test rig developed as an implementation of the methodology includes several sections, where each section is responsible for determining a specific DEM parameter. The use of a refinement test for the rupture and repose angles ensures that the material with the obtained unique set of DEM parameters adequately reproduces the material rheology in the DEM model. The presence of restrictions on the size and shape of particles impose specific features of the test rig design, as well as cameras for recording material movement. However, the test rig has wide applicability in various industries, from mining and metallurgy to pharmaceutical.

It is planned to further develop the project and conduct additional tests of other particle–material pairs in order to identify weaknesses in the test rig design and the approach as a whole. Other possible implementations of the approach will also be considered. The introduction and use of the approach and the test rig in the modeling of specific technological processes will increase the adequacy of the behavior of the material in the DEM models and simplify the solution of engineering problems using the discrete elements method software.

Author Contributions: Formal analysis, R.S.; Project administration, A.B.; Software, V.P.; Supervision, A.P. All authors have read and agreed to the published version of the manuscript.

Funding: This research received no external funding.

Institutional Review Board Statement: Not applicable.

Informed Consent Statement: Not applicable.

Acknowledgments: We would like to thank CADFEM CIS and personally Andrey Feoktistov for informational support, ideas, and assistance in work on this project.

Conflicts of Interest: The authors declare no conflict of interest.

References

1. Sizyakov, V.M.; Vlasov, A.A.; Bazhin, V.Y. Strategic tasks of Russian metallurgical complex. *Tsvetnye Met.* **2016**, 32–38. [CrossRef]
2. Gospodarikov, A.P.; Vykhodtsev, Y.N.; Zatsepin, M.A. Mathematical modeling of seismic explosion waves impact on rock mass with a working. *J. Min. Inst.* **2017**, *226*, 405–411.
3. Koteleva, N.; Frenkel, I. Digital Processing of Seismic Data from Open-Pit Mining Blasts. *Appl. Sci.* **2021**, *11*, 383. [CrossRef]
4. Iakovleva, E.; Belova, M.; Soares, A. Allocation of potentially environmentally hazardous sections on pipelines. *Geosciences* **2021**, *11*, 1–11.
5. Klyuev, R.; Bosikov, I.; Gavrina, O.; Madaeva, M.; Sokolov, A. Improving the energy efficiency of technological equipment at mining enterprises. *Adv. Intell. Syst. Comput.* **2021**, *1258*, 262–271.
6. Kalala, J.T.; Breetzke, M.; Moys, M.H. Study of the influence of liner wear on the load behaviour of an industrial dry tumbling mill using the Discrete Element Method (DEM). *Int. J. Miner. Process.* **2008**, *86*, 33–39. [CrossRef]
7. Wu, C.Y. DEM simulations of die filling during pharmaceutical tabletting. *Particuology* **2008**, *6*, 412–418. [CrossRef]
8. Ye, F.; Wheeler, C.; Chen, B.; Hu, J.; Chen, K.; Chen, W. Calibration and verification of DEM parameters for dynamic particle flow conditions using a backpropagation neural network. *Adv. Powder Technol.* **2019**, *30*, 292–301. [CrossRef]
9. Zhukovskiy, Y.L.; Suslikov, P.K.; Arapova, E.G.; Alieva, L.Z. Digital platform as a means of process optimization of integrating electric vehicles into electric power networks. *J. Phys. Conf. Ser.* **2020**, *1661*, 012162. [CrossRef]

10. Yan, Z.; Wilkinson, S.K.; Stitt, E.H.; Marigo, M. Discrete element modelling (DEM) input parameters: Understanding their impact on model predictions using statistical analysis. *Comput. Part. Mech.* **2015**, *2*, 283–299. [CrossRef]
11. Coetzee, C.J. Calibration of the discrete element method and the effect of particle shape. *Powder Technol.* **2016**, *297*, 50–70. [CrossRef]
12. Westbrink, F.; Elbel, A.; Schwung, A.; Ding, S. Optimization of DEM Parameters using Multi-Objective Reinforcement Learning. *Powder Technol.* **2021**, *309*, 602–616. [CrossRef]
13. Gröger, T.; André, K. On the numerical calibration of discrete element models for the simulation of bulk solids. *Comput. Aided Chem. Eng.* **2006**, *21*, 533–538.
14. Do, H.Q.; Aragón, A.M.; Schott, D.L. A calibration framework for discrete element model parameters using genetic algorithms. *Adv. Powder Technol.* **2018**, *29*, 1393–1403. [CrossRef]
15. Asaf, Z.; Rubinstein, D.; Shmulevich, I. Determination of discrete element model parameters required for soil tillage. *Soil Tillage Res.* **2007**, *92*, 227–242. [CrossRef]
16. Zhao, S.; Zhou, X.; Liu, W. Discrete element simulations of direct shear tests with particle angularity effect. *Granul. Matter* **2015**, *17*, 793–806. [CrossRef]
17. Turkia, S.; Wilke, D.; Pizette, P.; Govender, N.; Abriak, N. Benefits of virtual calibration for discrete element parameter estimation from bulk experiments. *Granul. Matter* **2019**, *21*, 110. [CrossRef]
18. Frankowski, P.; Morgeneyer, M. Calibration and validation of DEM rolling and sliding friction coefficients in angle of repose and shear measurements. *AIP Conf. Proc.* **2013**, *1542*, 851–854.
19. Zhou, H.; Hu, Z.; Chen, J.; Lv, X.; Xie, N. Calibration of DEM models for irregular particles based on experimental design method and bulk experiments. *Powder Technol.* **2018**, *332*, 210–223. [CrossRef]
20. Ghodki, B.M.; Patel, M.; Namdeo, R.; Carpenter, G. Calibration of discrete element model parameters: Soybeans. *Comput. Part. Mech.* **2019**, *6*, 3–10. [CrossRef]
21. Rackl, M.; Hanley, K.J. A methodical calibration procedure for discrete element models. *Powder Technol.* **2017**, *307*, 73–83. [CrossRef]
22. Al-Hashemi, H.M.B.; Al-Amoudi, O.S.B. A review on the angle of repose of granular materials. *Powder Technol.* **2018**, *330*, 397–417. [CrossRef]
23. Malone, K.F.; Xu, B.H. Determination of contact parameters for discrete element method simulations of granular systems. *Particuology* **2008**, *6*, 521–528. [CrossRef]
24. El-Kassem, B.; Salloum, N.; Brinz, T.; Heider, Y.; Markert, B. A multivariate regression parametric study on DEM input parameters of free-flowing and cohesive powders with experimental data-based validation. *Comput. Part. Mech.* **2020**, *8*, 87–111. [CrossRef]
25. Roessler, T.; Richter, C.; Katterfeld, A.; Will, F. Development of a standard calibration procedure for the DEM parameters of cohesionless bulk materials—Part I: Solving the problem of ambiguous parameter combinations. *Powder Technol.* **2019**, *343*, 803–812. [CrossRef]
26. Boikov, A.V.; Savelev, R.V.; Payor, V.A. DEM Calibration Approach: Design of experiment. *J. Phys. Conf. Ser.* **2018**, *1015*, 032017. [CrossRef]
27. Wang, L. Experimental determination of parameter effects on the coefficient of restitution of differently shaped maize in three-dimensions. *Powder Technol.* **2015**, *284*, 187–194. [CrossRef]
28. Hlosta, J.; Žurovec, D.; Rozbroj, J.; Ramírez-Gómez, Á.; Nečas, J.; Zegzulka, J. Experimental determination of particle–particle restitution coefficient via double pendulum method. *Chem. Eng. Res. Des.* **2018**, *135*, 222–233. [CrossRef]
29. Imre, B.; Räbsamen, S.; Springman, S.M. A coefficient of restitution of rock materials. *Comput. Geosci.* **2008**, *34*, 339–350. [CrossRef]
30. Google Patents. Available online: https://patents.google.com/patent/RU168916U1/ru (accessed on 15 April 2021).
31. Beloglazov, I.I.; Petrov, P.A.; Bazhin, V.Y. The concept of digital twins for tech operator training simulator design for mining and processing industry. *Eurasian Min.* **2020**, *2020*, 50–54. [CrossRef]
32. Grigorev, M.B.; Tananykhin, D.S.; Poroshin, M.A. Sand management approach for a field with high viscosity oil. *J. Appl. Eng. Sci.* **2020**, *18*, 64–69. [CrossRef]
33. Morenov, V.; Leusheva, E. Influence of the solid phase's fractional composition on the filtration characteristics of the drilling mud. *Int. J. Eng. Trans. B Appl.* **2019**, *32*, 794–798.
34. Beloglazov, I.I.; Stepanyan, A.S.; Feoktistov, A.Y.; Yusupov, G.A. Disintegration process modeling for a jaw crusher with complex jaws swing. *Obogashchenie Rud* **2018**, *2*, 3–8. [CrossRef]
35. Koteleva, N.; Buslaev, G.; Valnev, V.; Kunshin, A. Augmented reality system and maintenance of oil pumps. *Int. J. Eng. Trans. B Appl.* **2020**, *33*, 1620–1628.
36. Vasilyeva, N.V.; Erokhina, O.O. Post-impact recovery coefficient calibration in DEM modeling of granular materials. *Obogashchenie Rud* **2020**, *2020*, 42–48. [CrossRef]

Article

Synthetic Data Generation for Steel Defect Detection and Classification Using Deep Learning

Aleksei Boikov [1,*], Vladimir Payor [1], Roman Savelev [1] and Alexandr Kolesnikov [2]

1 Department of Mineral Process, Automation of Technological Processes and Production, St. Petersburg Mining University, 199106 St. Petersburg, Russia; s192087@stud.spmi.ru (V.P.); s192088@stud.spmi.ru (R.S.)
2 The Ministry of Education and Science of the Republic of Kazakhstan, M. Auezov South Kazakhstan University, Shymkent 160012, Kazakhstan; kas164@yandex.kz
* Correspondence: boykov_av@pers.spmi.ru

Abstract: The paper presents a methodology for training neural networks for vision tasks on synthesized data on the example of steel defect recognition in automated production control systems. The article describes the process of dataset procedural generation of steel slab defects with a symmetrical distribution. The results of training two neural networks Unet and Xception on a generated data grid and testing them on real data are presented. The performance of these neural networks was assessed using real data from the Severstal: Steel Defect Detection set. In both cases, the neural networks showed good results in the classification and segmentation of surface defects of steel workpieces in the image. Dice score on synthetic data reaches 0.62, and accuracy—0.81.

Keywords: computer vision; synthetic data; steel defect detection; machine learning

Citation: Boikov, A.; Payor, V.; Savelev, R.; Kolesnikov, A. Synthetic Data Generation for Steel Defect Detection and Classification Using Deep Learning. *Symmetry* **2021**, *13*, 1176. https://doi.org/10.3390/sym13071176

Academic Editors: Rudolf Kawalla and Beloglazov Ilya

Received: 15 June 2021
Accepted: 28 June 2021
Published: 29 June 2021

Publisher's Note: MDPI stays neutral with regard to jurisdictional claims in published maps and institutional affiliations.

Copyright: © 2021 by the authors. Licensee MDPI, Basel, Switzerland. This article is an open access article distributed under the terms and conditions of the Creative Commons Attribution (CC BY) license (https://creativecommons.org/licenses/by/4.0/).

1. Introduction

Machine learning algorithms for computer vision are widely used in various industries. A distinctive feature of such algorithms is the need for large arrays of labeled data on which to train them. The quality of a machine-learning-based automation system largely depends on the quality of the initial training sample. It should maximally reliably reflect the nature of the process under study, in other words, be representative [1]. Obtaining such a sample is very laborious; it is necessary to capture as many different variants of the object states under investigation as possible [2]. For example, if you want to classify an object, you have to include as many unique instances of each class in the sample as possible. However, this may cause difficulties because of the intraclass variation of the object, i.e., objects belonging to the same class may have a different representation (color, shape, size, etc.) [3].

In most cases, developers of industrial automation systems do not have at their disposal the necessary amount of production data sufficient to implement machine learning algorithms. This is due to the company not recording the necessary parameters beforehand nor doing it properly; automatic markup of production data being difficult, and manual markup requiring a high level of specialist competence; data collection must be performed in long time intervals (months and years) [4,5]. As a consequence, these limitations, taken together, significantly complicate the implementation of machine learning algorithms in automated control systems for technological processes [6].

One of these tasks is to control the surface condition of steel blanks and identify defects. Currently, machine learning methods applied as part of steel slab surface inspection systems require a large number of defect images for training. This in turn increases the time required to collect and markup the training dataset [7,8].

The use of synthesized datasets will solve these problems by accelerating the collection and partitioning of training data. The use of synthetic data for training machine learning algorithms has been gaining popularity recently. Artificial datasets based on computer graphics are already used for self-driving vehicles [9] and for cancer diagnostics [10]. This study considers the possibility of applying synthesized data for semantic segmentation and classification of defects in steel products. The developed approach is supposed to be used in automatic control systems of steel rolling production. These systems include vision-based quality control systems.

The task of determining defects on the workpiece surface is complex; it combines several independent vision tasks. First of all, it is necessary to determine the presence of surface defects in the image [11]. It is necessary to have a clear idea about the permissible visual deviations, which can lead to false positive recognitions. For example, grease residues, water drops, or fragments of slab markings can be such deviations (Figure 1).

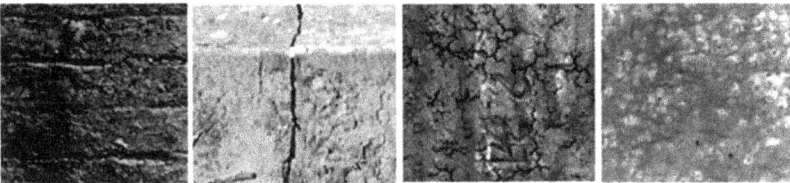

Figure 1. Examples of defects in steel workpiece. From left to right: scratch, surface crack, network cracks and caverns.

The next stage of slab surface analysis is the semantic classification of defects. The complexity of this task is due to the wide intraclass diversity of defects [12–14]. Most slab surface defects are cracks of various shapes, lengths, depths, and localization. An important problem is the technical side of defect detection. Current methods of metal surface scanning are based on optical systems: video imaging, laser triangulation, and their combination. Depth cameras have also recently begun to be used. The choice of the technical means of scanning the workpiece surface largely determines the further architecture of the system, the type of the classification algorithm, and the physical possibility of determining certain types of surface defects [15].

This publication presents the results of generating a synthetic dataset of steel defects for training a machine learning model. On the data generated during the work, neural networks of two types were trained—a classifier and a semantic segmentation network. Both models were also trained and evaluated on the dataset. The resulting models can be used in industrial quality control systems for rolled steel. Methods for evaluating neural networks are in Section 2. The dataset generation methodology and model training results are in Section 3.

2. Materials and Methods

To solve the issue described in the Introduction, a technique was developed that allows for generating training datasets for training neural networks. The implementation of the proposed methodology consists of the following stages. The process of building the above-described hardware and software complex can be divided into several sequential stages:

1. Collecting data and forming training samples. At this stage, the collection, systematization, and marking of data on surface defects of steel workpiece are carried out in a unified form [16].
2. Building a defect classifier model. A classifier model is built and trained based on the obtained ideas about the types of defects on the surfaces of rolled steel and variations in their manifestation [17].
3. Evaluating the quality of the classifier's work. The chosen classifier model is tested on a specially selected sample, and its samples were not part of the training one. Additionally, distortions can be introduced into the test sample images to test the robustness of the algorithm as a whole [18].

The freeware 3D editor Blender was used to generate the training sample. It is also equipped with built-in shader writing tools necessary for software generation of random slab defect textures.

To test the proposed methodology, two neural networks were trained on the synthesized data: Unet [19]—for segmentation of defects in the image and the Xception classifier [20]. Trained neural networks were tested on a real dataset Severstal: Steel Defect Detection [21] as a validation sample.

Metrics such as precision, recall, and Dice coefficient were used to evaluate the quality of the models [22–24].

Algorithm accuracy within one class or intraclass accuracy is a metric that characterizes the number of all records that really belong to a certain class, to the sum of all exemplars that were assigned to that class by the algorithm. The metric is calculated using the following Formula (1):

$$Precission = \frac{TP}{TP + FP} \quad (1)$$

where TP—number of true positive answers, and FP—number of false positives.

Recall is another important metric that is defined as the proportion of samples from a class that are correctly predicted by the model. This metric is the proportion of class instances recognized by the algorithm as related to the total number of instances of the class in the sample [25]. Recall is calculated using Formula (2):

$$Recall = \frac{TP}{TP + FN} \quad (2)$$

where TP—number of true positive answers, FN—number of false-negative responses.

Dice's coefficient [26] is used to compare the pixel match between the predicted segmentation and the corresponding ground truth [27]. The Dice coefficient is determined by Formula (3):

$$Dice(X, Y) = \frac{2 \cdot |X \cap Y|}{|X| + |Y|} \quad (3)$$

where X—predicted pixel set, Y—true meaning.

The Dice coefficient is primarily a statistical measure used to assess the similarity of two samples: the similarity coefficient [25].

The training and evaluating of the neural network model was carried out using the Keras framework and the Python programming language. To assess the model quality metrics, validation samples were fed to the input of the model, which the neural network had not previously processed during training. We compared the neural network's responses to the ground truth values according to the chosen metric. To automate the evaluation of the quality of the work of models, the function "evaluate", built into the Keras framework, was used.

The artificial training dataset was generated in the Blender 3 editor using the built-in shader tool; the program texture generation was done in the Blender API. This software product is widely used for generating artificial data for object detection using state-of-the-art deep learning models [26].

The process of generating an artificial dataset of defects includes the following steps:

- Setting the 3D scene of the object;
- Procedural generation of the surface texture (defect);
- Image rendering;
- Render of the mask.

To generate synthetic data containing surface defects of steel workpieces, a scene simulating the shooting of a steel by a camera was assembled in the Blender 3D graphical editor.

The slab model is a parallelepiped onto which the shader material is superimposed. Depending on the input parameters passed to the shader, the texture displayed on the surface of the parallelepiped changes. Thus, a unique combination of defects of the same kind can be reproduced with each new set of parameters. The disadvantage of this approach is the need to create a new shader for each type of defect. Therefore, in this work, the choice was limited to three basic types of defects: cracks, bubbles, foreign inclusions, and surface irregularities.

The conditions of shooting the slab surface in the 3D scene mimic real industrial conditions with cameras mounted vertically above the slab surface. The light source in the scene was placed slightly above the camera, thus simulating the illumination provided by the computer vision cameras (Figure 2).

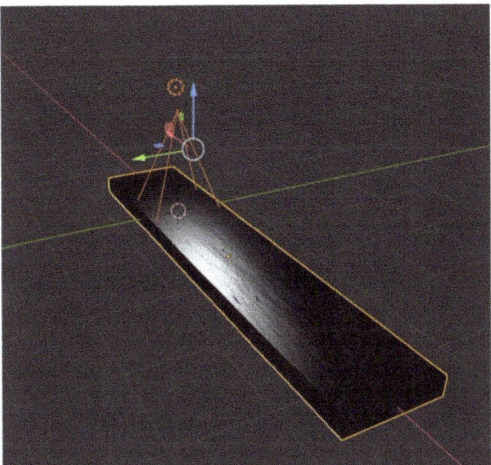

Figure 2. Defective steel sheet model in Blender.

The surface texture of the workpiece, the type, and frequency of appearance of defects on it were set through the shader of the material assigned to the workpiece model. Thus, we were able to determine in advance, even before generation, the composition (by defects) of our artificial dataset. Image generation for the dataset was performed automatically by sequentially shifting the slab model in the scene relative to the camera, thus simulating the movement of the workpiece along the roller conveyor. Shader parameters were also changed with each iteration to create a greater variety of defect shapes and locations. Thus, the effect of random distribution of surface defects was created, after which the image of the surface was rendered.

The main algorithm for creating a synthetic dataset is the procedural generation of a surface defect. It is a shader—a program that sequentially transforms the original noise texture. A separate shader was written for each of the four defect types. The variety of shapes of the generated defects was adjusted using the detorsion and noise parameter. For example, such a defect as a crack is based on a procedural texture—a spherical gradient. It, like the cracks themselves, has the shape of an ellipse, subjected in advance to numerous deformations through changes in its UV coordinates and the symmetry of the original figure. The fracture boundaries are subject to displacements along the normal. The textures for chipping generation were created by transforming the Perlin noise. An overall scheme of the procedural dataset generation algorithm is shown in Figure 3.

Parallel to the photorealistic images, their black and white masks are also created. The pixels containing the defects of the slab surface are highlighted in white. The masks are one of the variants of training data markup for segmenting architectures. They also can be used to automate the markup of classifiers. Thus, one of the main difficulties encountered in the preparation of real data—markup—was solved. In this approach, the partitioning was done automatically, in parallel with the generation of the images themselves.

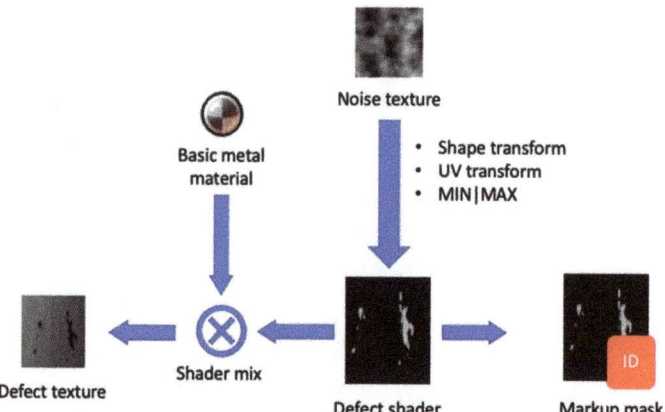

Figure 3. Scheme of the procedural dataset generation algorithm.

Since the data generation process for the dataset is fully controllable, we can predetermine the distribution of surface defect classes within the sample. In this case, it is necessary to ensure the most equal distribution between the classes of different defects. It is necessary to normalize the distribution of instances in the dataset. This will increase the accuracy of defect classification and reduce the influence of the predominant number of instances of individual classes in the sample on the classification result as a whole. Synthetic data have been tested over two artificial neural networks: U-Net and Xception.

U-Net is one of the standard CNN architectures for image segmentation tasks when you need to segment its areas by class and create a mask that will divide the image into several classes. The architecture consists of a contraction path for capturing context and an asymmetrical expanding path that allows precise object localization. U-Net achieves high results in various real-world problems using a small amount of data to achieve high segmentation accuracy [27].

The Xception is a compact modification of the Inception classifier architecture based on depthwise separable convolution. We used this architecture to classify defect types on original image areas with steel defects that previously were recognized with the U-Net model. This mode was chosen among many other classifiers because it requires less data for correct object classification.

As the result of combining both of these models, the semantic segmentation problem on steel defects models was solved.

3. Results

An artificial dataset consisting of 6000 defect images and including four defect classes was generated during the experiment. A total of 1500 images were generated for each type of defect to ensure an even distribution of samples in the sample.

Below, there are the results of generating synthetic data for different types of defects. Figure 4 shows examples of defects and their masks in the generated dataset.

Two neural network architectures were trained: Unet—for defect segmentation in the original image and Xception—for classification. Both neural networks were trained on a synthesized dataset and tested on real data.

Below are the results of training the Unet neural network on synthetic data with validation on real data. The neural network was trained entirely on a synthetic dataset for 30 epochs. Figure 5 shows charts of the change in the Dice coefficient for epochs for the test and validation samples.

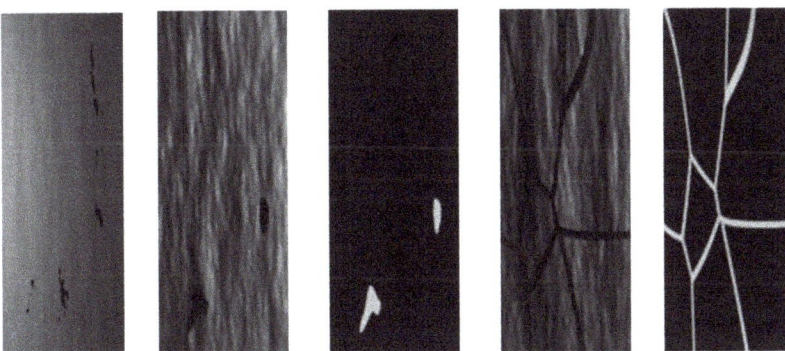

Figure 4. Examples of defect renders of various types and their masks.

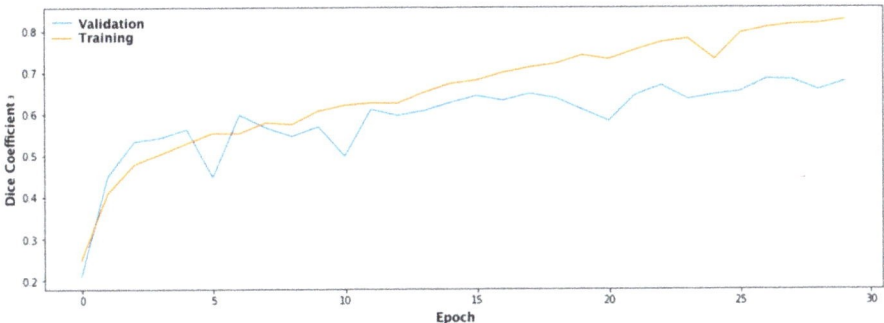

Figure 5. Dice Coefficient change graph.

As can be seen from the graph, the Dice coefficient for the training sample reaches 0.815 and 0.632 for the validation sample, represented by real defect images.

Figure 6 shows examples of segmentation of defects in an image from a real dataset by the Unet neural network trained on synthetic data.

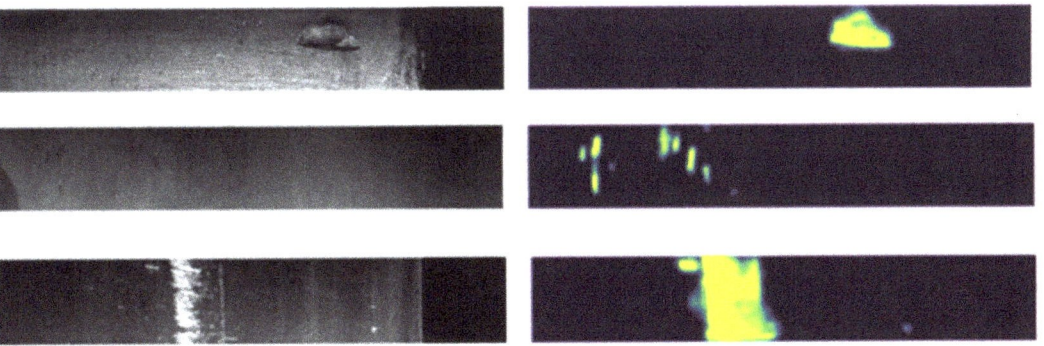

Figure 6. Defect segmentation by the Unet neural network.

As can be seen from the above images, the neural network with the Unet architecture quite accurately and clearly identifies defects in the original image of real defects in rolled steel.

The Xception architecture was used to classify defects. This neural network was also trained on synthetic data. The training was carried out in 15 epochs. As mentioned earlier, the main metrics for assessing the quality of classification are accuracy and recall.

Figures 7 and 8 show graphs of the accuracy of defect recognition on synthetic (training) data and on real data.

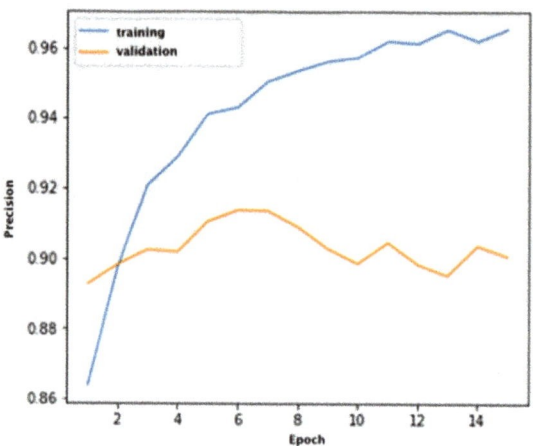

Figure 7. Precision graphs during neural network training.

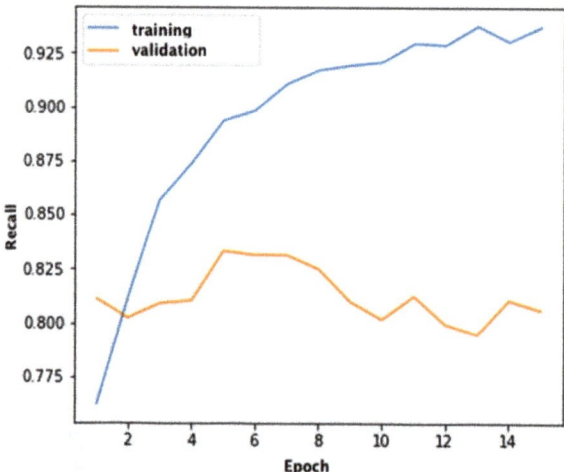

Figure 8. Plots of recall during neural network training.

As can be seen from the graphs, Xception classifies defects in training and validation samples with a sufficiently high accuracy. At the same time, the recall of the classification is somewhat lower and on the validation sample does not exceed 0.81, which indicates a large number of false positive recognitions (Figure 8).

Let us compare the performance of architectures trained on synthetic data and on real data. To do this, we train the presented Xception and Unet models on the real Severstal: Steel Defect Detection dataset, which includes 7095 samples and four classes of defects. Figure 9 shows the distribution of defects by type in the real dataset.

Defect Type: Count & Frequency

Figure 9. Defect types distribution in the real dataset.

Similar to the artificial dataset, the real data was divided into training and test dataset in the ratio of 80% for training and 20% for test dataset. Neural network training was also performed with the same settings as on synthetic data, i.e., 30 epochs for Unet and 15 epochs for Xception. Thus, the only different condition in this experiment was dataset. Table 1 shows the comparison of neural network quality metrics on real and synthesized data.

Table 1. Summary ANN performance on real and synthetic dataset.

	Unet	Xception	
	Dice Score	Precision	Recall
Real dataset	0.56	0.87	0.91
Synthetic dataset	0.63	0.81	0.89

4. Discussion

The proposed approach makes it possible to develop and debug computer vision algorithms without having access to the real object of research, as well as to automate the process of marking up training data for segmentation and classification tasks. The results of neural networks validation trained on artificial data were promising. This confirms the viability of the proposed methodology for working with different types of vision algorithms and the application of techniques for the development of industrial quality control and defectoscopy systems.

The variety of scenes that can be rendered using 3D graphics does not limit the scope of synthetic data to the steel industry. The proposed approach can be applied in other areas, for example, in medicine, analysis of satellite images, and autonomous vehicles.

Synthetic data made it possible to correctly train neural networks for such basic tasks of computer vision as image segmentation and image classification. During the variation of neural networks on real data, the accuracy of recognition and segmentation of defects noticeably decreased. This is primarily due to the fact that procedurally generated images of defects are not realistic enough in comparison with their real counterparts, which, of course, introduces certain distortions in the operation of the algorithm. In general, it should be noted that the quality of defect classification is lower than segmentation. This proves that the images of defects on artificial data are not realistic enough. This disadvantage can be compensated by combining synthetic and real data as part of one dataset, whenever possible, or by increasing the realism of generated images using computer graphics.

5. Conclusions

In the course of this work, we investigated the possibility of using synthesized datasets to train deep neural networks that solve the problems of computer vision on the example of segmentation and classification of surface defects in steel workpieces. A training dataset was generated using the 3D graphics editor Blender. Deep neural networks of two architectures Unet and Xception were trained on the synthetic data set. The performance of these neural networks was evaluated on real data from the Severstal:Steel Defect Detection dataset.

In both cases, neural networks showed good results in the classification and segmentation of surface defects of steel blanks in the image. The results obtained in the course of this experiment indicate the feasibility of applying the proposed methodology. These results are especially valuable when access to the object under study is difficult and the collection and markup of real data are time-consuming. In addition, the proposed technique can be used to increase the variety of existing datasets with real data.

The considered methodology, in addition to its use in industrial flaw detection, can also be useful in other computer vision tasks that require a large amount of data and are difficult to mark up.

Author Contributions: Formal analysis, R.S.; Project administration, A.B.; Software, V.P.; Supervision, A.K. All authors have read and agreed to the published version of the manuscript.

Funding: This research received no external funding.

Institutional Review Board Statement: Not applicable.

Informed Consent Statement: Not applicable.

Data Availability Statement: Not applicable.

Conflicts of Interest: The authors declare no conflict of interest.

References

1. Bazhin, V.Y.; Kulchitskiy, A.A.; Kadrov, D.N. Complex control of the state of steel pins in soderberg electrolytic cells by using computer vision systems. *Tsvetnye Met.* **2018**, *3*, 27–32. [CrossRef]
2. Bulatov, V.V.; Kulchitskii, A.A. Features of translucent materials and products defects detection with support of optical system. *J. Phys. Conf. Ser.* **2020**, *5*, 1–7. [CrossRef]
3. Long, J.; Shelhamer, E.; Darrell, T. Fully convolutional networks for semantic segmentation. In Proceedings of the 2015 IEEE conference on computer vision and pattern recognition, Boston, MA, USA, 7–12 June 2015; pp. 3431–3440.
4. Potapov, A.I.; Kondrat'ev, A.V.; Smorodinskii, Y.G. Nondestructive Testing of Structurally Inhomogeneous Composite Materials by the Method of Elastic-Wave Velocity Hodograph. *Russ. J. Nondestruct. Test.* **2019**, *55*, 434–442. [CrossRef]
5. Chen, L.-C.; Papandreou, G.; Kokkinos, I.; Murphy, K.; Yuille, A.L. Deeplab: Semantic image segmentation with deep convolutional nets, atrous convolution, and fully connected CRFs. *IEEE Trans. Pattern Anal. Mach. Intell.* **2017**, *40*, 834–848. [CrossRef] [PubMed]
6. Cordts, M.; Omran, M.; Ramos, S.; Rehfeld, T.; Enzweiler, M.; Benenson, R.; Franke, U.; Roth, S.; Schiele, B. The cityscapes dataset for semantic urban scene understanding. In Proceedings of the IEEE Computer Society Conference on Computer Vision and Pattern Recognition (CVPR), Las Vegas, NV, USA, 27–30 June 2016.
7. Sifre, L.; Mallat, S. Rotation, scaling and deformation invariant scattering for texture discrimination. In Proceedings of the 2013 IEEE Conference on Computer Vision and Pattern Recognition, Portland, OR, USA, 23–28 June 2013; pp. 1233–1240.
8. Girshick, R.; Donahue, J.; Darrell, T.; Malik, J. Rich feature hierarchies for accurate object detection and semantic segmentation. In Proceedings of the 2013 IEEE Conference on Computer Vision and Pattern Recognition (CVPR), Portland, OR, USA, 23–28 June 2013.
9. Hariharan, B.; Arbelez, P.; Girshick, R.; Malik, J. Hypercolumns for object segmentation and fine-grained localization. In Proceedings of the 2015 IEEE Conference on Computer Vision and Pattern Recognition (CVPR), Boston, MA, USA, 7–12 June 2015; pp. 447–456.
10. He, K.; Zhang, X.; Ren, S.; Sun, J. Delving deep into rectifiers: Surpassing human-level performance on imagenet classification. *arXiv* **2015**, arXiv:1502.01852.
11. Jia, Y.; Shelhamer, E.; Donahue, J.; Karayev, S.; Long, J.; Girshick, R.S.; Darrell, T. Caffe: Convolutional architecture for fast feature embedding. In Proceedings of the 22nd ACM international conference on Multimedia, Orlando, FL, USA, 3–7 November 2014.
12. Krizhevsky, A.; Sutskever, I.; Hinton, G.E. Imagenet classification with deep convolutional neural networks. *Commun. ACM* **2017**, *60*, 84–90. [CrossRef]

13. Fokina, S.B.; Petrov, G.V.; Sizyakova, E.V. Process solutions of zinc-containing waste disposal in steel industry. *Int. J. Civ. Eng. Technol.* **2019**, *10*, 2083–2089.
14. Romachev, A.; Kuznetsov, V.; Ivanov, E. Flotation froth feature analysis using computer vision technology. *EDP Sci.* **2020**, *192*, 02022. [CrossRef]
15. Koteleva, N.; Frenkel, I. Digital Processing of Seismic Data from Open-Pit Mining Blasts. *Appl. Sci.* **2021**, *11*, 383. [CrossRef]
16. Iakovleva, E.; Belova, M.; Soares, A. Allocation of potentially environmentally hazardous sections on pipelines. *Geosciences* **2021**, *11*, 3. [CrossRef]
17. Beloglazov, I.I.; Petrov, P.A.; Bazhin, V.Y. The concept of digital twins for tech operator training simulator design for mining and processing industry. *Eurasian Min.* **2020**, *9*, 50–54. [CrossRef]
18. Chollet, F. Xception: Deep learning with depthwise separable convolutions. In Proceedings of the IEEE Conference on Computer Vision and Pattern recognition, Honolulu, HI, USA, 21–26 July 2017; pp. 1251–1258.
19. Severstal: Steel Defect Detection. Available online: https://www.kaggle.com/c/severstal-steel-defect-detection (accessed on 21 May 2021).
20. Girshick, R. Fast R-CNN. In Proceedings of the IEEE International Conference on Computer Vision, Santiago, Chile, 7–13 December 2015; pp. 1440–1448.
21. Ronneberger, O.; Fischer, P.; Brox, T. U-net: Convolutional networks for biomedical image segmentation. In Proceedings of the International Conference on Medical Image Computing and Computer-Assisted Intervention, Munich, Germany, 5–9 October 2015; pp. 234–241.
22. Koteleva, N.; Buslaev, G.; Valnev, V.; Kunshin, A. Augmented reality system and maintenance of oil pumps. *Int. J. Eng. Trans. B Appl.* **2020**, *33*, 1620–1628.
23. Pryakhin, E.I.; Sharapova, D.M. Understanding the structure and properties of the heat affected zone in welds and model specimens of high-strength low-alloy steels after simulated heat cycles. *CIS Iron Steel Rev.* **2020**, *19*, 60–65. [CrossRef]
24. Vasilieva, N.V.; Fedorova, E.R. Process control quality analysis. *Tsvetnye Met.* **2020**, *2020*, 70–76. [CrossRef]
25. Vasilyeva, N.V.; Boikov, A.V.; Erokhina, O.O.; Trifonov, A.Y. Automated digitization of radial charts. *J. Min. Inst.* **2021**, *247*, 82–87. [CrossRef]
26. Bianco, S.; Ciocca, G.; Marelli, D. Evaluating the Performance of Structure from Motion Pipelines. *J. Imaging* **2018**, *4*, 98. [CrossRef]
27. Yan, Z.; Zhang, Z.; Liu, S. Improving Performance of Seismic Fault Detection by Fine-Tuning the Convolutional Neural Network Pre-Trained with Synthetic Samples. *Energies* **2021**, *14*, 3650. [CrossRef]

Article

Novel Approach to Collect and Process Power Quality Data in Medium-Voltage Distribution Grids

Sergei Kryltcov, Aleksei Makhovikov and Mariia Korobitcyna *

Department of Informatics and Computer Science, Faculty of Humanities and Sciences, Saint Petersburg Mining University, 2, 21st Line, 199106 St. Petersburg, Russia; Kryltsov_SB@pers.spmi.ru (S.K.); Makhovikov_AB@pers.spmi.ru (A.M.)
* Correspondence: Korobitsyna_MA@pers.spmi.ru; Tel./Fax: +7-812-328-9030

Abstract: The paper is devoted to the development of the structure of a fast and flexible data collecting system based on the proposed approach to measure power quality indicators in three-phase medium-voltage distribution grids with an example of a Mikhailovsky mining and processing plant. The approach utilizes the properties of a space vector, obtained from grid currents and voltages with disturbed waveform, to allow faster extraction of the harmonic components compared to traditional approaches, based on the direct Fourier-transform applied to a line or phase values. During the study, the concept of a universal measurement device was introduced, which allows fast estimation of the following values at the grid node: magnitudes and phases of voltage and current harmonic components, active and reactive power of harmonics and fundamental components, positive and negative instantaneous powers. The structure of interconnected measurement and control units for the considered grid node with simultaneous operation of two active variable frequency drives with active rectifiers was proposed in accordance with a concept of the Internet of things. The benefits of the proposed solution are shown by the example of the model of the grid node with two operating draglines and nonlinear load, which was developed in MATLAB/Simulink software. The proposed approach was utilized to produce distributed references for control systems of grid inverters to compensate nonlinear currents, which allowed to significantly improve THDi of the grid node input power.

Keywords: digital signal processing; control systems; smart grids; Internet of things; flexible ac transmission systems

Citation: Kryltcov, S.; Makhovikov, A.; Korobitcyna, M. Novel Approach to Collect and Process Power Quality Data in Medium-Voltage Distribution Grids. *Symmetry* **2021**, *13*, 460. https://doi.org/10.3390/sym13030460

Academic Editor: Rudolf Kawalla and Beloglazov Ilya

Received: 10 February 2021
Accepted: 9 March 2021
Published: 12 March 2021

Publisher's Note: MDPI stays neutral with regard to jurisdictional claims in published maps and institutional affiliations.

Copyright: © 2021 by the authors. Licensee MDPI, Basel, Switzerland. This article is an open access article distributed under the terms and conditions of the Creative Commons Attribution (CC BY) license (https://creativecommons.org/licenses/by/4.0/).

1. Introduction

The Internet of things (IoT) in the industry and the number of connected devices, and the amount of investment in IoT devices and infrastructure is growing at a tremendous pace [1–3]. According to Rostech, the global industrial IoT market will grow at an average annual rate of more than 14%, and by 2023, its volume will amount to US$ 700.38 billion [4]. Transport and industry will be the main drivers of growth. The greatest growth dynamics of the implemented IoT devices are expected in mining and industrial production [5,6]. The main areas of application of IoT in mining are the monitoring of equipment operating parameters, ensuring work safety, end-to-end digitization of production, the creation of a digital twin of production, the introduction of unmanned technologies, the introduction of AI for processing arrays of data from IoT sensors, the reduction of integral production costs [7,8].

Remote monitoring of equipment operating parameters allows to quickly identify work stoppages and make management decisions, which reduces production costs [1,9,10]. Large amounts of data on the operating parameters of a specific piece of equipment and data obtained from the same equipment throughout the world are the basis for the prediction system [5,11–13]. Predictive maintenance allows achieving significant economic benefits and production safety by reducing the number of sudden equipment failures, reducing equipment downtime, reducing service costs by planning repairs and optimizing spare parts logistics [14,15].

The growth of computing power and the increase in their availability accompanied by the ever-decreasing dimensions of digital components made it possible to significantly improve algorithms used to ensuring the controllability and safety of the technological processes [16,17]. The distribution of real-time algorithms, examples of which are given below, became integral parts of the control and information collection systems:

- Neural network, which is widely used to identify characteristic features of signals [18,19];
- Fast algorithms to identify spectra of signals [20,21];
- Adaptive filtering of signals that respond only to characteristic changes in signals [22,23].

These algorithms are widely used in the modern mining industry: from the control of the gas atmosphere in the mine to maintaining the proper operation of draglines [10,24,25]. The provision of mining operations is directly related to the supply of power of the required quality to the final consumers, whether it is mining equipment or heavily rated power units [26]. Special requirements are placed on the operation of powerful equipment since the continuity and safety of the process depend on their work. In order to achieve an uninterruptable technological process, the grid quality must meet local standards [27,28].

The variety of power equipment to provide necessary power quality is commercially available on the market–from passive capacitor banks aimed to reduce inductive currents of the loads to dynamic synchronous compensators of series, shunt, or mixed types [29,30]. The latter devices are able to compensate for current and voltage harmonics introduced by nonlinear loads and voltage imbalance caused by asymmetrical loads [31,32]. The uninterruptable power supply of heavy-rated power equipment also depends on the correct work of relay protection units and power quality monitoring systems [33–35].

To provide proper reaction for power quality disturbances, the control systems of relay protection units and compensation devices must be capable of fast and accurate tracking of both voltages and currents parameters in the industrial power grids [36–39]. To achieve this, well-known algorithms based on space vector and instantaneous power estimation are used [36,40,41]. In the presence of harmonics, the algorithms become more complicated utilizing short-time Fourier transform to estimate fundamental and harmonic components of signals [21,42].

The whole power supply system, therefore, generates large amounts of data, which should be transmitted across numerous control and monitoring systems. According to the Industry 4.0 concept, the interconnection of a variety of devices in a single network with mesh topology allows providing additional scalability to the system [43,44]. However, industrial networks usually consist of mediums with different bandwidth and reliability– from short and medium-range wireless connections for IoT sensors to unstable connections via LTE and power lines [45,46].

In such conditions, the ability of the power supply system to efficiently transmit and distribute power quality data between voltage/current sensors and control systems over different channels becomes its crucial property. In the recent literature, the real-time power quality analysis usually means obtaining voltages and currents spectrum components during one-half to one electrical period [25]. Such analysis has been typically used in power conditioning devices, which are able to mitigate nonlinear and asymmetrical currents flowing in the grid using onboard currents and voltage sensors. While there are recent studies indicating effective real-time transmission of the data in industrial networks via the protocols for time-critical applications [47], there is also a lack of studies that consider the benefits of implementing real-time power quality tracking being used in control systems of the power devices operating in different grid segments.

The paper is devoted to the development of an approach to collect and process power quality data within 1 period of mains voltage and transmit it to the control system of relay protection units and control systems of power conditioning devices. The novelty of the approach lies in the combination of:

- Cascade short-time Fourier transform used to estimate phase voltage and current spectra from the sensors data;
- Estimation of positive and negative voltages and currents components according to the instantaneous symmetrical components theory;
- Estimation of average and fluctuating power components;
- Transmitting the estimated power data via protocols for time-critical applications on the example of precision time protocol;
- Limiting the number of considered harmonics or switching to the transmission of average and oscillating power components depending on the transmission channel bandwidth and type of receiving device.

The benefits of the proposed approach are shown in the example of distributing references for mitigating harmonic currents between two simultaneously operating active frontends of draglines.

2. Materials and Methods

As a subject of modernization, the monitoring and control system of the mining and processing plant "Mikhailovsky GOK" is considered. The improvements are presented on the example of the grid node with three connected draglines of ES-15.90 type. The structure of the grid node is presented in Figure 1. The plant is supplied by power from a generation and distribution company via 35 kV overhead lines. The grid voltage is distributed from the main step-down substation 35/6 kV. Dragline #1 is connected near the transformer bus, while draglines #2 and #3 are connected to the grid node located 1.5 km from the substation.

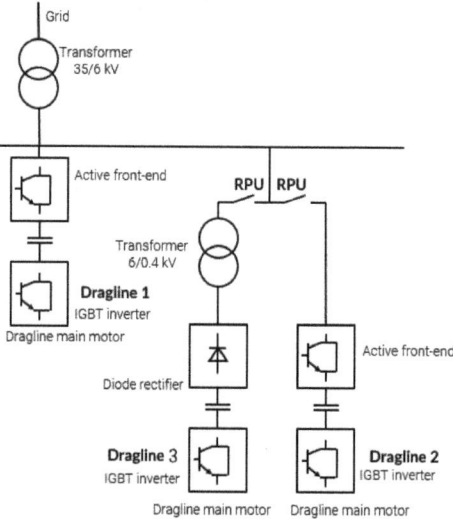

Figure 1. Structure of the site career distribution grid node.

Dragline contains several electrical motors to implement different operations: torso rotation, boom manipulation, ground movement (walking). All of them are connected to the grid drive, which is, in order, connected to the grid via variable frequency drive (VFD) with diode rectifier (dragline #3) or active rectifier (draglines #1 and #2). The diode rectifier (DR), despite its drawbacks, is still the most common rectifier used in VFD due to its low-cost. DR supplies DC-link in a noncontrollable way and consumes non-sinusoidal currents from the grid, introducing harmonics of 5, 7, 11, 13, ... orders [48,49]. Therefore, DR acts as a nonlinear load for the grid. Its structure is shown in Figure 2.

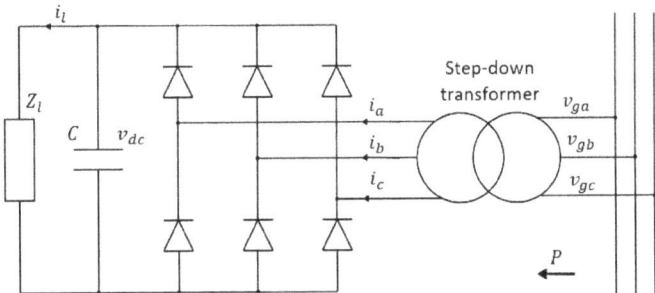

Figure 2. Structure of the two-level ES-15.90 VFD with diode rectifier. Z_l—equivalent impedance of the load (variable depending on the operation cycle); i_l —load current; C —capacitor of the DC-link; i_x —input current in phase x; v_{gx} —phase x to the neutral voltage at the PCC; v_{dc}—DC-link voltage.

Active rectifier, which is also known as active frontend (AFE) as a part of VFD, is a power converter with the ability to operate in four quadrants [50,51]. The power circuit structure of the AFE, which is built according to the three-level neutral point clamped topology, is shown in Figure 3 [52]. AFE is typically used to maintain the following functions:

- Bidirectional power flow, i.e., during regenerative braking [53,54];
- Correction of power factor at the input [55];
- Controllability of the DC-link voltage [56].

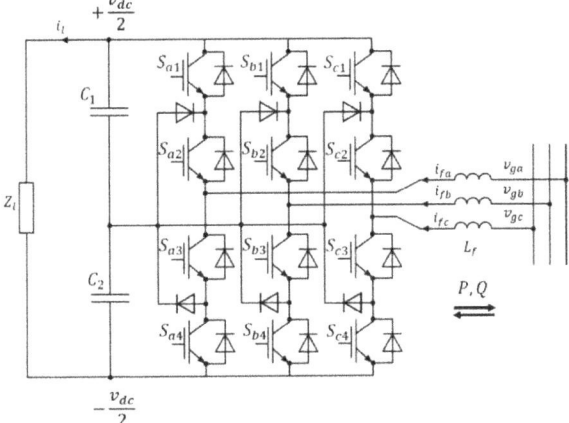

Figure 3. Structure of the three-level ES-15.90 VFD with active rectifier. Z_l—equivalent impedance of the load (variable depending on the operation cycle); i_l—load current; C_1, C_2—capacitors of the DC-link; S_{xn}—IGBT module in phase x with number n; i_{fx}—filter current in phase x; v_{gx}—phase x to the neutral voltage at the PCC; L_f—filter inductance, v_{dc}—DC-link voltage.

Draglines operate in a stochastic manner because of the relative randomness of excavation operations. The typical load profile of ES-15.90 draglines is shown in Figure 4, where rapid changes of both active and reactive power can be seen. Considering the remoteness of the dragline #2 and #3 from the transformer bus, the presented load profile will create a significant voltage drop in the cable lines, connecting the grid node with the substation bus, depending on the grid short-circuit impedance at the substation bus [57]. At the same time, dragline #3 will consume harmonic currents with arbitrary magnitude, depending on its load profile, therefore, introducing randomness to currents and voltages spectra at the PCC [38,58,59].

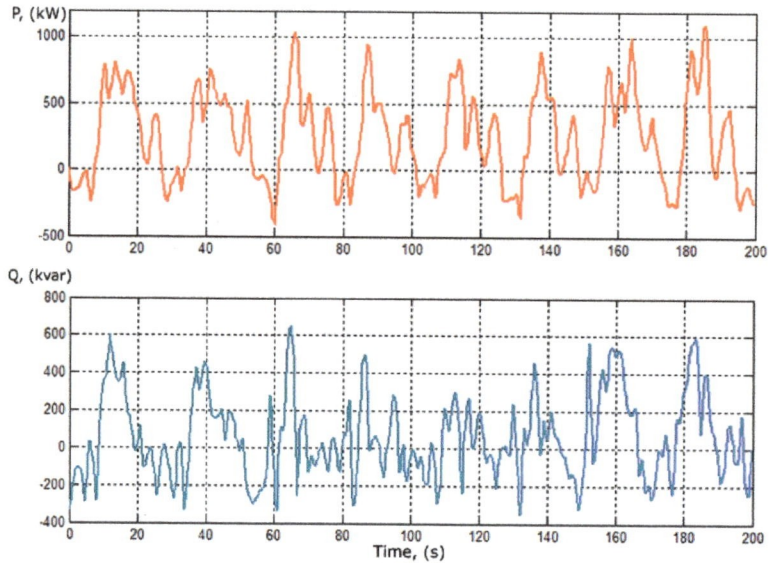

Figure 4. Load profile of ES-15.90 during operation cycles.

To maintain power quality within the acceptable limits, which are regulated according to GOST (acronym for State Standard or Governmental Standard in Russian) 32144–2013, the dynamic compensators are typical to be installed at the nodes depending on the grid and load configuration. The most common device, used to mitigate harmonic currents and rapid voltage fluctuations, is a STATCOM–four-quadrant power converter with a DC-link, a part of flexible AC transmission systems family [60]. While STATCOM is a standalone device for reducing grid power distortions of various factors, its similarity to AFE increases interest in providing the ability to improve the grid power quality by the use of VFD with AFE, which would reduce capital costs to install and maintain STATCOMS at the grid nodes.

To maintain such functionality, AFE requires available current reserve, i.e., it should not be fully loaded by the active current flowing to the load [23,61]. The AFE control system also requires the implementation of special algorithms to be able to release available current to improve the grid power quality and at the same time maintain normal operation of the ES-15.90 grid motor. Such control algorithms rely on fast and accurate estimation of current and voltage spectrum at the dragline PCC [62].

Dragline's AFE sensors typically include current and voltage sensors per phase at the grid side and voltage sensors at the DC-link side. Based on information from grid-side sensors, it is possible to estimate current and voltage spectra via short-time Fourier transform (STFT). According to Fourier transform, every non-sinusoidal periodical signal can be represented as a sum of sine and cosine waves:

$$x_p = \frac{a_0}{2} + \sum_{n=1}^{\infty} a_n \cos(n\omega t) + b_n \sin(n\omega t), \qquad (1)$$

where x_p–instantaneous phase-to-neutral voltage; a_0–DC Fourier coefficient; a_n, b_n–sine and cosine Fourier coefficients for n-th harmonic; $\omega = 2\pi f$–angular frequency of the grid voltage, equals to 100π rad/s for f = 50 Hz.

Parameters of each harmonic component relate to a_n and b_n values as follows:

$$X_p^{(n)} = \sqrt{a_n^2 + b_n^2}; \psi_x^{(n)} = \operatorname{atan2}(b_n, a_n), \qquad (2)$$

where $X_p^{(n)}$, $\psi_x^{(n)}$—magnitude and phase shift of n-th harmonic in p-th phase; atan2–2-argument arctangent.

According to STFT, it is possible to estimate parameters of each harmonic component by accumulating the signal within some observation period–T_f:

$$\begin{aligned} a_n &= \tfrac{2}{T_f} \int_0^{T_f} x_p \cos(n\omega t) dt; \\ b_n &= \tfrac{2}{T_f} \int_0^{T_f} x_p \sin(n\omega t) dt. \end{aligned} \qquad (3)$$

The obtained coefficients a_n and b_n are substituted into expression (2) to calculate the magnitude and phase shift for each harmonic of the phase voltages or currents [63]. The latency of the STFT algorithm is determined by the observation period of the signal T_f. Moreover, if the period of consideration of the signal T_f is not equal and/or is not a multiple of the period of the main signal, then there will be a loss of power of the spectrum and the values of the calculated coefficients a_n, b_n will be unreliable. Thus, the minimum delay of the algorithm based on the Fourier transform will be determined by the period of one oscillation of the mains voltage T_f = 20 ms.

To affect grid power quality in the case of the presence of voltages or currents unbalance, it is also necessary to calculate the positive and negative components of each harmonic, which are required to identify and mitigate voltage and current unbalance between phases. This is achieved according to the instantaneous symmetrical components theory [64].

Instantaneous symmetrical components of each harmonic extracted according to:

$$X^{+(n)} = x_\alpha^{(n)} + x_\beta^{(n)} j90^0; \qquad (4)$$

$$X^{-(n)} = x_\beta^{(n)} - x_\alpha^{(n)} j90^0,$$

where $j90^0$–quadrature operator, which is typically implemented as a digital delay for $\tfrac{1}{4}$ period of the signal; $X^{+(n)}$, $X^{-(n)}$–magnitudes of positive and negative components of harmonic. However, as STFT provides information about the magnitude and phase of each frequency components, it is possible to directly calculate $X^{+(n)}$ and $X^{-(n)}$.

To maintain monitoring of grid power quality and take proper control actions, it is necessary to collect information about power flow. Akagi's theory of instantaneous powers suits the most complicated power calculations, which include harmonics and symmetrical components data. According to the theory, active–p, and reactive–q powers can be determined from the instantaneous projections of voltages and currents space vectors onto $\alpha\beta$ plane as follows:

$$p = v_\alpha i_\alpha + v_\beta i_\beta; \quad q = v_\alpha i_\beta - v_\beta i_\alpha. \qquad (5)$$

However, in the case of harmonic distortions, it is useful to distinguish average–$\bar{p}$, $\bar{q}$–and oscillatory–$\tilde{p}$, $\tilde{q}$–components of powers [65]. Average active power $\bar{p}$ is used to maintain power flow between generators and loads and, in the ideal case, is the only power that makes actual work and should pass through the grid. It is calculated based on the fundamental components of currents and voltages as follows:

$$\bar{p} = v_\alpha^{(1)} i_\alpha^{(1)} + v_\beta^{(1)} i_\beta^{(1)}. \qquad (6)$$

Average reactive power is used to estimate reactive power flow between power plants and stabilize voltage by injecting or absorbing the reactive power. It is calculated as follows:

$$\bar{q} = v_\alpha^{(1)} i_\beta^{(1)} - v_\beta^{(1)} i_\alpha^{(1)} \tag{7}$$

In a similar way, average powers may be calculated for specific harmonics.

Oscillatory components of powers are represented as high harmonics and should be mitigated by the compensators and filters if possible [23]:

$$\tilde{p} = \sum_n^N v_\alpha^{(n)} i_\alpha^{(n)} + v_\beta^{(n)} i_\beta^{(n)}; \tag{8}$$

$$\tilde{q} = \sum_n^N v_\alpha^{(n)} i_\beta^{(n)} - v_\beta^{(n)} i_\alpha^{(n)}.$$

Based on the described equations, the concept of a multipurpose measurement unit (MU) can be introduced, which collects enough information about power quality at the grid node and transfers it to control devices, such as control systems of VFDs STATCOMs, RPUs et cetera. The structure of the data packet is shown in Table 1:

Table 1. Values in the data packet generated by the measurement unit (MU).

Harmonic	Currents	Voltages	Active Power	Reactive Power
Instantaneous	I, θ_i	V, θ_v	p	q
1	$I^{+(1)}, \theta_i^{+(1)}, I^{-(1)}, \theta_i^{-(1)}$	$V^{+(1)}, \theta_v^{+(1)}, V^{-(1)}, \theta_v^{-(1)}$	$\bar{p}$	$\bar{q}$
5	$I^{+(5)}, \theta_i^{+(5)}, I^{-(5)}, \theta_i^{-(5)}$	$V^{+(5)}, \theta_v^{+(5)}, V^{-(5)}, \theta_v^{-(5)}$	$p^{(5)}$	$q^{(5)}$
39		Similar to the 5th harmonic		

Each data packet will contain 186 values, which equals 744 bytes of payload if each value is considered as a floating-point of 4 bytes. To use the benefit of developed fast algorithms, such packets should be generated by the MU at least every millisecond, which allows to provide proper reaction for transients, improve grid power quality and prevent emergency situations. The considered amount of data leads to approximately 1 MB/s of data produced by one MU. In the case of a reliable connection with decent bandwidth, such a system will work properly. However, if we consider unreliable channels or channels with unpredictable bandwidth, such as 4G or power line communication, it is necessary to reduce the amount of transmitted data and to shift part of calculations to controllers. Depending on the receiving unit and channel bandwidth, it is possible to choose which data to share between the MU and controller. For example, in the worst-case MU can share only average and oscillatory power components per cycle. Considering each value is a 2-byte integer, this is only 400 bytes per second.

The flowchart of the algorithm to operate the proposed MU is shown in Figure 5. The inputs for the algorithm are sampled instantaneous values, measured from current and voltage sensors and passed through an analog to a digital converter (ADC). A typical performance of ADC converters may vary from a few to hundreds of kHz. While 1 kHz (1 measurement per millisecond) is enough for proper operation of MU, operating on higher ADC frequencies allows adding filtering and predictive algorithms. After this, sampled three-phase voltage and currents (6 measurements per cycle of calculations) are transformed into voltage and currents space vectors according to Clarke transform (4, 6).

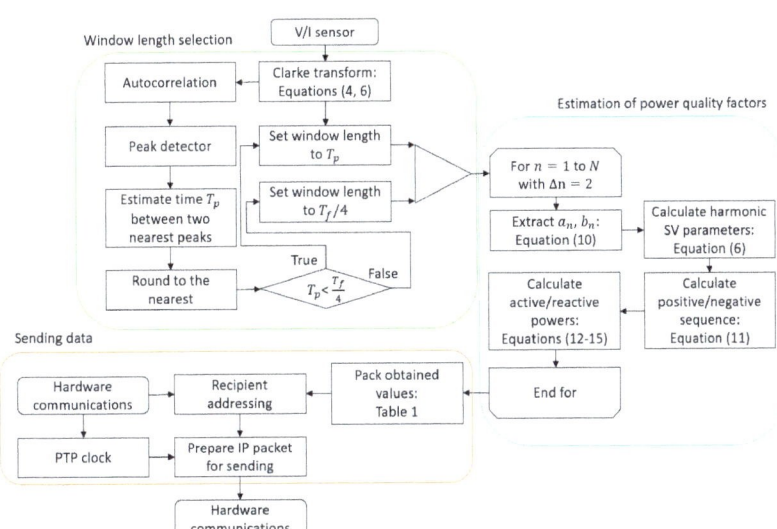

Figure 5. The flowchart of the algorithm for estimating power components at the grid node and transmits them across the network.

Based on the calculated magnitude of the voltage space vector, the autocorrelation signal is continuously produced. The time between the two most recent peaks of the autocorrelation function is counted and is used to determine the length of the window for Fourier transform. If two peaks are found lesser than in $\frac{1}{4}$ of the fundamental period T_f ($T_f = 0.02$ s for $f^{(1)} = 50$ Hz), the time between peaks T_p is rounded to the nearest in the series $\frac{1}{f^{(1)}}, \frac{1}{2f^{(1)}}, \frac{1}{3f^{(1)}} \ldots$ s, which is required to avoid interference of different harmonic components. Then window length T_{SV} is set to T_p value. Otherwise T_{SV} is set to $\frac{T_f}{4}$.

When window length is set, the consequent Fourier transform is performed for every odd harmonics to extract sine and cosine Fourier coefficients of each harmonic according to (3). Then magnitude and phase of each component are calculated from coefficients according to (2). These values are then used to estimate positive and negative sequence components according to (4) and corresponding active and reactive instantaneous, average and oscillatory components of power (6–8). The calculated values are used to build a data packet according to Table 1.

The MU collects requests for transferring data packets to other devices in a network segment, therefore, storing requesting devices' addresses in the memory. The data are transferred via protocols for time-critical applications. One of the good examples of such protocol that may be utilized is a precision time protocol (PTP), which allows to synchronization of clocks between devices in a network segment on a microsecond level. The clock master may be selected automatically via built-in algorithms, i.e., best master clock algorithm, or may be selected manually, and therefore, usually nearest controller unit is chosen to be clock master. The PTP is suitable for any IP compatible network via wired or wireless mediums and allows to ensure precise measurements of power quality indicators.

The effective joint operation of the power converters in the distribution grid segment is determined by the possibility of distributing tasks between them depending on their workload according to the active power consumed by the load (16):

$$p^*_{AFE} = v_{DC} \cdot k_{PI}(V^*_{DC} - v_{DC}) - p^*_{GC}; \tag{9}$$

$$q^*_{AFE} = q^*_{GC},$$

where p_{GC}^*, q_{GC}^*—references for active and reactive powers for grid converter; v_{DC}—DC-link voltage of the AFE; k_{PI}—proportional/integral function of the v_{DC} regulator, which was designed according to [66].

Let us express the instantaneous total power distortion S_{GC}^* (17):

$$s_{GC}^* = \sqrt{\left(p_{GC}^*\right)^2 + \left(q_{GC}^*\right)^2}. \quad (10)$$

The total available instantaneous power of the distortion s_{GCmax}^* is determined by the load on the active current:

$$s_{GCmax}^* = v_{DC} \cdot |i_{max} - i_l|, \quad (11)$$

where i_{max}—maximum available current through the IGBT module.

It is obvious that during the formation of tasks p_{AFE}^* and q_{AFE}^* for AFE, the condition $s_{GC}^* \leq s_{GCmax}^*$ must be satisfied at each moment of time. In this case, it is effective to decompose the signals p_{GC}^* and q_{GC}^* into separate harmonics $p_{GC}^{*(n)}$ and $q_{GC}^{*(n)}$, as well as extract the constant component of the reactive power responsible for maintaining the voltage level of the network. Then:

$$p_{AFE}^* = \sum_{n=5}^{N} p^{(n)}; q_{AFE}^* = \bar{q} + \sum_{n=5}^{N} q^{(n)}. \quad (12)$$

In this case, addition by individual harmonics is performed, while the condition $s_{GC}^* \leq s_{GCmax}^*$ is met. Overall, the structure of the AFE control system is shown in Figure 6.

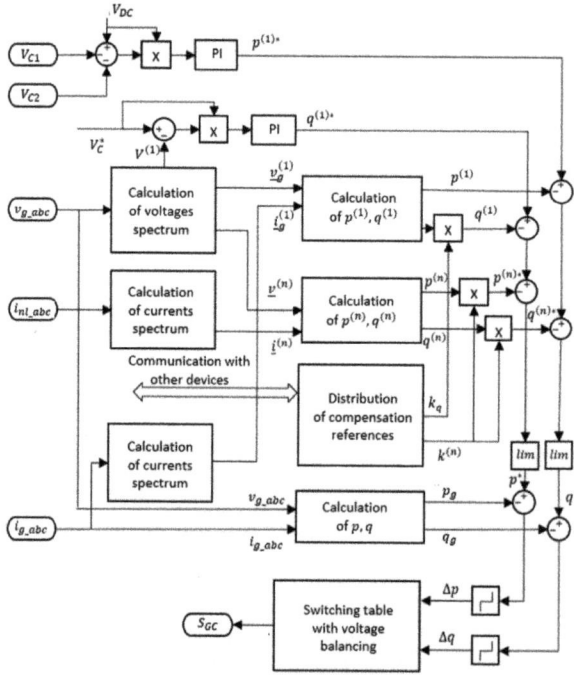

Figure 6. Structure of control system of the active frontend.

Local MUs send the processed information packages to the controller units as well as to any unit, which requests the information and is allowed to access it. Controllers are placed in accordance with hierarchy, so local controllers produce control signals for endpoint devices, while the main controller maintains the whole surface mine operation [62]. MU are typically placed at each power or protection device, where MU usually measures the voltage at the device's PCC and current going through the device. Typical examples are transformer buses, compensators, VFD. MU usually provides collected information to the local control unit, which depends on the device. For example, for STATCOM, the control system, which operates switches, obtains information from local measurement units.

Let us consider short-circuit at the arbitrary grid node to illustrate the advantages of gathering information by MUs that might trigger control signals for different power devices: control of RPU, control of VFD, control of compensation device, on the example of STATCOM.

RPUs are essential devices that may break fault circuits include power grid branches and segments as well as faulty loads. The most common use case of RPUs is the isolation of circuits with short circuits. Therefore, using the fast estimation of negative sequence voltage according to (4), MU positioned close to RPU may trigger it to isolate circuit with the delay of 10–20 ms, which is much faster than the traditional use of RPUs.

At the same time, information about the negative sequence is to be used by STATCOM to mitigate the negative effects of short circuits for all loads across the grid. STATCOM in 6–10 kV grids is able to partially compensate unbalanced voltages and currents during several periods without severe DC-link voltage fluctuations by injection of reactive and active currents in each phase. If the STATCOM's DC-link is supplied by a constant voltage source, such as a battery or flywheel, the amount of injected active power gradually increases.

The VFD with AR obtaining information about short circuits may produce two main functions. First of all, the control scheme is triggered to maintain low-field operation at the load side of the converter to increase the voltage sag drive-through ability of the drive. At the same time, the grid-side inverter may be used as a local STATCOM device to mitigate short-circuit consequences for loads located nearby.

If we consider the usual grid operation, the information from MUs is to be used by STATCOM and VFDs to improve grid quality by eliminating harmonic currents and stabilize voltage levels by injection of reactive power to the grid nodes. It is also important that the universalization of MUs allows for the production of compensation currents, which will target the source of harmonic and/or reactive currents, therefore, increasing the effect of compensation devices.

According to the proposed control schemes, the power units achieve autonomous operation, as each device carries the local MU, which is able to produce enough information to maintain fault protection and the ability to increase power quality at the load PCC. This, according to the Internet of things (IoT), is considered as operation at the device level. At the same time, the interconnection of MUs and controllers allows introducing the fog level device–master controller (MC) of the power grid, which provides the following functionality to maintain the effectiveness and safety of the open cast mining technological process:

- Gathering of information from all MUs;
- Monitoring situation at every grid node, which has MU installed as well as monitoring loads status;
- Distribution of reference signals for compensation devices to effectively stabilize grid voltages across the whole grid and mitigate harmonic currents;
- Prediction of escalating the emergency situations, such as short-circuits and according to the reaction by the generating control signals for loads, compensators and RPUs;
- Logging necessary part of gathering information as well as sending the whole information to cloud storage.

While the device level provides individual operability of the power appliances, the for level allows optimizing grid power distribution and maintaining necessary power quality at the main step-down transformer buses. Fog level control also allows transmitting necessary analytical data to display at the operators' workstations via SCADA software or web-interfaces. Therefore, complete monitoring of the grid situation is achieved at the fog level. Fog devices usually store logs for several days to a week to achieve a proper response of grid devices and operators for estimated trends.

The cloud level devices are used to store a massive amount of information collected by the MC, which allows analyzing emergency incidents in detail as well as to further optimize the mining process using statistical processing of gathered logs. Cloud level includes backup and analytics servers that are leased from the cloud hosting providers.

The modern development of communication systems allows a sufficient variety of device interconnection approaches. At the device level, the interconnection of MUs and device controller may be used via twisted pairs, optical links, CAN buses, etc. At the same time, protocols to exchange measurement data are also presented in a wide variety: MODBUS, ProfiBus, ProfiNet, standard TCP/IP stacks. However, as it is important to maintain transmission of information packages, as the data calculated by MUs changes at microseconds level, it is advised to use time-synchronized protocols, such as precision time protocol, time-sensitive protocol.

At the fog level, it is necessary to monitor and maintain interconnection topology and hierarchy as well as to maintain guaranteed collecting of all available signals by the MC. Therefore, the main principles here are providing backup data channels and the application of protocols that utilize grid topology. Data channels for transmitting information from MUs to MC and control signals from MCs to device controllers are direct links where possible (typically twisted pair and optical links) and radio communication. However, in the recent decade, the power line communication concept has been significantly developed and is to be used as a backup data channel across the grid. The MC is connected to cloud servers via the leased primary link and one to several backup data links if possible.

3. Results

Based on the proposed algorithms and described structural features of the monitoring and communications between power devices, aimed to improve grid power quality as well as to mitigate consequences of emergency operation of the grid, the concept of the signal collecting systems in an open-pit mining grid was developed. Its structure based upon the power scheme of the open-pit mining grid node is shown in Figure 7.

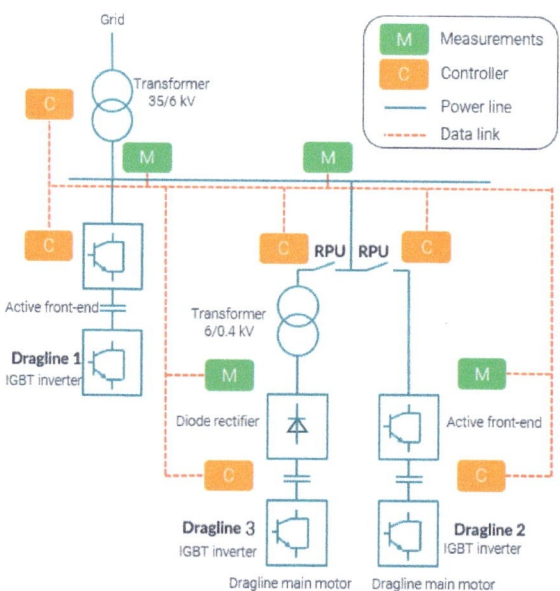

Figure 7. Structure of the system to collect signals in the open suite mining network.

All digital devices are divided into two groups–MUs and controllers, which are usually work in pairs. For example, MU at the dragline input first sends data to the dragline controller. That pairs form the domains, interconnected and limited by the industrial switching equipment. Devices are interconnected with the optical fiber data link. In the case of damaging the cable, the reserve link is always maintained via PLC, however, with significantly lower bandwidth. While optical fiber between MU and nearest controller is operational, MU sends the full amount of gathered and computed data about the power flows, voltage and current spectra.

In the case of malfunctioning of the optical link between the controller and MU, the reserve channel via PLC becomes uplink. As the bandwidth of the PLC link is significantly lower than that of the optical fiber, the devices measure the average bandwidth of the channel and negotiate about the amount of information processed by MU. The whole topology of the grid can be achieved by the use of standard neighbor discovery protocol (NDP), which is perfectly suitable for enterprise networks [67].

All controllers are numbered in the hierarchy, so the controller with a higher available priority always becomes a master controller in negotiations. For example, the controller at the substation has the highest priority number and becomes the master controller. For all negotiating devices, it becomes the clock master to realize time-sensitive protocol throughout the network. At the same time, the master controller (MC) implements links between the MUs and controllers if it is not overridden in a particular controller. Such a scheme provides scalability and the possibility to make redundant connections to provide whole network functionality in the case of MC failure.

To illustrate some of the benefits of the proposed system for monitoring and gathering digital signals, the Simulink model of grid node of open suite mining was developed. Its structure is shown in Figure 8. The main purpose of the model is to demonstrate modes of operation of draglines' VFDs, which are not available with traditional control and measurement systems.

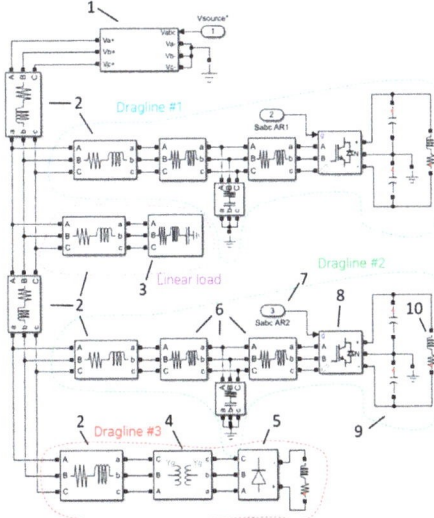

Figure 8. Structure of the grid model to test signal collecting in the open suite mining network. 1—a model of main step-down substation 35/6 kV—ideal voltage source with finite short-circuit resistance; 2—cable lines models; 3—linear load model, implemented to vary relation between non-sinusoidal and sinusoidal currents; 4—transformer 6/0.4 kV (star—star); 5—diode rectifier of the dragline #3; 6—LCL filters of dragline #1 and #2; 7—signals from the control system of AFE for dragline #1 and #2; 8—three-level IGBT AFE; 9—DC-link of VFD of draglines #1 and #2; 10—equivalent load of draglines #1 and #2.

The dragline #3 becomes an unpredictable nonlinear load for the grid, which introduces harmonics inherent for diode rectifiers, with a rapidly changing amount of absorbed active and reactive power. Draglines #1 and #2 are able to operate as active filters for such harmonics as well as to stabilize voltage fluctuations if they have enough current reserve to release it into the grid node. However, as draglines #1 and #2 are located at the different grid nodes, they sense the distortions caused by dragline #3 at the different periods of time, which leads to either mutual compensation or uncontrollable overcompensation. This situation is illustrated in Figure 9, where both draglines try to compensate fifth harmonics as the most dominant, and their AFEs have not enough current reserve to compensate it completely; instead, they try to react to each other's actions.

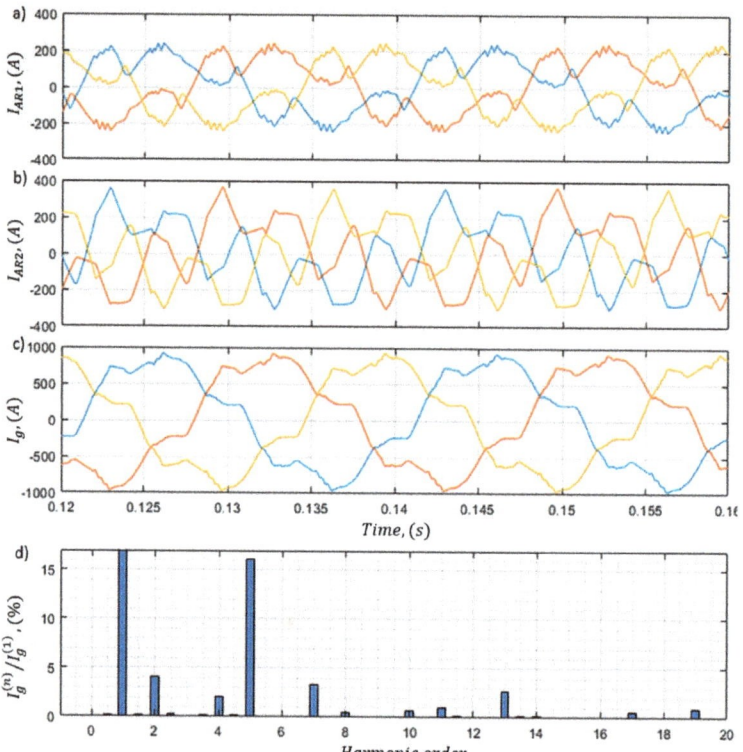

Figure 9. Draglines operating in non-synchronized mode. Waveforms of phase currents at the input of: dragline 1—(**a**), dragline 2—(**b**), grid node—(**c**); spectrum of the grid node input currents—(**d**).

Figure 9a,b shows the currents absorbed by the draglines #1 and #2. Summary current, absorbed by the substation, is shown in Figure 9c. The spectrum of absorbed current by the substation is shown in Figure 9d—it can be seen that the 5th harmonic reaches a 15% value, which is quite high for 2 VFDs working in the active filtering mode. That is explained by their remoteness from each other's, which leads to dealing with each other's effects rather than working with the harmonic content.

The simplest solution to improve the situation is to distinguish reference currents for the elimination of specific harmonics between devices. Figure 10 shows the result of such reference distribution. The latency introduced by communications between the MU and AFE controllers is simulated as a discrete delay of 1 ms to every external reference produced for each AFE controller.

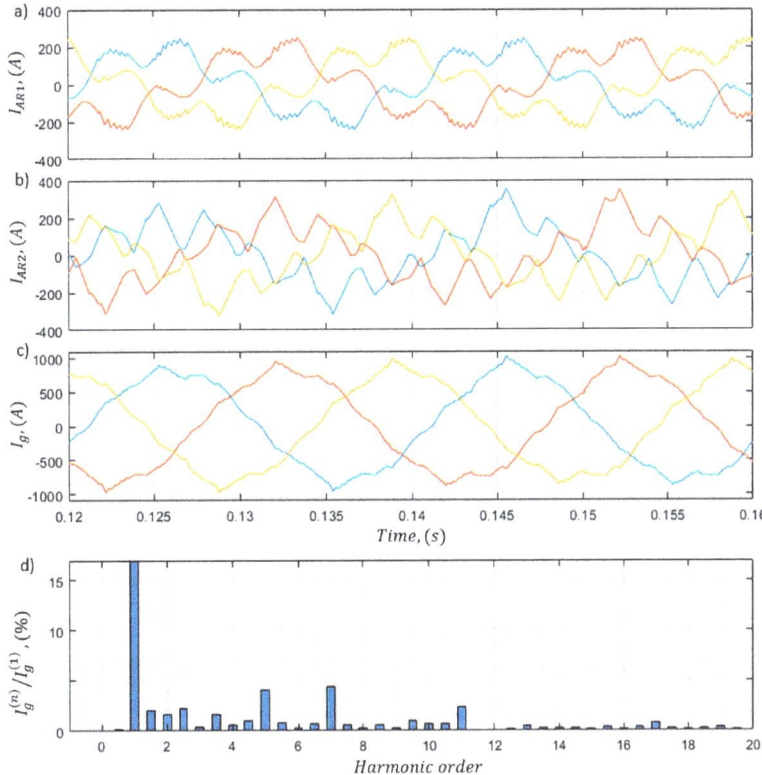

Figure 10. Draglines operating in synchronized mode. Waveforms of phase currents at the input of: dragline 1—(**a**), dragline 2—(**b**), grid node—(**c**); spectrum of the grid node input currents—(**d**).

While dragline #1 deals with the 5th harmonic in the current, dragline #2 handles the 7th harmonic component, as can be seen from Figure 10a,b. Comparing Figures 9d and 10d, it can be seen that in the case of distinguished references, the 5th harmonic magnitude at the substation bus does not exceed 4% of fundamental, in comparison with 15% in the case of local references setup.

4. Discussion

It was shown that the simultaneous operation of two VFDs partially loaded by the active current in the filtering mode of nonlinear currents does not effectively reduce the current harmonic distortion at the input of the network node, which is a consequence of the oscillatory process due to the overlapping of currents consumed by both joint ventures and subsequent overcompensation in those parts of the electric period, where the form of the current consumed by the network section is closer to the sinusoid and undercompensation on other sites. The curves of the currents consumed by each of the AFEs, as well as the current curve and its spectrum at the input of the distribution network section, are given to form tasks for compensating all distortions (Figure 9) and separately for compensating the fifth harmonic for AFE #1 and seventh harmonic for AFE #2 (Figure 10). From the obtained graphs, it can be seen that in the first case, there is under-and over-compensation of currents in the lines, which leads to a value of THDi current at the input of the network section equal to 17.42%. In the case of separate tasks for harmonic compensation for each AFE, such processes are not observed, and the THDi value of the current at the input of the network section decreases to 8.16%.

In the simulation, the reference signals are generated for each AFE with the frequency of one electrical period and delayed by 1 ms, which simulates constant delay of using PTP during the transmission of data packets. However, in real hardware, the AFE controller will obtain measurements with different frequencies but with information accurate to the microseconds when the packet was produced by the MU. This allows us to utilize prediction strategies to further reduce the negative effects of communication over long lines. Adaptive strategies of the measurements are to be used in the case of unreliable and cluttered connections, which is a subject of further research.

The results of the simulation highlight the potential benefits of utilizing the proposed approach to develop more complex control strategies for power conditioning units based on data obtained from MUs placed at different grid nodes. However, extending the approach to large-scale grids is expected to raise issues with communicating over different channels while providing low latencies. The simple master-slave hierarchy used in a considered network is to be improved for large-scale applications. Particular application cases of utilizing approach in complex grids require further investigation.

5. Conclusions

During the study, the approach to fast and accurately determine power quality factors of the three-phase grid was developed. The approach is based on the introduction of a multipurpose measurement unit, which calculates the following qualities from the input current and voltage sensors: magnitudes of each current and voltage harmonics component; symmetrical components of currents and voltages; instantaneous active and reactive powers, as well as powers of specific harmonics and symmetrical components. The novelty of the approach lies in the combination of measurement unit with time-critical protocols, which allows producing packets with timestamp accurate to microseconds and power quality data only necessary for a particular receiving device, which is suitable in the case of low-bandwidth networks or a significant number of communicating devices.

The proposed approach utilizes a simple master-slave hierarchy, which, however, is to be extended in further studies on large-scale grids. To verify the effectiveness of the proposed solution, a computer model of the grid node with two simultaneously operating VFDs was developed in Simulink. The results of the simulation have shown the potential to develop complex control strategies based on the proposed approach, which in the case of separating references for harmonic currents mitigations for simultaneous operating variable-frequency drives with active rectifiers allowed to significantly reduce harmonic distortions of currents flowing into the grid node.

Therefore, the proposed structure of the signaling system introducing the IoT concept to a particular open cast mining suite is a viable and flexible solution, which implementation is cost-effective in terms of technological process continuity given the low costs of its implementation. While simulation proves the proposed approach to collect and process power quality data, such an approach is to be investigated on the real hardware, especially in the case of power line and wireless communications.

Author Contributions: Conceptualization, S.K. and M.K., methodology, A.M., software, S.K., validation, S.K., A.M., and M.K., formal analysis, M.K., investigation, S.K., resources, M.K., writing—original draft preparation, S.K., writing—review and editing, M.K., visualization, S.K., supervision, A.M., project administration, A.M., funding acquisition, A.M. All authors have read and agreed to the published version of the manuscript.

Funding: This research was carried out within the state assignment of the Ministry of Science and Higher Education of the Russian Federation (theme No. FSRW-2020–0014).

Conflicts of Interest: The authors declare no conflict of interest. The funders had no role in the design of the study, in the collection, analyses, or interpretation of data, in the writing of the manuscript, or in the decision to publish the results.

Abbreviations

AC	Alternate current
ADC	Analog to a digital converter
AFE	Active front–end
AI	Artificial intelligence
AR	Active rectifier
DC	Direct current
DR	Diode rectifier
FFT	Fast Fourier transform
IGBT	Insulated–gate bipolar transistor
IoT	Internet of Things
IP	Internet protocol
MC	Master controller
MU	Measurements unit
NDP	Neighbor discovery protocol
PCC	Point of common coupling
PLC	Power line communications
PTP	Precision time protocol
RPU	Relay protection unit
SCADA	Supervisory control and data acquisition
STATCOM	Static synchronous compensator
STFT	Short-time Fourier transform
VFD	Variable-frequency drive

References

1. Cherepovitsyn, A.; Fedoseev, S.; Tcvetkov, P.; Sidorova, K.; Kraslawski, A. Potential of Russian regions to implement CO_2-enhanced oil recovery. *Energies* **2018**, *11*, 1528. [CrossRef]
2. Tom, R.J.; Sankaranarayanan, S. IoT based SCADA integrated with fog for power distribution automation. In Proceedings of the 2017 12th Iberian Conference on Information Systems and Technologies (CISTI), Lisbon, Portugal, 21–24 June 2017; pp. 1–4.
3. Zhukovskiy, Y.; Batueva, D.; Buldysko, A.; Shabalov, M. Motivation towards energy saving by means of IoT personal energy manager platform. *J. Phys. Conf. Ser.* **2019**, *1333*, 062033. [CrossRef]
4. TADVISER. Available online: http://tadviser.com/index.php/Article:IIoT_2018:_The_market_of_industrial_Internet_of_Things_in_Russia. (accessed on 2 February 2021).
5. Litvinenko, V.S. Digital economy as a factor in the technological development of the mineral sector. *Nat. Resour. Res.* **2020**, *29*, 1521–1541. [CrossRef]
6. Makhovikov, A.B.; Katuntsov, E.V.; Kosarev, O.V.; Tsvetkov, P.S. Digital transformation in oil and gas extraction. In Proceedings of the 11th conference of the Russian–German Raw Materials, Potsdam, Germany, 7–8 November 2018; pp. 531–538.
7. Akbar, A.; Khan, A.; Carrez, F.; Moessner, K. Predictive analytics for complex IoT data streams. *IEEE Internet Things J.* **2017**, *4*, 1571–1582. [CrossRef]
8. Zhukovskiy, Y.; Malov, D. Concept of smart cyberspace for smart grid implementation. *J. Phys. Conf. Ser.* **2018**, *1015*, 042067. [CrossRef]
9. Abramovich, B.; Sychev, Y. Problems of ensuring energy security for enterprises from the mineral resources sector. *J. Min. Inst.* **2016**, *217*, 132–139.
10. Zhukovskiy, Y.L.; Starshaia, V.V.; Batueva, D.E.; Buldysko, A.D. Analysis of technological changes in integrated intelligent power supply systems. In Proceedings of the 11th conference of the Russian–German Raw Materials, Potsdam, Germany, 7–8 November 2018; pp. 249–258.
11. Bosch, S.; Staiger, J.; Steinhart, H. Predictive current control for an active power filter with LCL-filter. *IEEE Trans. Ind. Electron.* **2017**, *65*, 4943–4952. [CrossRef]
12. Mazakov, E.B. Representation and processing of knowledge in information automated systems of intelligent field. *J. Min. Inst.* **2014**, *208*, 256.
13. Svetlana, V.; Razmanova, O.; Andrukhova, V. Oilfield service companies as part of economy digitalization: Assessment of the prospects for innovative development. *J. Min. Inst.* **2020**, *244*, 482–492. [CrossRef]
14. Nordhaus, W.D. Two centuries of productivity growth in computing. *J. Econ. Hist.* **2007**, *67*, 128–159. [CrossRef]
15. Ugolnikov, A.V.; Makarov, N.V. Application of automation systems for monitoring and energy efficiency accounting indicators of mining enterprises compressor facility operation. *J. Min. Inst.* **2019**, *236*, 245. [CrossRef]
16. Safiullin, R.N.; Afanasyev, A.S.; Reznichenko, V.V. The concept of development of monitoring systems and management of intelligent technical complexes. *J. Min. Inst.* **2019**, *237*, 322. [CrossRef]

17. Maksarov, V.V.; Leonidov, P.V. Modeling and control of dynamical properties of the technological systems. *J. Min. Inst.* **2014**, *209*, 71.
18. Fei, J.; Chu, Y. Double hidden layer output feedback neural adaptive global sliding mode control of active power filter. *IEEE Trans. Power Electron.* **2019**, *35*, 3069–3084. [CrossRef]
19. Güler, N.F.; Übeyli, E.D.; Güler, I. Recurrent neural networks employing Lyapunov exponents for EEG signals classification. *Expert Syst. Appl.* **2005**, *29*, 506–514. [CrossRef]
20. Gough, P.T. A fast spectral estimation algorithm based on the FFT. *IEEE Trans. Signal. Process.* **1994**, *42*, 1317–1322. [CrossRef]
21. Wang, X.; Ying, T.; Tian, W. Spectrum Representation Based on STFT. In Proceedings of the 2020 13th International Congress on Image and Signal Processing, BioMedical Engineering and Informatics (CISP-BMEI), Chengdu, China, 17–19 October 2020; pp. 435–438.
22. Evensen, G. The ensemble Kalman filter: Theoretical formulation and practical implementation. *Ocean. Dyn.* **2003**, *53*, 343–367. [CrossRef]
23. Wu, W.; Liu, Y.; He, Y.; Chung, H.S.H.; Liserre, M.; Blaabjerg, F. Damping methods for resonances caused by LCL-filter-based current-controlled grid-tied power inverters: An overview. *IEEE Trans. Ind. Electron.* **2017**, *64*, 7402–7413. [CrossRef]
24. Carrizosa, M.J.; Stankovic, N.; Vannier, J.C.; Shklyarskiy, Y.E.; Bardanov, A.I. Multi-terminal dc grid overall control with modular multilevel converters. *J. Min. Inst.* **2020**, *243*, 357. [CrossRef]
25. El Kadi, Y.A.; Baghli, F.Z.; Lakhal, Y. Energy quality optimization in smart grids Faults monitoring by the space vector signature analysis method. In Proceedings of the 2020 IEEE 6th International Conference on Optimization and Applications (ICOA), Beni Mellal, Morocco, 20–21 April 2020; pp. 1–8.
26. Zakaryukin, V.; Kryukov, A.; Cherepanov, A. Intelligent Traction Power Supply System. In *Energy Management of Municipal Transportation Facilities and Transport*; Springer: Cham, Switzerland, 2017; pp. 91–99. Available online: https://link.springer.com/chapter/10.1007/978-3-319-70987-1_10 (accessed on 11 March 2021).
27. GOST 32144-2013 Electrical Energy. Electromagnetic Compatibility of Technical Equipment. Standards of Electric Power Quality in General-Purpose Power Supply Systems. Available online: http://docs.cntd.ru/document/1200104301 (accessed on 2 February 2021).
28. Pankov, I.A.; Frolov, V.Y. Increase of electric power quality in autonomous electric power systems. *J. Min. Inst.* **2017**, *227*, 563. [CrossRef]
29. Liu, X.; Lv, J.; Gao, C.; Chen, Z.; Chen, S. A novel STATCOM based on diode-clamped modular multilevel converters. *IEEE Trans. Power Electron.* **2016**, *32*, 5964–5977. [CrossRef]
30. Mosaad, M.I. Model reference adaptive control of STATCOM for grid integration of wind energy systems. *IET Electr. Power Appl.* **2018**, *12*, 605–613. [CrossRef]
31. Khramshin, T.R.; Krubtsov, D.S.; Kornilov, G.P. Mathematical model of the active rectifier under unbalanced voltage operating conditions. *Russ. Internet J. Electr. Eng.* **2016**, *1*, 3–9.
32. Svensson, J. Synchronisation methods for grid-connected voltage source converters. *IEEE Proc. Gener. Transm. Distrib.* **2001**, *148*, 229–235. [CrossRef]
33. Alam, M.R.; Bai, F.; Yan, R.; Saha, T.K. Classification and visualization of power quality disturbance-events using space vector ellipse in complex plane. *IEEE Trans. Power Deliv.* **2020**, *1*, 1. [CrossRef]
34. Bollen, M.H. Understanding Power Quality Problems: Voltage Sags and Interruptions. 2000. Available online: https://ieeexplore.ieee.org/book/5270869 (accessed on 11 March 2021).
35. Liang, X. Emerging power quality challenges due to integration of renewable energy sources. *IEEE Trans. Ind. Appl.* **2016**, *53*, 855–866. [CrossRef]
36. Akagi, H.; Watanabe, E.H.; Aredes, M. *Instantaneous Power Theory and Applications to Power Conditioning*; John Wiley & Sons, 2017; Available online: https://onlinelibrary.wiley.com/doi/book/10.1002/0470118938 (accessed on 3 March 2021).
37. Arrillaga, J.; Watson, N.R. *Power System Harmonics*; John Wiley & Sons, 2003; p. 412. Available online: https://onlinelibrary.wiley.com/doi/book/10.1002/0470871229 (accessed on 11 March 2021).
38. Shklyarskiy, Y.; Hanzelka, Z.; Skamyin, A. Experimental Study of Harmonic Influence on Electrical Energy Metering. *Energies* **2020**, *13*, 5536. [CrossRef]
39. Vorontsov, A.G.; Glushakov, V.V.; Pronin, M.V.; Sychev, Y.A. Cascade frequency converters control features. *J. Min. Inst.* **2020**, *241*, 37. [CrossRef]
40. Vasiliev, B.Y.; Kozyaruk, A.E.; Mardashov, D.V. Increasing the Utilization Factor of an Autonomous Inverter under Space Vector Control. *Russ. Electr. Eng.* **2020**, *91*, 247–254. [CrossRef]
41. Zhan, L.; Liu, Y.; Liu, Y. A clarke transformation-based DFT phasor and frequency algorithm for wide frequency range. *IEEE Trans. Smart Grid* **2016**, *9*, 67–77. [CrossRef]
42. Chikkerur, S.; Cartwright, A.N.; Govindaraju, V. Fingerprint enhancement using stft analysis. *Pattern Recognit.* **2007**, *40*, 198–211. [CrossRef]
43. Ilyushin, Y.; Golovina, E. Stability of temperature field of the distributed control system. *ARPN J. Eng. Appl. Sci.* **2020**, *15*, 664–668.
44. Wollschlaeger, M.; Sauter, T.; Jasperneite, J. The future of industrial communication: Automation networks in the era of the internet of things and industry 4.0. *IEEE Ind. Electron. Mag.* **2017**, *11*, 17–27. [CrossRef]

45. De Francisci Morales, G.; Bifet, A.; Khan, L.; Gama, J.; Fan, W. Iot big data stream mining. Available online: https://dl.acm.org/doi/10.1145/2939672.2945385 (accessed on 11 March 2021).
46. Luo, L.; Gu, W.; Zhang, X.P.; Cao, G.; Wang, W.; Zhu, G.; You, D.; Wu, Z. Optimal siting and sizing of distributed generation in distribution systems with PV solar farm utilized as STATCOM (PV-STATCOM). *Appl. Energy* **2018**, *210*, 1092–1100. [CrossRef]
47. Gallo, D.; Landi, C.; Rignano, N. Real-time digital multifunction instrument for power quality integrated indexes measurement. *IEEE Trans. Instrum. Meas.* **2008**, *57*, 2769–2776. [CrossRef]
48. Shklyarskiy, Y.; Skamyin, A.; Vladimirov, I.; Gazizov, F. Distortion load identification based on the application of compensating devices. *Energies* **2020**, *13*, 1430. [CrossRef]
49. Shklyarskiy, Y.E.; Pirog, S. Impact of the load curve on losses in the power supply network of the company. *J. Min. Inst.* **2016**, *222*, 859–863.
50. Hoon, Y.; Mohd Radzi, M.A.; Hassan, M.K.; Mailah, N.F. Control algorithms of shunt active power filter for harmonics mitigation: A review. *Energies* **2017**, *10*, 2038. [CrossRef]
51. Terriche, Y.; Guerrero, J.M.; Vasquez, J.C. Performance improvement of shunt active power filter based on non-linear least-square approach. *Electr. Power Syst. Res.* **2018**, *160*, 44–55. [CrossRef]
52. Rodriguez, J.; Bernet, S.; Steimer, P.K.; Lizama, I.E. A survey on neutral-point-clamped inverters. *IEEE Trans. Ind. Electron.* **2009**, *57*, 2219–2230. [CrossRef]
53. Hossain, E.; Tür, M.R.; Padmanaban, S.; Ay, S.; Khan, I. Analysis and mitigation of power quality issues in distributed generation systems using custom power devices. *IEEE Access* **2018**, *6*, 16816–16833. [CrossRef]
54. Padiyar, K.R. FACTS Controllers in Power Transmission and Distribution; New Age International. 2007, p. 549. Available online: https://pdfslide.net/documents/facts-controllers-in-power-transmission-and-distribution-55845a9210575.html (accessed on 11 March 2021).
55. Mousavi, S.Y.M.; Jalilian, A.; Savaghebi, M.; Guerrero, J.M. Coordinated control of multifunctional inverters for voltage support and harmonic compensation in a grid-connected microgrid. *Electr. Power Syst. Res.* **2018**, *155*, 254–264. [CrossRef]
56. Sirjani, R.; Jordehi, A.R. Optimal placement and sizing of distribution static compensator (D-STATCOM) in electric distribution networks: A review. *Renew. Sustain. Energy Rev.* **2017**, *77*, 688–694. [CrossRef]
57. Pedersen, K.O.H.; Nielsen, A.H.; Poulsen, N.K. Short-circuit impedance measurement. *IEEE Proc. Gener. Transm. Distrib.* **2003**, *150*, 169–174. [CrossRef]
58. Pirog, S.; Shklyarskiy, Y.E.; Skamyin, A.N. Non-linear electrical load location identification. *J. Min. Inst.* **2019**, *237*, 317. [CrossRef]
59. Woo, D.J.; Lee, T.K. Suppression of harmonics in Wilkinson power divider using dual-band rejection by asymmetric DGS. *IEEE Trans. Microw. Theory Tech.* **2005**, *53*, 2139–2144.
60. Peng, F.Z. Flexible AC transmission systems (FACTS) and resilient AC distribution systems (RACDS) in smart grid. *Proc. IEEE* **2017**, *105*, 2099–2115. [CrossRef]
61. Wu, X.H.; Panda, S.K.; Xu, J.X. Design of a plug-in repetitive control scheme for eliminating supply-side current harmonics of three-phase PWM boost rectifiers under generalized supply voltage conditions. *IEEE Trans. Power Electron.* **2010**, *25*, 1800–1810. [CrossRef]
62. Khokhar, S.; Zin, A.A.M.; Memon, A.P.; Mokhtar, A.S. A new optimal feature selection algorithm for classification of power quality disturbances using discrete wavelet transform and probabilistic neural network. *Measurement* **2017**, *95*, 246–259. [CrossRef]
63. Yacamini, R. Power system harmonics. IV. Interharmonics. *Power Eng. J.* **1996**, *10*, 185–193. [CrossRef]
64. Tummuru, N.R.; Mishra, M.K.; Srinivas, S. Multifunctional VSC controlled microgrid using instantaneous symmetrical components theory. *IEEE Trans. Sustain. Energy* **2013**, *5*, 313–322. [CrossRef]
65. Skamyin, A.N.; Vasilkov, O.S. Power Components Calculation and Their Application in Presence of High Harmonics. In Proceedings of the 2019 Electric Power Quality and Supply Reliability Conference (PQ) & 2019 Symposium on Electrical Engineering and Mechatronics (SEEM), Kardla, Estonia, 12–15 June 2019; pp. 1–4.
66. Alcalá, J.; Bárcenas, E.; Cárdenas, V. Practical methods for tuning PI controllers in the DC-link voltage loop in Back-to-Back power converters. In Proceedings of the 12th IEEE International Power Electronics Congress, San Luis Potosi, Mexico, 22–25 August 2010; pp. 46–52. Available online: https://ieeexplore.ieee.org/document/5598898 (accessed on 11 March 2021).
67. Wei, L.; Zhou, B.; Ma, X.; Chen, D.; Zhang, J.; Peng, J.; Luo, Q.; Sun, L.; Li, D.; Chen, L. Lightning: A high-efficient neighbor discovery protocol for low duty cycle WSNs. *IEEE Commun. Lett.* **2016**, *20*, 966–969. [CrossRef]

Article

Virtual Soft Sensor of the Feedstock Composition of the Catalytic Reforming Unit

Natalia Koteleva * and Ilya Tkachev

Department of Mineral Process, Automation of Technological Processes and Production,
St. Petersburg Mining University, 199106 St. Petersburg, Russia; tka4ev.ilia@yandex.ru or s175067@stud.spmi.ru
* Correspondence: Koteleva_NI@pers.spmi.ru

Abstract: The paper discusses a method for obtaining a matrix of individual and group composition of a hydrotreated heavy gasoline fraction in industrial conditions based on the fractional composition obtained by the distillation method according to the ASTM D86 (the Russian analogue of such a standard is GOST 2177). A method for bounds estimation of the retention index (RI) change is considered on the basis of the symmetry of the RI change range relative to its arithmetic mean. Implementation of this method is performed by simulation of individual composition of C6–C12 feedstock of the catalytic reforming unit in the software package. For this purpose, the boiling curve of individual composition of hydrocarbon mixture is converted into the corresponding curve of fractional composition. The presented technique of creating a virtual soft sensor makes it possible to establish a correct relationship between the fractional composition and the individual hydrocarbon composition obtained according to the IFP 9301 (GOST R 52714) (Russian GOST R 52714 and international IFP 9301 standards for the determination of individual and group composition of hydrocarbon mixtures by capillary gas chromatography). The virtual soft sensor is based on chemical and mathematical principles. The application of this technique on the data of a real oil refinery is shown. Obtaining accurate data by means of a virtual soft sensor on the individual composition of feedstock will make it possible to optimize the catalytic reforming process and thus indirectly improve its environmental friendliness and enrichment efficiency.

Keywords: virtual soft sensor; naphtha; composition model; method of pseudo-components; fractional composition; simulated distillation; boiling point; gas chromatography

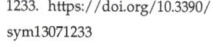

Citation: Koteleva, N.; Tkachev, I. Virtual Soft Sensor of the Feedstock Composition of the Catalytic Reforming Unit. *Symmetry* **2021**, *13*, 1233. https://doi.org/10.3390/sym13071233

Academic Editors: Rudolf Kawalla and Beloglazov Ilya

Received: 25 May 2021
Accepted: 7 July 2021
Published: 9 July 2021

Publisher's Note: MDPI stays neutral with regard to jurisdictional claims in published maps and institutional affiliations.

Copyright: © 2021 by the authors. Licensee MDPI, Basel, Switzerland. This article is an open access article distributed under the terms and conditions of the Creative Commons Attribution (CC BY) license (https://creativecommons.org/licenses/by/4.0/).

1. Introduction

Digitalization of the economy in general [1] and industry in particular [2] is a top national priority of the Russian Federation. Digitalization of technological processes in this case is associated with their advancement [3]. Currently, development of technological processes of oil refining is carried out with the help of improvement of technology [4,5] and control systems and control principles of these technological processes [6]. In this case, technological development means everything that is related to technology: advancement of apparatus design, replacement of equipment, reagents, etc. Improvement of control systems and principles means creation of new control algorithms and principally new by structure and functionality automated control systems. The development of primary oil refining processes is mainly due to the introduction of so-called advanced control systems (APC), which have already been proven to bring substantial profits to oil refineries [3].

However, secondary oil refining processes are directly related to improvements in technology [7,8]. For example, moving bed catalyst reactors are used instead of a fixed bed reactor or development of new types of catalysts that increase conversion and efficiency of processes in chemical reactors [5]. Meanwhile, improving the control systems and control principles of secondary oil refining processes is not considered a priority task. This is due to several reasons: (1) Significant profit from technological advances overshadows the profit from system advances. (2) New techniques do not allow the formation of significant experience in the automation of these processes, and therefore decisions concerning advancements of systems can be considered hasty and lacking adequate substantiation. (3) Low flexibility of the process, most parts of which can rather be perceived as a black box with no chance to change the contents. (This is due to the peculiarity of reactor processes. As a rule, the controls are made in such a way that those control actions that are applied to the reactor input give their result at the output of the apparatus. We can only change something with a loss of quality for a period of time. The change occurs intuitively, because there are no control actions while the substance is in the apparatus; however, there are many influencing factors: coke formation, reduction of the reactivity of the catalyst, etc. Therefore, from the point of view of control, the apparatus is a black box, since it is impossible to monitor the state of the substances inside the unit.) (4) The complexity of chemical processes that are difficult to determine. (5) High cost of equipment for the study of these processes, etc. However, taking into account these issues, the use of APC algorithms along with technological developments will certainly increase the efficiency of secondary oil refining processes, as well as bring additional profit to oil refineries [9,10]. Although advanced control systems are based upon mathematical models, it is difficult to obtain accurate mathematical models describing a process in petroleum or a related field [11]. This applies to both mathematical kinetic and empirical models. For kinetic models, it is difficult to obtain a complete list of reactions of the process. For empirical models, it is insufficient information about the process, which makes it complicated to accumulate data to build empirical models. In this regard, the work aimed at improving the information component of the system is relevant.

Data about the hydrocarbon components contained in naphtha is used to monitor the catalytic reforming process, assess product quality, and control composition. Extended hydrocarbon composition can be obtained by chromatography. If chromatography is used to identify compounds, the retention time should be independent of the amount of sample and the chromatographic peaks should be symmetrical to ensure correct identification of the compounds. The extended hydrocarbon composition is also used as input for mathematical modeling of the process. It should be kept in mind that data obtained by chromatography cannot be extracted in real time. Usually, they are received in the laboratory over a period of at least two hours with human participation. Soft-sensing technology is used in various industries and technological facilities. The application, algorithmic and mathematical bases for these sensors are very diverse and are mainly based on neural networks, regression methods, and composition prediction. The paper by Tian et al. (2021) [12] presents soft sensor applied in the monitoring system of a typical 330 MW CHP plant. This approach uses the turbine's Flugel formula as a static model, the turbine's heat balance characteristic to correct the coefficient in the model and the butterfly valve characteristic to realize dynamic compensation to realize the soft sensor. The work Niño-Adan and colleagues (2021) [13] discusses soft-sensor for class prediction of the percentage of pentanes in butane at a debutanizer column. It includes the autoML approach that selects among different normalization and feature weighting preprocessing techniques and various well-known machine learning (ML) algorithms. The article by Winkler et al. (2021) [14] presents soft sensor for real-time process monitoring of multidimensional fractionation in tubular centrifuges. Reference [15] describes Soft sensor for industrial distillation column. The authors Hsiao et al. (2021) propose soft sensor development methodology combining first-principle simulations, and transfer learning was used to address these problems.

One of the elements of advanced control systems is the virtual sensor [16]. Virtual sensors calculate parameter values using statistical dependencies (a polynomial), a neural network, or other mathematical tools to determine correlation between variables [17,18]. This method involves the accumulation of a large volume of data and its further processing using various approaches [19] including those mentioned earlier. For a catalytic reformer, various variables can act as deterministic parameters for the virtual sensor. However, in some cases, the creation and implementation of virtual sensors for some variable process is highly difficult and even impossible. This is due to the fact that the large sample of data history for this segment does not exist, or their synchronization is troublesome. In particular, to be more specific, the process of creating a virtual soft sensor of the feedstock composition is a challenging task. The reason for this is the mismatch between the company's capabilities to measure individual hydrocarbon composition in a number of industrial processes and the data requirements of the virtual sensor. In this case, data obtained on the individual hydrocarbon composition of the feedstock in real time is an effective tool for optimizing technological processes that take place in a catalytic reforming unit. The need to optimize technological processes in this matter is caused by tough requirements for environment protection [20] and the influence of the modern trends in the development of the global energy sector [21,22].

It is important to reduce the uncertainty arising from infrequent composition control in processes such as catalytic reforming where the individual and group composition of the feedstock determines the target performance of the unit and the catalyst lifespan. Such uncertainty in the feedstock composition can complicate the application of mathematical models in the loop of an advanced control system or as an advisor to the operator [23], which can result to fluctuations in product target performance over the specification limits in the absence of the advanced control system. Studies of naphtha catalytic reforming process have been carried out for a long period of time [24]. During this period, a large number of [25] complex, highly precise, and detailed mathematical models of the catalytic reforming process, simulating different naphthas with various amount of detail, have been developed. The following steps were highlighted in the study of research and work: the effect of changes in feedstock composition at the naphtha catalytic reforming unit is considered [26]; consider the parameters of the working process of coke combustion, comparing the results with industrial data [27]; conduct a comprehensive sensitivity analysis of the quality and quantity of the product [28] without taking into account the impact of changes in the composition of raw materials of the process; the influence of the design parameters of a catalytic reforming reactor, the molar flow rate on the hydrodealkylation side, the molar ratio of hydrogen to hydrocarbons, the impact of catalyst deactivation on the system performance are subjected to the research [29]; the modes of incoming and outgoing flows in reactors with thermal coupling are analyzed [30].

A certain technological level of the unit that meets the requirement of the mathematical model for the size of the input matrix is needed to introduce the developed mathematical models in the existing production facilities. The model input matrix can be obtained from the results of analytical control of the individual hydrocarbon composition of raw materials, but inline control is not applied at all refineries. This raises the question of how to provide the mathematical model with up-to-date input information about changes in the composition of the workflow under operating production conditions, and whether this control of the feedstock composition of a catalytic reforming unit can be performed more frequently at an operating production facility.

A review Ren and colleagues (2019) [31] of methods for converting individual composition into fractional composition and vice versa showed several approaches. Most of the approaches are formed on a multidimensional base for controlling several parameters besides composition, which implies a preparatory stage of model development. Incomplete data and checking their correctness results in the use of data processing and recovery methods. The researchers consider the dependences of the mixture properties on the compound identification parameters [32–34], individual constants, and characteristics of the compound [35], which is an important and necessary basis for this study.

The paper discusses a method for obtaining a matrix of the carbon number and group composition of the feedstock of a catalytic reforming unit in industrial conditions. A group composition of petroleum fractions during an oil refining processes is the most important factor influencing in the yield and composition of products, as well as an efficiency of the catalysts. The fuels ASTM D86 distillation temperature distribution is divided into equal-volume pseudo-component cuts, each of which is assigned a property volume blending index the aggregation of which provides an accurate estimation of the global property of the whole petroleum fuel, or portions thereof. The list of these pseudo-components is the group composition of petroleum fractions [36]. It is envisaged that it is possible to find a matrix of carbon number and group composition of hydrotreated catalytic reforming naphtha close to the experimental one by expressing [37] the desired composition through close fractions of known individual hydrocarbon compositions. The evaluation of the fraction proximity is determined by the associated boiling points. This is known due to the fact that the heavier in molecular weight individual components that make up the fractions have higher boiling points than the lighter ones.

The retention index is a common type of data used to identify chemical compounds by gas chromatography. The retention index system is a widely used and recognized system in gas chromatography for the identification of compounds. The paper by Yan et al. (2015) [38] describes that the database retention indices of over 300 aroma compounds that were determined on three capillary columns of different polarity can be used for qualitative identification. The work [39] shows that retention indices of 28 polychlorinated biphenyls in capillary gas chromatography referred to 2,4,6-trichlorophenyl alkyl ethers as RI-standards. The paper by Morosini and Ballschmiter (1994) [39] presents that on the basis of the TCPE, the retention indices of 28 polychlorinated biphenyls were determined using the ECD, a 95% dimethyl 5% phenyl polysiloxane phase and six different temperature programs. In addition, there are a number of studies in practice that have generated a system of retention indices in different ways [40–42].

2. Materials and Methods

The development of a model for a virtual soft sensor of the feedstock composition can be divided into two stages: preparatory and computational. The preparatory stage includes the analysis and processing of the obtained data, determination of the method of obtaining fractions from the individual composition, and the formation of a database of individual components and associated boiling points of fractions. The description of the preparatory stage is formed on the lack of information on the chromatographic system and the fractional composition control system based only on the available measurement data. A chromatographic system is defined as a set of hardware and methods that allow chromatography to be performed. The need of these operations at each stage will be discussed further.

According to the technological regulations of the enterprise, the individual and group composition is controlled according to the IFP 9301 standard, which recommends the use of gas chromatography with a 100 m long fused-silica capillary column with an inner diameter of 0.25 mm. According to the standard, the capillary column is coated with methylsilicone elastomer or dimethylsiloxane, 0.5 μm thick, and has to be equivalent to at least 6000 theoretical plates/m; a linear retention index (n-alkane) is used to identify the components. The fractional composition is controlled according to the ASTM D86 method.

2.1. Preparatory Stage

Check the presence and repeatability of the distribution law in the IFPi homologous series. If the data obey the distribution law, then composition models based on these laws can be used. Determine the retention time of non-absorbent substance and possible parameters of the chromatographic system for the identification of compounds [37]. However, reference sources on retention indices provide single values for individual substances and there are no confidence interval limits of their measurement, which leads to uncertainty in identification [43]. If the report on the control of individual and group composition of raw materials records the given time, then calculate the matrix of minimum ΔRI from all reports for each homologous group by carbon number by Equation (1):

$$\Delta RI = RI_i - RI_{i-1}, \tag{1}$$

where ΔRI is the difference in the retention indices of adjacent compounds in the report, RI_i is the retention index of the i-th compound, and RI_{i-1} is the retention index of the previous compound to the i-th. The chromatographic system identifies a component by its retention index, and therefore it is important that the maximum deviation from the mean in the retention index of each compound in different reports does not exceed the ΔRI value for the corresponding homologous group of a matrix of minimum ΔRI. If the value of deviation of the retention index exceeds the corresponding ΔRI, then this indicates that the data are incorrect, and that compound cannot be correctly identified. Moreover, the matrix of minimum ΔRI and average values of the retention indices can be used as an indicator of the chromatographic system performance, automatically checking the deviations of the new composition measurement, since visual assessment of the chromatogram allows for human error.

For identified compounds with unknown boiling point the experimental values of the parameter are taken from the reference sources [35]. Construct the function between the normal boiling point of a compound and its retention index within one homologous series [33,44]. For unidentified compounds, determine its boiling point according to the constructed mathematical relation.

Determine actual ASTM boiling point intervals (min and max) for a given period of unit operation. In this case, the period of operation of the unit should be representative (historical data should cover the entire range of variation in the feedstock composition). This will allow for assessment of the range of change in the fractional feedstock composition.

Construct theoretical curves [45] corresponding to the mixture distillation simulated curves. The obtained simulated distillation curves are set in the Hysys/Pro II simulation program, specifying the composition of the mixture, which is the beginning of its boiling. Calculate the D86 boiling curve and enter the obtained values into the database as an associated fractional composition with an individual and group composition.

Theoretical curves are derived from the characteristic boiling points of the mixture from the individual hydrocarbon composition of the feedstock. The characteristic boiling points of a mixture are close values to the boiling points of the mixture at the corresponding cumulative fractions of the mixture. They uniquely characterize the entire mixture fraction taken in the interval of the corresponding cumulative fractions of the mixture by considering the boiling point of each compound of the fraction in accordance with the fraction occupied by this component in the given fraction of the given hydrocarbon com-position. Cumulative fractions are calculated in accordance with the principle of additivity of fractions of mixture components. The fraction taken from the individual hydrocarbon composition is considered separated from the rest of the mixture, and equated to 100%, the fractions of individual components in it are recalculated and used as weight coefficients when adding temperatures of each compound in the taken fraction. Thus, we obtain a unique temperature characterizing the fraction through the temperatures of the compounds of its constituents and close to the experimental boiling point of the mixture at the corresponding cumulative fraction of the mixture. The beginning of boiling of the mixture is determined on the basis of the algorithm of finding the experimental boiling points of the mixture. The obtained characteristic boiling points of a mixture of individual hydrocarbon composition are taken as a simulated distillation curve (SD) and, using the procedure 3A.3.2 API-TDB 1997 [46], convert them to an ASTM fractional boiling curve. We estimate the belonging of the obtained ASTM boiling curve according to the available actual boiling point ranges according to ASTM.

The prepared IFPi and their corresponding boiling points of the fractional composition are recorded in the non-relational database as the key value. The key in this case is the date of chromatography, associating the data of the two compositions, and the values are the report of the individual hydrocarbon composition and the corresponding boiling curve.

2.2. Computational Stage

Compare each point of the measured D86 boiling curve with the corresponding point by volume fraction point of the boiling curve from the prepared database. For comparison, we use the module of the difference between the measured and associated boiling point from the prepared database. A reference book with the keys of delta temperatures and values of chromatography dates with a length equal to the number of keys in the prepared database is created in the operating memory of the computer.

In the temperature delta reference book, search for the minimum temperature delta for each boiling point of the hydrocarbon mixture. As a result, one obtains a list consisting of an ordered sequence of dates and the corresponding boundary cumulative fraction of the hydrocarbon mixture.

The IFPi fractions sequence is determined from the list of dates. To obtain a sequence of fractions, we use the algorithm for obtaining a fraction from IFPi by cumulative fractions of the mixture by referring by date to the IFPi in the prepared IFPi database and the boundary cumulative fraction of the hydrocarbon mixture. We obtain a list of sequences of individual mixture components expressed from the nearest IFPi fractions. The resulting sequence is recorded in the database of estimated compositions for the possibility of performing analysis and statistical assessment of changes in the composition over time.

Obtaining the MTHS matrix (MTHS—molecular type and homologous series). We find the scoring matrix of the carbon number and group composition of the mixture. The method used to assess the proximity of the sought individual composition and the experimentally obtained composition requires reducing the IFPi to a matrix form. This covers the cases of repeating the dates at step 2 and possible duplicates of the names of the boundary components of the IFPi fractions. In this case, the values of the fractions of the components, for which the individual composition was incremented, are not repeated for the duplicate names, and do not violate the additivity principle of the mixture.

The Figure 1 shows the block diagram of the model for assessing MTHS composition by the ASTMi boiling.

The measured ASTMi boiling curve of size 1×7 is fed to the input to the model. On the basis of the minimum temperature difference, the model determines the closest associated boiling point for each ASTMi boiling point fed to the input. According to the mixing rule, the MTHS matrix of the hydrocarbon mixture composition is calculated on the basis of the nearest boiling points of fractions found in the BPi virtual soft sensor database.

The presented virtual model of the soft sensor can be verified using four available reports of individual and group composition of the hydrocarbon mixture. These reports were created by monitoring the composition of the hydrotreated heavy gasoline fraction of a catalytic reforming unit (CCR) in different months of different years according to IFP 9301.

Let us conduct an experiment with the model, taking one of the four IFPi as unknown, and feeding the associated ASTMi boiling curve, taken as unknown associated IFPi, to the input to the model. As a result of the experiment with the model, we obtain the estimated MTHS matrix of the unit feedstock composition, taken as unknown. The estimated matrix is compared with the experimental matrix via reducing to the PIONA (paraffins, iso-paraffins, olefins, naphthenes, aromatics) vector, obtained by adding the respective fractions of compounds belonging to one of the five types of compound groups.

IFPi are represented by adsorption sequences of various lengths without repeating names, consisting of a list of individual components with diverse fractions of compounds in the mixture, with different boiling points. The various lengths of the reports and the difference in the positions of the same compound complicate assessing the proximity of the compositions in this form. However, the report on the considered raw materials can be reduced to an 11×5 matrix. The columns are the homological series, while the rows are the carbon numbers of the compound or several compounds of the same group. This approach will allow us to quantitatively assess the proximity of compositions by the components of the vector PIONA.

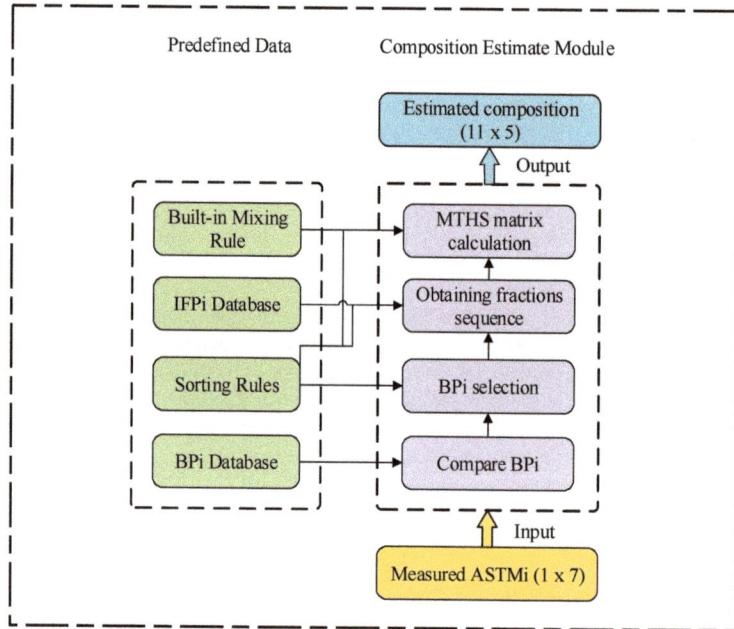

Figure 1. Block diagram of the model for assessing MTHS composition by the ASTMi boiling curve. BPi Database is a list of associated boiling curves; sorting rules—sorting rules used to obtain the desired elements; IFPi Database—list of associated reports on the individual hydrocarbon composition of the mixture; built-in-mixing rule—incrementing the fractions of individual components is performed only with the corresponding fractions according to the principle of additivity of the mixture fractions; measured ASTMi (1 × 7)—boiling points (minimum 7 boiling points of a mixture), obtained during the in-process control of the fractional composition of the hydrocarbon mixture; compare BPi—calculation of deltas of measured and prepared boiling points of the hydrocarbon mixture; BPi selection—determination of the minimum deltas for each boundary value of the cumulative fraction of the mixture; obtaining fractions sequence—generation of a sequence of fractions of individual components; MTHS matrix calculation—calculation of the estimated MTHS matrix; estimated composition (11 × 5)—the resulting estimated MTHS matrix.

The accuracy of the data taken is determined by the accuracy of the DCS (distributed control system) and LIMS (laboratory information management system) systems operating on the unit, as well as by the accuracy of the sensor equipment used.

In addition, when describing the experiment, it is worth noting that the enterprise has internal standards that describe the required accuracy of the system operation and the laboratory tests carried out, which indirectly indicates the sufficient reliability of the data obtained in this manner.

3. Results

3.1. Statistical Descriptive Analysis of the Samples

Before developing the model, we subjected the IFPi data obtained at the enterprise to statistical analysis. In particular, for each homologous series, a distribution histogram was constructed for four samples of the same catalytic reforming feedstock process stream, tested by the IFP 9301 method at different times (Figure 2a–e).

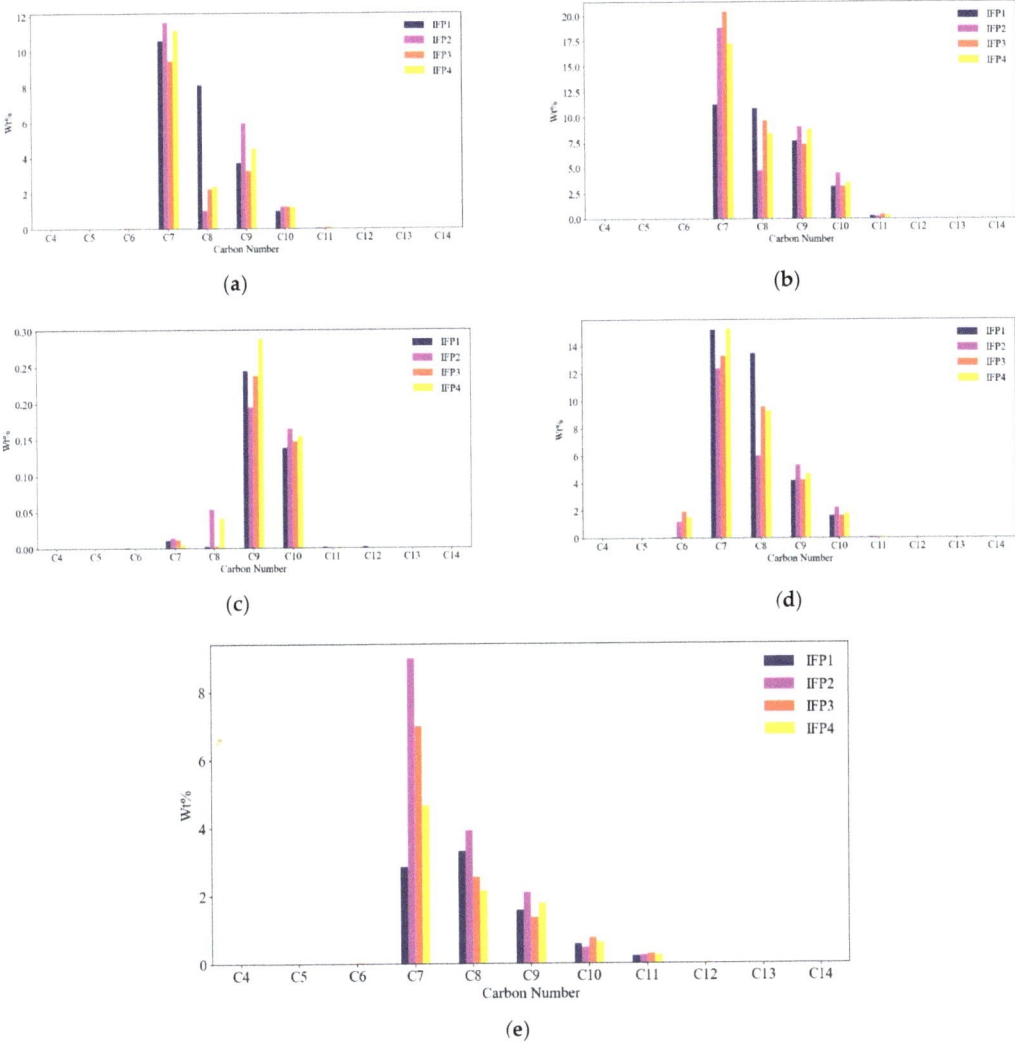

Figure 2. Distribution histograms: (**a**) paraffins; (**b**) iso-paraffins; (**c**) olefins; (**d**) naphthenes; (**e**) aromatics.

As can be seen from the graphs, the distribution within each homologous group (paraffins, iso-paraffins, olefins, naphthenes, and aromatics) did not statistically obey any distribution function. This made it impossible to apply known models [9,47–50] based on the assumption of a change in composition in accordance with the known statistical distribution within the homologous group. The unevenness in the composition of raw materials and distribution by homologous groups can also be seen. At the same time, the low frequency of analysis of raw materials was associated with a stable composition; however, Figure 2 shows a contradiction. This fact additionally indicates the relevance of this work.

3.2. Retention Indices as a Marker for Component Identification in Homologous Groups

It was not possible to set the time for non-adsorbent compound, because the report recorded the adjusted retention time. When determining the matrix of minimum ΔRI, the values given in Table 1 were obtained.

Table 1. Matrix ΔRI_{min} for homologous groups of IFP1–IFP4.

	I	O	N	A
C6	3.8	-	32.37	-
C7	1.47	2.99	0.8	-
C8	0.48	50.26	0.8	1.13
C9	0.97	1.06	0.47	1.95
C10	0.7	1.12	0.96	1.07
C11	1.47	-	19.36	0.92
C12	35.79	-	-	0.91
C13	-	-	-	42.46

The first column of the table contains the numbers of carbon atoms; the title of the table contains the name of the homologous group. The least values of ΔRI from Table 1 are contained in I8 and N9. These and other cases are shown in Figure 3.

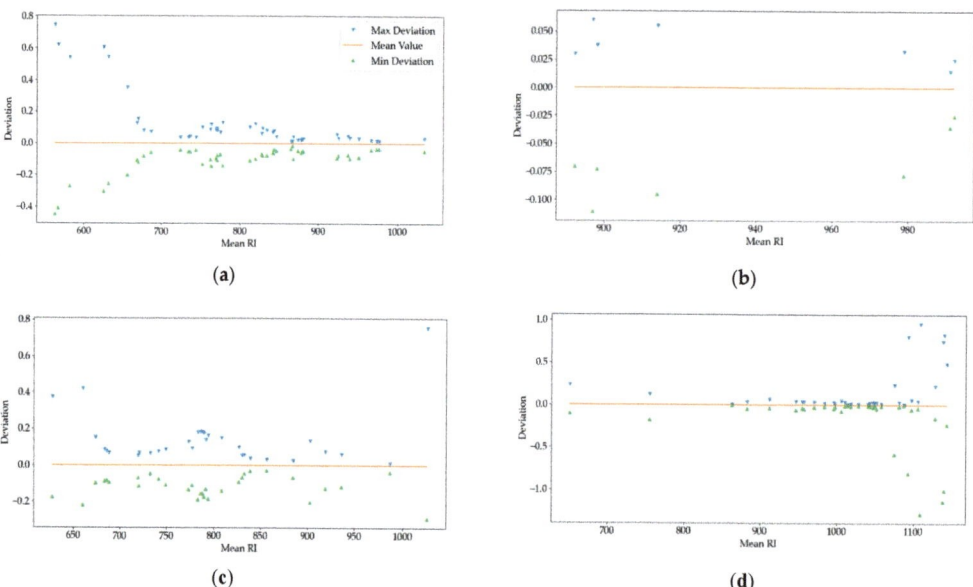

Figure 3. Maximum deviation from the RI mean value for the identified components: (**a**) iso-paraffins; (**b**) olefins; (**c**) naphthenes; (**d**) aromatics.

Figure 3 shows the RI range from its arithmetic mean for each identified compound present in each IFPi. The RI ranges of the retention indices of the different compounds in the various homologous groups show the differentiation in the ranges of the RI retention indices of each compound and the inferred RI limits for the compounds. A symmetry with respect to the arithmetic mean RI can be observed. The deviation values show a tendency towards an increase in the spread of RI for light and heavy compound. The reason for this may be the methods and algorithms used to calculate the RI, as well as methods and instructions for performing the composition control procedure in production.

Let us consider the case of I8 with RI in the range of mean values from 724.503 to 777.97, where the maximum upper and lower boundaries for this group were reached at point 777.97 and its value was 0.27, which was less than 0.48 from Table 1. In the case of N9 with RI in the range of mean values from 830.515 to 936.827, the maximum upper and lower boundaries for this group were reached at point 902.905, with the value of maximum deviations of 0.34, which was less than 0.47 from Table 1. The inequality was valid for all PIONA corresponding pairs of RI values of all homologous series with the exception of a few aromatics and one olefin. Thus, the retention index is considered a reliable parameter for model development, therefore the reported data are valid. The retention index of the identified components were close and coincided with the retention index obtained in [51–53].

3.3. Identifying Components with "Drifting" RIs

The Figure 4 shows the search algorithm for component with "drifting" RI.

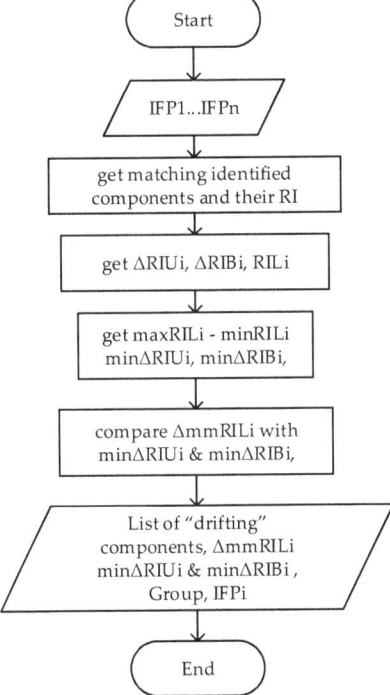

Figure 4. Search algorithm for component with "drifting" RI. $\Delta RI_U i$—difference between the retention index of the current component and the retention index of the next component, $\Delta RI_B i$—difference between the retention index of the current component and the retention index of the previous component, $RI_L i$—list of retention indices of the current component, $maxRI_L i$—the maximum value of the retention index of the current component, $min\Delta RI_L i$—the minimum value of the retention index of the current component, $\Delta mmRI_L i$—delta between the maximum and minimum value of the retention index of the current component ($\Delta mmRI_L i = max\Delta RI_L i - min\Delta RI_L i$), $min\Delta RI_B i$—the minimum difference between the retention indices of the current compound name and the previous value in all reports, $min\Delta RI_u i$—the minimum difference between the retention indices of the current compound name and the next value in all reports.

Table 2 shows the result of the algorithm for finding drifting retention indices on experimental data. Components with drifting retention indices were identified. They all belonged to groups A10, A11, A12, and O11.

Table 2. Search result for components with "drifting" RI.

Component	Group	Report	$\Delta mmRI_L i$	$min\Delta RI_u i$	$min\Delta RI_B i$
1,2-Dimethyl-4-ethylbenzene	A10	IFP4	0.81	0.85	0.79
Undecene-1	O11	IFP4	1.02	1.28	0.98
1,2-Dimethyl-3-ethylbenzene	A10	IFP4	1.61	1.28	1.42
1,2,3,5-Tetramethylbenzene	A10	IFP4	2.24	1.27	1.83
1,2-Ethyl-n-propylbenzene	A11	IFP4	1.83	1.7	1.62
4-Methylindan	A10	IFP4	1.89	1.62	1.86
n-Hexylbenzene	A12	IFP4	2.44	1.76	14.79

3.4. Evaluation of a Chromatographic System

The change in the properties of the column during aging was assessed by the change in the retention index and the capacity factor k of benzene. Experimental methods were also used with a previously known composition of the mixture. Since the retention index is a reproducible parameter within a single chromatographic system, it can be used to evaluate a chromatographic system and change its properties over time. The Figure 5 shows the algorithm for evaluating the chromatographic system.

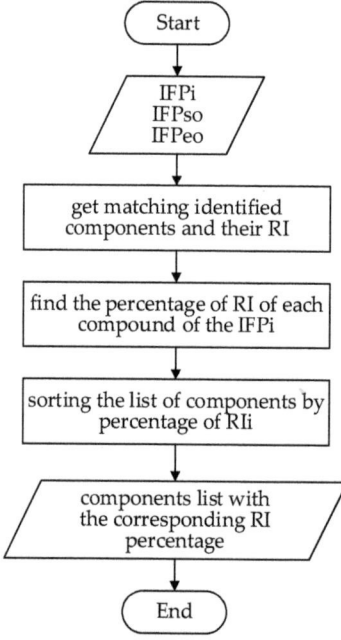

Figure 5. Algorithm for evaluating the chromatographic system. IFPso—start of operation of the chromatographic column, IFPeo—the last measurement before replacing the chromatographic column (end of operation). Input reports should be on the same process stream. Only the corresponding reports on the control of the composition were submitted to the entrance.

3.5. Predicting Normal Boiling Points from RIs

In order to use the retention index as a parameter for assessing the normal boiling points of compounds, we carried out an analysis of the reports. The IFPi analysis identified three categories of data: unidentified compounds with unknown boiling points, unidentified compounds with known boiling points, and identified compounds with unknown boiling points. The component contribution to the mixture by category is shown in Tables 3–5.

Table 3. Unidentified C7-C13 compounds with unknown boiling point.

IFPi	Numb.	Summarized Unidentified (numb. | wt %)				
		I	O	N	A	Summarized
IFP1	245	31 | 3.3334	4 | 0.0128	39 | 4.7344	7 | 0.0565	81 | 8.1371
IFP2	246	31 | 3.3705	3 | 0.0552	40 | 5.9527	11 | 0.0637	85 | 9.4421
IFP3	256	34 | 3.4353	2 | 0.0044	38 | 4.6287	16 | 0.0948	90 | 8.1632
IFP4	247	34 | 3.9115	4 | 0.0434	38 | 6.0251	10 | 0.0632	86 | 10.0432

Numb.—the number of components.

Table 4. Unidentified C9-C13 compounds with known boiling point.

IFPi	Summarized Unidentified with Known Temperature (numb. | wt %)				
	I	O	N	A	Summarized
IFP1	4 | 0.6811	1 | 0.0018	15 | 1.3249	14 | 0.1695	34 | 2.1773
IFP2	5 | 0.9755	0 | 0	17 | 1.9265	12 | 0.188	34 | 3.09
IFP3	5 | 0.6672	0 | 0	14 | 1.3254	17 | 0.2039	36 | 2.1965
IFP4	5 | 0.7675	0 | 0	14 | 1.442	11 | 0.1745	30 | 2.384

Table 5. Identified C9-C12 compounds with unknown boiling point.

IFPi	Summarized Identified with Unknown Temperature (numb. | wt %)				
	I	O	N	A	Summarized
IFP1	1 | 0.0665	7 | 0.1991	1 | 0.3499	6 | 0.0093	15 | 0.6248
IFP2	2 | 0.0998	6 | 0.1927	3 | 0.5018	5 | 0.0084	16 | 0.8027
IFP3	2 | 0.1599	7 | 0.2405	1 | 0.367	10 | 0.0208	20 | 0.7882
IFP4	2 | 0.1161	8 | 0.2675	2 | 0.3968	7 | 0.01	19 | 0.7904

These tables show the estimated normal boiling points contribution to the theoretical curves shown in Figures 6 and 7.

The restored theoretical curves are shown in the Figure 6. In the Figure 7, the D86 boiling curves obtained from the theoretical curves by the pseudo-component method are shown as solid lines. The triangular marker indicates the points of the D86 boiling curves obtained by the procedure 3A.3.2 from API–TDB 1997 on the basis of a sample of experimental data. The weight and volume percent of the mixture are located along the ordinate axis, and the temperature is located along the abscissa axis. Blue color was chosen for IFP1, green for IFP2, yellow for IFP3, and black for IFP4. The resulting D86 boiling curves corresponded to the D86 boiling curves obtained by the method of converting simulated distillation according to the ASTM D86. The difference in boiling points D86 from 10% to 90% inclusively did not exceed 1 °C. Differences more than 1 °C between curves can be observed at the beginning and end of the mixture boiling, since the correlation error for the beginning and end of boiling is more than 1 °C. That is due to the accuracy of the fractional composition measurements according to the ASTM D86 method, used equipment and possible way of processing data of the theoretical curve. When the sample was tested according to the ASTM D86 method, statistically the mixture boiled off by 98 vol %. The presented D86 curves fell within the range of ASTMi boiling points obtained during the analysis of fractional composition statistics. It was seen that three boiling curves were located close to each other on the segment of 10–70 vol %, and the boiling points at the points of 10 vol %, 30 vol %, and 50 vol % were repeated in different curves. Thus, it can be assumed that reducing the sampling interval of the measurements will provide a more accurate difference in close compositions with the use of the presented method. This can be seen from the D86 curves obtained by the method of pseudo-components.

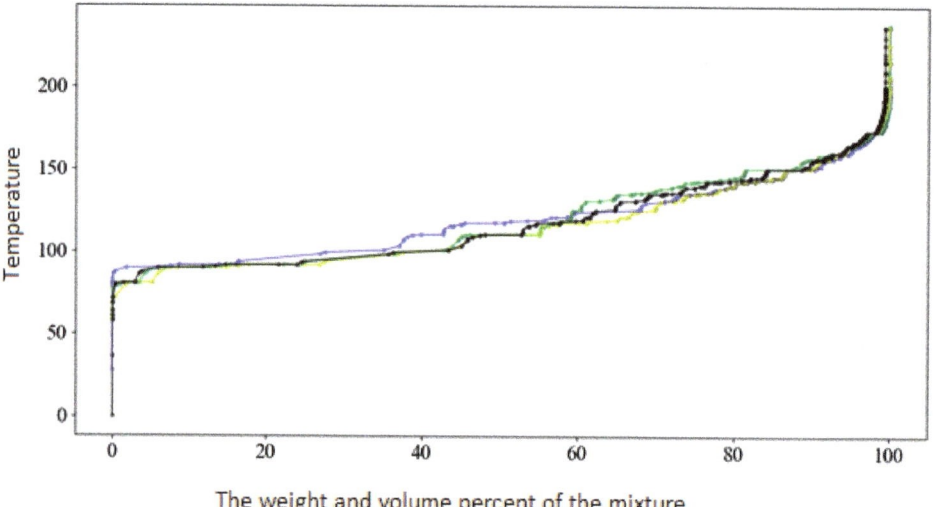

Figure 6. The restored theoretical curves. Blue color—IFP1, green—IFP2, yellow—IFP3, and black—IFP4.

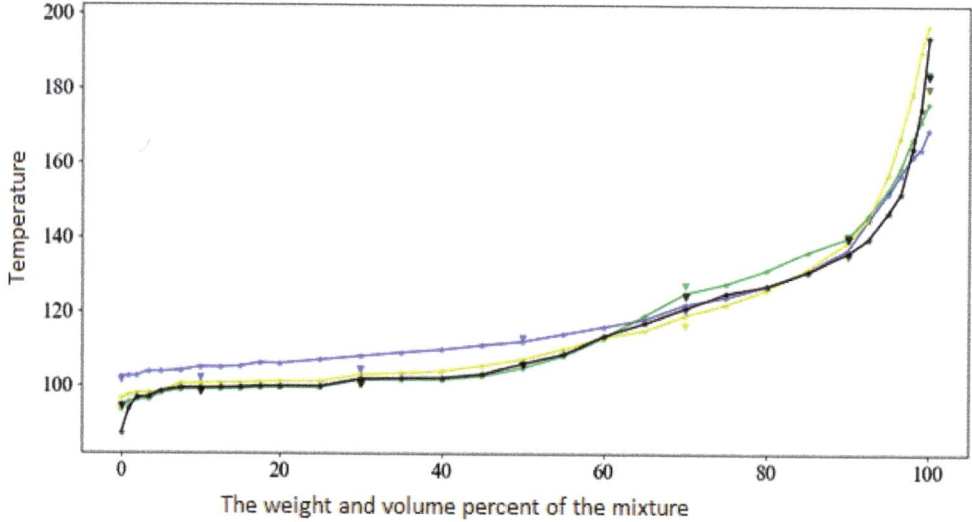

Figure 7. The D86 boiling curves obtained from the theoretical curves by the pseudo-component method. Blue color—IFP1, green—IFP2, yellow—IFP3, and black—IFP4.

During the preparatory stage, the boiling curves were analyzed for a year and a half of the unit's operation (see Table 6).

Table 6. Boiling point intervals according to the ASTMi.

	IBP, vol %	10, vol %	50, vol %	90, vol %	FBP, vol %
Min	93.0	100.0	109.0	135.0	156.0
Max	103.0	110.0	127.0	160.0	183.0

IBP—initial boiling point; FBP—final boiling point.

The range of variation in the feedstock composition of the catalytic reforming was finite and corresponded to the established specification limits of the technological regulations for the catalytic reforming unit feedstock. This fact further indicates the relevance of the research.

Let us take for unknown composition, for example, IFP3. We can feed the corresponding D86 boiling curve to the input of the developed model. The result (Table 7) obtained is not optimal in terms of possible combinations of fractions in order to minimize the resulting error of the composition, and the result depends on the proximity of each fraction through which the desired composition was expressed.

Table 7. The model calculation result.

	Calculation	Experiment	Δ
P[wt %]	18.6676	16.2217	2.4459
I[wt %]	38.3471	40.8639	−2.5168
O[wt %]	0.4319	0.3978	0.0341
N[wt %]	30.0788	30.6024	−0.5235
A[wt %]	12.4747	11.9142	0.5604
RMSE = 2.581194; R^2 = 0.991234046			

4. Conclusions

The presented model of the virtual soft sensor is designed to reduce production costs by using information about the composition stored in the databases of the catalytic reformer, with the possibility of implementing advanced control systems with high-precision mathematical models into the control loop. The main hypothesis of this work is the hypothesis about the possibility of establishing the correct relationship between the boiling curves of ASTM D86 (GOST 2177) and the individual hydrocarbon composition of the mixture obtained by the IFP 9301 method (GOST R 52714). In the course of the study, it was possible to show the consistency of the hypothesis put forward, develop a method, and convert the boiling curve of D86 into MTHS. Thus, a virtual soft sensor based on the developed technique can evaluate the composition of the feedstock in real time from the D86 boiling curves. The following results were obtained:

(1) The quantitative change in the individual composition of catalytic reforming naphtha over time did not obey the distribution laws.
(2) Methods for evaluating the results of the chromatographic system operation were presented, which made it possible to determine compounds with a large "drift" of the retention index, which can be used when setting up and operating the chromatographic system, as well as in analyzing and processing data from the reports of the chromatographic system.
(3) The data used were correct, since the retention index (n-alkane) was reproduced for the corresponding components of the mixture in the same chromatographic system and was repeated in the indicated studies for such components as benzene, 2,4-

dimethylpentane, and methylcyclopentane with a difference of no more than 0.4 units retention index.
(4) An algorithm for evaluating the chromatographic system and changing its properties with time was proposed.
(5) A method for converting the fractional composition into a matrix of individual and group composition was presented.

In addition, it should be noted that the developed model requires a more thorough test on a larger sample of IFPi to determine the sensitivity in cases of close compositions.

Author Contributions: Conceptualization, methodology, gathering and processing experimental data, writing—original draft, I.T.; supervision, writing—review and editing N.K. All authors have read and agreed to the published version of the manuscript.

Funding: This research received no external funding.

Institutional Review Board Statement: Not applicable.

Informed Consent Statement: Not applicable.

Data Availability Statement: Not applicable.

Acknowledgments: The authors are indebted to Head of the Department of Automation of Technological Processes and Production, Bazhin V.Yu.; Dean of the Faculty of Mineral Raw Material Processing, Petrov P.A.; and postgraduate student of the Department of Automation of Technological Processes, Snegirev N.V., for help in obtaining production data. Special thanks to Yu. V. Sharikov.

Conflicts of Interest: The authors declare no conflict of interest. The funders had no role in the design of the study; in the collection, analyses, or interpretation of data; in the writing of the manuscript; or in the decision to publish the results.

Abbreviations

IFP	sample test method according to the IFP 9301 (GOST R 52714)
IFPi	report/data on the sample test results according to the IFP 9301 (GOST R 52714)
ASTM	sample test method according to the ASTM D86 (GOST 2177)
MTHS	molecular type and homologous series
MES	manufacturing execution system
ERP	enterprise resource planning
PIONA	paraffins, iso-paraffins, olefins, naphthenes, aromatics
IBP	initial boiling point
FBP	final boiling point
t_m	retention time of non-absorbable substance
DCS	distributed control system
LIMS	laboratory information management system

References

1. Litvinenko, V.S. Digital Economy as a Factor in the Technological Development of the Mineral Sector. *Nat. Resour. Res.* **2020**, *29*, 1521–1541. [CrossRef]
2. Makhovikov, A.B.; Katuntsov, E.V.; Kosarev, O.V.; Tsvetkov, P.S. Digital transformation in oil and gas extraction (2019) Innovation-Based Development of the Mineral Resources Sector: Challenges and Prospects. In Proceedings of the 11th Conference of the Russian-German Raw Materials, Potsdam, Germany, 7–8 November 2018; pp. 531–538.
3. Nicolae, N.; Popescu, M.; Patrascioiu, C. Implementation of advanced process control in refineries. In Proceedings of the 2019 23rd International Conference on System Theory, Control and Computing, Sinaia, Romania, 9–11 October 2019; ICSTCC 2019—Proceedings. Institute of Electrical and Electronics Engineers Inc.: New York, NY, USA, 2019; pp. 95–100.
4. Anchita, J. HYDRO-IMP Technology for Upgrading of Heavy Petroleum. *J. Min. Inst.* **2017**, *224*, 229–234. [CrossRef]
5. Alabdullah, M.A.; Gomez, A.R.; Vittenet, J.; Bendjeriou-Sedjerari, A.; Xu, W.; Abba, I.A.; Gascon, J. A Viewpoint on the Refinery of the Future: Catalyst and Process Challenges. *ACS Catal.* **2020**, *10*, 8131–8140. [CrossRef]
6. Robinson, P.R.; Cima, D. Advanced Process Control. In *Practical Advances in Petroleum Processing*; Chang, S.H., Paul, R.R., Eds.; Springer: New York, NY, USA, 2006; pp. 695–703.

7. Tian, Y.; Demirel, S.E.; Hasan, M.M.F.; Pistikopoulos, E.N. An overview of process systems engineering approaches for process intensification: State of the art. *Chem. Eng. Process. Process. Intensif.* **2018**, *133*, 160–210. [CrossRef]
8. Shakeri, M.; Iranshahi, D.; Naderifar, A. Optimization of a novel multifunctional reactor containing m-xylene hydrodealkylation and naphtha reforming. *Int. J. Hydrog. Energy* **2019**, *44*, 21882–21895. [CrossRef]
9. Cui, C.; Billa, T.; Zhang, L.; Shi, Q.; Zhao, S.; Klein, M.T.; Xu, C. Molecular Representation of the Petroleum Gasoline Fraction. *Energy Fuels* **2018**, *32*, 1525–1533. [CrossRef]
10. Tipler, S.; Parente, A.; Coussement, A.; Contino, F.; Symoens, S.; Djokic, M.; Van Geem, K. Prediction of the PIONA and oxygenate composition of unconventional fuels with the Pseudo-Component Property Estimation (PCPE) method. Application to an Automotive Shredder Residues-derived gasoline. *SAE Tech. Pap.* **2018**, 1–15. [CrossRef]
11. Boikov, A.V.; Savelev, R.V.; Payor, V.A.; Erokhina, O.O. The control method concept of the bulk material behavior in the pelletizing drum for improving the results of DEM-modeling. *CIS Iron Steel Rev.* **2019**, *17*, 10–13. [CrossRef]
12. Tian, L.; Liu, X.; Luo, H.; Deng, T.; Liu, J.; Zhou, G.; Zhang, T. Soft Sensor of Heating Extraction Steam Flow Rate Based on Frequency Complementary Information Fusion for CHP Plant. *Energies* **2021**, *14*, 3474. [CrossRef]
13. Niño-Adan, I.; Landa-Torres, I.; Manjarres, D.; Portillo, E.; Orbe, L. Soft-Sensor for Class Prediction of the Percentage of Pentanes in Butane at a Debutanizer Column. *Sensors* **2021**, *21*, 3991. [CrossRef]
14. Winkler, M.; Gleiss, M.; Nirschl, H. Soft Sensor Development for Real-Time Process Monitoring of Multidimensional Fractionation in Tubular Centrifuges. *Nanomaterials* **2021**, *11*, 1114. [CrossRef]
15. Hsiao, Y.-D.; Kang, J.-L.; Wong, D.S.-H. Development of Robust and Physically Interpretable Soft Sensor for Industrial Distillation Column Using Transfer Learning with Small Datasets. *Processes* **2021**, *9*, 667. [CrossRef]
16. Martin, D.; Kühl, N.; Satzger, G. Virtual Sensors. *Bus. Inf. Syst. Eng.* **2021**, *63*, 315–323. [CrossRef]
17. Zhukovskiy, Y.L.; Korolev, N.A.; Babanova, I.S.; Boikov, A.V. The prediction of the residual life of electromechanical equipment based on the artificial neural network. In Proceedings of the IOP Conference Series: Earth and Environmental Science, Shanghai, China, 19–22 October 2017; Institute of Physics Publishing: Bristol, UK, 2017; Volume 87, p. 32056.
18. Khodabakhsh, A.; Ari, I.; Bakir, M.; Ercan, A.O. Multivariate Sensor Data Analysis for Oil Refineries and Multi-mode Identification of System Behavior in Real-time. *IEEE Access* **2018**, *6*, 64389–64405. [CrossRef]
19. Vasilieva, N.V.; Fedorova, E.R. Process control quality analysis. *Tsvetnye Met.* **2020**, 70–76. [CrossRef]
20. Vasilenko, N.V.; Linkov, A.J.; Tokareva, O.V. Clustering of services amid a growth in green consumption and digital technology use. In Proceedings of the E3S Web of Conferences, Online, 15 April 2020; Volume 161, p. 01028. [CrossRef]
21. Iakovleva, E.; Guerra, D.; Shklyarskiy, A. Alternative Measures to Reduce Carbon Dioxide Emissions in the Republic of Cuba. *J. Ecol. Eng.* **2020**, *21*, 55–60. [CrossRef]
22. Litvinenko, V.; Tsvetkov, P.; Dvoynikov, M.; Buslaev, G. Barriers to implementation of hydrogen initiatives in the context of global energy sustainable development. *J. Min. Inst.* **2020**, *244*, 428–438. [CrossRef]
23. Cannon, M.; Couchman, P.; Kouvaritakis, B. *Assessment and Future Directions of Nonlinear Model Predictive Control*; Springer: Berlin/Heidelberg, Germany, 2007; Volume 358, ISBN 978-3-540-72698-2.
24. Rodríguez, M.A.; Ancheyta, J. Detailed description of kinetic and reactor modeling for naphtha catalytic reforming. *Fuel* **2011**, *90*, 3492–3508. [CrossRef]
25. Rahimpour, M.R.; Jafari, M.; Iranshahi, D. Progress in catalytic naphtha reforming process: A review. *Appl. Energy* **2013**, *109*, 79–93. [CrossRef]
26. Belinskaya, N.; Ivanchina, E.; Ivashkina, E.; Silko, G. Effect of Feed Composition Changing at Naphtha Catalytic Reforming Unit Due to Involvement of Gasoline Fraction Obtained by Diesel Fuels Hydrodewaxing into the Processing. *Procedia Chem.* **2014**, *10*, 267–270. [CrossRef]
27. Mehraban, M.; Hashemi Shahraki, B. A mathematical model for decoking process of the catalyst in catalytic naphtha reforming radial flow reactor. *Fuel Process. Technol.* **2019**, *188*, 172–178. [CrossRef]
28. Yusuf, A.Z.; John, Y.M.; Aderemi, B.O.; Patel, R.; Mujtaba, I.M. Modelling, simulation and sensitivity analysis of naphtha catalytic reforming reactions. *Comput. Chem. Eng.* **2019**, *130*, 106531. [CrossRef]
29. Shakeri, M.; Iranshahi, D.; Naderifar, A. Analysis of combined heat and mass transfer in membrane-assisted thermally coupled reactors containing naphtha reforming and m-xylene hydrodealkylation. *Chem. Eng. Process. Process. Intensif.* **2020**, *148*, 107724. [CrossRef]
30. Ebrahimian, S.; Iranshahi, D. An investigative study on replacing the conventional furnaces of naphtha reforming with chemical looping combustion for clean hydrogen production. *Int. J. Hydrog. Energy* **2020**, *45*, 19405–19419. [CrossRef]
31. Ren, Y.; Liao, Z.; Sun, J.; Jiang, B.; Wang, J.; Yang, Y.; Wu, Q. Molecular reconstruction: Recent progress toward composition modeling of petroleum fractions. *Chem. Eng. J.* **2019**, *357*, 761–775. [CrossRef]
32. Willis, D.E. Retention Time-Boiling Point Correlations during Programmed Temperature Capillary Column Analysis of C8-C12 Aromatic Compounds. *Anal. Chem.* **1967**, *39*, 1324–1326. [CrossRef]
33. Panneerselvam, K.; Antony, M.P.; Srinivasan, T.G.; Vasudeva Rao, P.R. Estimation of normal boiling points of trialkyl phosphates using retention indices by gas chromatography. *Thermochim. Acta* **2010**, *511*, 107–111. [CrossRef]
34. De Lima Ribeiro, F.A.; Ferreira, M.M.C. QSPR models of boiling point, octanol-water partition coefficient and retention time index of polycyclic aromatic hydrocarbons. *J. Mol. Struct. THEOCHEM* **2003**, *663*, 109–126. [CrossRef]

35. Boethling, R.S.; Howard, P.H.; Meylan, W.M. Finding and estimating chemical property data for environmental assessment. *Environ. Toxicol. Chem.* **2004**, *23*, 2290–2308. [CrossRef] [PubMed]
36. Tareq, A. Albahri Developing correlations for the properties of petroleum fuels and their fractions. *Fluid Phase Equilibria* **2012**, *315*, 113–125. [CrossRef]
37. Zhang, J.; Fang, A.; Wang, B.; Kim, S.H.; Bogdanov, B.; Zhou, Z.; McClain, C.; Zhang, X. IMatch: A retention index tool for analysis of gas chromatography-mass spectrometry data. *J. Chromatogr. A* **2011**, *1218*, 6522–6530. [CrossRef]
38. Yan, J.; Liu, X.B.; Zhu, W.W.; Zhong, X.; Sun, Q.; Liang, Y.Z. Retention Indices for Identification of Aroma Compounds by GC: Development and Application of a Retention Index Data-base. *Chromatographia* **2015**, *78*, 89–108. [CrossRef]
39. Morosini, M.; Ballschmiter, K. Retention indices of 28 polychlorinated biphenyls in capillary gas chromatography referred to 2,4,6-trichlorophenyl alkyl ethers as RI-standards. *Fresenius J. Anal. Chem.* **1994**, *348*, 595–597. [CrossRef]
40. Podmaniczky, L.; Szepesy, L.; Lakszner, K.; Schomburg, G. Determination of retention indices in LPTGC. *Chromatographia* **1986**, *21*, 387–391. [CrossRef]
41. Škrbić, B.D.; Cvejanov, J.D. Unified retention indices of alkylbenzenes on OV-101 and SE-30. *Chromatographia* **1993**, *37*, 215–217. [CrossRef]
42. Aparkin, A.M.; Pashinin, V.A. Linear Correlation between Kovats Retention Indices I and the Sum of 13C Nuclear Magnetic Resonance Chemical Shifts in the Structural Isomers of Saturated Hydrocarbons. *Russ. J. Phys. Chem.* **2021**, *95*, 101–105. [CrossRef]
43. Arutyunov, Y.I.; Kudryashov, S.Y.; Onuchak, L.A. Analysis of mixtures containing unknown components by gas chromatography: Determination of molecular mass. *J. Anal. Chem.* **2004**, *59*, 358–365. [CrossRef]
44. Meeks, O.R.; Rybolt, T.R. Correlations of adsorption energies with physical and structural properties of adsorbate molecules. *J. Colloid Interface Sci.* **1997**, *196*, 103–109. [CrossRef]
45. Green, L.E.; Schmauch, L.J.; Worman, J.C. Simulated Distillation by Gas Chromatography. *Anal. Chem.* **1964**, *36*, 1512–1516. [CrossRef]
46. Daubert, T.E.; Danner, R.P. (Eds.) *API Technical Data Book—Petroleum Refining*, 6th ed.; American Petroleum Institute (API): Washington, DC, USA, 1997.
47. Xue, Y.; Wang, Y.; Sun, B. Asymmetric Probability Distribution Function-Based Distillation Curve Reconstruction and Feature Extraction for Industrial Oil-Refining Processes. *Energy Fuels* **2020**, *34*, 2533–2544. [CrossRef]
48. Sánchez, S.; Ancheyta, J.; McCaffrey, W.C. Comparison of probability distribution functions for fitting distillation curves of petroleum. *Energy Fuels* **2007**, *21*, 2955–2963. [CrossRef]
49. Liu, L.; Hou, S.; Zhang, N. Incorporating numerical molecular characterization into pseudo-component representation of light to middle petroleum distillates. *Chem. Eng. Sci. X* **2019**, *3*, 100029. [CrossRef]
50. Ren, Y.; Liao, Z.; Sun, J.; Jiang, B.; Wang, J.; Yang, Y.; Wu, Q. Molecular Reconstruction of Naphtha via Limited Bulk Properties: Methods and Comparisons. *Ind. Eng. Chem. Res.* **2019**, *58*, 18742–18755. [CrossRef]
51. Zhang, X.; Qi, J.; Zhang, R.; Liu, M.; Hu, Z.; Xue, H.; Fan, B. Prediction of programmed-temperature retention values of naphthas by wavelet neural networks. *Comput. Chem.* **2001**, *25*, 125–133. [CrossRef]
52. Miermans, C.J.H.; van de Velde, L.E.; Frintrop, P.C.M. Analysis of volatile organic compounds, using the purge and trap injector coupled to a gas chromatograph/ion-trap mass spectrometer: Review of the results in Dutch surface water of the Rhine, Meuse, Northern Delta Area and Westerscheldt, over the period 1992–1997. *Chemosphere* **2000**, *40*, 39–48. [CrossRef] [PubMed]
53. Van Langenhove, H.; Schamp, N. Identification of volatiles in the head space of acid-treated phosphate rock by gas chromatography-mass spectrometry. *J. Chromatogr. A* **1986**, *351*, 65–75. [CrossRef]

Article

Big Data as a Tool for Building a Predictive Model of Mill Roll Wear

Natalia Vasilyeva [1,*], Elmira Fedorova [1] and Alexandr Kolesnikov [2]

[1] Department of Economics, Organization and Management, Saint Petersburg Mining University, 199106 St. Petersburg, Russia; fedorova_er@pers.spmi.ru
[2] Non-Profit Joint Stock Company «M. Auezov South Kazakhstan University», Shymkent 160012, Kazakhstan; kas164@yandex.kz
* Correspondence: vasileva_nv@pers.spmi.ru; Tel.: +7-921-441-51-78

Citation: Vasilyeva, N.; Fedorova, E.; Kolesnikov, A. Big Data as a Tool for Building a Predictive Model of Mill Roll Wear. *Symmetry* 2021, 13, 859. https://doi.org/10.3390/sym13050859

Academic Editors: Rudolf Kawalla, Beloglazov Ilya and Basil Papadopoulos

Received: 23 April 2021
Accepted: 9 May 2021
Published: 12 May 2021

Publisher's Note: MDPI stays neutral with regard to jurisdictional claims in published maps and institutional affiliations.

Copyright: © 2021 by the authors. Licensee MDPI, Basel, Switzerland. This article is an open access article distributed under the terms and conditions of the Creative Commons Attribution (CC BY) license (https://creativecommons.org/licenses/by/4.0/).

Abstract: Big data analysis is becoming a daily task for companies all over the world as well as for Russian companies. With advances in technology and reduced storage costs, companies today can collect and store large amounts of heterogeneous data. The important step of extracting knowledge and value from such data is a challenge that will ultimately be faced by all companies seeking to maintain their competitiveness and place in the market. An approach to the study of metallurgical processes using the analysis of a large array of operational control data is considered. Using the example of steel rolling production, the development of a predictive model based on processing a large array of operational control data is considered. The aim of the work is to develop a predictive model of rolling mill roll wear based on a large array of operational control data containing information about the time of filling and unloading of rolls, rolled assortment, roll material, and time during which the roll is in operation. Preliminary preparation of data for modeling was carried out, which includes the removal of outliers, uncharacteristic and random measurement results (misses), as well as data gaps. Correlation analysis of the data showed that the dimensions and grades of rolled steel sheets, as well as the material from which the rolls are made, have the greatest influence on the wear of rolling mill rolls. Based on the processing of a large array of operational control data, various predictive models of the technological process were designed. The adequacy of the models was assessed by the value of the mean square error (MSE), the coefficient of determination (R^2), and the value of the Pearson correlation coefficient (R) between the calculated and experimental values of the mill roll wear. In addition, the adequacy of the models was assessed by the symmetry of the values predicted by the model relative to the straight line Ypredicted = Yactual. Linear models constructed using the least squares method and cross-validation turned out to be inadequate (the coefficient of determination R^2 does not exceed 0.3) to the research object. The following regressions were built on the basis of the same operational control database: Linear Regression multivariate, Lasso multivariate, Ridge multivariate, and ElasticNet multivariate. However, these models also turned out to be inadequate to the object of the research. Testing these models for symmetry showed that, in all cases, there is an underestimation of the predicted values. Models using algorithm composition have also been built. The methods of random forest and gradient boosting are considered. Both methods were found to be adequate for the object of the research (for the random forest model, the coefficient of determination is $R^2 = 0.798$; for the gradient boosting model, the coefficient of determination is $R^2 = 0.847$). However, the gradient boosting algorithm is recognized as preferable thanks to its high accuracy compared with the random forest algorithm. Control data for symmetry in reference to the straight line Ypredicted = Yactual showed that, in the case of developing the random forest model, there is a tendency to underestimate the predicted values (the calculated values are located below the straight line). In the case of developing a gradient boosting model, the predicted values are located symmetrically regarding the straight line Ypredicted = Yactual. Therefore, the gradient boosting model is preferred. The predictive model of mill roll wear will allow rational use of rolls in terms of minimizing overall roll wear. Thus, the proposed model will make it possible to redistribute the existing work rolls between the stands in order to reduce the total wear of the rolls.

Keywords: big data; rolling mill; rolled steel; rolling mill roll wear; mathematical model; correlation coefficient

1. Introduction

The metallurgical industry is one of the leading sectors of the Russian economy. The products manufactured by this industry are used in construction, mechanical engineering, the chemical industry, and many other industries [1–3].

Rolled steel production is one of the most important items of Russian export. By deforming the metal in the space between the rotating rolls, you can get almost any kind of metal product from steel and other alloys. This process is called metal rolling. One of the major problems of rolled products is the wear of rolls that deform the metal.

In this work, wear refers to qualitative and quantitative changes in the roll surface caused by physical and chemical processes, as well as mechanical effects of one body on another [4–6].

Current trends in the development of metallurgy are characterized by the development and implementation of information systems and technologies, which are based on computers and computer networks with the richest software, as well as database management systems and computer decision support systems, the methodological basis of which is systems theory and systems analysis.

Scientific and technological progress creates prerequisites for improving the quality of management through the use of computer technology, mathematical methods of data processing, control theory, and control automation. All this has found concrete implementation in automated control systems. Owing to the development of information technology (IT), there are modern software products and database management systems (DBMS) for solving production management problems. Modern software and microprocessor technology makes it possible to create high-level control systems with the inclusion of powerful control algorithms.

The relevance of the work is thanks to the fact that the construction of linear and multidimensional regression models based on a large data set does not provide a high-quality result, as it does not allow taking into account complex and multi-connected dependencies between the input variables. In this case, compositional models that are resistant to overtraining, noise, and outliers show themselves in the best way. However, with less data that can be described by a simple model, it makes more sense to use multivariate regression.

The aim of the work is to develop a predictive model of rolling mill roll wear based on a large array of operational control data containing information about the time of filling and unloading of rolls, rolled assortment, roll material, and the time during which the roll is in operation.

To achieve the set objective, it is necessary to solve the following tasks:

1. Prepare data for modeling (filter and aggregate data).
2. Conduct a correlation analysis of the data to identify the factors that have the greatest impact on the wear of the mill rolls.
3. Build various models for predicting mill roll wear (linear models, multidimensional models, and intelligent models). Test their adequacy and identify the most accurate one.

The predictive model of mill roll wear will allow rational use of rolls in terms of minimizing overall roll wear. Thus, the proposed model will make it possible to redistribute the existing work rolls between the stands in order to reduce the total wear of the rolls.

2. Theoretical Basis

In the technical literature, data on the durability and wear of mill rolls are extremely rare. The amount and nature of work roll wear depend on many factors. The main factors are as follows: force, temperature and speed conditions of rolling, properties and amount of rolled metal, hardness, and diameter of rolls. However, it is extremely difficult to study the individual influence of each factor on roll wear [7,8].

The presence of a large number of factors makes it difficult to obtain dependencies that would take them into account and makes it possible to calculate the wear of the rolls.

Based on the literature review, wear is associated with the number (length) of rolled strips and this dependence is described using empirical equations, the coefficients of which are determined experimentally at each rolling mill. The main disadvantage of these dependencies is that they take into account the influence of a small number of factors and cannot be used when changing the rolling conditions.

The existing theoretical methods are based on determining the path of friction in the deformation zone and contact stresses or on calculating the work of deformation. They are quite complex and lengthy, and often give a high error [9].

Therefore, to assess the wear of mill rolls, it is more convenient to use the methods of statistical analysis and mathematical modeling, which make it possible to use statistical data accumulated during operation to assess the condition and predict further roll behavior. Here, the methods of statistical analysis and mathematical modeling are understood as a certain computational algorithm implemented on computers and simplified simulating of the functioning of objects.

Statistical analysis is divided into three sequential stages [10]:

- Statistical observation, i.e., collection of primary statistical material;
- Summary and development of observation results, i.e., their processing;
- Analysis of the received overall materials.

With the development of Big Data and IIoT technologies, finding dependencies between the parameters of the technological process can provide a company with a greater effect than just methods of statistical analysis.

Big Data and data analysis technologies allow the following [11–13]:

- To find patterns that appear in mass phenomena under the influence of the law of large numbers;
- To systematize and classify data based on similarities and differences;
- To analyze the overall material, identify patterns and relationships in the studied facts, and calculate generalizing indicators (total, relative, and average values, as well as statistical coefficients).

3. Object and Problem Statement

The data of the operational control of the technological process are characterized by a different origin and are measured in different quantitative and qualitative scales. Bringing operational control data to a form suitable for developing a model of a technological process is a prerequisite for the effectiveness of the modeling process [14].

Initial data are presented in five sheets (Figure 1) in a Microsoft Office Excel file. The data contains information about roll material (500 lines), roll workflow for 9 months of rolling mill operation (18,080 lines), roll suppliers (25 lines), and rolled assortment (269,968 lines).

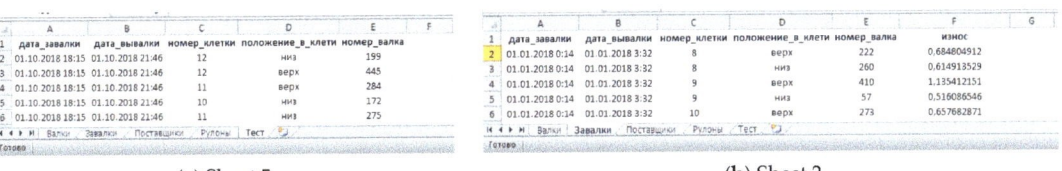

(a) Sheet 5   (b) Sheet 2

Figure 1. Fragment of a file with initial data.

The following were considered as initial data for modeling: minutes (time of rolling of a batch of products); stand number (set by a number); mill stand position (top or bottom); number and material of the roll (in coded form, each of the parameters); the number of sheets rolled by a certain roll; gauge, width, and weight of the sheet; grade of rolled products; and roll wear.

The column «mill stand position» is problematic, as it contains text data («top»–«bottom»). For convenience, they are encoded with numbers 0 and 1.

To correctly prepare data for the development of a predictive model, you first need to find out the data types presented in the source file and check them for integrity. It is easiest to delete «empty» values, but if there are a lot of them, it makes sense to replace the missing data with some number, for example, the arithmetic average of the entire column.

As a result of the check, it was found that there are no gaps in the columns. In addition, some lines were found to contain zero roll wear after rolling steel. Such records should be disregarded, because, even if such «outliers» are not errors, but are rare exceptional situations, they can still hardly be used [15–17].

Calculation of the difference between filling up and unloading times allows to obtain the roll operating time for one rolled batch. By analyzing the rolling time of coils with the ranges of filling up and unloading of rolls indicated in the «rolls» sheet, it is possible to calculate the average weight, width, gauge, and number of coils rolled through these rolls. The resulting features can be used to build models.

To determine the influence of each investigated factor on roll wear, the Pearson correlation criteria (R) were calculated, characterizing the linear effects of the factors, and a cross-correlation matrix was constructed. With an insignificant value of the coefficient, certain features can be ignored when building models (Table 1).

Table 1. Feature correlation diagram.

	Minutes	Stand Number	Mill Stand Position	Roll Number	Roll Material	Sheets	Gauge	Width	Steel Grades	Weight	Wear
minutes	1										
stand number	0.0037	1									
mill stand position	0.00012	-4×10^{-5}	1								
roll number	0.0089	0.0086	0.0041	1							
roll material	0.009	0.0021	3×10^{-5}	−0.014	1						
sheets	**0.87**	0.0034	-9×10^{-5}	0.0033	0.0046	1					
gauge	**−0.34**	−0.0011	4.2×10^{-5}	−0.003	−0.0069	−0.025	1				
width	**−0.27**	0.00049	−0.00085	−0.0026	−0.0035	−0.016	**0.35**	1			
steel grades	**0.12**	0.002	−0.00046	0.00047	−0.012	**0.16**	**0.1**	−0.032	1		
weight	**−0.16**	−0.00079	-4.1×10^{-5}	−0.0091	−0.0045	**−0.23**	−0.0021	**0.14**	−0.087	1	
wear	**0.28**	**−0.35**	0.0011	−0.0029	0.063	**0.17**	**−0.23**	−0.037	0.094	−0.021	1

(significant coefficients are in bold).

Checking the significance of the correlation coefficients according to the Student's test showed that the correlation coefficients are significant, the absolute value of which exceeds 0.1; that is, the condition $|R| \geq 0.1$ must be satisfied.

From the data obtained, it follows that the position of the roll in the stand ($R = 0.0011$) and the serial number of the roll ($R = -0.0029$) do not have a linear effect on the wear of the rolls. In addition, the serial number of the roll (from 1 to 500) is not a technological parameter and is only for informational purposes. The position of the roll in the stand (top or bottom) is also for informational purposes only. These signs will not be taken into account in the construction of the future model.

Despite the fact that such operational parameters as the roll material, width, weight, and grade of rolled steel also do not satisfy the condition $|R| \geq 0.1$, it was decided not to exclude these parameters from consideration.

Thus, the next stage of the study is to develop a predictive model of rolling mill roll wear based on a large array of operational control data containing information about the time of filling and unloading of rolls, rolled assortment, roll material, and time during which the roll is in operation [18].

4. Algorithm

The algorithm for the development of a predictive model of mill roll wear based on a large array of operational control data is presented in Figure 2.

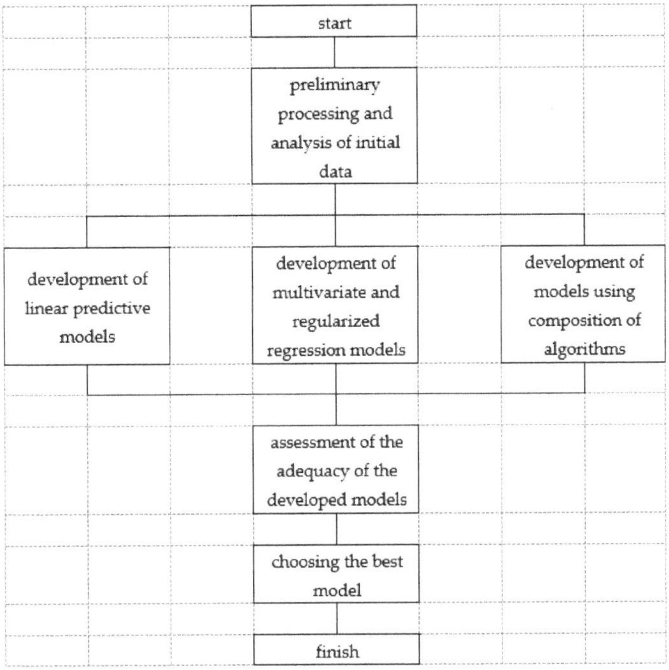

Figure 2. Algorithm for developing a predictive model of mill roll wear.

4.1. Using Big Data to Develop Linear Predictive Models

Cross-validation (CV) and least squares are used to develop a linear predictive model.

The essence of the least squares method is that the sum of the squares of deviations of the experimental values from the smoothing curve is reduced to a minimum:

$$\sum_{i=1}^{N}[y_i - \varphi(x_i)]^2 = \min$$

where y_i and x_i—experimental data values in the i-th experiment, N—number of experiments, $\varphi(x)$—desired linear regression y of x of the form $\varphi(x) = b_0 + b_1 x_1 + b_2 x_2 + b_3 x_3 + \ldots + b_k x_k$, and k—number of factors.

The essence of the CV method is that the entire array of operational control data is divided into a certain number of subsamples (blocks). One of the blocks is used to test the model (check the model for adequacy to the process under study), while the others are used for training. Then, the test block is used for training, and the next block is selected for the test. The cross-validation scheme is shown in Figure 3 (open blocks are model training blocks, filled block is a test subsample). This method allows you to obtain an unbiased estimate of the probability of error in the predictive model and to prevent optimistic overestimation of the quality of the above-mentioned.

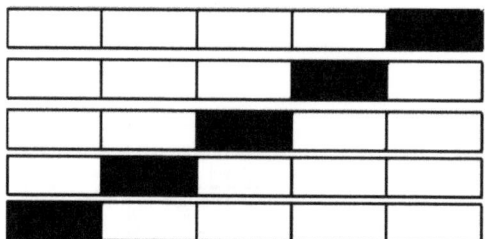

Figure 3. «Cross-validation» operation scheme.

4.2. Using Big Data to Develop Multi-Dimensional and Regularized Regression Models

The essence of regularization is to impose additional constraints on various parameters or to add a priori information, thus reducing the model error as its complexity increases [19,20].

Based on the same operational control database, the following were built: multivariate regression with L1 regulator (Lasso), multivariate regression with L2 regulator (Ridge), and multivariate regression with mixed regulator (ElasticNet).

Regularization is a way to reduce the complexity of a model in order to prevent overtraining or to fix an incorrectly posed problem. This is usually achieved by adding some a priori information to the problem statement.

The essence of L1 regularization is to select from the entire array of factors only a small number of the most important ones that set the trend, and to remove all the rest, which are just noise. Thus, L1 regularization is aimed at decreasing the dimension of the model.

L2 regularization is aimed at reducing the dimension of space by prohibiting disproportionately large weight coefficients, which prevents overtraining of the model.

The development of multivariate regression using both L1 and L2 regularization is called a mixed regulator (ElasticNet) and takes into account the effectiveness of both methods: decreasing the model dimension and decreasing the dimension of the factor space.

4.3. Algorithm Composition for Model Development Based on Big Data

The main method of composing algorithms is to combine a large number of models into one composition. The final quality of the resulting model will be significantly improved owing to the fact that the individual ones will correct the errors of each other.

This study explores such methods as random forest and gradient boosting [21–23].

The random forest method is one of the most professional and high-quality machine learning methods. The key idea of this method for finding regression dependencies is averaging the result of several models built independently of each other on random subsamples of one data array. Thus, a set of low-precision algorithms when combined into one composition give an impressive result, despite the significant amount of randomness represented in this method.

The advantage of the random forest method is its resistance to overfitting. As all algorithms are developed independently of each other, an increase in their number in a composition does not complicate the final model [24,25].

In this study, the random forest algorithm uses feature space dimensionality reduction using principal component analysis (PCA). Using the technique of reducing the dimensionality of the feature space, it is possible to represent the initial data set in terms of fewer variables and, at the same time, reduce the amount of computing resources required to ensure the operation of the model.

Gradient boosting method. The difference between this method and the previous one is that, in this algorithm, when building a composition, all models are not independent, but follow each other. Moreover, each subsequent algorithm tries to correct and compensate for the errors of the previous one. So it takes less time to get the correct answer.

In this study, gradient boosting uses a gradient descent technique to minimize the error function right in these sequential models. This approach makes it possible to expand the range of problems solved by this algorithm, as well as often leading to a gain in prediction accuracy.

4.4. Assessment of the Model Quality

Model quality is assessed using the mean squared error (MSE) between the predicted and actual roll wear, the correlation coefficient (R) between the actual and predicted mill roll wear values, and the determination coefficient (R^2) between the actual and the predicted values of rolling mill roll wear.

The coefficient of determination clearly shows how the constructed model is more accurate than the mean value of the target variable, and is in accordance with the following expression:

$$R^2 = 1 - \frac{\sum_i (y_i - \hat{y}_i)^2}{\sum_i (y_i - \bar{y})^2} \approx 1 - \frac{MSE}{VAR(y)}$$

where y_i—actual value of roll wear, $\hat{y}_i$—model predicted roll wear, and $\bar{y}$—average roll wear according to the initial data. If the coefficient of determination R^2 is equal to 1, then the values of the rolling mill roll wear calculated by the model exactly repeat the actual values, which indicate the adequacy of the mathematical model to the object of the research. If the coefficient of determination R^2 is close to zero, then this means that the model is imperfect and it would be better to take the average value $\bar{y}$. Models are recognized as adequate if the coefficient of determination is $R^2 \geq 0.7$.

5. Results

Figure 4 shows the results of comparing the actual and predicted roll wear for different models.

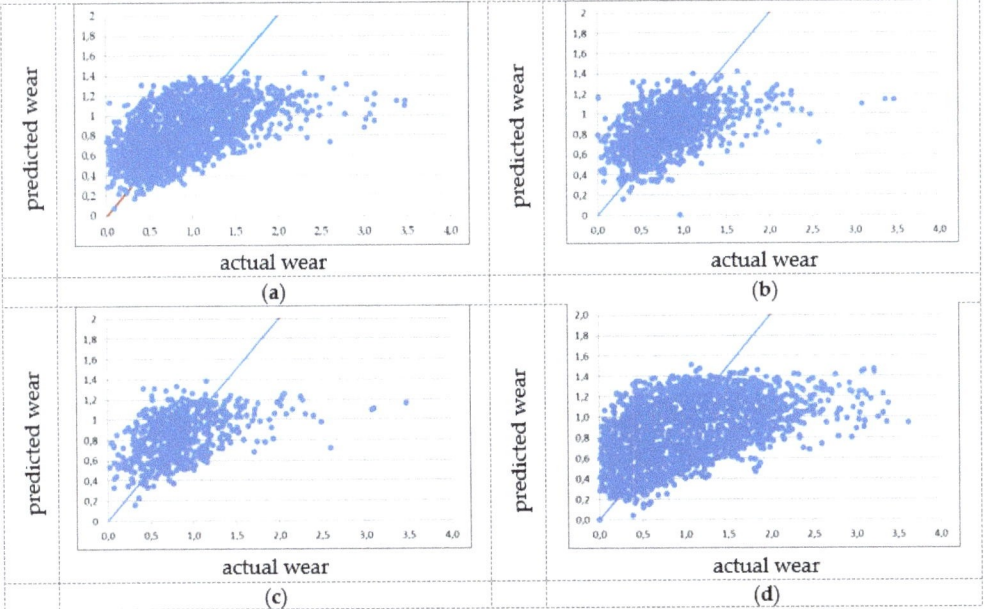

Figure 4. Comparison of predicted and actual rolling mill roll wear: (**a**) 30% test sample; (**b**) 10% test sample; (**c**) 5% test sample; (**d**) cross-validation.

For clarity, you can compare the models built with and without cross-validation.

Instead of cross-validation, the entire array of operational control data is divided into training and test samples by mixing all the features and choosing a certain percentage between the training and test samples. Linear regression, found by the method of least squares, is used as a model.

Analysis of the graphs (Figure 4) for symmetry regarding the straight line Ypredicted = Yactual shows that, in all cases, there is an underestimation of the predicted values. With real wear values of 0–4, the predicted values do not exceed 0–1.6.

In this case, the quality of the model changes depending on the amount of data selected for training the model and test validation. More data per test reduces the amount of training data and leads to a decrease in model accuracy, and vice versa [26,27].

The results of assessing the adequacy of the obtained models are shown in Table 2.

Table 2. Assessment of the adequacy of multivariate and regularized regression models. MSE, mean square error.

Model	Assessment	MSE	R^2	R
30% test sample		0.109	0.257	0.513
10% test sample		0.112	0.257	0.505
5% test sample		0.108	0.253	0.503
Cross-validation		0.113	0.256	0.507
Lasso		0.113	0.253	0.504
Ridge		0.113	0.256	0.506
ElasticNet		0.113	0.256	0.507
Random forest		0.021	0.798	0.933
Gradient boosting		0.021	0.847	0.927

Thus, the results of this analysis indicate insignificant differences in the simulation results. All models cannot be considered suitable for predicting the amount of roll wear in a rolling mill. Therefore, it is necessary to choose another type of dependence [28,29].

The introduction of a regularizer into a linear or multidimensional model did not lead to an increase in the accuracy of predicting the wear of the rolling mill rolls. It can be clearly seen that the proposed models predict the value of the target parameter not more accurately than the arithmetic mean of the wear of the rolling mill roll.

Based on the data obtained, it can be stated that, in this case, either rethinking or intellectualization of the initial data is required, or the use of more complex models [30].

A comparison of the predicted by the random forest method and the actual values of rolling mill roll wear is shown in Figure 5a. A comparison of the predicted by the gradient boosting method and the actual values of the rolling mill roll wear is shown in Figure 5b.

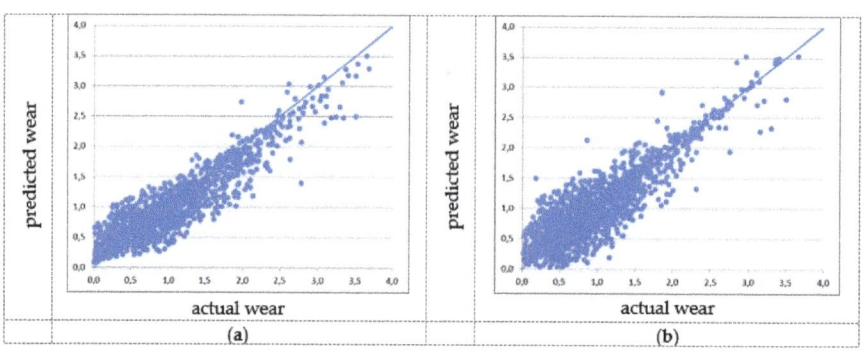

Figure 5. Comparison of predicted and actual rolling mill roll wear: (**a**) by the random forest model; (**b**) by the gradient boosting model.

The results of assessing the adequacy of the random forest model and gradient boosting model are far superior to previous models (Table 2).

Compared with linear, multivariate, and regularized models, the root mean square error (MSE) has decreased by about five times, and the coefficients of determination and correlation approximated to unity. That is to say that the random forest model can be recognized as adequate to the object of research and can be used to predict the degree of wear of the rolls of a rolling mill in the steel industry.

In terms of the coefficient of determination R^2, gradient boosting is a more accurate model compared with the random forest model (the coefficient of determination is closer to unity). The root mean square errors of both models are equal, but, according to Figure 5, it can be seen that, when using the gradient boosting method, there is a greater number of coincidences of predicted and actual wear than when using the random forest method.

Analysis of the graphs (Figure 5) for symmetry regarding the straight line Ypredicted = Yactual shows that, in the case of developing the random forest model, there is a tendency to underestimate the predicted values. It is apparent that most of the values are located below the straight line (Figure 5a). In the case of developing the gradient boosting model, the predicted values are located symmetrically in reference to the straight line Ypredicted = Yactual (Figure 5b). Therefore, the gradient boosting model is preferred.

If necessary, carrying out additional optimization of the model, it is possible to achieve an even greater decrease in the forecast error [31]. Thus, the gradient boosting forecast model is preferable.

6. Conclusions

Based on the above study, the following conclusions can be drawn.

1. The hypothesis of using a large volume of production data (Big Data) to find statistically significant dependencies turned out to be completely consistent [32]. Operational control data are an inexhaustible source of information. Extracting useful information from Big Data is an important production task [33].
2. To improve the accuracy of the models, it is necessary to prepare statistical material in advance (remove outliers, «odd», and random measurement results; filter the data; identify different modes of operation; and consider them separately) and select the appropriate type of mathematical dependence. The quality of the developed models directly depends on the quality of training material preparation [34].
3. The analysis of the correlation dependences of the data showed that the most significant factors affecting the wear of the rolls are the dimensions and brands of rolled steel sheets. In addition, not least important is the material from which the rolls are made.
4. The construction of linear and multivariate regression models based on a large data set does not provide a qualitative result, as it does not allow taking into account complex and multi-connected dependencies between the input variables. Compositional models that are resistant to overfitting, noise, and outliers perform best. However, with a smaller amount of data that can be described by a simple model, it makes more sense to use multivariate regression.
5. Thus, a predictive model of rolling mill roll wear will allow rational use of rolls in terms of minimizing overall roll wear. The proposed model will make it possible to redistribute the existing work rolls between the stands in order to reduce the total wear of the rolls.

Author Contributions: Conceptualization, N.V.; methodology, N.V.; software, E.F.; validation, N.V. and E.F. data curation, A.K.; visualization, A.K. All authors have read and agreed to the published version of the manuscript.

Funding: This research received no external funding.

Institutional Review Board Statement: Not applicable.

Informed Consent Statement: Not applicable.

Data Availability Statement: Not applicable.

Conflicts of Interest: The authors declare no conflict of interest.

References

1. Abrosimov, A.A.; Shelyago, E.V.; Yazynina, I.V. Justification of Representative Data Volume of Porosity and Permeability Properties for Obtaining Statistically Reliable Petrophysical Connections. *J. Min. Inst.* **2018**, *233*, 487–491. [CrossRef]
2. Sharikov, Y.V.; Snegirev, N.V.; Tkachev, I.V. development of a control system based on predictive mathe-matical model of the C5–C6 isomerization process. *J. Chem. Technol. Metall.* **2020**, *55*, 335–344.
3. Kadyrov, E.D.; Koteleva, N.I. Introducing neural-network algorithms into an automated system designed to control metal-lurgical processes. *Metallurgist* **2011**, *54*, 799–802. [CrossRef]
4. Demidovich, V.B.; Chmilenko, F.V.; Rastvorova, I.I. Utilization of induction heating in the line of continuous casting-continuous rolling of steel. *Acta Technica CSAV* **2015**, *60*, 107–118.
5. Zhukovskiy, Y.L.; Korolev, N.A.; Babanova, I.S.; Boikov, A.V. The prediction of the residual life of electromechanical equipment based on the artificial neural network. *IOP Conf. Ser. Earth Environ. Sci.* **2017**, *87*, 032056. [CrossRef]
6. Oprea, G.; Andrei, H. Power quality analysis of industrial company based on data acquisition system, numerical algorithms and compensation results. In Proceedings of the 2016 International Symposium on Fundamentals of Electrical Engineering, ISFEE, Bucharest, Romania, 30 June–2 July 2016; p. 7803232.
7. Galkin, V.; Koltyrin, A. Investigation of probabilistic models for forecasting the efficiency of proppant hydraulic fracturing technology. *J. Min. Inst.* **2021**, *246*, 650–659. [CrossRef]
8. Vasilyeva, N.V.; Koteleva, N.I.; Fedorova, E.R. Real-time control data wrangling for development of mathematical control models of technological processes. *J. Phys. Conf. Ser.* **2018**, *1015*, 032067. [CrossRef]
9. Bazhin, V.Y.; Kulchitskiy, A.A.; Kadrov, D.N. Complex control of the state of steel pins in Soderberg electrolytic cells by using computer vision systems. *Tsvetnye Met.* **2018**, 27–32. [CrossRef]
10. Utekhin, G. Use of statistical techniques in quality management systems. In Proceedings of the 8 International Conference Reliability and Statistics in Transportation and Communication–2008, Riga, Latvia, 17–20 October 2018; pp. 329–334.
11. Boikov, A.V.; Savelev, R.V.; Payor, V.A.; Erokhina, O.O. The control method concept of bulk material behaviour in the pelletizing drum for improving the results of DEM-modeling. *CIS Iron Steel Rev.* **2019**, *17*, 10–13. [CrossRef]
12. Leonidovich, Z.Y.; Urievich, V.B. The development and use of diagnostic systems and estimation of residual life in industrial electrical equipment. *Int. J. Appl. Eng. Res.* **2015**, *10*, 41150–41155.
13. Milyuts, V.G.; Tsukanov, V.V.; Pryakhin, E.I.; Nikitina, L.B. Saint Petersburg Mining University Development of Manufacturing Technology for High-Strength Hull Steel Reducing Production Cycle and Providing High-Quality Sheets. *J. Min. Inst.* **2019**, *239*, 536–543. [CrossRef]
14. Thombansen, U.; Purrio, M.; Buchholz, G.; Hermanns, T.; Molitor, T.; Willms, K.; Schulz, W.; Reisgen, U. Determination of process variables in melt-based manufacturing processes. *Int. J. Comput. Integr. Manuf.* **2016**, *29*, 1147–1158. [CrossRef]
15. Servin, R.; Arreola, S.A.; Calderón, I.; Perez, A.; Miguel, S.M.S. Effect of Crown Shape of Rolls on the Distribution of Stress and Elastic Deformation for Rolling Processes. *Metals* **2019**, *9*, 1222. [CrossRef]
16. Li, H.-J.; Xu, J.-Z.; Wang, G.-D.; Shi, L.-J.; Xiao, Y. Development of strip flatness and crown control model for hot strip mills. *J. Iron Steel Res. Int.* **2010**, *17*, 21–27. [CrossRef]
17. Zhao, N.; Cao, J.; Zhang, J.; Su, Y.; Yan, T.; Rao, K. Work roll thermal contour prediction model of nonoriented electrical steel sheets in hot strip mills. *J. Univ. Sci. Technol. Beijing Miner. Met. Mater.* **2008**, *15*, 352–356. [CrossRef]
18. Turk, R.; Fajfar, P.; Robic, R.; Perus, I. Prediction of hot strip mill roll wear. *Metalugija* **2002**, *41*, 47–51.
19. Taimasov, B.T.; Sarsenbayev, B.K.; Khudyakova, T.M.; Kolesnikov, A.S.; Zhanikulov, N.N. Development and testing of low-energy intensive technology of receiving sulfate-resistant and road Portland cement. *Eurasian Chem. Technol. J.* **2017**, *19*, 347–355. [CrossRef]
20. Abdulaev, E.K.; Makharatkin, P.N.; Kuzhelev, A.I.; Grudinin, N.N. Assessment of technical condition of gearbox-motor-wheels and tires according to heating wear criterion when transporting building materials. *IOP Conf. Series Mater. Sci. Eng.* **2020**, *775*, 012001. [CrossRef]
21. Bolobov, V.; Chupin, S.; Binh, L.T. On the Wear Intensity Ratio of a Striker under Dynamic and Static Conditions. *IOP Conf. Ser. Earth Environ. Sci.* **2020**, *459*, 062085. [CrossRef]
22. Krasnyy, V.; Maksarov, V.V.; Maksimov, D. Improving the Wear Resistance of Piston Rings of Internal Combustion Engines when Using Ion-Plasma Coatings. *Key Eng. Mater.* **2020**, *854*, 133–139. [CrossRef]
23. Ratra, R.; Gulia, P. Big Data Tools and Techniques: A Roadmap for Predictive Analytics. *Int. J. Eng. Adv. Technol.* **2019**, *9*, 4986–4992.
24. Thillaieswari, B. Comparative Study on Tools and Techniques of Big Data Analysis. *Int. J. Adv. Netw. Appl.* **2017**, *8*, 61–66.
25. George, G.; Lavie, D. Big data and data science methods for management research. *Acad. Manag. J.* **2016**, *59*, 1493–1507. [CrossRef]
26. Maratea, A.; Petrosino, A.; Manzo, M. Extended Graph Backbone for Motif Analysis. In Proceedings of the 18th International Conference on Hybrid Systems: Computation and Control, Seattle, WA, USA, 14–16 April 2015; pp. 36–43.

27. Nguyen, T.L. A Framework for Five Big V's of Big Data and Organizational Culture in Firms. In Proceedings of the 2018 IEEE International Conference on Big Data (Big Data), Seattle, WA, USA, 10–13 December 2018; pp. 5411–5413.
28. Kaur, N.; Singh, G. A Review Paper On Data Mining And Big Data. *Int. J. Adv. Res. Comput. Sci.* **2017**, *8*, 407–409.
29. Rao, J.N.; Ramesh, M. A Review on Data Mining & Big Data, Machine Learning Techniques. *Int. J. Recent Technol. Eng.* **2019**, *7*, 914–916.
30. Kaisler, S.; Armour, F.; Espinosa, J.A.; Money, W. Big data: Issues and challenges moving forward. System sciences (HICSS). In Proceedings of the 2013 46th Hawaii International Conference on System Sciences, Maui, HI, USA, 7–10 January 2013; pp. 995–1004.
31. Dean, J.; Ghemawat, S. Mapreduce: Simplified data processing on large clusters. *Commun. ACM* **2008**, *51*, 107–113. [CrossRef]
32. Katal, A.; Wazid, M.; Goudar, R.H. Big data: Issues, challenges, tools and Good practices. In Proceedings of the 2013 Sixth International Conference on Contemporary Computing (IC3), Noida, India, 8–10 August 2013; pp. 404–409.
33. Wu, X.; Zhu, X.; Wu, G.-Q.; Ding, W. Data mining with big data. *IEEE Trans. Knowl. Data Eng.* **2014**, *26*, 97–107. [CrossRef]
34. Lindell, Y.; Pinkas, B. Privacy Preserving Data Mining. *J. Cryptol.* **2002**, *15*, 177–206. [CrossRef]

Article

Estimation of Electricity Generation by an Electro-Technical Complex with Photoelectric Panels Using Statistical Methods

Anna Turysheva [1,*], Irina Voytyuk [2] and Daniel Guerra [3]

1. Department of Electric Power Engineering and Electromechanics, Saint-Petersburg Mining University, 199106 Saint-Petersburg, Russia
2. Department of General Electrical Engineering, Saint-Petersburg Mining University, 199106 Saint-Petersburg, Russia; voytuk_irina@mail.ru
3. Solar Energy Research Center, 90400 Santiago de Cuba, Cuba; dgd210386@gmail.com
* Correspondence: anna_turysheva_21@mail.ru

Citation: Turysheva, A.; Voytyuk, I.; Guerra, D. Estimation of Electricity Generation by an Electro-Technical Complex with Photoelectric Panels Using Statistical Methods. *Symmetry* **2021**, *13*, 1278. https://doi.org/10.3390/sym13071278

Academic Editor: Anthony Harriman

Received: 4 May 2021
Accepted: 13 July 2021
Published: 16 July 2021

Publisher's Note: MDPI stays neutral with regard to jurisdictional claims in published maps and institutional affiliations.

Copyright: © 2021 by the authors. Licensee MDPI, Basel, Switzerland. This article is an open access article distributed under the terms and conditions of the Creative Commons Attribution (CC BY) license (https://creativecommons.org/licenses/by/4.0/).

Abstract: This paper presents a computational tool for estimating energy generated by low-power photovoltaic systems based on the specific conditions of the study region since the characteristic energy equation can be obtained considering the main climatological factors affecting these systems in terms of the symmetry or skewness of the random distribution of the generated energy. Furthermore, this paper is aimed at determining any correlation that exists between meteorological variables with respect to the energy generated by 5-kW solar systems in the specific climatic conditions of the Republic of Cuba. The paper also presents the results of the influence of each climate factor on the distribution symmetry of the generated energy of the solar system. Studying symmetry in statistical models is important because they allow us to establish the degree of symmetry (or skewness), which is the probability distribution of a random variable, without having to make a graphical representation of it. Statistical skewness reports the degree to which observations are distributed evenly and proportionally above and below the center (highest) point of the distribution. In the case when the mentioned distribution is balanced, it is called symmetric.

Keywords: solar power; solar systems; photovoltaic panel; mathematical modeling; statistics; correlation; skewness; symmetry; random variable distribution

1. Disadvantages and Advantages of Renewable Energy Sources

The world's population growth, as well as the development of industry and production technologies, is accompanied by a significant increase in power consumption. To meet the needs of the population, power-generating enterprises are forced to consume an increasing number of fossil organic resources [1,2] since energy generation is usually provided through the combustion of hydrocarbons (oil, gas, coal). However, over time, reserves of this type of raw material are depleted, green fields are in increasingly complex mining, geological, and climatic conditions [3,4], and projects for the implementation of hydrocarbon production require the construction of several infrastructures: industrial facilities for preparation, drilling, production, and transportation of oil, gas, and coal [5]. This results not only in significant investments but also in a negative impact on the environment, due to construction and installation works, road embankments, trenching for pipelines, and emissions arising from machine operation, resulting in soil disturbance, pollution, littering, destruction of the soil cover, changes and destruction of animal habitats, and occurrence of the greenhouse effect [6].

Therefore, the issue of transitioning from traditional energy production to alternative methods of generating electricity becomes more and more relevant [7]. Methods of generating electric energy based on the use of renewable resources have the following advantages: non-depletion, availability, no need for complex related infrastructure, as well as reduction or complete elimination of carbon dioxide emissions [8]. However, despite all the advantages, the man-made impact on the environment still exists; this fact is confirmed by studies conducted within the framework of China—United States cooperation [9]. According to the report, negative factors include changes to animal habitats and emission of toxic substances from some photovoltaic cells of solar panels.

However, despite the disadvantages of renewable energy sources, it has a much less significant impact on the environment than traditional types of electricity generation [10]. Therefore, the use of alternative types of energy, including solar power, has recently taken a leading position in the global energy industry. From year to year, new problems arise, and new tasks are assigned to improve systems [11,12] that use alternative energy sources facilitated by the development of other fields of science and technology—automation, materials science, and production technology. Furthermore, for today's society, the problem of reducing the negative impact on the environment is a burning issue that requires an immediate solution [13].

In order to attract enterprises to transition to renewable types of electricity generation, many countries are taking measures of state, political, legislative, and economic support, including:

1. Increased funding from the state budgets of the United States, Japan, Germany, Italy, and India [14];
2. Introduction of a system of "Green Certificates", which operates in the European Union and the United States, ensuring the implementation of the mechanism for granting quotas for the generation/acquisition of energy from renewable sources;
3. Tax credits and benefits for renewable energy producers; grants and tenders for the development of new projects and expansion of existing production facilities.

2. The Feasibility of Using Solar Energy

This paper discusses aspects of the use of solar power in electro-technical complexes. The choice of solar power as a source is supported by the fact that the sun emits about 1 kW/m^2 on the Earth's surface per day, and within seven days, the energy entering the planet exceeds the energy of all global reserves of fossil organic resources. According to some estimates, the economic potential of solar power is 20 billion tons of standard fuel, and this figure is two times greater than the production of all hydrocarbons per year [15]. In addition, the raw-material base for producing photovoltaic panels has significant resources: the amount of silicon, from which most solar cells are currently made, is 100,000 times greater than the reserves of uranium used when generating electricity in nuclear power plants.

Based on the above, it should be concluded that it is advisable to use solar energy [16] and convert it into electrical energy [17] using solar panels (photovoltaic panels).

3. Factors Affecting the Efficiency of a Photovoltaic Panel

A photovoltaic panel is a direct-current generator, which principle of operation is based on the physical property of semiconductors: photons of light knock electrons out from the outer orbit of the semiconductor atoms, creating enough free electrons to generate an electric current. When the circuit is closed, an electric current occurs [18]. To obtain the required power, individual solar cells are combined in panels, where they are connected in parallel or in series to obtain the required current and voltage parameters. Since the electricity produced is directly proportional to the area of the panels, photovoltaic panels occupy a large amount of space.

The efficiency of converting solar energy into electrical energy depends primarily on the intensity of sunlight and the angle of incidence of the rays. The efficiency of the panel depends on its location (latitude), climatic characteristics, time of year, and time of day. Since the surface of the panel has reflective properties, not all of the sun's rays are captured by the module. However, it should be noted that since the panel has the ability to convert not only direct solar radiation, but also scattered, into electrical energy, the photoelectric module can also capture the radiation reflected from neighboring surfaces. According to the current-voltage characteristic of solar modules, the no-load voltage OSV depends inversely on the operating temperature of the module, so the output power decreases when the module is heated.

In addition, power is also lost when a current passes through the volumetric resistance of the semiconductor [19], thereby heating the module, which leads to a decrease in its energy efficiency [20–22]. The number of failures of PV power plants during operation also affects the amount of electricity produced. The number of faults is small for about ten years of operation but then rises rapidly [23]. The factors described above are the main reasons that reduce the efficiency of photovoltaic panels. Therefore, theoretically, a silicon solar cell has an efficiency of about 20%, but in practice–less [24].

Currently, increasing the efficiency of sunlight-to-electricity conversion is a highly relevant task [25]. Widely known are two methods for increasing the generation of electricity [26] obtained from a photovoltaic installation: improving the structure of a photovoltaic panel to increase its performance [27] and increasing the amount of solar radiation captured by the panel [28]. The first method is directly related to the development of new technological solutions for creating materials and combining various semiconductor materials that can capture a different spectrum. For example, in [29], an increase in the efficiency of a photovoltaic module is achieved by creating multilayer panels, the so-called heterostructures. The paper [30] describes the use of thin films for two-sided silicon solar cells. The second method includes technical solutions for the use of solar tracking systems–solar radiation concentrators, or, in a word, the component composition of the equipment included in a solar power plant.

This paper is aimed at determining the correlation that exists between climatological factors in systems that use solar power with respect to the energy generated by these systems. This is due to the fact that the efficiency of generation is affected by climatological factors, for both increasing and decreasing efficiency. This research work is focused on determining the impact of various climatological factors on electricity production, taking into account the subject matter's geographic location. Studying statistical models is important because it allows us to establish the degree of symmetry (or skewness), which is the probability distribution of a random variable, without having to make a graphical representation of it.

Based on the analysis of statistical data, accounting for the greatest impact on the production of energy by a solar power plant at the design stage, it will be possible to determine the most efficient geographical location of the power plant [31] or its component composition. The obtained dependencies will allow one to increase the productivity of direct conversion solar power plants.

This paper presents an analysis of an electro-technical complex with a low-power solar power plant (5 kW) connected to the electrical network of the Santiago de Cuba Province, the Republic of Cuba. To estimate the energy generated by a five-kilowatt solar system, studies with different climatic conditions should be conducted. This approach will make it possible to determine the dependence of climatic factors that affect electricity generation in photovoltaic systems.

4. Modeling an Electro-Technical Complex with a Photovoltaic System

During previous studies, a model implemented via Matlab software for simulation of a five-kilowatt photovoltaic system, as shown in Figure 1, was developed [32]. This model allows us to study the main electrical variables, such as the energy generated by the system in certain climatic conditions. The model includes the response surface equations to estimate the energy generated. Thus, it is possible to compare the generated energy calculated based on the mathematical model of the complex with the response surface equations obtained using statistical models, as well as to check their efficiency when estimating the energy generated. The system under study is located in the territory of Santiago de Cuba (latitude 20.0208° N and longitude 75.8267° W).

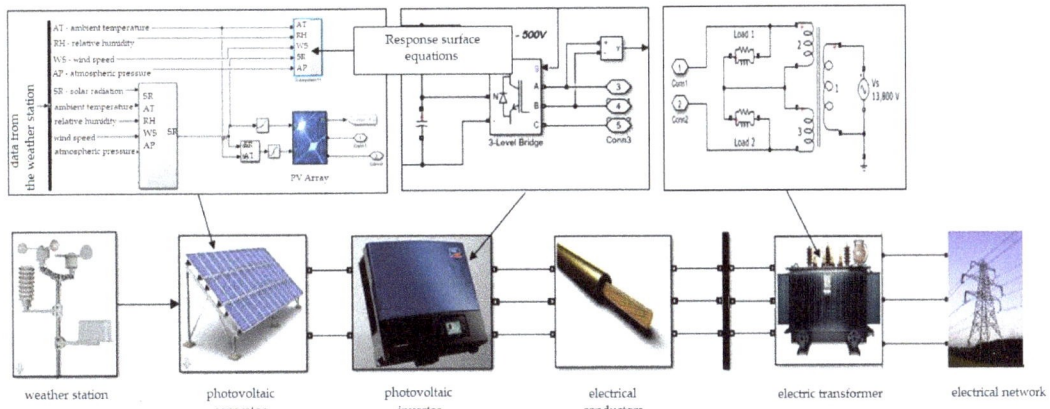

Figure 1. Model of an electro-technical complex with a 5-kW photovoltaic system.

The panels used in this photovoltaic energy system are from the NUMEN SOLAR brand, model DSM-240-C, which are interconnected, allowing the generation of electricity. Table 1 shows the technical parameters of the panels with emissions of 1000 W/m² and an ambient temperature of 25 °C.

Table 1. Technical characteristics of the solar module DSM-240-C.

Variables	Technical Data
Module type	polycrystalline
Open circuit voltage (V_{OC})	37
Short circuit current (I_{SC})	8.54
MPP voltage (V_{MPPT})	29.8
MPP current (I_{MPPT})	8.19
Efficiency (%)	16

Using a weather station installed within the study region, the following data were obtained (2020):

- Horizontal global radiation;
- Wind speed;
- Ambient temperature;
- Relative humidity;
- Atmospheric pressure.

The measurement results were entered into the developed computer model. The math needed for the photovoltaic generator simulation, and introduced into the solar generator unit, included as follows: the response surface equations, found via the Minitab Statistical Software; data, measured by the weather station. Next, the energy values obtained by both models were compared. This approach made it possible to check the statistical model efficiency.

In the automatic calculations of the developed program, the solar radiation is calculated in the inclined plane in correspondence with the inclination of the solar generator.

5. Correlation of Meteorological Variables

To determine the relationship between different variables, a correlation study was carried out. For this purpose, the Pearson's correlation coefficient (P) was calculated for each of the selected variables (horizontal global radiation, wind speed, ambient temperature, relative humidity, and atmospheric pressure) via Matlab (version R2018a) and Minitab Statistical Software (version 18.0) packages. Based on the calculations, it was determined whether the correlation between the studied variables is significant so that the p-value is less than 0.05.

The results obtained via both software packages are presented in Tables 2 and 3. The first table presents the values for the correlation between the meteorological variables and electrical energy, coming from a low-power solar system, calculated via the Matlab and Minitab statistical software packages, and the second table presents the values for the correlation between the meteorological variables of both software packages.

Table 2. Coefficients of correlation between energy and atmospheric variables, calculated via Matlab and Minitab software.

Variables	E	E (kW) (Matlab)	E (kW) (Minitab)
Ambient temperature	AT (°C)	0.75005	0.750
Wind speed	WS (m/s)	0.54787	0.548
Relative humidity	RH (%)	−0.72428	−0.725
Solar radiation	SR (W/m^2)	0.69986	0.700
Atmospheric pressure	AP (bar)	−0.13067	−0.131

Table 3. Calculations of correlation coefficients via the Matlab and Minitab software.

V	Mat AT (°C)	Min AT (°C)	Mat WS (m/s)	Min WS (m/s)	Mat RH (%)	Min RH (%)	Mat SR (W/m^2)	Min SR (W/m^2)
WS	0.407/0°	0.41	—	—	—	—	—	—
RH	−0.91/0°	−0.91	−0.39/0°	−0.39	—	—	—	—
SR	0.74/0°	0.74	0.38/0°	0.38	−0.73/0°	−0.73	—	—
AP	−0.05/0.85°	−0.05	−0.2/0°	−0.20	−0.01/0°	−0.01	0.12/0°	0.12

Based on the results presented in Table 2, it is possible to conclude as follows:
1. The results of the correlation between the variables, found via both software packages, are the same.
2. There are four meteorological variables having a greater correlation with electrical energy generated by a solar power plant, solar radiation, ambient temperature, and relative humidity, and to a lesser extent with wind speed.
3. There is a direct relationship between solar radiation and ambient temperature with energy, which means they are directly proportional.
4. There is an inverse correlation between relative humidity and energy, which means they are inversely proportional.
5. Atmospheric pressure has a very low correlation with the electrical energy coming from the solar system produced by the solar power plant.

Table 3 presents the differences in the calculations of the correlation coefficients obtained via the Matlab and Minitab software packages. As seen from the table, the results for both software packages are the same.

Based on the results presented in Table 2, it is possible to conclude as follows:
1. There is a high and inverse correlation (K = −0.91) between relative humidity and ambient temperature.
2. There is a high and direct relationship (K = 0.74) between solar radiation and ambient temperature.
3. There is a high and inverse correlation (K = −0.73) between solar radiation and relative humidity.
4. There is an average and direct correlation (K = 0.407) between ambient temperature and wind speed.
5. Other correlations, marked in red, are low or zero.
6. Atmospheric pressure has a low or zero correlation with other meteorological variables.

Figure 2 shows a graphical representation of the relationship between the meteorological variables obtained from a meteorological station located within the study region in the Santiago de Cuba Province, the Republic of Cuba.

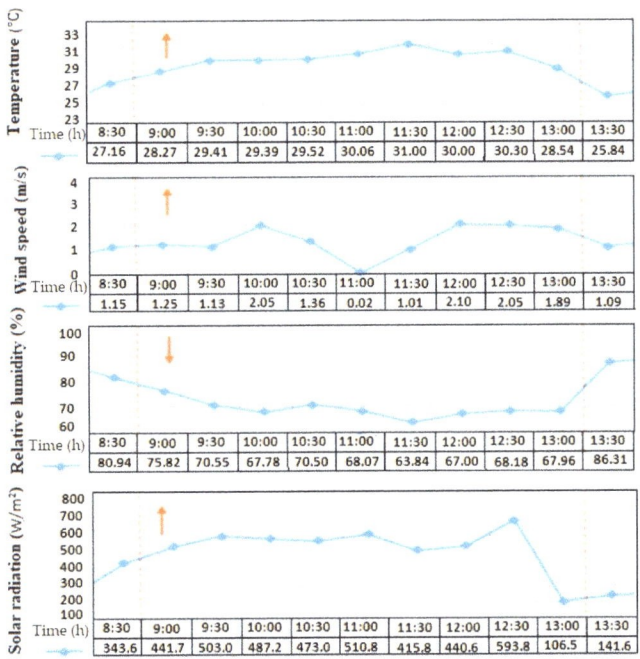

Figure 2. The behavior of meteorological variables on an ordinary day (23 October 2020).

The behavior of the measured variables confirms the results obtained according to Table 3 since the following phenomenon is observed—with an increase in solar radiation in the time interval from 9:00 to 13:00, the ambient temperature also increases proportionally and to a lesser extent, so does the wind speed. Relative humidity shows the opposite behavior, decreasing, as previously obtained (Table 3).

The results of the correlation calculations confirm the efficiency of the mathematical model since they coincide with the measurements by the weather station.

6. Calculation of the Main Partials

In statistics, principal component analysis (PCA) is a method used for a data set definition in terms of new uncorrelated variables ("components") [33]. The components are ordered by the amount of initial variance they define; therefore, this method is effective for reducing the data set dimensionality [34].

Technically, PCA is searching for a prediction, according to which data is best represented in terms of least squares [35]. It converts a set of observations of possibly correlated variables into a set of values of linearly uncorrelated variables called principal components.

As for its application, the principal component method is considered a method for reducing the number of initial variables that were taken into account while analyzing [36].

This method is needed to determine five meteorological variables, the relationship between which must be studied (solar radiation, ambient temperature, relative humidity, wind speed, and atmospheric pressure). It is necessary to determine which variables have the greatest impact on the electricity generation by the complex. This method allows one to determine the most affecting variables; therefore, it is these variables that must be taken into account when calculating. Ultimately, it will be possible to reduce the number of variables in the equation, thereby reducing estimation errors.

There are two main modes of PCA use:

A method based on a correlation matrix is used when the data is not uniform dimensionally, or the order of the measured random variables is not the same [37].

A method based on covariance, used when the data is uniform dimensionally and has similar mean values [38].

For the purposes of this study, the first PCA method was used since the variable data are heterogeneous.

The method starts with a correlation matrix. Next, the values of each of m random variables Fj^β are considered. For each of n individuals, the values of these variables were taken, and the data set was written in matrix form [39]:

$$(F_j^\beta) \quad \begin{matrix} \beta = 1, \ldots .n \\ j = 1, \ldots .m \end{matrix} \quad (1)$$

where each set:

$$M_j = \left\{ F_j^\beta \middle| \beta = 1, \ldots, n \right\} \quad (2)$$

can be considered a random sample for the variable F_j. From the $m \times n$ data, corresponding to m random variables, one can construct a sample correlation matrix, which is defined as follows:

$$R = [r_{ij}] \epsilon\ M_{mxm} \quad (3)$$

$$r_{ij} = \frac{cov(F_i, F_j)}{\sqrt{var(F_i) * var(F_j)}} \quad (4)$$

Since the correlation matrix is symmetric, it is diagonalizable, and its eigenvalues λ_i, are checked:

$$\sum_{i=1}^{m} \lambda_i = m \quad (5)$$

Due to the previous property, these eigenvalues are called the weights of each of m principal components. The main mathematically identified factors are represented by the base of the eigenvectors of the matrix R. Each of the variables can be expressed as a linear combination of eigenvectors or principal components [40].

Using the PCA method, the AP coefficient (%) that contains the percentage of the total variance, which in turn explains each principal component of the dependent variable being studied, was calculated via Matlab software.

According to the results obtained in Table 4, from the calculation of the main components, it can be concluded that the meteorological variables with the highest correlation with the energy delivered by photovoltaic systems are solar radiation, ambient temperature, and wind speed. Being solar radiation and ambient temperature, the climatic variables with the highest correlation with the energy delivered by photovoltaic systems.

On the other hand, relative humidity greatly affected the behavior of ambient temperature (see Table 2), so both ambient temperature and solar radiation are the main meteorological variables that are taken into account when estimating the energy delivered by photovoltaic systems.

Table 4. Calculations of the principal components were obtained by the statistical program Minitab software.

Variables	E	PC1	PC2	PC3	PC4	PC5
Ambient temperature	AT (°C)	0.488	0.076	0.283	0.367	0.067
Wind speed	WS (m/s)	0.322	−0.39	−0.81	0.20	0.18
Relative humidity	RH (%)	−0.482	−0.13	−0.24	−0.47	−0.073
Solar radiation	SR (W/m^2)	0.451	0.23	0.01	−0.67	0.53
Atmospheric pressure	AP (bar)	−0.03	0.86	−0.44	0.12	−0.16
Energy	E (kWh)	0.470	−0.1	−0.03	−0.35	−0.8

7. Response Surface Method

The concept of a response surface includes a dependent variable Y, called a response variable, and several independent or controlled variables. If a provision is made that all these variables are measurable, the response surface can be expressed as:

$$Y = f(X_1, X_2, \ldots, X_n) \tag{6}$$

To obtain the response surface equation, several special experimental plans aimed at an approximation of this equation using the smallest possible number of experiments were developed.

In a two-dimensional problem, the simplest surface is the plane defined by the equation [41]:

$$Y = B_0 * X_0 + B_1 * X_1 + B_2 * X_2 + \varepsilon \tag{7}$$

where X is the values of the independent variable, and B is the coefficients calculated for each of the independent variables. The observed response is taken to be equal to one, and the estimates for B should be determined by the least-squares method, which minimizes the sum of squared errors. This equation is called a first-degree equation since the exponent of each independent variable is equal to one.

If there is any reason to believe that the surface is not flat, then the most suitable model may be a second-degree equation with two unknowns [42]:

$$Y = B_0 * X_0 + B_1 * X_1 + B_2 * X_2 + B_{11} * X_1^2 + B_{12} * X_1 * X_2 + B_{22} * X_2^2 + \varepsilon \tag{8}$$

In order to effectively assess the model parameters, it is necessary to apply an appropriate experimental plan to collect the required data [43]. Some of the key features are as follows:

1. Provides a reasonable distribution of data points and, therefore, information.
2. Does not require a large number of experiments.
3. Allows one to study the model adequacy.
4. Provides accurate estimates of the model coefficients.
5. Provides internal error estimation.
6. Allows one to conduct experiments in blocks.
7. Does not require too many levels of independent variables.

As the surface becomes more complex, a larger number of coefficients must be estimated, and the number of experimental points will inevitably increase [44].

Based on the results obtained, the response surface equation was found for two factors, namely, for two independent variables and one dependent variable, using the Minitab 18 software. The results of the simulation, on the basis of which it can be concluded that in order to obtain the response equation, it is necessary to use only two independent variables, which will be the ambient temperature and solar radiation, since more than 85% of the response variable, in this case, energy, can be explained with two independent variables only.

Based on the calculations made, it is possible to conclude as follows:

1. To determine the change in the energy generated by a solar power plant, taking into account the five meteorological variables studied (wind speed, relative humidity, ambient temperature, solar radiation, atmospheric pressure), the model used will explain only 58% of the response.
2. If four meteorological variables (wind speed, relative humidity, ambient temperature, solar radiation) are taken into account, the model used will explain only 67% of the response.
3. If three meteorological variables (wind speed, ambient temperature, solar radiation) are taken into account, the model used will explain only 85% of the response.
4. If only two meteorological variables (ambient temperature, solar radiation) are taken into account, the model used will explain only 87% of the response.

Therefore, based on the results obtained, it can be concluded that in order to estimate the energy generated by the complex in the specific climatic and geographical conditions of the region, the three most affecting variables include: ambient temperature and solar radiation (with an explanation of the dependent variable at 87%).

Where EC is the average energy per month, calculated using Matlab software, EE is the calculated average energy per month according to the response surface equations, D is the difference between the average energy obtained by both methods in October.

8. Results and Discussion

The results obtained give rise to the following conclusion: for two response surface equations, the equation that relates the independent variables, ambient temperature, and solar radiation, gives the best answer with respect to the equation that relates the independent variables, ambient temperature, and relative humidity.

The results from Table 4 show that equation two (solar radiation and ambient temperature) gives the best estimate of the energy produced by a five-kilowatt system.

In Figure 3, the average energy generated by an electro-technical complex with a five-kilowatt photovoltaic plant per day, and calculated according to equation (Table 1), is represented via red columns. The average energy, produced by an electro-technical complex with a five-kilowatt photovoltaic plant per day, and calculated using a mathematical model (Figure 1), is represented via blue columns.

The results obtained give rise to the following conclusions:

1. The obtained energy values are estimated by the response surface equation in Table 5 (red columns); it approximates with high accuracy to the energy obtained using the mathematical model of a five-kilowatt photovoltaic system, simulated via the Matlab/Simulink software (blue columns).
2. Low average values of energy, generated per day, as shown in Figure 3 (area 1), are the result of low average values of solar radiation and low average values of ambient temperatures, associated with high average values of relative humidity and a decrease in average wind speed during the day.
3. According to Figure 3 (area 2), the average energy produced on days 9, 10, 11, and 14, despite the fact that the values of solar radiation and wind speed are lower than on days 12, 13, and 15, by about 100 W/m^2, represents slightly higher values for the energy produced on days 12, 13, and 15. On days 9, 10, 11, and 14, higher values of relative humidity, which affect the decrease in ambient temperature, are observed. The latter is directly related to the operating temperature of the solar panel.
4. The highest average values of energy, generated per day, as shown in Figure 3 (area 3), are the result of high average values of solar radiation and high average values of ambient temperature, associated with low average values of relative humidity and an increase in average wind speed during the day.
5. When estimating the energy of a system, it is sufficient when only two meteorological variables (ambient temperature and solar radiation) are taken into account since both explain more than 85% of the system's response and introduce a significant skewness in the random variable distribution of the generated energy (Figure 3).

6. Figure 3 shows that at high wind speeds, photovoltaic systems receive additional cooling since it is known that with an increase in the operating temperature, the efficiency of the photovoltaic module decreases. This circumstance also introduces a certain skewness of energy.
7. There is a direct correlation between ambient temperature and solar radiation and an inverse relationship between relative humidity with solar radiation and ambient temperature.
8. It can be proved that the atmospheric pressure has little or almost no impact on the energy performance of photovoltaic systems in the conditions under consideration, which indicates that there is no random change in energy, but there is a theoretical possibility that the atmospheric pressure affects the energy performance when the geographical location of the subject matter changes.

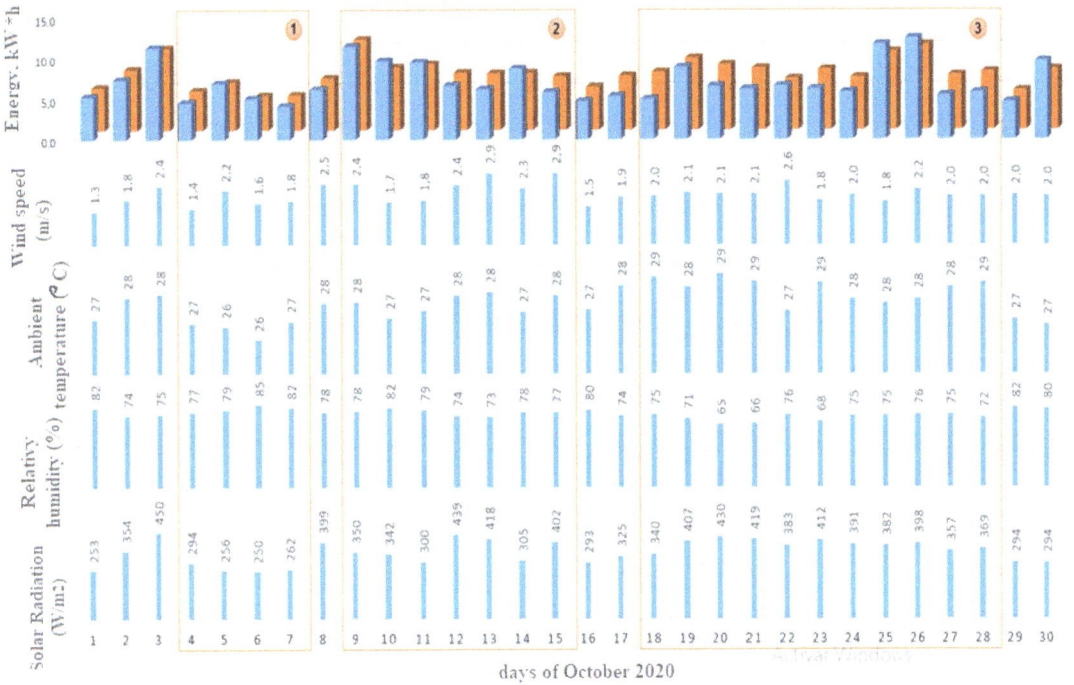

Figure 3. Energy produced per day by a 5-kW photovoltaic system (October 2020) with respect to meteorological variables (ambient temperature, solar radiation, relative humidity, wind speed).

Table 5. Response surface equations.

No.	Equation	EC (kWh)	EE (kWh)	D (kWh)
1	$E = (604 - 117.7 * T_a + 1.4 * G_h + 3.84 * T_a^2) * 10$	214	213.6	−0.4

There are a number of articles devoted to the estimation of electricity generation by solar panels depending on various factors, including climatic conditions, for example, work [45–48]. In these studies, only solar radiation is taken into account; other climatic factors are not represented. Also, these works do not provide a detailed description of the calculation models, a statistical analysis of the influence of climatic factors on the energy produced. Article [49] describes a model for determining the tilt angle with the horizon (with respect to the ground) of the solar energy system by estimating the monthly mean daily global solar radiation on tilted surfaces facing directly towards the equator, which is based on monthly average daily global solar radiation data produced from typical meteorological year (TMY) data. The disadvantage of the proposed model is the lack of correlation with other climatic factors, which can also randomly change and affect solar radiation. The same assessment can be given to the model of the photovoltaic system presented in article [50].

Furthermore, the article [51] presents a model and a self-learning system for dust estimation of photovoltaic panels based on data on solar radiation, ambient temperature, and output power generated by solar panels, as well as the amount of dust in these conditions. This approach has many advantages, but data on wind speed and humidity, which have a great influence on dust formation, are not used when constructing the model.

There are also currently clear sky models that take into account the influence of clouds on solar radiation and do not take into account other climatic factors.

In solar applications, the most common CSI models provide broadband irradiance predictions based on a number of simplifications and/or empirical components compared to the rigorous radiative transfer models used in atmospheric sciences. Thus, these common CSI models have to undergo continuous quality assurance evaluations to delineate the range of validity of such simplifications. Traditionally, these evaluations have consisted of direct comparisons against high-quality ground observations [52].

Taking into account the results of these studies and the limited experience of existing systems and models for estimation of electricity generation by solar panels depending on climatic conditions, it should be concluded that the proposed methods are appropriate for use in specific geographical conditions.

9. Conclusions

The computational tool proposed in this paper is designed to estimate the energy produced by low-power photovoltaic systems based on the specific conditions of the study region. This approach will make it possible to determine the relationship between climatic factors that affect energy production in photovoltaic systems operating in any region. This approach allows us to evaluate the most favorable geographical location of photovoltaic panels, which contributes to increasing the efficiency of converting solar energy into electricity. The approach to assessing the significance of climate parameters described in this paper will also allow us to determine the component composition of a solar power plant from the point of view of automation and its algorithm of operation. The energy estimation results, derived using the response surface equations, and obtained during this study for the specific climatic conditions of the Republic of Cuba, correspond to one month of the study (October 2020), which is a small sample. For an adequate estimation of energy, annual meteorological data and the energy generated are needed.

According to the results obtained during this study, when estimating the energy generated by an electro-technical complex with a five-kilowatt photovoltaic plant, by statistical methods, it can be stated that statistical skewness reports the degree to which observations are distributed evenly and proportionally above and below the center (highest) point of the distribution. In the case when the mentioned distribution is balanced, it is called symmetric. Thus, based on the presented studies, three climatic factors contribute to the skewness and the greatest influence in the random variable distribution of the generated energy: ambient temperature, solar radiation and wind speed.

Author Contributions: Conceptualization, A.T. and I.V.; methodology, D.G.; software, D.G.; validation, A.T., I.V. and D.G.; formal analysis, I.V.; investigation, I.V.; resources, D.G.; data curation, A.T.; writing—original draft preparation, A.T.; writing—review and editing, I.V.; visualization, D.G.; supervision, A.T.; project administration, A.T. All authors have read and agreed to the published version of the manuscript.

Funding: This research received no external funding.

Data Availability Statement: Not applicable.

Acknowledgments: We acknowledge support by the Solar energy research center in Santiago de Cuba and the department of General Electrical Engineering of the Saint-Petersburg Mining University.

Conflicts of Interest: The authors declare no conflict of interest.

Abbreviations

The following abbreviations are used in this article:

AT	Ambient temperature
WS	Wind speed
RH	Relative humidity
SR	Solar radiation
AP	Atmospheric pressure
SR	Solar radiation
PCA	Principal component analysis
CSI	Clear sky irradiance
TMY	Typical meteorological year

References

1. Pirog, S.; AGH Scientific and Technical University; Shklyarskiy, Y.; Skamyin, A. Saint Petersburg Mining University Non-linear Electrical Load Location Identification. *J. Min. Inst.* **2019**, *237*, 317–321. [CrossRef]
2. Bolshunova, O.; Kamyshian, A.; Bolshunov, A. Diagnostics of career dump truck traction induction motors technical condition using wavelet analysis. In Proceedings of the 2016 Dynamics of Systems, Mechanisms and Machines, Dynamics, Omsk, Russia, 15–17 November 2016. [CrossRef]
3. Malarev, V.; Kopteva, A.; Koptev, V.; Gotsul, Y. Improvement of Efficiency of Steam-Thermal Treatment of High-Viscous Oil Formations Using Downhole Electric Steam Generators. *J. Ecol. Eng.* **2021**, *22*, 17–24. [CrossRef]
4. Iakovleva, E.; Belova, M.; Soares, A. Specific Features of Mapping Large Discontinuous Faults by the Method of Electromagnetic Emission. *Resources* **2020**, *9*, 135. [CrossRef]
5. Koteleva, N.; Buslaev, G.; Valnev, V.; Kunshin, A. Augmented Reality System and Maintenance of Oil Pumps. *Int. J. Eng.* **2020**, *33*, 1620–1628. [CrossRef]
6. Eder, L.; Provornaya, I.; Filimonova, I.; Kozhevin, V.; Komarova, A. World energy market in the conditions of low oil prices, the role of renewable energy sources. *Energy Procedia* **2018**, *153*, 112–117. [CrossRef]
7. Munoz-Guijosa, J.M.; Kryltcov, S.B.; Solovev, S.V. Application of an active rectifier used to mitigate currents distortion in 6–10 KV distribution grids. *J. Min. Inst.* **2019**, *236*, 229–238.
8. Rassõlkin, A.; Sell, R.; Leier, M. Development case study of the first estonian self-driving car, iseauto. *Electr. Control. Commun. Eng.* **2018**, *14*, 81–88. [CrossRef]
9. National Research Council. *The Power of Renewables: Opportunities and Challenges for China and the United States*; The National Academies Press: Washington, DC, USA, 2011; pp. 1–240. [CrossRef]
10. Kozioł, J.; Mendecka, B. Evaluation of Economic, Energy-environmental and Sociological Effects of Substituting Non-renewable Energy with Renewable Energy Sources. *J. Sustain. Dev. Energy Water Environ. Syst.* **2015**, *3*, 333–343. [CrossRef]
11. Boikov, A.V.; Savelev, R.V.; Payor, V.A.; Potapov, A.V. Evaluation of bulk material behavior control method in technological units using DEM. Part 2. *CIS Iron Steel Rev.* **2020**, *20*, 3–6. [CrossRef]
12. Bardanov, A.I.; Pudkova, T.V. Control of D-STATCOM for asymmetric voltage dips compensation. In Proceedings of the 2019 IEEE Conference of Russian Young Researchers in Electrical and Electronic Engineering, ElConRus, St. Petersburg and Moscow, Russia, 28–31 January 2019; pp. 430–433. [CrossRef]
13. Ragazzi, M.; Ionescu, G.; Cioranu, S.; Brebbia, C.A.; Polonara, F.; Magaril, E.R.; Passerini, G. Assessment of environmental impact from renewable and non-renewable energy sources. *Int. J. Energy Prod. Manag.* **2017**, *2*, 8–16. [CrossRef]
14. Furlan, C.; Mortarino, C. Forecasting the impact of renewable energies in competition with non-renewable sources. *Renew. Sustain. Energy Rev.* **2018**, *81*, 1879–1886. [CrossRef]
15. Baranes, E.; Jacqmin, J.; Poudou, J.-C. Non-renewable and intermittent renewable energy sources: Friends and foes? *Energy Policy* **2017**, *111*, 58–67. [CrossRef]
16. Lakatos, L.; Hevessy, G.; Kovács, J. Advantages and Disadvantages of Solar Energy and Wind-Power Utilization. *World Futur.* **2011**, *67*, 395–408. [CrossRef]
17. Bardanov, A.I.; Vasilkov, O.S.; Pudkova, T.V. Modeling the process of redistributing power consumption using energy storage system with various configurations to align the electrical loads schedule. *J. Physics Conf. Ser.* **2021**, *1753*, 012013.
18. Carrizosa, M.J.; Stankovic, N.; Vannier, J.-C.; Shklyarskiy, Y.E.; Bardanov, A.I. Multi-terminal dc grid overall control with modular multilevel converters. *J. Min. Inst.* **2020**, *243*, 357. [CrossRef]

19. Ivanchenko, D.I.; Belsky, A.A.; Dobush, V.S. Application of Kalman filter for prevention of unrequired operation of power transformer differential protection. *J. Phys. Conf. Series* **2020**, *1652*, 012001. [CrossRef]
20. Peng, Z.; Herfatmanesh, M.R.; Liu, Y. Cooled solar PV panels for output energy efficiency optimisation. *Energy Convers. Manag.* **2017**, *150*, 949–955. [CrossRef]
21. Buonomano, A.; Calise, F.; D'Accadia, M.D.; Vicidomini, M. A hybrid renewable system based on wind and solar energy coupled with an electrical storage: Dynamic simulation and economic assessment. *Energy* **2018**, *155*, 174–189. [CrossRef]
22. Fakouriyan, S.; Saboohi, Y.; Fathi, A. Experimental analysis of a cooling system effect on photovoltaic panels' efficiency and its preheating water production. *Renew. Energy* **2019**, *134*, 1362–1368. [CrossRef]
23. Poulek, V.; Safrankova, J.; Cerna, L.; Libra, M.; Beranek, V.; Finsterle, T.; Hrzina, P. PV Panel and PV Inverter Damages Caused by Combination of Edge Delamination, Water Penetration, and High String Voltage in Moderate Climate. *IEEE J. Photovolt.* **2021**, *11*, 561–565. [CrossRef]
24. Setiawan, E.A.; Setiawan, A.; Siregar, D. Analysis on solar panel performance and PV-inverter configuration for tropical region. *J. Therm. Eng.* **2017**, *3*, 1259–1270. [CrossRef]
25. Ngoc, T.N.; Phung, Q.N.; Tung, L.N.; Sanseverino, E.R.; Romano, P.; Viola, F. Increasing efficiency of photovoltaic systems under non-homogeneous solar irradiation using improved Dynamic Programming methods. *Sol. Energy* **2017**, *150*, 325–334. [CrossRef]
26. Zamyatina, E.N.; Zamyatin, E.O.; Shafkhatov, E.R. Criteria for Assessing the Energy Efficiency of the Electrical Complex. In Proceedings of the 2020 IEEE Conference of Russian Young Researchers in Electrical and Electronic Engineering, EIConRus, St. Petersburg and Moscow, Russia, 27–30 January 2020; pp. 1344–1346.
27. Liu, H.-D.; Lin, C.-H.; Pai, K.-J.; Lin, Y.-L. A novel photovoltaic system control strategies for improving hill climbing algorithm efficiencies in consideration of radian and load effect. *Energy Convers. Manag.* **2018**, *165*, 815–826. [CrossRef]
28. Zhang, L.; Yu, S.S.; Fernando, T.; Iu, H.H.-C.; Wong, K.P. An online maximum power point capturing technique for high-efficiency power generation of solar photovoltaic systems. *J. Mod. Power Syst. Clean Energy* **2019**, *7*, 357–368. [CrossRef]
29. Alferov, Z.I.; Andreev, V.M.; Rumyantsev, V.D. III-V heterostructures in photovoltaics. In *Concentrator Photovoltaics*; Luque, A., Viacheslav, A., Eds.; Springer: Berlin/Heidelberg, Germany, 2007; Volume 130, pp. 25–50.
30. Untila, G.; Kost, T.; Chebotareva, A.; Zaks, M.; Sitnikov, A.; Solodukha, O.; Shvarts, M. Concentrator bifacial Ag-free LGCells. *Sol. Energy* **2014**, *106*, 88–94. [CrossRef]
31. Alves, P.; Fernandes, J.F.; Torres, J.P.N.; Branco, P.C.; Fernandes, C.; Gomes, J. From Sweden to Portugal: The effect of very distinct climate zones on energy efficiency of a concentrating photovoltaic/thermal system (CPV/T). *Sol. Energy* **2019**, *188*, 96–110. [CrossRef]
32. Gerra, D.D.; Iakovleva, E. Sun tracking system for photovoltaic batteries in climatic conditions of the Republic of Cuba. *IOP Conf. Series: Mater. Sci. Eng.* **2019**, *643*, 012155. [CrossRef]
33. Zhukovskiy, Y.L.; Korolev, N.A.; Babanova, I.S.; Boikov, A.V. The prediction of the residual life of electromechanical equipment based on the artificial neural network. *IOP Conf. Series: Earth Environ. Sci.* **2017**, *87*, 032056. [CrossRef]
34. Abdi, H.; Williams, L.; Valentin, D. Multiple factor analysis: Principal component analysis for multitable and multiblock data sets. *Wiley Interdiscip. Rev. Comput. Stat.* **2013**, *5*, 149–179. [CrossRef]
35. Cardot, H.; Degras, D. Online Principal Component Analysis in High Dimension: Which Algorithm to Choose? *Int. Stat. Rev.* **2017**, *86*, 29–50. [CrossRef]
36. Ma, Z. Sparse principal component analysis and iterative thresholding. *Ann. Stat.* **2013**, *41*, 772–801. [CrossRef]
37. Happ, C.; Greven, S. Multivariate Functional Principal Component Analysis for Data Observed on Different (Dimensional) Domains. *J. Am. Stat. Assoc.* **2018**, *113*, 649–659. [CrossRef]
38. Fan, J.; Liao, Y.; Wang, W. Projected principal component analysis in factor models. *Ann. Stat.* **2016**, *44*, 219–254. [CrossRef]
39. Chiou, J.-M.; Yang, Y.-F.; Chen, Y.-T. Multivariate functional principal component analysis: A normalization approach. *Stat. Sin.* **2014**, *24*, 1571–1596. [CrossRef]
40. Aït-Sahalia, Y.; Xiu, D. Principal Component Analysis of High-Frequency Data. *J. Am. Stat. Assoc.* **2019**, *114*, 287–303. [CrossRef]
41. Yu, J. Local and global principal component analysis for process monitoring. *J. Process. Control.* **2012**, *22*, 1358–1373. [CrossRef]
42. Lu, C.; Feng, Y.-W.; Fei, C.-W. Weighted Regression-Based Extremum Response Surface Method for Structural Dynamic Fuzzy Reliability Analysis. *Energies* **2019**, *12*, 1588. [CrossRef]
43. Rezk, H.; Hasaneen, E.-S. A new MATLAB/Simulink model of triple-junction solar cell and MPPT based on artificial neural networks for photovoltaic energy systems. *Ain Shams Eng. J.* **2015**, *6*, 873–881. [CrossRef]
44. Sofi, A.; Muscolino, G.; Giunta, F. Propagation of uncertain structural properties described by imprecise Probability Density Functions via response surface method. *Probabilistic Eng. Mech.* **2020**, *60*, 103020. [CrossRef]
45. Al-Badi, A.H. Measured performance evaluation of a 1.4 kW grid connected desert type PV in Oman. *Energy Sustain. Dev.* **2018**, *47*, 107–113. [CrossRef]
46. Eke, R.; Demircan, H. Performance analysis of a multi crystalline Si photovoltaic module under Mugla climatic conditions in Turkey. *Energy Convers. Manag.* **2013**, *65*, 580–586. [CrossRef]
47. Adaramola, M.S.; Vågnes, E.E. Preliminary assessment of a small-scale rooftop PV-grid tied in Norwegian climatic conditions. *Energy Convers. Manag.* **2015**, *90*, 458–465. [CrossRef]
48. Sundaram, S.; Babu, J.S.C. Performance evaluation and validation of 5MWp grid connected solar photovoltaic plant in South India. *Energy Convers. Manag.* **2015**, *100*, 429–439. [CrossRef]

49. Zang, H.; Guo, M.; Wei, Z.; Sun, G. Determination of the Optimal Tilt Angle of Solar Collectors for Different Climates of China. *Sustainability* **2016**, *8*, 654. [CrossRef]
50. Markos, F.M.; Sentian, J. Potential of Solar Energy in Kota Kinabalu, Sabah: An Estimate Using a Photovoltaic System Model. *J. Phys Conf. Ser.* **2016**, *710*, 12032. [CrossRef]
51. Shaaban, M.F.; Alarif, A.; Mokhtar, M.; Tariq, U.; Osman, A.H.; Al-Ali, A.R. A New Data-Based Dust Estimation Unit for PV Panels. *Energies* **2020**, *13*, 3601. [CrossRef]
52. Ruiz-Arias, J.A.; Gueymard, C.A. Worldwide inter-comparison of clear-sky solar radiation models: Consensus-based review of direct and global irradiance components simulated at the earth surface. *Sol. Energy* **2018**, *168*, 10–29. [CrossRef]

Article

Monitoring of the Behaviour and State of Nanoscale Particles in a Gas Cleaning System of an Ore-Thermal Furnace

Vladimir Bazhin and Olga Masko *

The Automation of Technological Processes and Production Department, Saint Petersburg Mining University, 2, 21st Line, 199106 St Petersburg, Russia; bazhin-alfoil@mail.ru
* Correspondence: olgamasko.17@gmail.com or s205017@stud.spmi.ru

Abstract: The aim of this paper is to define and select stable zones in the off-gas duct of an ore-thermal furnace using a mathematical model. This is needed to increase the effectiveness of exhaust gas composition control in metallurgical silicon production. **Methods.** The goals of this study were achieved by means of computational fluid dynamics. A model with a water-cooled furnace roof as well as a model comprising steel gas passes with a sliding shutter was developed using ANSYS Fluent software. Both models were symmetrical to ensure a uniform gas-dust distribution, which allowed us to test the adequacy of the obtained models. The models were based on the Navier–Stokes equations system as well as on a discrete phase model (DPM) that was developed using the Euler–Lagrange method. **Results.** As a result of the modelling, a transition flow mode (Re 0-7437) was revealed behind the sliding shutter. As such, it can be assumed that the most suitable place for measuring equipment to be installed is directly behind the closed part of the sliding shutter.

Keywords: silicon production; nanoparticles; ore-thermal furnace (OTF); gas cleaning; symmetry; carbon footprint; CFD; ANSYS fluent

Citation: Bazhin, V.; Masko, O. Monitoring of the Behaviour and State of Nanoscale Particles in a Gas Cleaning System of an Ore-Thermal Furnace. *Symmetry* 2022, 14, 923. https://doi.org/10.3390/sym14050923

Academic Editor: Toshio Tagawa

Received: 24 February 2022
Accepted: 27 April 2022
Published: 1 May 2022

Publisher's Note: MDPI stays neutral with regard to jurisdictional claims in published maps and institutional affiliations.

Copyright: © 2022 by the authors. Licensee MDPI, Basel, Switzerland. This article is an open access article distributed under the terms and conditions of the Creative Commons Attribution (CC BY) license (https://creativecommons.org/licenses/by/4.0/).

1. Introduction

A large number of fine particles with various compositions are emitted into the atmosphere during carbothermic silicon reduction. Analyses of waste gases show that most emissions are related to the consumption of carbon materials that contribute to the overall carbon balance. These are carbon-graphite electrodes that are used for heating quartz and charcoal to reduce the amount of silicon released from oxides (quartz) [1–3]. The main component of waste fume emissions is SiO_2 microsilica (up to 85 percent), which is present in a mixture of solid carbon in various forms and states (7–8 percent) and in silicon carbide (5 percent) [4,5]. As a rule, industrial emissions are not controlled, and dust is collected from gas pass systems and from deposits on equipment and building structures.

Granulometric analyses of the fumes captured by GCS electro-filters indicate the presence of particles in microsilica fumes that are 200–250 μm in size and have an elevated carbon nanoparticle content (up to 8 percent) that can be removed with the off-gas.

Currently, carbon-free microsilica is widely used as a modifying additive to base materials in the construction industry. Thus, the use of microsilica makes it possible to produce concrete with special properties: increased durability (resistance to the action of weak acids and seawater) and increased compression strength. Production methods for silicon-carbide powder materials, such as micronized carbide (particle size < 1 m) for ceramics and nanocarbides (particle size < 1 nm) for high-quality structural ceramics and galvanics, are being intensively developed, as they create a high-value of the final product [6,7].

The main sources of exhaust gas carbon emissions are carbon electrodes, activated carbon, and carbonaceous materials.

For electrodes, the main components of carbon flow are arc heating fractures, the main quartz reduction reaction (stoichiometry), the decrease and oxidation of the lateral faces, and the destruction of the electrode soles upon contact with the charge. The key factor in electrode mass erosion is the oxygen concentration in the furnace atmosphere. As a result of the increased formation and oxidation of carbon monoxide, the oxygen concentration in the furnace atmosphere will decrease [8–10].

There is scientific and technical interest in modelling the distribution of waste gas concentration fields during carbothermic silicon reduction. It is necessary to ensure that the furnace's thermal conditions and the balance of consumable carbon are controlled effectively [11].

2. Problem Overview

2.1. Causes of Carbon Nanoparticle Formation during Carbothermic Silicon Reduction in Ore-Thermal Furnaces

At present, reducing the carbon footprint in pyrometallurgical processes [6] is relevant to the resolution of global decarbonization issues. The manufacturing process in ore-thermal furnaces (OTFs) involves multi-component carbon systems (carbon electrodes and lining, activated charcoal, modifying additives) that affect the overall carbon balance during smelting. Activated carbon is consumed by the main silicon reduction reaction by means of stoichiometry, as well as by the side reactions caused by interactions with the impurities in quartz that take place according to thermodynamic conditions. For example, one of these irrevocable losses can be attributed to the transfer of active carbon into the crust and the subsequent production of silicon carbide when there are temperature disturbances of more than 1700–1900 °C [12]. Additionally, thermal disturbances in the furnace and increased carbon consumption are associated with carbon oxidation (an increase in CO and CO_2 content) or with the abrupt release of soot and carbon particles into the atmosphere of the furnace and into the gaseous space [13].

Charge materials are consumed for the main silicon reduction reaction to form silicon dioxide, which may be accompanied by a transition into carbon monoxide in parallel with the formation of intermediate silicon monoxide, as well as silicon carbide during overheating, especially at the start of the smelting process and during the primary arc [14]. A separate consumption item is the unresponsive carbon that is derived from charcoal, which forms nanoparticles in the form of amorphous carbon, active pure carbon, or fullerenes.

The carbon resulting from electrode chipping and falling passes into a fume mixture together with microsilica. In this case, carbon particles without interaction are adsorbed on the highly developed surface of the silica fumes to form microsilica, the main form of silicon waste. This is an item of consumption due to the changes in the silicon balance that range from 380 to 450 kg per ton of produced silicon and requires operational control. In this instance, sampling and relevant data on the chemical composition of the microsilica captured in the GCS are needed for analytical comparison with the source quartz and impurities to ultimately determine the quality of silicon products [15–17].

2.2. Microsilica Monitoring and Nanoparticle Capture in the Ore-Thermal Furnace Gas Cleaning System

The main problem with capturing and controlling nanoscale particles in the OTF GSC is the timely determination of the emission composition of the gas fumes (in mass). Conventional GSC implements a detailed analysis after the end of the electric filter cycle and after the filter has been cleaned and the sediment has been weighed according to the time. As a result, there is a delay in the response when the electric and technological modes of the furnace are disrupted and when the electrodes are burned, which is indicated by an increase in the carbon content in the waste gases [18]. Monitoring the waste composition during the production of silicon and its alloys is associated with a number of industry-specific problems:

- The temperatures of the gases in the immediate vicinity of the furnace roof are very high (600–850 °C), resulting in the need to cool and ventilate the gas-dust flow before it makes contact with the sensitive instruments when taking extractive measurements;

- The high concentration of particulates in front of the filter can cause rapid abrasive damage to the measuring instruments in the gas streams that are in contact with the particles and can also affect the measured data [19,20];
- The turbulent mode of gas flow has a wide range of time and space scales for the pulsations of all of the flow characteristics. This makes the gas flow faster than the laminar flow and results in intensive mass exchanges with high-impulse and energy levels between different stream regions due to the intensive mixing of the dispersed medium. This results in the substance having an uneven distribution in the gas flow and a consequent distortion of the measurement results.

Taking into account the described flow conditions in the furnace atmosphere and in the gas duct system of GCSs, the question of how to determine the temperature and velocity control points of the particles arises. For this purpose, it is necessary to define stable zones on the mass transfer interaction path.

To effectively control the electric mode of the furnace, installing a gas analyzer between the gas duct and the gas purification equipment in the stable flow region of the gas stream is recommended. This allows additional data to be obtained to create a digital database of information about the process [21].

The continuous growth of computing capacities and measuring technologies in recent years has opened up radically new possibilities for the computer modelling of large production units [22].

The novelty of the proposed solution is in justifying the location of the gas analyzer installation with the aid of the created computational fluid dynamics (CFD) model. The ANSYS software package, specifically its CFD modelling module ANSYS Fluent, was used for the mathematical model.

2.3. Main Features of Flue Gas Movement in the Ore-Thermal Furnace Gas Cleaning System

In most cases, when taking the fundamental laws of gas-fluid dynamics [4] in the furnace gas duct into account, the flue flow has a high Reynolds value and is turbulent due to different densities.

This movement of gases with dust is accompanied by an intensive mixing with velocity and pressure pulsations, and in addition to the main longitudinal movement, transverse movements and rotational movements are observed in individual flow volumes, especially in the vortex zones that are close to the filters and ejectors. As a result, the local cross-sectional velocities of the entire gas content flow from the furnace vault to the GCS during the mixing process under the influence of a temperature gradient between the layers for the entire mixing period.

It should be noted that turbulence has a continuous influence on the main flow parameters such as the concentration of components, temperature, velocity, and heat state. Thus, each turbulent vortex volume has its own substance and temperature concentration [23].

To avoid components and pulsations mixing and to thus obtain adequate data on flow parameters and the adequacy of the matrix, it is necessary to define data for the transient flow by taking the measurements into account in practice. On the other hand, the transient flow mode is characterized by the low mixing rate of the pulsation particles compared with the turbulence mode. In this instance, the key value for determining the flow of gas is the Reynolds number (Re) that characterizes the mode changes.

For this process, it has been experimentally determined that the Re for straight, smooth pipes with the most perturbed flow at the entrance of the pipe is 2300. However, at Re values above this value and up to a certain limit, a transient (mixed) flow mode is observed, and after this limit, turbulent flow is more likely [24]. In cylindrical receptacles (pipes), this transition interval can be varied significantly by reducing the initial disturbance of the medium by up to 50,000. For this process, we determined the factors influencing the turbulent state of the system in the gas pass system from the furnace:

- The current state of the fume environment (kinetics, thermodynamics, etc.): compressibility (velocity of motion of silica fume) taking into account multi-phase flow (interphase exchange).
- The outer limits of gas flow by zone: the movement along the side lining into the vault and output into the gas channel without the influence of the channel geometry.
- The process limit stage and GCS outlet (GCS electric filter surface pressure): the flow area on the surface of the electric filter and the pressure.

The Reynolds criteria for the different flow mode models are as follows:

1. At $Re < 2 \times 10^3$ laminar flow is observed.
2. At $Re > 10^4$ the flow becomes turbulent, but when gases begin to exit the furnace vault and move into the gas channel, it is preserved.
3. At $Re > 5 \times 10^4$ a turbulent boundary layer begins to form during the beginning of the gas flow process due to a sharp change in the temperature.
4. At $2 \times 10^4 < Re\ 10^4$ a transient flow and heat exchange mode are observed when the flow approaches the electric filter. Thus, given the turbulent flow conditions, the ratio of the average to maximum velocity increases with the turbulence. In the Re, this ratio is asymptotically close to 1 [25–27].

3. Materials and Methods

3.1. Computer Simulation of the Dispersion Fluid Dynamics

Offsetting the limit values for transient flows is a major difficulty in determining the flow parameters of a multi-component gas. This problem is particularly pronounced in the case of flow limits since the existing standard models can only estimate the average flow rate of a gas duct when averaging the Reynolds criteria values in ANSYS Fluent [28].

The exhaust ducts and flows of the carbothermic silicon reductions in the OTF were simulated to detect stable flow zones in which the control point for determining the concentration of the exhaust gases could be installed.

The classification of existing methods and approaches for the numerical modelling of turbulent flows is based on the level of detail required to refine and detect turbulent pulsations, as well as their energy spectrum and type of flow. Depending on this, methods can be divided into three groups (DNS—direct numerical simulation, LES—large eddy simulation, and RANS—Reynolds-averaged Navier–Stokes) [29].

For the current task, the best solution to account for large-scale turbulent vortices and flows in the boundary layer is a hybrid approach in which an RANS model is activated in a wall area with an LES model close to it. This is a detached eddy simulation (DES) method for simulating disconnected vortices that takes into account the reduction in turbulent vortices near a solid surface [30]. This method requires significant computational resources but ensures its adequacy compared to others.

In the considered case, taking the influence of the boundary layer in the gas flow transition zones on turbulence into account, the explicit resolution of even the largest vortices in the boundary layer requires considerable grinding in the calculation grid, resulting in an increase in the calculation time. Thus, a wall-adapted local eddy-viscosity model (WALE) [31] can solve this problem, taking the particularities of the gas flow and its thermal potential into consideration.

The WALE method requires a high-quality grid. The number of grid elements should be more than 1,000,000 at least, and boundary layers should be used for inflation. Otherwise, it is possible that uncorrected data will be obtained as a result of the numerical simulation.

3.2. Problem Statement: Modelling the Off-Gas Mixture under Ore-Thermal Furnace Conditions

The symmetry of the gas duct system ensures uniform flow separation. An increase in the waste gas concentration in one part of the duct will result in changes in the pressure drops in another part. This will consequently lead to asymmetric flows, making it impossible to define a stable flow area. Gas duct system symmetry allows us to evaluate the adequacy of the resulting models.

The following boundary conditions (Tables 1–3) were used as input components for modelling the furnace exhaust gas system: the water-cooled roof of the furnace and the steel gas passes. A sliding shutter was placed at a 45-degree angle at the fork of the two gas passes.

Table 1. Initial model data.

Parameter	Unit	Value
Volume (gas)	Nm^3/h *	1000
Temperature (gas)	°C	500
Pressure (water)	kPa	250,000
Volume (water)	Nm^3/h *	250,000
Temperature (water)	°C	35–45

*—m^3/h under normal conditions (0 °C, 100 kPa).

Table 2. Average composition of the waste gases in percentages [6].

Mixture Component	Percent
CO	88.6
CO$_2$	4.81
CH$_4$	1.42
N$_2$	2.5
H$_2$	2.67

Table 3. Average composition of the fumes in percentages [7].

Mixture Component	Percent
SiO$_2$	85.41
Al$_2$O$_3$	0.46
Fe$_2$O$_3$	0.30
CaO	1.50
MgO	1.24
C	6.09
Na$_2$O	0.08
SO$_3$	0.16
P$_2$O$_5$	0.12
K$_2$O	0.31
TiO$_2$	0.02
SiC	5.03

The average values of the fumes in the off-gas mixture are 10–12 percent. According to the goals of this research, two models were developed:
- A system with a water-cooled portion of the roof for gas passes.
- A gas pass system without water cooling.

3.3. Governing Equations

The mathematical modelling of turbulence is based on the set of ratios used to describe the movement of a fluid/gas. The basic governing Navier–Stokes equation system consists of the equation of continuity (1) and the equation of motion (2):

$$\frac{\partial \rho}{\partial t} + \frac{\partial \rho \cdot u_j}{x_j} = 0 \tag{1}$$

$$\frac{\partial \rho \cdot u_i}{\partial t} + \frac{\partial \rho \cdot u_j \cdot u_i}{x_i} = -\frac{\partial P}{x_i} + \frac{\partial \tau_{ij}}{x_j}$$

where:

P—pressure of the gas mixture;
μ—gas mixture density;
t—time;
$u_{i,j}$—velocity components in the i and j directions; $\tau_{i,j}$—shear strain tensor.

To simulate the particulate matter (fume), a discrete phase model (DPM) was developed using the Euler–Lagrange method. It was constructed by solving the time-averaged Navier–Stokes equations for the liquid phase, which was treated as a continuum, while the dispersed phase was described by tracing the trajectory of a large number of particles through the calculated flow fields. The dispersed phase can exchange momentum, mass, and energy with the liquid phase.

The balance of the forces acting on a particle predicts the trajectory of the discrete phase particles by integrating the balance of the forces on the particle, which is written in the Lagrangian reference frame. This force balance equates inertia with the forces acting on the particle and can be written (based on the directions in the Cartesian coordinate system) as:

$$\frac{\partial U_p}{\partial t} = F_D(U - U_p) + \frac{g_x \cdot (\rho_p - \rho)}{\rho_p} + F_x \qquad (2)$$

where $F_D(U - U_p)$ is the drag force per unit mass of the particle.

4. Results and Discussion

4.1. Model 1: Combination of the Furnace's Roof and Water-Cooled Gas Passes

As initial data, in addition to the variables specified in Tables 1–3 as well as the dimensions, the following parameters were made available: water-cooled thickness, 0.06 m; side lining thickness, 0.05 m; and thickness of the non-water-cooled part of the roof made of chamotte bricks, 0.5 m.

The grid of this model consisted of 2,037,611 elements to obtain adequate simulation accuracy and had a minimum orthogonal quality of at least 0.1 (Figure 1). The LES WALE turbulence model was used to solve the variable-density subsonic flow problem by means of a pressure–based coupled solver. The real Soave–Redlich–Kwong gas model [32,33] was used for the gas mixture.

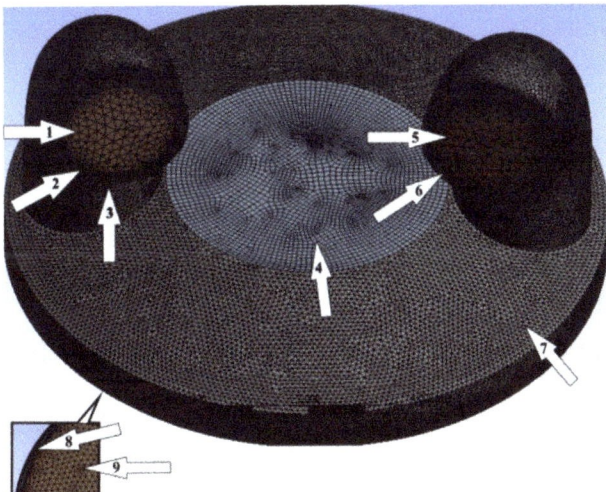

Figure 1. Furnace roof model. (1, 5—exhaust gas outputs; 2, 6—cooling water outputs; 3, 7—concrete refractory; 4—chamotte refractory; 8—exhaust gas input; 9—cooling water input.)

The boundary conditions for both streams (exhaust gases and cooling water) are shown in Tables 4–6.

Table 4. Model 1 boundary conditions for exhaust gas mixture.

Parameter	Input	Output
Type of boundary conditions	Mass-flow inlet	Pressure outlet
Hydraulic diameter, m	10.34	3
Mass flow rate, kg/s	29.16	-
Gauge pressure, Pa	-	0
Temperature, °C	500	-
Re	60,889.4	236,962.6
Turbulence intensity, percentage	10.34	3

Table 5. Model 1 boundary conditions for cooling water.

Parameter	Input	Output
Type of boundary conditions	Mass-flow inlet	Pressure outlet
Hydraulic diameter, m	0.06	0.06
Mass flow rate, kg/s	278	-
Gauge pressure, Pa	-	0
Temperature, °C	35	-
Re	150,075	150,075
Turbulence intensity, percent	0.06	0.06

Table 6. Model 2 boundary conditions.

Parameter	Input	Output
Type of boundary conditions	Mass-flow inlet	Pressure outlet
Hydraulic diameter, m	3	2.7
Mass flow rate, kg/s	15.54	-
Gauge pressure, Pa	-	0
Temperature, °C	430	0
Re	117,255.6	266,330
Turbulence intensity, percent	3.72	3.35

As a consequence of simulation, the temperature distribution and gas velocity profiles were obtained to define the boundary conditions for the second model as the area in which the intended gas analyzer could be installed.

At the outlet from the water-cooled part of the gas pass system, the gas flow rate was 5.5 m/s, which is equivalent to a mass flow rate of 15.54 kg/s. The temperature of the mixture was 450 °C.

Because the model had a horizontal symmetry, we were able to evaluate the temperature and velocity distribution using the cross-sectional area at the centre of one of the water-cooled parts of gas ducts 2 (Figure 2). This model makes it possible to determine the input parameters to assess possible variation among them. In this way, a prediction story was created for the next part of the GCS, in which the steel gas passes through a sliding shutter model. This provides stable initial characteristics for further modelling tasks.

4.2. Model: 2 Gas Passes without Water-Cooling

The simulated part of the exhaust gas system consists of gas passes with a rigid steel frame and a sliding shutter, which acts as a gas velocity regulator and is located at the gas pass junction. This part is of greatest interest for modelling and further analysis because stable zones were predicted to be here.

There were 2,739,629 grid elements in this model (Figure 3). The grid had an acceptable average orthogonal quality of 0.79.

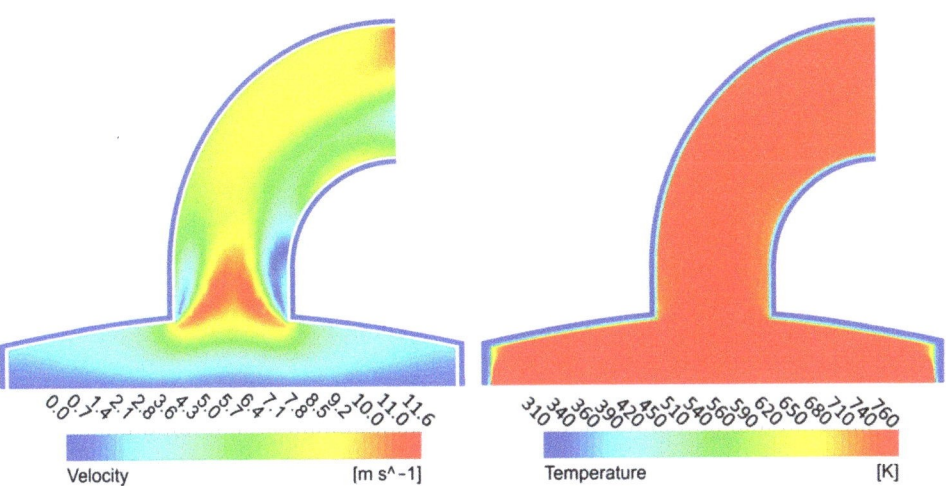

Figure 2. Sectional view of temperature and velocity distribution contours of model 1.

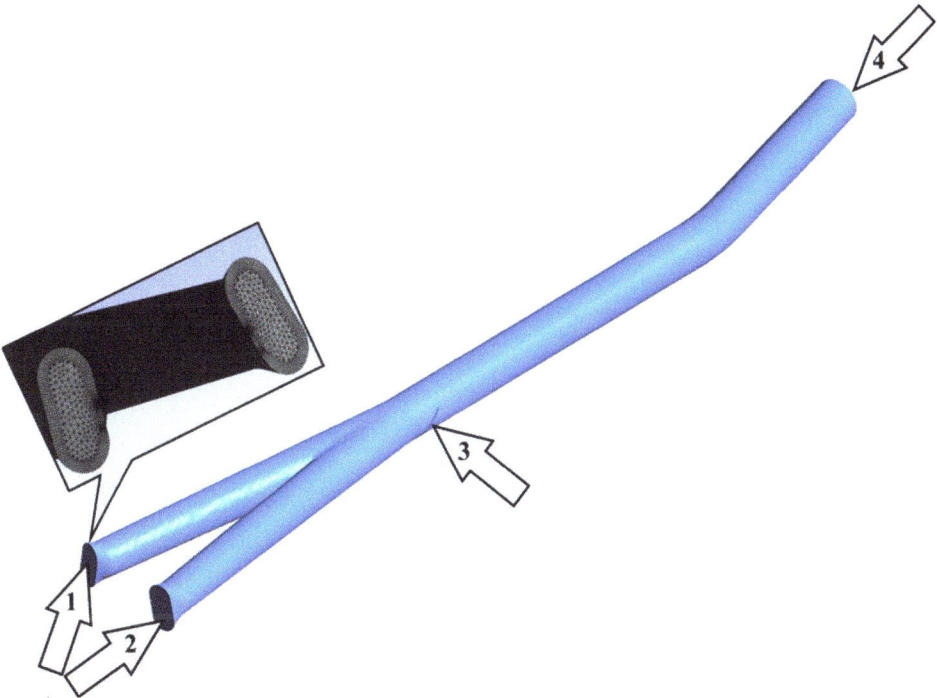

Figure 3. Pass model. (1, 2—exhaust gas inputs; 3—sliding shutter; 4—exhaust gas output.)

Based on the fact that the most stable flows in the models will not be laminar ones because of the high velocities, considering the transient mode that was identified by means of ANSYS Fluent is advised. The Re ratio was calculated using the conventional equation:

$$\mathrm{Re} = \frac{u \cdot d_{mix} \cdot \rho_{mix}}{\mu_{mix}} \qquad (3)$$

where:

u—velocity, m/s;
d_{mix}—hydraulic diameter, m;
ρ_{mix}—mixture density, kg/m^3;
μ_{mix}—dynamic viscosity of the gas mixture, Pa · s;
d_{mix}—hydraulic diameter, m;
ρ_{mix}—mixture density, kg/m^3;
μ_{mix}—dynamic viscosity of the gas mixture, Pa · s.

Sutherland's formula was used to determine the dynamic viscosity:

$$\mu_t = \mu_0 \cdot \frac{273+C}{T+C} \cdot \frac{T^{\frac{3}{2}}}{273} \tag{4}$$

where:

μ_t—dynamic viscosity of the gas at the temperature, Pa · s;
μ_0—dynamic viscosity of the gas at 0 °C, Pa · s;
T—the absolute temperature of the gas, K;
C—Sutherland's constant.

Thus, the dynamic viscosity of the gas mixture can be found using the following equation:

$$\frac{M_{mix}}{\mu_{mix}} = \frac{a_1 \cdot M_1}{\mu_1} + \frac{a_2 \cdot M_2}{\mu_2} + \ldots + \frac{a_n \cdot M_n}{\mu_n} \tag{5}$$

where M_{mix}, M_1, M_2, and M_n are the molecular masses of the gas mixtures and their components; a_1, a_2, and a_n are the volumetric fractions of the components in the gas mixtures; and μ_{mix}, μ_1, μ_2, and μ_n are the dynamic viscosities of the gas mixtures and their components, Pa · s [34,35].

The density of the furnace gas mixture is a very important indicator for determining the concentration field profile that is repeated on the GCS electric filters:

$$\rho_{mix} = y_1 \cdot \rho_1 + y_2 \cdot \rho_2 + \ldots + y_n \cdot \rho_n \tag{6}$$

where y_1, y_2, and y_n are the volumetric fractions, and ρ_1, ρ_2, and ρ_n are the densities of the components, kg/m^3.

$$\rho_0 \cdot \frac{273}{273+t} \tag{7}$$

The kinematic viscosity was calculated using the following formula:

$$v = \frac{\mu_{mix}}{\rho_{mix}} \tag{8}$$

As a result of calculating the required auxiliary parameters in ANSYS CFD-Post, the contours of the main off-gas parameters, such as velocity and kinematic viscosity, were obtained. These parameters have a direct impact on the Re as a key criterion for the flow conditions.

Any obstacle in the gas flow path changes the dynamic flow characteristics. As such, it is necessary to know what happens before and after the gas flow encounters the sliding shutter to evaluate any changes in the cross-section of the gas path. Knowing this, we can determine the control actions for the system.

Figure 4 illustrates the variations in the dynamic characteristics of the gas-dust flowover and the volume of the gas duct. A transient flow mode can be observed in the volume-rendering region behind the closed part of the sliding shutter (shown by the pointer) with the smallest Re. Taking into account the initial conditions of developing the best possible environment (laminar flow) for measurements to be taken in because of the high velocities, the transition mode revealed here can be considered to be an appropriate result of the modelling.

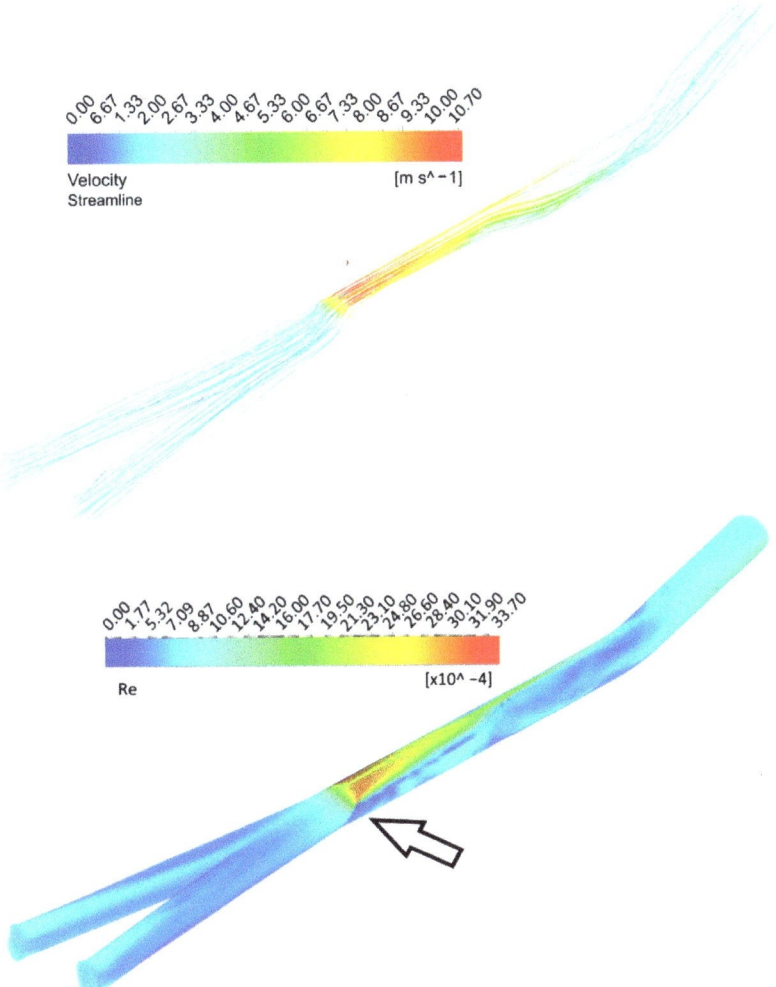

Figure 4. Velocity and Re distribution contours in the gas passes.

The flow velocity is the most significant parameter affecting both the flow mode and Re. The linear dependence of the Re on the flow velocity, as shown in Figure 5, allows us to estimate the flow mode using the volumetric velocity profile alone for future calculations. Based on this chart, the appropriate velocity should be less than 1 m/s to reach the transient Re.

Histograms, such as those in Figure 6, are needed to confirm the existence of a transitional mode and to estimate the proportion of its volumetric distribution in particular figures. A small fraction of transient off-gas flow (red column on the histogram (0–7437) Re) can be observed. These values are appropriate for minimizing turbulent pulsations in this case.

Thus, despite the wide variety of turbulence models in ANSYS Fluent, in cases where there is strong turbulence, considering transient flow modes is advised.

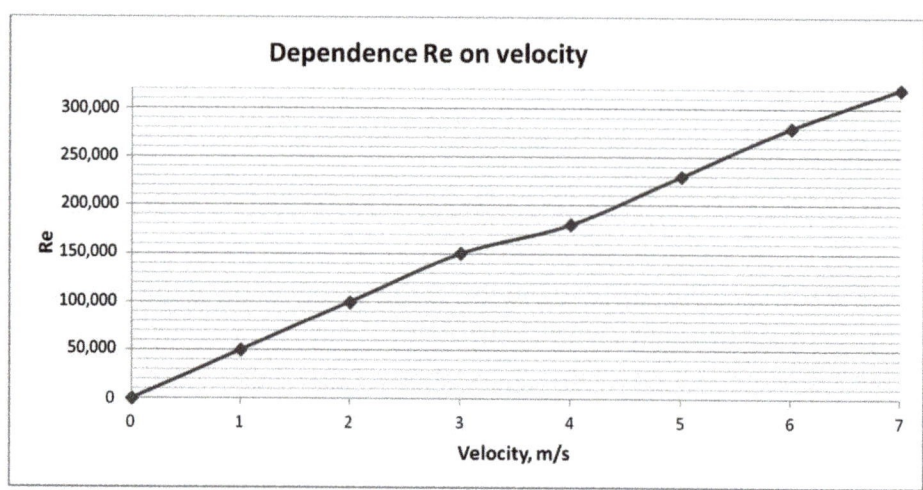

Figure 5. Re/velocity dependence chart.

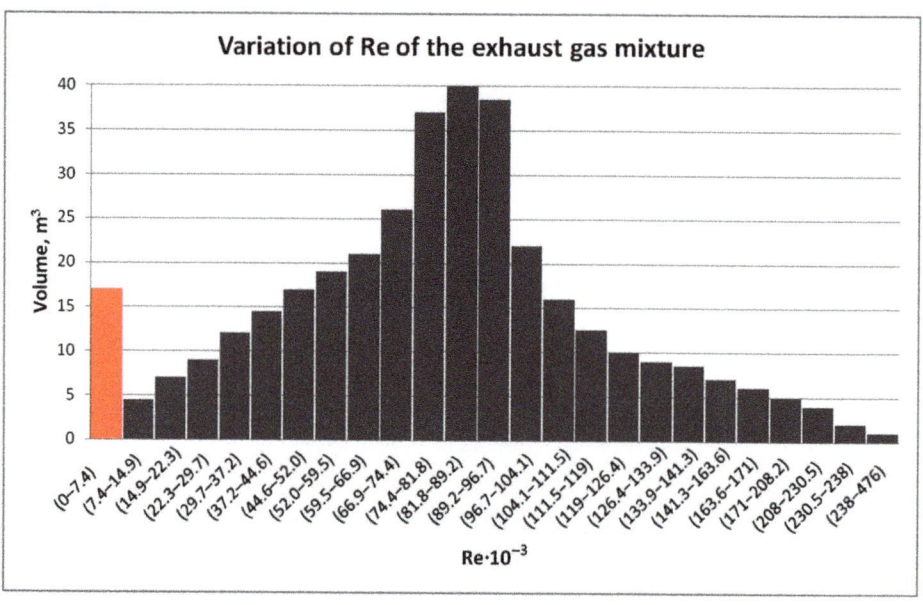

Figure 6. Histograms showing the variations in the Re of the exhaust gas mixture.

5. Conclusions

The silicon smelting process in OTFs is only controlled in the furnace and at the inlets and outlets of the gas duct. Thus, everything that goes into the gas ducts is a "black box". Emissions can only be controlled when the electrostatic precipitators are clogged. Modelling allows us to look inside the process and to react to the changes that take place in a short period of time.

Something else that is important for process control is minimizing the effects of turbulent pulsations on measurements in the gas duct. The main innovation of this paper is the determination of stable zones by means of CFD modelling to avoid measurement errors. All of the methods mentioned above can profoundly increase the transparency and controllability of the silicon production process.

When producing silicon in an OTF when the exhaust gas was at a volume flow rate of 250,000 m^3/h (under normal conditions), strong turbulence developed in the gas ducts, preventing the adequate measurement of the concentrations of each gas mixture component. In order to control the velocity at the fork of the two gas passes, a sliding shutter was installed in one of them at a 45° angle. This resulted in a 4–5-fold reduction in the velocity at the exit of the gas duct. A transient flow mode (Re < 10,000) was formed directly behind the closed part of the shutter, allowing the concentrations of the flue gas components to be measured with the required accuracy and to be controlled using an additional parameter.

In modern conditions, the production of silicon from quartz raw materials in OTFs needs to address energy efficiency issues by taking into account the distribution of gas-fume streams. As a result of the simulation presented here:

- The contours of the main parameters defining the flow mode in the exhaust gas transfer line, namely the kinematic viscosity and velocity, were obtained.
- The flow mode was determined by calculating the Reynolds criterion along the exhaust gas transfer line from the OTF to the GCS.
- It was revealed that the most suitable place for the installation of measuring equipment is directly behind the closed part of the sliding shutter. In this area, there is a transient flow mode with the lowest velocity and lowest Reynolds criterion value. In this location, the flow is influenced by turbulent forces at least, allowing the concentrations of the flow components to be measured with the required accuracy.

Author Contributions: The conceptualization and methodology of this research have been developed by V.B.; the model development and validation have been performed by O.M. As for writing, the original text has been written by O.M.; editing of the article, as well as supervision, has been done by V.B. All authors have read and agreed to the published version of the manuscript.

Funding: This research was funded by Russian Science Foundation grant no. 22-29-00397.

Institutional Review Board Statement: The study was conducted according to the guidelines of Saint Petersburg Mining University and approved by the University Review Board (or Ethics Committee) of Saint Petersburg Mining University.

Data Availability Statement: The results was obtained during the authours investigation and were not published in other papers.

Conflicts of Interest: The authors declare no conflict of interest.

References

1. Nedosekin, A.O.; Rejshahrit, E.I.; Kozlovskij, A.N. Strategic approach to assessing economic sustainability objects of mineral resources sector of Russia. *J. Min. Inst.* **2019**, *237*, 354–360. [CrossRef]
2. Litvinenko, V.; Tcvetkov, P.; Molodstov, K.V. The social and market mechanism of sustainable development of public companies in the mineral resource sector. *Eurasian Min.* **2019**, *1*, 36–41. [CrossRef]
3. Litvinenko, V. Digital Economy as a Factor in the Technological Development of the Mineral Sector. *Nat. Resour. Res.* **2019**, *29*, 1521–1541. [CrossRef]
4. Cheremisina, O.V.; Al-Salim, S.Z. Modern Methods of Ananlytical Control of Industrial Gases. *J. Min. Inst.* **2017**, *228*, 726–730.
5. Ivanchik, N.N.; Balanovsky, A.E.; Kondratyev, V.V.; Tyutrin, A.A. Research of silicon waste processing products as ultradispersed activating fluxes of arc welding. *J. Sib. Fed. Univ.* **2018**, *11*, 155–167. [CrossRef]
6. Nemchinova, N.V.; Tyutrin, A.A.; Sokolnikova, Y.V.; Fereferova, T.T. Analytical Investigations of Silicon Silicon Production Raw Materials and Products. *J. Sib. Fed. Univ.* **2017**, *10*, 37–48. [CrossRef]
7. Nemchinova, N.V.; Mineev, G.G.; Tyutrin, A.A.; Yakovleva, A.A. Utilization of Dust from Silicon Production. *Steel Transl.* **2017**, *47*, 763–766. [CrossRef]
8. Chigondo, F. From Metallurgical-Grade to Solar-Grade Silicon: An Overview. *Silicon* **2018**, *10*, 789–798. [CrossRef]
9. Liu, Y.; Kong, J.; Zhuang, Y.; Xing, P.; Yin, H.; Luo, X. Recycling high purity silicon from solar grade silicon cutting slurry waste by carbothermic reduction in the electric arc furnace. *J. Clean. Prod.* **2019**, *224*, 709–718. [CrossRef]

10. Karlina, A.I.; Kondrat'ev, V.V.; Balanovsky, A.E.; Kolosov, A.D.; Ivanchik, N.N. Results of modification of cast iron by carbon nanostructures of gas cleaning dust of silicon production. Advances in Engineering Research. In Proceedings of the International Conference on Aviamechanical Engineering and Transport (AviaENT 2018), Irkutsk, Russia, 21–26 May 2018; pp. 169–173.
11. Vasilyeva, N.V.; Boikov, A.V.; Erokhina, O.O.; Trifonov, A.Y. Automated digitization of radial charts. *J. Min. Inst.* **2021**, *247*, 82–87. [CrossRef]
12. Gembitskaya, I.M.; Gvozdetskaya, M.V. Transformation of grains of technological raw materials in the process of obtaining fine powders. *J. Min. Inst.* **2021**, *249*, 401–407. [CrossRef]
13. Bartie, N.; Cobos-Becerra, L.; Froehling, M.; Reuter, M. The resources, exergetic and environmental footprint of the silicon photovoltaic circular economy: Assessment and opportunities. *Resour. Conserv. Recycl.* **2021**, *169*, 24. [CrossRef]
14. Yolkin, K.S.; Yolkin, D.K.; Kolosov, A.D.; Ivanov, N.A.; Shtayger, M.G. Technologies, which allow to reduce an impact of metal silicon production on the environment. *IOP Conf. Ser. Mater. Sci. Eng.* **2018**, *411*, 012028. [CrossRef]
15. Saevarsdottir, G.; Magnusson, T.; Kvande, H. Reducing the Carbon Footprint: Primary Production of Aluminum and Silicon with Changing Energy Systems. *J. Sustain. Metall.* **2021**, *7*, 848–857. [CrossRef]
16. Legemza, J.; Findorák, F.; Bul'ko, B.; Briančin, J. New Approach in Research of Quartzes and Quartzites for Ferroalloys and Silicon Production. *Metals* **2021**, *11*, 23. [CrossRef]
17. Rozhikhina, I.D.; Nokhrina, O.I.; Yolkin, K.S.; Golodova, V.A. Ferroalloy production: State and development trends in the world and Russia. *IOP Conf. Ser. Mater. Sci. Eng.* **2020**, *866*, 012004. [CrossRef]
18. Asaniv, D.A.; Zapasnyi, V.V.; Ermekova, A.T.; Maratova, G.; Ivanov, A.A.; Cherepanov, N.I. Current Status of Dust Collection Systems in Aksu Ferroalloy Plant Smelting Shop 1 and Functional Improvement to These Systems. *Metallurgist* **2018**, *62*, 391–400. [CrossRef]
19. Danilov, A.; Smirnov, Y.; Korelsky, D.S. Effective methods for reclamation of area sources of dust emission. *J. Ecol. Eng.* **2017**, *18*, 1–7. [CrossRef]
20. Kero, I.; Dahl, S.; Tranell, G. Airborne Emissions from Si/FeSi Production. *J. Met.* **2017**, *69*, 365–380.
21. Pashkevich, M.A.; Petrova, T.A. Development of an operational environmental monitoring system for hazardous industrial facilities of Gazprom Dobycha Urengoy. *J. Phys. Conf. Ser.* **2019**, *1384*, 012040. [CrossRef]
22. Koteleva, N.; Kuznetsov, V.; Vasileva, N.V. Simulator for Educating the Digital Technologies Skills in Industry. Part One. Dynamic Simulation of Technological Processes. *Appl. Sci.* **2021**, *11*, 10885. [CrossRef]
23. Qili, W.; Binbin, J.; Mingquan, Y.; Min, H.; Xiaochuan, L.; Komarneni, S. Numerical simulation of the flow and erosion behavior of exhaust gas and particles in polysilicon reduction furnace. *Sci. Rep.* **2020**, *10*, 1909. [CrossRef] [PubMed]
24. Vasilyeva, M.A.; Vöth, S. Multiphysical Model of heterogeneous flow moving along a channel of variable cross-section. *J. Min. Inst.* **2017**, *227*, 558–562.
25. Beloglazov, I.; Morenov, V.A.; Leusheva, E.L. Flow modeling of high-viscosity fluids in pipeline infrastructure of oil and gas enterprises. *Egypt. J. Pet.* **2021**, *30*, 43–51. [CrossRef]
26. Belolgazov, I.I.; Petrov, P.A.; Martynov, S.A. Application of Production Processes Control Algorithm Using Adaptive Control System. In Proceedings of the International Russian Automation Conference (RusAutoCon), Sochi, Russia, 9–16 September 2018; pp. 1–4.
27. Hamzehloo, A.; Lusher, D.J.; Laizet, S.; Sandham, N.D. Direct numerical simulation of compressible turbulence in a counter-flow channel configuration. *Phys. Rev. Fluids* **2021**, *6*, 094603. [CrossRef]
28. Sandham, N.D.; Johnstone, R.; Jacobs, T.C. Jacobs Surface-sampled simulations of turbulent flow at high Reynolds number. *Int. J. Numer. Methods Fluids* **2017**, *85*, 25. [CrossRef]
29. Modeling Transient Compressible Flow. *ANSYS Fluent Tutorial Guide*; Release 18.0; ANSYS, Inc.: Canonsburg, PA, USA, 2017; pp. 267–310.
30. Zhao, Y.; Akolekara, H.; Weatheritta, J.; Michelassib, V.; Sandberg, R. RANS Turbulence Model Development using CFD-Driven Machine. *J. Comput. Phys.* **2020**, *411*, 109413. [CrossRef]
31. Mishra, P.; Aharwal, K.R. A review on selection of turbulence model for CFD analysis of air flow within a cold storage. In Proceedings of the 2nd International Conference on Advances in Mechanical Engineering (ICAME 2018), Kattankulathur, India, 22–24 March 2018; Volume 402, pp. 1–9.
32. Kuhnen, J.; Song, B.; Scarselli, D.; Budanur, N.B.; Riedl, M.; Willis, A.; Avila, M.; Hof, B. Destabilizing turbulence in pipe. *Nat. Phys.* **2018**, *14*, 386–390. [CrossRef]
33. Salama, A. Velocity Profile Representation for Fully Developed Turbulent Flows in Pipes: A Modified Power Law. *Fluids* **2021**, *6*, 369. [CrossRef]
34. Duraisamy, K.; Iaccarino, G.; Xiao, H. Turbulence modeling in the age of data. *Annu. Rev. Fluid Mech.* **2019**, *51*, 357–377. [CrossRef]
35. Tania, S.; Ferreira, K.; Arts, T.; Croner, E. On the Influence of High Turbulence on the Convective Heat Flux on the High-Pressure Turbine Vane LS89. *Int. J. Turbomach. Propuls. Power* **2019**, *4*, 37.

Article

A Study of the Critical Velocity of the Droplet Transition from the Cassie to Wenzel State on the Symmetric Pillared Surface

Zhulong Wu, Yingqi Li, Shaohan Cui, Xiao Li, Zhihong Zhou * and Xiaobao Tian

College of Architecture and Environment, Sichuan University, Chengdu 610065, China
* Correspondence: zhouzhihong@scu.edu.cn; Tel.: +86-199-8334-5630

Abstract: A droplet hitting a superhydrophobic surface will undergo the Cassie to Wenzel transition when the wetting force exceeds the anti-wetting force. The critical velocity of the droplet's Cassie to Wenzel state transition can reflect the wettability of the surface. However, the critical velocity research is still at the microscale and has not been extended to the nanoscale mechanism. A cross-scale critical velocity prediction model for superhydrophobic surfaces with symmetric structures is proposed here based on a mechanical equilibrium system. The model's applicability is verified by experimental data. It demonstrates that the mechanical equilibrium system of droplet impact with capillary pressure and Laplace pressure as anti-wetting forces is more comprehensive, and the model proposed in this study predicts the critical velocity more precisely with a maximum error of 12% compared to the simulation results. Furthermore, the correlation between the simulation at the nanoscale and the evaluation of the macroscopic symmetrical protrusion surface properties is established. Combined with the model and the correlation, the relationship between the microscopic mechanism and the macroscopic examination of droplet dynamics on the superhydrophobic surface be presented, and the wettability evaluation method of macroscopic surfaces based on the molecular simulation mechanism can be realized.

Keywords: droplet impact; superhydrophobic surface; critical velocity; Cassie to Wenzel transition; cross-scale

Citation: Wu, Z.; Li, Y.; Cui, S.; Li, X.; Zhou, Z.; Tian, X. A Study of the Critical Velocity of the Droplet Transition from the Cassie to Wenzel State on the Symmetric Pillared Surface. *Symmetry* **2022**, *14*, 1891. https://doi.org/10.3390/sym14091891

Academic Editors: Rudolf Kawalla and Beloglazov Ilya

Received: 1 August 2022
Accepted: 5 September 2022
Published: 9 September 2022

Publisher's Note: MDPI stays neutral with regard to jurisdictional claims in published maps and institutional affiliations.

Copyright: © 2022 by the authors. Licensee MDPI, Basel, Switzerland. This article is an open access article distributed under the terms and conditions of the Creative Commons Attribution (CC BY) license (https://creativecommons.org/licenses/by/4.0/).

1. Introduction

Cassie states and Wenzel states are two typical states of droplet impact on a superhydrophobic surface [1], as shown in Figure 1. A droplet that has transitioned from the Cassie state to the Wenzel state (C-W) shows bigger contact angle hysteresis and slip angle, which results in the gaps on the surface being occupied by droplets and the surface losing its superhydrophobic properties [2]. When the superhydrophobic properties of the surface are weakened, the surface is easily contaminated in the case of foreign body viscosity. It has been verified that the wetting force of the droplet will be larger than the anti-wetting force of the surface under a high enough impact velocity of the droplet, which causes the C-W transition of the droplet [3]. The study of the critical velocity of the droplet at the C-W transition is very important for many applications, such as anti-fogging of windshield glasses [4], medical cooling spray [5], anti-icing of aircraft and circuit surfaces [6,7], and anti-fouling of photovoltaic panels [8].

Therefore, efforts have been made to understand the mechanism of the C-W transition of the droplet using experimental methods, and many models have been proposed to predict the critical velocity of the C-W transition of the droplet. Reyssat et al. [3] found that the critical velocity of the C-W transition of the droplet was closely related to the structure distribution through an experiment of a droplet's impact on a pillared surface, and proposed a critical velocity model ($V = \sqrt{\gamma_{lv} h / \rho d^2}$, where γ is the surface tension of the droplet; h is the pillar height; ρ is the droplet density; d is the pillar spacing). Barolo et al. [9] analyzed the droplet impact on a model microfabricated surface and established a semi-quantitative model to predict the critical velocity of the C-W transition of the droplet based on the surface resistance. Jung et al. [10] observed the wetting behavior of the droplet impact on a pillared surface and proposed the critical velocity prediction model ($V = \sqrt{16\gamma_{lv}h/\rho d^2}$) by the relationship between the impact velocity of the droplet and the surface parameters, as shown in Figure 2b. Liu et al. [11] studied the critical parameter of the C-W transition of the droplet and established physical and mathematical models of the C-W transition of the droplet from the perspective of energy balance. The above models were based on the equilibrium between the inertial force and the Laplace pressure of the droplet. However, Shi et al. [12] concluded that whether a droplet underwent the C-W transition was determined by the competition between the inertia force of the droplet and the capillary force. Malla et al. [13] studied the wetting behavior of the droplet impact on a micro-grooved surface and established a critical velocity model based on the relationship between the impact velocity of the droplet and the groove spacing. Recently, Wang et al. [14] found in their experiments that the actual critical velocity of the C-W transition of the droplet was nearly 10 times higher than the theoretical value of the above models and proposed a standard for the C-W transition of the droplet based on the height of the droplet meniscus, as shown in Figure 2c.

Figure 1. The Cassie state and Wenzel state of a droplet on a pillared surface.

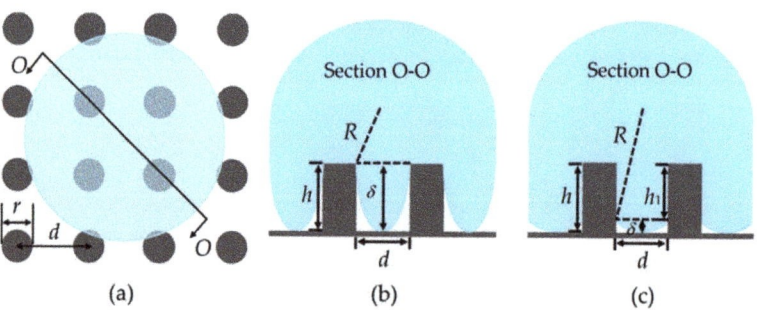

Figure 2. Diagram of meniscus height of the droplet: (**a**) Section position diagram; (**b**) the theoretical model by Jung [10]; (**c**) the theoretical model by Wang [14].

Although many critical velocity prediction models have been proposed, there is still a lack of tests available to evaluate the applicability of the models for a variety of superhydrophobic surfaces. In addition, such trial-and-error research is costly, time-consuming, and a waste of resources. Molecular dynamics (MD) simulation has been widely used to study the dynamics of droplets on superhydrophobic surfaces due to the advantages of high reliability, low cost, and a short research period [15,16]. Furthermore, the effects of droplet impact velocity, height, width, and spacing of the protrusion structure on the droplet wetting state have been studied deeply by MD simulation [17–20]. However, no critical velocity prediction model at the nanoscale has been reported so far. Furthermore, the results of MD simulation at the nanoscale are not practical because of the lack of correlation with the macroscale, which means the results of MD simulation cannot directly evaluate superhydrophobic surface properties at the macroscale. Thus, it is very important to establish the critical velocity prediction model of the C-W transition of a droplet at the nanoscale and explore the correlation between the nanoscale and the macroscale of a droplet's wetting behavior on superhydrophobic surfaces.

In this paper, the MD simulation method was employed to study the effects of nanopillar spacing and the droplet radius on the critical velocity of the C-W transition of a droplet. It was found that the capillary pressure and the Laplace pressure must be considered in the calculation of the critical velocity, and the critical velocity prediction model was established based on the mechanical equilibrium system at the C-W transition of a droplet, while its applicability was verified by the experiment data. In addition, the correlation between the nanoscale and the macroscale of the C-W transition of the droplet was proposed based on the model. Using the critical velocity prediction model and the correlation between the nanoscale and the macroscale of the C-W transition of the droplet, the MD simulation results can directly evaluate superhydrophobic surface properties at the macroscale.

2. Simulation Methodology

In this paper, the wetting behavior of droplets on a superhydrophobic surface was calculated by the MD simulation method. The impact model consists of a spherical droplet model and a substrate model with a nanopillar structure. Furthermore, the dimensions of the model box are 20 nm, 20 nm, and 25 nm in the x, y, and z directions, respectively, as shown in Figure 3. In the initial case, the positions of the centroid of the droplet and the nanopillar top surface are 0 and −50 Å, respectively. The eight-atom chain liquid molecular model that was often used to establish the molecular models of the polymer [21], silicone oil [22], and water [23] was used to establish the droplet model. It has been proven that the model can reflect the dynamic behavior and physical parameters of the liquid well and has been widely used in molecular dynamic simulation of wetting and flow at the solid–liquid interface. After the relaxation of the droplet model, the interatomic bond length of the chain liquid molecule is 1.54 Å, the bond angle of the chain liquid molecule is 109.5°, and the dihedral angle of the chain liquid molecule is 0. The extra interaction forces of the chain molecule model can force the atoms in a molecule together and reduces evaporation [24]. In addition, we used carbon atoms as monomers in chain molecules, which can significantly reduce the computational burden of the Coulomb force calculation. This method of building chain molecules using uncharged particles was used in many similar studies [23,25,26]. The single crystal Cu structure was used to establish the substrate model, and the lattice type of the substrate model is a face-centered cubic lattice, while the lattice constant is 3.615 Å.

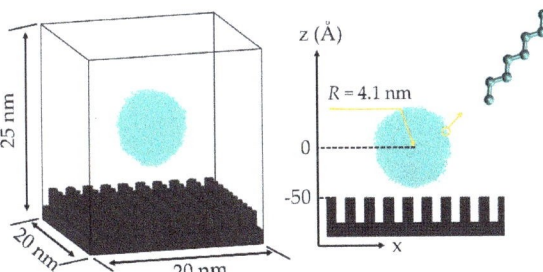

Figure 3. The three−dimensional droplet impact model.

In the process of MD simulation, the Velocity-verlet method [27] was employed to solve Newton's equation of motion of the particles in the system to obtain the velocities and positions of the particles, and the Lennard–Jones (LJ) potential was employed to calculate the force between unbonded atoms. The function is

$$U_{ij} = 4\varepsilon_{ij}\left[\left(\frac{\sigma_{ij}}{r_{ij}}\right)^{12} - \left(\frac{\sigma_{ij}}{r_{ij}}\right)^{6}\right], \quad (1)$$

where ε_{ij} is the interatomic interaction strength coefficient, r_{ij} is the distance between atoms, and σ_{ij} is the distance between atoms at equilibrium. In this paper, the interaction strength coefficients of liquid–liquid (ε_{ll}), solid–solid (ε_{ss}), and liquid–solid (ε_{ls}) atoms are 0.931, 0.582, and 0.087 kcal/mol, respectively, and the distance between atoms at equilibrium is 3.5 Å.

The Finite Extensible Nonlinear Elastic (FENE) potential was employed to calculate the force between bonded atoms, and the function is

$$E_{FENE}(r) = \begin{cases} -0.5KL_0^2 \ln\left[1 - \left(\frac{r}{L_0}\right)^2\right] & r \leq L_0 \\ \infty & r > L_0 \end{cases}, \quad (2)$$

where L_0 is the maximum distance the chain can extend and K is the elasticity modulus. In this paper, L_0 and K were calculated as $L_0 = 1.5\sigma_{ij}, K = 30\varepsilon_{ij}/\sigma_{ij}^2$ according to Ref. [21]. The surface tension of the droplet (γ_{lv}) was calculated by the Test-area method [28], and the surface tension of the droplet model at 298 K was calculated as 59.0×10^{-3} N/m.

LAMMPS software [29] was used to perform the MD simulations based on the above potential functions and parameters, and the NVT ensemble was used in the simulation process. The Nose–Hoover thermostat was used to keep the system temperature at 298 K, and the temperature damping coefficient was 100 fs. The base atoms remained fixed, and the truncation radius was set to 10 Å. The x and y directions were periodic boundaries, and the z direction was an aperiodic boundary. The time step was 1.0 fs. After the relaxation of 200 ps at 298 K, the droplet was loaded at a given initial velocity and the loading lasted 200 ps.

3. Results and Discussion

The effect of nanopillar spacing and the droplet radius on the critical velocity of the C-W transition of the droplet was investigated via MD simulation. Due to the scale effect, the nanoscale droplets require a higher initial impact velocity to deform similarly to the macroscale droplets [30]. As a result, in the MD simulation calculations, the initial velocity of droplets is nearly three orders of magnitude greater than that of macroscopic droplets to produce the Weber number (We) of droplets close to the macroscopic situation. In the calculations, the droplet impact velocity ranged from 180 m/s to 730 m/s. The contact angle was measured using the simulation results. To reduce the measurement error, the contact angle of the droplet on each surface was measured five times, and the final value was taken within the error range. Figure 4 shows the contact angle and the statistical error of each case in Table 1.

Table 1. The parameters of surfaces.

Case	Pillar Width r (Å)	Pillar Spacing d (Å)	Solid Area Fraction ϕ	Contact Angle θ
1	10.8 Å	9.0 Å	0.29	160
2	10.8 Å	12.6 Å	0.21	155
3	10.8 Å	16.2 Å	0.16	152
4	10.8 Å	19.8 Å	0.12	151
5	10.8 Å	23.5 Å	0.09	150.5

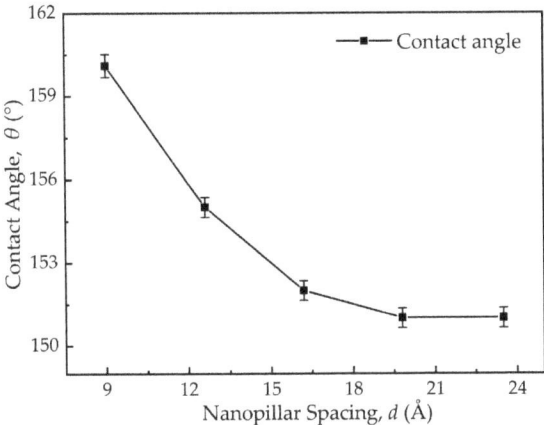

Figure 4. Measurement results and statistical errors of the contact angles of the droplet on the surface with different nanopillar spacing.

3.1. Effect of Different Pillar Spacing

Table 1 shows the parameters of different surfaces. Five cases were calculated to investigate the effect of different pillar spacing on the critical velocity of the droplet. The height of the pillar is 18 Å and the droplet models consist of 800 chain molecules with a radius of 41 Å in all cases. The impact process was recorded in the first 40 ps with a 10 ps interval as shown in Figure 5. It shows that the varying pillar spacing affects the wetting behavior of droplets significantly compared with the state of the five cases in 20 ps, and the droplet cannot wet the pillar gap when the spacing is 9.0 Å. Furthermore, the droplet's wetting state transitions from the Cassie state to the Wenzel state when the spacing increases to 19.8 Å. The calculation results are similar to that in Ref. [31]. The wetting state of the droplet impact on the nano-pillared surface was controlled by varying the initial impact velocity of the droplet. The impact velocity at which the droplet undergoes the C-W transition is the critical velocity. It also shows that the greater the nanopillar spacing, the smaller the critical velocity of the C-W transition of the droplet.

Then, the variation trend of the critical velocity and the capillary pressure were compared, as shown in Figure 6. The capillary pressure [32] can be calculated by

$$P_C = \frac{-4\gamma_{lv}\cos\theta_Y \phi}{r(1-\phi)}, \tag{3}$$

where ϕ is the area fraction of nanopillar structure on the surface, θ_Y is Young's contact angle, γ_{lv} is the surface tension of the droplet, and r is the pillar width. The results show that the capillary pressure decreases with the increase in the nanopillar spacing, and the variation trend is similar to that of the critical velocity. The air in the nanopillar gap is more easily replaced by the droplet as the nanopillar spacing increases, which reduces the hydrophobic properties of the surface. As a result, there is great relevance between the critical velocity of the C-W transition of the droplet and the capillary pressure of the surface. Therefore, capillary pressure plays an indispensable role in determining the critical velocity of the droplet.

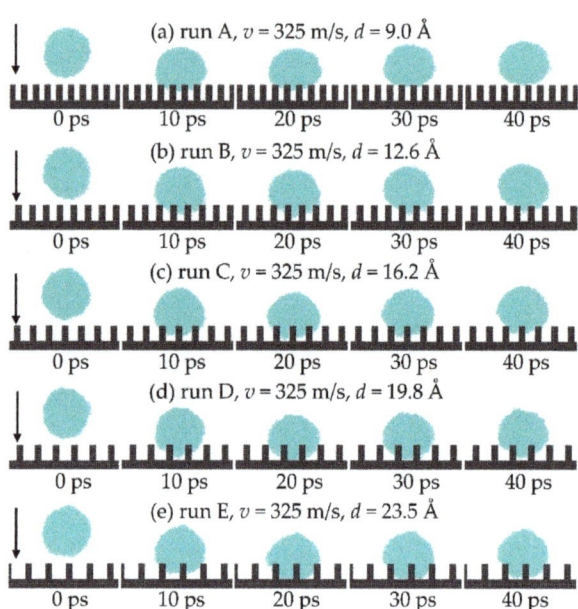

Figure 5. Comparison of the impact process for different nanopillar spacing: (**a**) 9.0 Å; (**b**) 12.6 Å; (**c**) 16.2 Å; (**d**) 19.8 Å; (**e**) 23.5 Å.

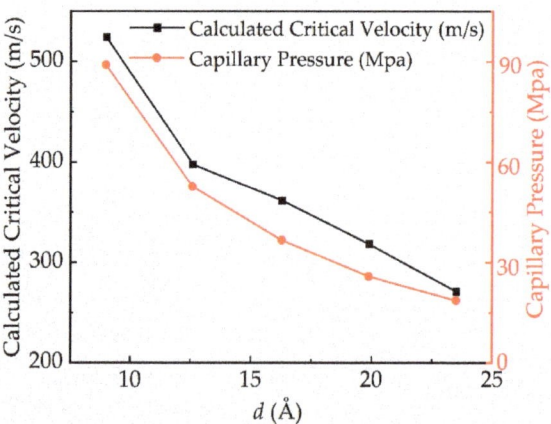

Figure 6. Curves of the critical velocity and capillary pressure with pillar spacing.

3.2. Effect of the Droplet Radius

Table 2 shows the parameters of the droplets. The droplet radius was varied by controlling the number of chain molecules. In cases 6 to 10, the nanopillar height, spacing, and width are 18 Å, 10.8 Å, and 12.6 Å on the surface, which are the same as in case 2.

The impact process was recorded in the first 40 ps with a 10 ps interval, as shown in Figure 7. The comparison of the wetting state of the droplet at 20 ps shows that the droplet can only wet the part of the gap on the surface when its droplet radius is 24 Å but reaches the Wenzel state when 41 Å. The phenomenon is the same as in Ref. [33]. As a result, the droplet radius significantly influences the wetting behavior of the droplet on the surface.

Table 2. The parameters of surfaces and droplets.

Case	Number of Atoms	Droplet Radius R (Å)
6	200	24
7	400	31
8	600	37
9	800	41
10	2000	45

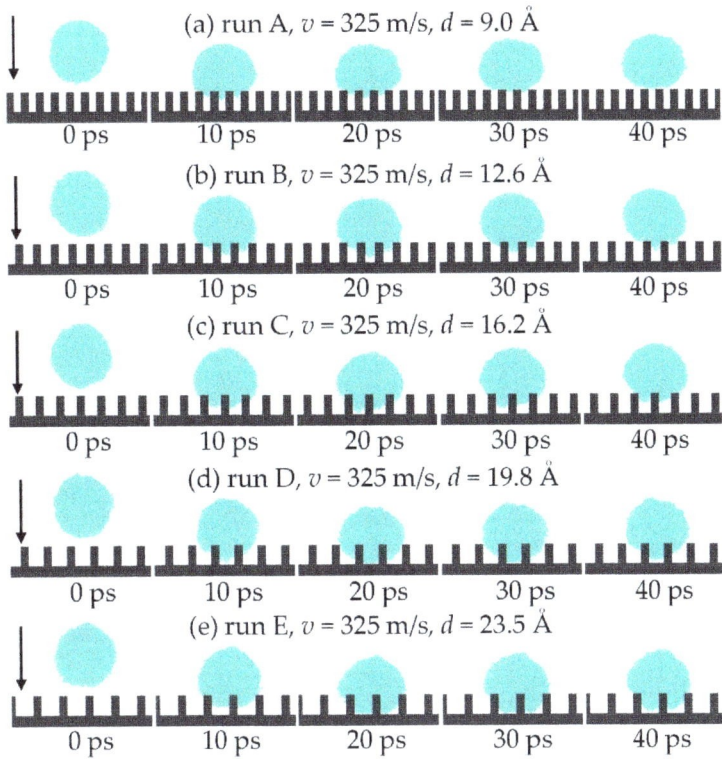

Figure 7. Comparison of the impact process for different droplet radius: (a) 24 Å; (b) 31 Å; (c) 37 Å; (d) 41 Å; (e) 45 Å.

The change in droplet critical velocity, Laplace pressure, and capillary pressure with droplet radius was calculated as shown in Figure 8. The Laplace pressure can be calculated by

$$P_L = \frac{2\gamma_{lv}}{R}, \qquad (4)$$

where the R is the droplet radius. The result shows that the bigger droplet can readily pin the gap in the surface and show the Wenzel state on the surface. The changing trend of the critical velocity and the Laplace pressure of the droplet is the same. Besides, the Laplace pressure and the capillary pressure are of the same order of magnitude. Thus, the Laplace pressure is part of the anti-wetting pressure and must be taken into account in the mechanical equilibrium system of the C-W transition of the droplet.

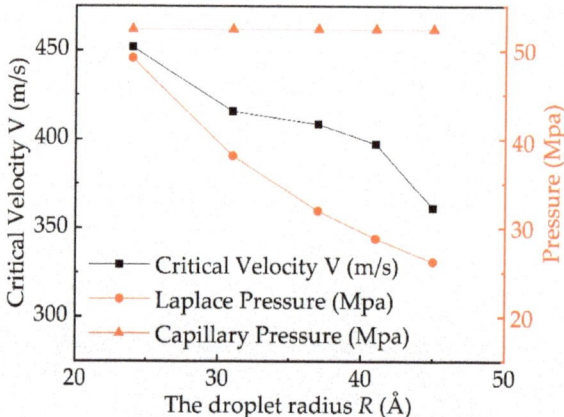

Figure 8. Curves of the critical velocity, Laplace pressure, and capillary pressure with droplet radius.

3.3. Components Critical Velocity Prediction Model

It is well known that the water hammer pressure generated by high-speed impact and the dynamic pressure generated by inertial force are the wetting forces during the process of droplet impact on a superhydrophobic surface. Furthermore, the expressions of the dynamic pressure and the water hammer pressure are

$$P_D = 0.5\rho V^2, \quad (5)$$

$$P_{WH} = k\rho CV, \quad (6)$$

where k is the coefficient of the water hammer pressure (obtained using k = 0.003 in Ref. [34]), ρ is the density of the impact droplet (obtained using ρ = 0.997 g/m³ in Ref. [35]), and C is the sound velocity in the liquid (obtained using C = 1497 m/s in Ref. [36]). In previous experiments, it was found that the action time of the water hammer pressure was shorter, but the magnitude of the water hammer pressure was much larger than that of dynamic pressure [10]. However, the maximum wetting depth of droplet impact on the surface can also be achieved in a short time [37]. Therefore, the water hammer pressure should not be neglected due to the short action time. In addition, the capillary pressure and the Laplace pressure are the anti-wetting forces. However, whether the capillary pressure or the Laplace pressure is used as the anti-wetting force, the mechanical equilibrium system is incomplete. It shows that considering the capillary pressure (the Laplace pressure) as the anti-wetting force alone means that the change in the droplet radius (the surface parameters) is independent of the anti-wetting force and the critical velocity of the C-W transition of the droplet based on Equations (3) and (4). This is contrary to some reports [31,33] and the calculation results in this paper.

Figure 9 shows the comparison of the critical velocity between the calculations in this paper and the predicted values of the five existing models, as shown in Table 3. "Model in study" presents the theoretical values of the model proposed in this study, and "Calculation" presents the calculated values by the MD method in Figure 9. The results show a significant difference. It is worth noting that model 1 and model 4 show a similar trend to the calculated results. Model 1 is established based on the competition between the dynamic pressure and the Laplace pressure. It causes that the predicted values of model 1 to be smaller than the calculations due to neglecting the capillary pressure. For model 4, the height of the protrusion structure is considered in the calculation of the capillary pressure, which results in the capillary pressure in model 4 being larger than the calculated value. Therefore, its predicted critical velocity values are larger than the calculated results. Compared with the calculation results, the model in this study has higher accuracy in predicting the critical velocity, with a maximum error of 12%.

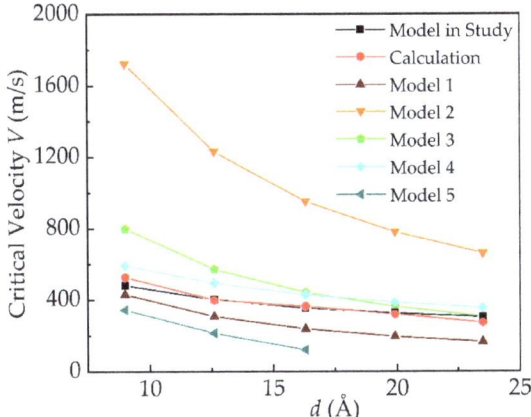

Figure 9. Comparison of the critical velocity between the calculated results and the predicted values of each model.

Table 3. Existing models for the critical velocity V based on impact parameters.

Model	Model Expression	Reference
1	$V = \sqrt{\gamma_{lv} h / \rho d^2}$	Reyssat et al. [3]
2	$V = \sqrt{16 \gamma_{lv} h / \rho d^2}$	Jung et al. [9]
3	$V = \sqrt{16 \gamma_{lv} (h - h_1) / \rho d^2}$	Wang et al. [10]
4	$V = \sqrt{-4\gamma_{lv}(r + h) \cos\theta_Y / \rho b h}$	Shi et al. [13]
5	$0.5\rho V^2 + k\rho C V + 2\gamma_{lv}/R = -4\gamma_{lv} \cos\theta_Y \phi / r(1 - \phi)$	Hu et al. [31]

Thus, the critical velocity prediction model of the C-W transition of the droplet was established based on the mechanical equilibrium system of $P_D + P_{WH} = P_C + P_L$ in this paper (P_D is the dynamic pressure, P_{WH} is the water hammer pressure, P_C is the capillary pressure, and P_L is the Laplacian pressure), as shown in Figure 10a, and the expression is

$$V = \sqrt{k^2 C^2 + \frac{4\gamma_{lv}}{\rho R} - \frac{8\gamma_{lv} \cos\theta\phi}{\rho r(1 - \phi)}} - kC, \qquad (7)$$

Figure 10b compares the balance of wetting pressure and anti-wetting pressure between the prediction models and the experimental data in Ref. [32]. It must be noted that not all models include the dynamic pressure, the water hammer pressure, the capillary pressure, and the Laplace pressure, but these models are based on a balance between the wetting force and resistance to wetting. The model proposed in this paper shows better agreement with the experimental data. Therefore, the critical velocity prediction model is applicable at the macroscale. However, the model can predict the critical velocity only when the contact angle of a droplet on the surface is known in practice. The most common method of obtaining the contact angle is test measurement, which is very troublesome. Fortunately, MD simulation can be employed to measure the contact angle of the droplet on the surface, which is consistent with the material and the solid area fraction (ϕ) of the macroscopic surface. As proposed by Cassie in the study of surface wetting [38], the contact angle of the droplet on a rough surface is unchanged when the material and the solid area fraction of the surface remain unchanged. Therefore, it is feasible to measure the contact angle of a droplet on a macroscopic surface using MD simulation and calculate the critical velocity according to Equation (7). In other words, the correlation between the simulation at the nanoscale and the evaluation of the macroscopic surface properties are valid.

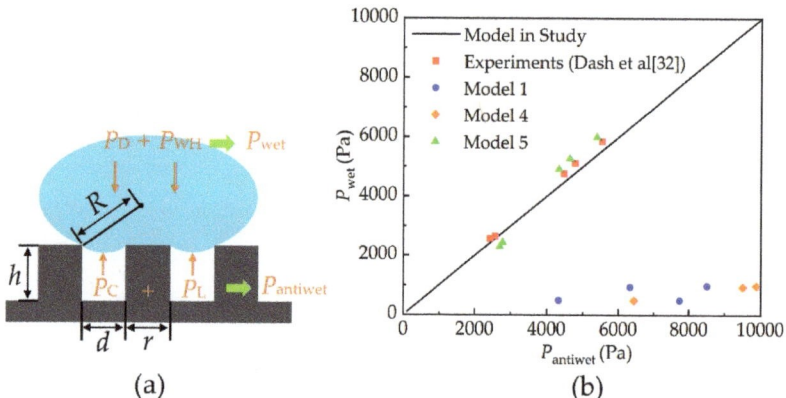

Figure 10. (a) Schematic diagram of mechanical equilibrium mechanism of droplet wetting surface; (b) comparison of the balance of wetting pressure and anti-wetting pressure between the prediction models and the experiment data in Ref. [32].

Based on the model and the correlation, the transformation relationship between the macroscopic test and micro-nano-scale mechanism of the studies of the wetting behavior of a droplet on a surface and the coupling relationship between molecular-scale calculation mechanism and macroscopic experimental performance were realized, and the wettability evaluation method of a macroscopic surface based on the molecular simulation mechanism was presented. By predicting the critical velocity, the wetting resistance of superhydrophobic surfaces can be rapidly evaluated. In addition, the impact velocity of pollutants on the surface of different applications is different in different environments, and this model can provide a theoretical basis for the design of superhydrophobic surfaces for different applications.

However, it must be noted that this model can only be applied to surfaces with symmetric structures. When a droplet impacts an asymmetric surface, the capillary pressure will change with the location of the droplet impact, which is the factor that cannot be calculated by this model.

4. Conclusions

In this paper, the effect of the nanopillar spacing and the droplet radius on the critical velocity of the C-W transition of the droplet was examined. In addition, the critical velocity prediction model was proposed based on the mechanical equilibrium system of the C-W transition of the droplet. The study conclusions are as follows:

1. The capillary pressure and the Laplace pressure should be considered in the calculation of the critical velocity of the C-W transition of the droplet. Furthermore, a critical velocity prediction model was proposed based on the mechanical equilibrium system including the capillary pressure and the Laplace pressure. The model can predict the critical velocity more accurately and be applied across scales.
2. The correlation between the simulation at the nanoscale and the evaluation of the macroscopic symmetrical protrusion surface properties were presented. This correlation can be used to guide the parameters set in the MD simulation.
3. This study established a method to directly evaluate the wettability of a surface based on the results of the MD simulation and has practical application value for the design and research of superhydrophobic surfaces.

Author Contributions: Conceptualization, Z.W. and Z.Z.; methodology, Y.L. and X.L.; software, S.C.; validation, Z.W. and S.C.; investigation, Z.W.; resources, Y.L. and Z.Z.; data curation, X.T.; writing—original draft preparation, Z.W., Z.Z. and X.T.; writing—review and editing, Z.W., X.L. and S.C.; visualization, S.C. All authors have read and agreed to the published version of the manuscript.

Funding: This research was funded by the National Natural Science Foundation of China, grant number 12072213, the National Science and Technology Major Project, grant number J2019-III-0010-0054, and the National Numerical Windtunnel, grant number NNW2019-JT01-023, Open Project of Key Laboratory of Icing and Anti/De-icing, grant number IDAL202001.

Institutional Review Board Statement: Not applicable.

Informed Consent Statement: Not applicable.

Data Availability Statement: Not applicable.

Acknowledgments: I am grateful to Zhihong Zhou, Yingqi Li, Xiao Li, Xiaobao Tian, and Shaohan Cui for their strong support.

Conflicts of Interest: The authors declare no conflict of interest.

References

1. Li, X.M.; Reinhoudt, D.; Crego-Calama, M. What Do We Need for a Superhydrophobic Surface? A Review on the Recent Progress in the Preparation of Superhydrophobic Surfaces. *Chem. Soc. Rev.* **2007**, *38*, 1350–1368. [CrossRef] [PubMed]
2. Geyer, F.; D'Acunzi, M.; Sharifi-Aghili, A.; Saal, A.; Gao, N.; Kaltbeitzel, A.; Sloot, T.; Berger, R.; Butt, H.J.; Vollmer, D. When and how self-cleaning of superhydrophobic surfaces works. *Sci Adv* **2020**, *6*, eaaw9297. [CrossRef] [PubMed]
3. Reyssat, M.; Pépin, A.; Marty, F.; Chen, Y.; Quéré, D. Bouncing transitions on microtextured materials. *EPL* **2006**, *74*, 306–312. [CrossRef]
4. Yasmeen, S.; Yoon, J.; Moon, C.H.; Khan, R.; Gaiji, H.; Shin, S.; Oh, I.; Lee, H. Self-Formation of Superhydrophobic Surfaces through Interfacial Energy Engineering between Liquids and Particles. *Langmuir* **2021**, *37*, 5356–5363. [CrossRef] [PubMed]
5. Zhang, X.; Liu, X.; Wu, X.; Min, J.C. Impacting-freezing dynamics of a supercooled water droplet on a cold surface: Rebound and adhesion. *Int. J. Heat Mass Transf.* **2020**, *158*, 119997. [CrossRef]
6. Morita, K.; Kimura, S.; Sakaue, H. Hybrid System Combining Ice-Phobic Coating and Electrothermal Heating for Wing Ice Protection. *Aerospace* **2020**, *7*, 102. [CrossRef]
7. Dalili, N.; Edrisy, A.; Carriveau, R. A review of surface engineering issues critical to wind turbine performance. *Renew. Sust. Energ. Rev.* **2009**, *13*, 428–438. [CrossRef]
8. Bergin, M.H.; Ghoroi, C.; Dixit, D.; Schauer, J.J.; Shindell, D.T. Large Reductions in Solar Energy Production Due to Dust and Particulate Air Pollution. *Env. Sci. Tech. Let.* **2017**, *4*, 339–344. [CrossRef]
9. Bartolo, D.; Bouamrirene, F.; Verneuil, É.; Buguin, A.; Silberzan, P.; Moulinet, S. Bouncing or sticky droplets: Impalement transitions on superhydrophobic micropatterned surfaces. *EPL* **2006**, *74*, 299–305. [CrossRef]
10. Jung, Y.C.; Bhushan, B. Dynamic Effects of Bouncing Water Droplets on Superhydrophobic Surfaces. *Langmuir* **2008**, *24*, 6262–6269. [CrossRef]
11. Liu, T.Q.; Li, Y.J.; Li, X.Q.; Sun, W. Theoretical analysis of droplet transition from Cassie to Wenzel state. *Chin. Phys. B* **2015**, *24*, 116801. [CrossRef]
12. Shi, S.; Lv, C.; Zheng, Q. Drop Impact on Two-Tier Monostable Superrepellent Surfaces. *ACS Appl. Mater. Interfaces* **2019**, *11*, 43698–43707. [CrossRef] [PubMed]
13. Malla, L.K.; Patil, N.D.; Bhardwaj, R.; Neild, A. Droplet Bouncing and Breakup during Impact on a Microgrooved Surface. *Langmuir* **2017**, *33*, 9620–9631. [CrossRef] [PubMed]
14. Wang, L.Z.; Zhou, A.; Zhou, J.Z.; Chen, L.; Yu, Y.S. Droplet impact on pillar-arrayed non-wetting surfaces. *Soft Matter* **2021**, *17*, 5932–5940. [CrossRef]
15. Lv, S.H.; Yang, Z.; Duan, Y.Y. Retraction kinetics of impacting nanodroplets on hydrophobic surfaces: A molecular dynamics simulation study. *J. Mol. Liq.* **2021**, *341*, 116936. [CrossRef]
16. Karplus, M.; McCammon, J.A. Molecular dynamics simulations of biomolecules. *Nat. Struct. Biol.* **2002**, *9*, 646–652. [CrossRef]
17. Ambrosia, M.S.; Ha, M.Y.; Balachandar, S. The effect of pillar surface fraction and pillar height on contact angles using molecular dynamics. *Appl. Surf. Sci.* **2013**, *282*, 211–216. [CrossRef]
18. Wang, L.W.; Zhang, R.; Zhang, X.W.; Hao, P.F. Numerical simulation of droplet impact on textured surfaces in a hybrid state. *Microfluid. Nanofluid.* **2017**, *21*, 61. [CrossRef]
19. Di, J.W.; Yang, Z.; Duan, Y.Y. Molecular dynamics simulation of nanosized water droplet spreading on chemically heterogeneous surfaces. *Langmuir* **2019**, *9*, 125105. [CrossRef]
20. Hiratsuka, M.; Emoto, M.; Konno, A.; Ito, S. Molecular Dynamics Simulation of the Influence of Nanoscale Structure on Water Wetting and Condensation. *Micromachines* **2019**, *10*, 587. [CrossRef]

21. Kurt, K.; Gary, S.G. Dynamics of entangled linear polymer melts: A molecular-dynamics simulation. *J. Chem. Phys.* **1990**, *92*, 5057–5086. [CrossRef]
22. Fan, J.C.; Wang, F.C.; Chen, J.; Zhu, Y.B.; Lu, D.T.; Liu, H.; Wu, H.A. Molecular mechanism of viscoelastic polymer enhanced oil recovery in nanopores. *Roy. Soc. Open Sci.* **2018**, *5*, 180076. [CrossRef] [PubMed]
23. Chen, H.; Nie, Q.C.; Fang, H.S. Many-body dissipative particle dynamics simulation of Newtonian and non-Newtonian nanodroplets spreading upon flat and textured substrates. *Appl. Surf. Sci.* **2020**, *519*, 146250. [CrossRef]
24. de Ruijter, M.J.; Blake, T.D.; De Coninck, J. Dynamic Wetting Studied by Molecular Modeling Simulations of Droplet Spreading. *Langmuir* **1999**, *15*, 7836–7847. [CrossRef]
25. Theodorakis, P.E.; Amirfazli, A.; Hu, B.; Che, Z.Z. Droplet Control Based on Pinning and Substrate Wettability. *Langmuir* **2021**, *37*, 4248–4255. [CrossRef]
26. Li, Z.; Liao, K.; Liao, F.Y.; Xiao, Q.X.; Jiang, F.; Zhang, X.R.; Liu, B.; Sun, C.Y.; Chen, G.J. Wetting and Spreading Behaviors of Nanodroplets: The Interplay Among Substrate Hydrophobicity, Roughness, and Surfactants. *J. Phy. Chem. C* **2016**, *120*, 15209–15215. [CrossRef]
27. Maroo, S.C.; Chung, J.N. Nano-Droplet Impact on a Homogenous Surface Using Molecular Dynamics. In Proceedings of the ASME 2008 3rd Energy Nanotechnology International Conference Collocated with the Heat Transfer, Fluids Engineering, and Energy Sustainability Conferences, Jacksonville, FL, USA, 5 June 2008; pp. 113–121.
28. Nair, A.R.; Sathian, S.P. A molecular dynamics study to determine the solid-liquid interfacial tension using test area simulation method (TASM). *J. Chem. Phys.* **2012**, *137*, 084702. [CrossRef]
29. Thompson, A.P.; Aktulga, H.M.; Berger, R.; Bolintineanu, D.S.; Brown, W.M.; Crozier, P.S.; in 't Veld, P.J.; Kohlmeyer, A.; Moore, S.G.; Nguyen, T.D.; et al. LAMMPS—A flexible simulation tool for particle-based materials modeling at the atomic, meso, and continuum scales. *Comput. Phys. Commun.* **2022**, *271*, 108171. [CrossRef]
30. Hu, H.B.; Chen, L.B.; Bao, L.Y.; Huang, S.H. Molecular dynamics simulations of the nano-droplet impact process on hydrophobic surfaces. *Chin. Phys. B* **2014**, *23*, 074702. [CrossRef]
31. Hu, A.J.; Liu, D. 3D simulation of micro droplet impact on the structured superhydrophobic surface. *Int. J. Multiphas. Flow* **2022**, *147*, 103887. [CrossRef]
32. Dash, S.; Alt, M.T.; Garimella, S.V. Hybrid surface design for robust superhydrophobicity. *Langmuir* **2012**, *28*, 9606–9615. [CrossRef]
33. Thanh-Vinh, N.; Isao, S. Maximum Pressure Caused by Droplet Impact is Dependent on the Droplet Size. In Proceedings of the IEEE 2019 20th International Conference on Solid-State Sensors, Actuators and Microsystems & Eurosensors XXXIII, Berlin, Germany, 23 June 2019; pp. 813–816.
34. Dae, H.K.; Sang, J.L. Impact and wetting behaviors of impinging microdroplets on superhydrophobic textured surfaces. *Appl. Phys. Lett.* **2012**, *100*, 171601. [CrossRef]
35. Koishi, T.; Kenji, Y.; Shigenori, F.; Toshikazu, E.; Zeng, X.C. Coexistence and transition between Cassie and Wenzel state on pillared hydrophobic surface. *Proc. Natl. Acad. Sci. USA* **2009**, *106*, 8435–8440. [CrossRef] [PubMed]
36. Martin, K.; Spinks, D. Measurement of the speed of sound in ethanol/water mixtures. *Ultrasound Med. Biol.* **2001**, *27*, 289–291. [CrossRef]
37. Khojasteh, D.; Kazerooni, M.; Salarian, S.; Kamali, R. Droplet impact on superhydrophobic surfaces: A review of recent developments. *J. Ind. Eng. Chem.* **2016**, *42*, 1–14. [CrossRef]
38. Cassie, A.B.D.; Baxter, S. Wettability of porous surfaces. *Trans. Faraday. Soc.* **1944**, *40*, 546–551. [CrossRef]

Article

Self-Optimizing Path Tracking Controller for Intelligent Vehicles Based on Reinforcement Learning

Jichang Ma, Hui Xie *, Kang Song and Hao Liu

State Key Laboratory of Engines, Tianjin University, Tianjin 300072, China; majichang@tju.edu.cn (J.M.); songkangtju@tju.edu.cn (K.S.); hao.liu@uisee.com (H.L.)
* Correspondence: xiehui@tju.edu.cn

Citation: Ma, J.; Xie, H.; Song, K.; Liu, H. Self-Optimizing Path Tracking Controller for Intelligent Vehicles Based on Reinforcement Learning. *Symmetry* 2022, 14, 31. https://doi.org/10.3390/sym14010031

Academic Editors: Rudolf Kawalla and Beloglazov Ilya

Received: 17 November 2021
Accepted: 17 December 2021
Published: 27 December 2021

Publisher's Note: MDPI stays neutral with regard to jurisdictional claims in published maps and institutional affiliations.

Copyright: © 2021 by the authors. Licensee MDPI, Basel, Switzerland. This article is an open access article distributed under the terms and conditions of the Creative Commons Attribution (CC BY) license (https://creativecommons.org/licenses/by/4.0/).

Abstract: The path tracking control system is a crucial component for autonomous vehicles; it is challenging to realize accurate tracking control when approaching a wide range of uncertain situations and dynamic environments, particularly when such control must perform as well as, or better than, human drivers. While many methods provide state-of-the-art tracking performance, they tend to emphasize constant PID control parameters, calibrated by human experience, to improve tracking accuracy. A detailed analysis shows that PID controllers inefficiently reduce the lateral error under various conditions, such as complex trajectories and variable speed. In addition, intelligent driving vehicles are highly non-linear objects, and high-fidelity models are unavailable in most autonomous systems. As for the model-based controller (MPC or LQR), the complex modeling process may increase the computational burden. With that in mind, a self-optimizing, path tracking controller structure, based on reinforcement learning, is proposed. For the lateral control of the vehicle, a steering method based on the fusion of the reinforcement learning and traditional PID controllers is designed to adapt to various tracking scenarios. According to the pre-defined path geometry and the real-time status of the vehicle, the interactive learning mechanism, based on an RL framework (actor–critic—a symmetric network structure), can realize the online optimization of PID control parameters in order to better deal with the tracking error under complex trajectories and dynamic changes of vehicle model parameters. The adaptive performance of velocity changes was also considered in the tracking process. The proposed controlling approach was tested in different path tracking scenarios, both the driving simulator platforms and on-site vehicle experiments have verified the effects of our proposed self-optimizing controller. The results show that the approach can adaptively change the weights of PID to maintain a tracking error (simulation: within ±0.071 m; realistic vehicle: within ±0.272 m) and steering wheel vibration standard deviations (simulation: within ±0.04°; realistic vehicle: within ±80.69°); additionally, it can adapt to high-speed simulation scenarios (the maximum speed is above 100 km/h and the average speed through curves is 63–76 km/h).

Keywords: autonomous vehicle; path tracking; reinforcement learning; adaptive PID; self-optimizing controller; vehicle control

1. Introduction

Autonomous driving is an active research topic that has attracted considerable attention from both academic institutions and manufacturing companies, owing to its broad application prospects in intelligent transportation systems. Automated vehicle software mainly involve environmental perception, decision planning, and motion control. Intelligent vehicles are non-linear motion systems, and their dynamic parameters change significantly with different speeds and road conditions, especially at high speeds of motion and during complex trajectories. This makes the path tracking control problem one of the most challenging aspects of this field. A closed-loop control system, which is composed of people, vehicles, and roads, as shown in Figure 1, is influenced by inevitable disturbances both inside and outside the vehicle, such as road adhesion coefficients, driving air resistance, and power output device, etc. As a result, the vehicle's model parameters change in real time, and there is a dynamic deviation between the vehicle's operating state and the desired state. Therefore, the human driver needs to constantly adjust the vehicle's state of motion to keep it on the desired path. The development process of the intelligent controller should learn the control mechanism of the human driver. With that in mind, the question of whether the path tracking controller can realize online self-optimization, according to the changes of the environment, is a key point for research.

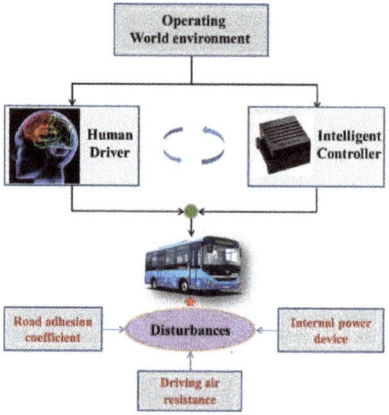

Figure 1. Closed-loop control system for vehicles.

There are many methods of providing state-of-the-art tracking performance, which can be divided into three typical categories, as follows: traditional classical control, model-based control, and intelligent adaptive control.

With regard to classic approaches, proportional–integral–derivative (PID) control is one of the most widely used methods in actual systems, with the advantages of a simple structure and easy implementation [1]. Previous studies [2,3] have presented an algorithm for using a PID controller to solve the path tracking problem for autonomous ground robots. Their results showed that the PID controller was capable of tracking a path. Regarding the traditional proportional–integral–derivative control strategy, due to the fixed constant PID control parameters, its application scenarios have limitations. A detailed analysis shows that a PID controller inefficiently reduces the lateral error under complex trajectories and variable speed conditions; when the road curvature is large, or when the vehicle is driving at high speeds, it is easy to deviate from the expected trajectory—as shown by the red arrows in Figure 2.

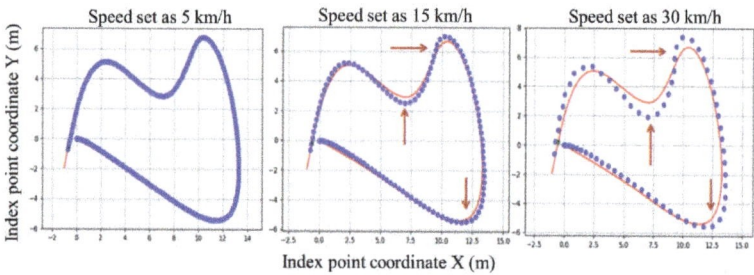

Figure 2. The performance of traditional PID control in different speed conditions.

As for the model-based categories, most of the proposed methods for path tracking control are based on modeling the vehicle dynamics [4–6], including the tire forces and the moments generated by the wheels. Some previous studies [7–9] have used model predictive control (MPC), in which an autonomous vehicle was directed to follow a pre-planned trajectory and a dynamic model of the system was used to predict an optimal sequence. However, MPC requires a heavy computational load, owing to its complex design. Therefore, this algorithm is unsuitable for high-speed autonomous driving and complex road trajectories. In [10], the authors modified the lateral dynamics of a vehicle and used a linear quadratic regulator (LQR) controller. A bicycle model was used to obtain the feedforward and feedback parts of the steering input. The optimal control parameters were obtained, based on a cost function. The authors of [11] compared and analyzed various control strategies for path tracking applications by running a vehicle model in a prescribed environment. In general, as described in the literature, the results may vary when additional control inputs, such as brake control and accelerator control, are brought into the system. We can conclude that complex trajectories and high-speed driving have important impacts on a vehicle motion model; thus, model-based controllers have limitations and can only be applied to simple roads in low-speed driving scenarios. In addition, intelligent driving vehicles are highly non-linear objects and a high-fidelity model is unavailable in most autonomous systems. As for the model-based controller (MPC or LQR), the complex modeling process may increase the computational burden; moreover, changes in model parameters may lead to a decrease in control performance. Therefore, for the vehicle motion control system, it is urgent to develop a tracking method with an adaptive and effective control framework for real-time implementation.

More recently, approaches in the third category—i.e., intelligent adaptive approaches—have been proposed to mitigate the aforementioned problems. These types of methods provide the ability to adapt; for example, they can undertake corrective control actions based on changes in the environment. Several studies have been conducted based on these methods, aiming to solve the problems noted above. A fuzzy controller with a parameter PID self-tuning module was introduced in [12,13] to provide a mobile robot with complete path tracking control; this showed advantages in providing a rapid response, high stability, and high tracking accuracy. However, the design of fuzzy adaptive PID control requires a significant amount of prior knowledge, and, in reality, it is difficult to obtain such comprehensive prior knowledge when a vehicle travels in unknown situations. An adaptive PID control method, based on neural networks, was presented in [14,15]. Nevertheless, a neural network generally uses supervised learning to optimize parameters, so it is also limited by some application conditions; for instance, it is difficult to obtain the exact teacher signal for supervised learning. Moreover, it does not work in real-time in the context of line optimization.

In order for automated vehicles to improve their adaptability, it is essential for them to interact with their environments and promote the natural evolution of a control policy. The essence of reinforcement learning is to learn an optimal control policy through interaction with the environment, which provides an effective way to solve the online optimization control problem of path tracking. In recent years, many exciting RL applications have been proposed in the context of self-driving vehicle control; for example, previous studies [16–18] proposed a framework for autonomous driving using deep RL. They adopted the deep deterministic policy gradient (DDPG) algorithm to manage complex road curvatures, states, and action spaces in a continuous domain and tested the approach in an open-source 3D car racing simulator called "TORCS" [19]. The Robotics and Perception Group at the University of Zurich created an autonomous agent for a GT Sport car racing simulator [20] that matched or outperformed human experts in time trials; this worked by defining a reward function for formulating the racing problem and a neural network policy for mapping input states to actions, then, the policy parameters were optimized by maximizing the reward function using the soft actor–critic algorithm [21]. Reference [22] introduced a robust drift controller based on an RL framework with a soft actor–critic algorithm and used a "CARLA" simulator [23] for training and validation. The controller was capable of making the vehicle drift through various sharp corners quickly and stably in an unseen map and was further shown to have excellent generalization ability. It could directly manage unseen vehicle types with different physical properties, such as mass and tire friction. Reinforcement learning, as a method for solving the optimization problem of continuous action space under uncertain environments, has also been extensively researched in the path tracking control process of UAVs and robots [24–30]. It is a data-driven control strategy that does not depend on the precise model of the controlled object [31]; therefore, the path-following control problem of autonomous vehicles can be quantitatively described as a sequential data optimization control problem [32–36].

The success of the deep RL algorithms proves that control problems can be naturally solved by optimizing policy-guided agents in a continuous state and action space. However, so far, RL research on automated vehicle control is mainly limited to simulation environments, such as TORCS, GT Sport, and CARLA, and only a few, comparably simple examples have been deployed in real systems, such as in references [37,38], which demonstrated the first applications of deep RL to realistic autonomous driving. In those studies, the RL agent evaluated and improved its control policy in a trial-and-error manner; thus, it would be dangerous and costly to train such an agent on a real vehicle; moreover, particularly with dynamically balancing systems, such a process is complicated and expensive.

Nevertheless, the generality of RL makes it a useful framework for autonomous driving. Most importantly, it provides a corrective mechanism for improving an online control policy, based on interacting with the environment. Thus, in this paper, a novel RL-based method is proposed for use in path tracking control. We demonstrate a self-optimizing controller structure incorporating a simple physics-based model and adaptive PID control based on RL; additionally, we present a newly developed approach for training an actor–critic network policy on a simulator and transferring it to a state-of-the-art realistic vehicle. This system can be used to track a path under complex trajectories and different speed conditions, and its performance is comparable to that of professional drivers. The main contributions of this paper are as follows:

- In this paper, we propose a self-optimized PID controller with a new adaptive updating rule, based on a reinforcement learning framework for autonomous vehicle path tracking control systems, in order to track a predefined path with high accuracy and, simultaneously, provide a comfortable riding experience.
- According to the pre-defined path geometry and the real-time status of the vehicle, the environment interactive learning mechanism, based on RL framework, can realize the online self-tuning of PID control parameters.
- In order to verify the stability and generalizability of the controller under complex paths and variable speed conditions, the proposed self-optimizing controller was tested in different path tracking scenarios. Finally, a realistic vehicle platform test was carried out to validate the practicability.

The remainder of this paper is organized as follows. In Section 2, we introduce the vehicle dynamics and kinetics models and define the state–action spaces and reward function. In Section 3, we provide an overview of the proposed self-optimizing controller structure and then introduce the actor–critic framework and algorithm. In Section 4, we introduce the simulation system and realistic autonomous platform, describe the experimental settings, and analyze the test results. Finally, we draw conclusions in Section 5 and propose future work in Section 6.

2. Vehicle Dynamic Constraints and Reference Trajectory Generation

An intelligent vehicle is a multi-input and multi-output electrical system with non-linear characteristics, and it is difficult to construct an accurate dynamic model for it. In addition, the dynamic characteristics of the system are also affected by the operating speed and environment, especially for unmanned vehicles running at high speeds, and the dynamic parameters will change significantly with the vehicle speed. When accounting for the non-linearity and time-varying characteristics of an intelligent vehicle system, traditional control methods, based on PID, LQR, and MPC, experience difficulties in meeting the current control requirements. Moreover, the design of a path tracking controller should provide online learning and self-optimization abilities. Therefore, the development of intelligent control algorithms combining mechanism models and data-driven methods has become a popular research topic in the field of control engineering applications. Here, we discuss a self-optimizing controller, based on online RL, and show that a simple path tracking architecture can enable an automated vehicle to track a path accurately, while using a complex trajectory. The essence of this approach is to reduce the error between the vehicle and reference path by controlling the lateral and longitudinal movement of the vehicle. Therefore, the key is to calculate control variables that satisfy the constraints of the dynamic model and the geometric constraints of the actuator. The proposed self-optimizing control structure, based on RL, begins with the vehicle dynamic constraints, which are based on a simplified bicycle model. Schematics of the vehicle dynamic model and kinematic state model are shown in Figure 3a,b, respectively. As shown in Figure 3, XOY is the inertial coordinate system fixed on the ground and xoy is the vehicle coordinate system fixed on the vehicle body.

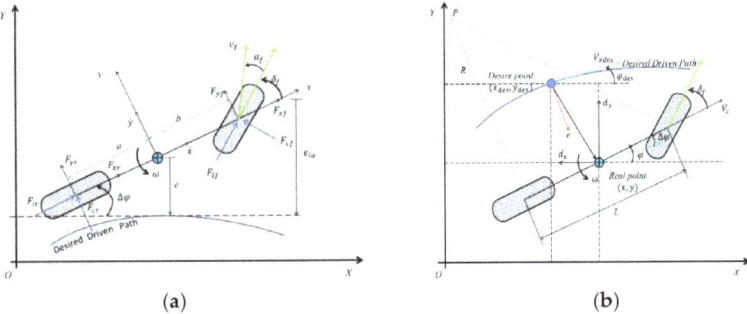

Figure 3. Schematic diagram of the vehicle model and description of the path tracking states. (**a**) Vehicle dynamics model; (**b**) vehicle kinematics model.

We can construct a 2 degrees of freedom (2-DOF) vehicle dynamic model for describing the motion of the vehicle, based on the following key assumptions [39,40]:

1. By ignoring the movement in the Z-axis direction, only the movement in the XY horizontal plane is considered; this is referred to as the planar bicycle model.
2. By assuming that the rotation angles of the tires on the left and right sides of the vehicle body are identical, the tires on both sides can be combined into one tire.
3. The rear wheels are not considered as steering wheels; only the front wheels are.
4. The aerodynamic forces are ignored.

The actuation of the steering angle, δ_f, at the front wheel results in the generation of lateral tire forces. According to Figure 3a, F_{cf} and F_{cr} are the two lateral forces acting on the front and rear tires, respectively, while a_f is the slip angle of the front wheel. The two lateral forces cause the vehicle to produce the yaw rate ω, which describes the angular rotation of the vehicle. In addition to the vehicle dynamics model constraints, two additional state variables are required, to account for the vehicle kinematics model, which shows the vehicle's position relative to the desired driven path. As shown in Figure 3b, the lateral path deviation, also referred to as the lateral error, e, is the distance from the vehicle's center of gravity to the closest point on the desired driven path. The vehicle heading deviation, also referred to as the heading error, $\Delta\varphi$, is defined as the angle between the vehicle's center line and a tangent line drawn on the desired driven path at the closest point. The specific descriptions and meanings of the remaining parameters are listed in Table 1.

Table 1. Specific definitions and meanings of the vehicle model parameters.

Symbol	Parameter	Units
F_{lf}, F_{lr}	Front and rear tires longitudinal force	N
F_{cf}, F_{cr}	Front and rear tires lateral force	N
F_{xf}, F_{xr}	Front and rear tires force in the x direction	N
F_{yf}, F_{yr}	Front and rear tires force in the y direction	N
a	Front axle to center of gravity (CG)	m
b	Rear axle to CG	m
δ_f	Steer angle input	Rad
a_f	Front tire slip	rad
ω	Yaw rate	rad/s
e	Lateral path deviation	m
$\Delta\varphi$	Vehicle heading deviation	rad
V_x	Longitudinal velocity	m/s

Figure 1 depicts a diagram of the two-wheel vehicle model, which considers the longitudinal, lateral, and yaw motions. By analyzing the forces on the x-axis, y-axis, and z-axis, respectively, the equations of motion for the 2-DOF states are given as follows:

$$X - \text{axis direction } ma_x = 2\left(F_{xf} + F_{xr}\right) \quad Y - \text{axis direction } ma_y = 2\left(F_{yf} + F_{yr}\right) \quad Z - \text{axis direction } I_z\dot{\omega} = 2aF_{yf} - 2bF_{yr} \quad (1)$$

The acceleration in the Y-axis direction consists of two aspects: the displacement acceleration, $\ddot{y}$, and centripetal acceleration, $V_x \cdot \omega$. Then, Formula (1) can be rewritten as follows:

$$m(\ddot{y} + V_x \cdot \omega) = 2\left(F_{yf} + F_{yr}\right) \quad (2)$$

According to the lateral force of the tire, the slip angle of the front wheel is $\alpha_f = \delta - \delta_f$, where δ is front wheel angle, and δ_f is the angle between the front wheel speed direction and the vehicle speed direction. Then, the lateral force experienced by the front wheels can be expressed as follows:

$$F_{yf} = C_{af}\left(\delta - \delta_f\right) \quad (3)$$

Similarly, the lateral force of the rear wheel can be expressed as $F_{yr} = C_{ar}(-\delta_r)$, where C_{af} and C_{ar} are the cornering stiffness values of the front and rear wheels, respectively. δ_f and δ_r can be approximated by the following formula:

$$\delta_f = (V_y + a\omega)/V_x \quad \delta_r = (V_y - b\omega)/V_x \quad (4)$$

As shown in Figure 3b, e is the lateral path deviation, $\Delta\varphi$ is the vehicle heading deviation, φ is vehicle heading angle, and φ_{des} is the road desired heading angle. According to the kinematic formula, the desired angular velocity required by the vehicle at the turning radius R can be denoted as the following formula:

$$\Delta\varphi = \varphi - \varphi_{des} \quad \dot{\varphi}_{des} = V_x/R \quad (5)$$

The desired lateral acceleration required by the vehicle at the turning radius R can be written as the following formula:

$$a_{ydes} = V_x^2/R \quad (6)$$

The lateral acceleration error is recorded as $\ddot{e}$, $\omega = \dot{\varphi}$.

$$\ddot{e} = a_y - a_{ydes} = (\ddot{y} + V_x\Delta\omega) - V_x^2/R = \ddot{y} + V_x(\dot{\varphi} - \dot{\varphi}_{des}) \quad (7)$$

That is:

$$\ddot{e} = \ddot{y} + V_x\Delta\dot{\varphi} \quad (8)$$

φ_{des} is the desired heading angle of the reference driven path and is calculated using the path planning formula, as follows:

$$\dot{\varphi}_{des} = V_x/R = V_x * K \quad (9)$$

where K is the desired road curvature, which can be obtained from the collected high-precision map data. Substituting Formulas (5) and (9) into Formula (1) can obtain the following expression of $\Delta\ddot{\varphi}$:

$$\Delta\ddot{\varphi} = \frac{2aF_{yf} - 2bF_{yr}}{I_z} - K\dot{V}_x - \dot{K}V_x \tag{10}$$

$$\begin{cases} e = d_x * \cos\varphi_{des} + d_y * \sin\varphi_{des} \\ \dot{e} = V_x * \sin\Delta\varphi \\ \Delta\varphi = \varphi - \varphi_{des} \\ \Delta\dot{\varphi} = \dot{\varphi} - \dot{\varphi}_{des} \end{cases} \tag{11}$$

Here, e is the lateral error, $\dot{e}$ is the rate of the lateral error, $\Delta\varphi$ is the heading error, and $\Delta\dot{\varphi}$ is the rate of the heading error. φ is the heading angle of the vehicle body, which can be obtained using a vehicle-mounted inertial measurement unit (IMU) sensor.

$$\begin{cases} \dot{X} = AX + Bu \\ Y = CX + Du \end{cases} \tag{12}$$

According to the state space Equation (12), the dynamic model of the steering wheel control can be obtained as follows:

$$\frac{d}{dt}\begin{bmatrix} e \\ \dot{e} \\ \Delta\varphi \\ \Delta\dot{\varphi} \end{bmatrix} = \begin{bmatrix} 0 & 1 & 0 & 0 \\ 0 & A_1/V_x & -A_1 & A_2/V_x \\ 0 & 0 & 0 & 1 \\ 0 & A_3/V_x & -A_3 & A_4/V_x \end{bmatrix}\begin{bmatrix} e \\ \dot{e} \\ \Delta\varphi \\ \Delta\dot{\varphi} \end{bmatrix} + \begin{bmatrix} 0 \\ B_1 \\ 0 \\ B_2 \end{bmatrix}\delta + \begin{bmatrix} 0 \\ \frac{A_2}{V_x} - V_x \\ 0 \\ A_4/V_x \end{bmatrix}\dot{\varphi}_{des} \tag{13}$$

For the above calculations, a, b, and c are, respectively, determined as follows:

$$\begin{cases} A_1 = -2(C_{af} + C_{ar})/m \\ A_2 = -2(C_{af}l_f - C_{ar}l_r)/m \\ A_3 = -2(C_{af}l_f - C_{ar}l_r)/I_z \\ A_4 = -2(C_{af}l_f^2 + C_{ar}l_r^2)/I_z \end{cases} \tag{14}$$

$$\begin{cases} B_1 = 2C_{af}/m \\ B_2 = 2C_{af}l_f/I_z \end{cases} \tag{15}$$

The time series data, e, $\dot{e}$, $\Delta\varphi$, $\Delta\dot{\varphi}$, are taken as the state variables, while δ is the control variable. Aiming at the path tracking control problem of automatic driving, the conventional PID control law is expressed as follows:

$$u(t) = K_{p1}e(t) + K_{d1}\dot{e}(t) - K_{p2}\Delta\varphi(t) - K_{d2}\Delta\dot{\varphi}(t) \tag{16}$$

Here, K_p and K_d are the proportional and differential gain coefficients, respectively.

The above traditional PID control is just a preliminary approach under ideal dynamics models; however, the dynamic characteristics of the system will, in fact, be affected by the operating speed and environment. Especially for unmanned vehicles running at a high speed, the dynamic parameters can change significantly with the vehicle speed, making it difficult for automatic path tracking control to guarantee performance and stability over a wide range of parameter changes. A key point of this paper is to set the path tracking process of an autonomous vehicle as a Markov decision process (MDP) of sequence data. Therefore, we need to accurately define the state space (S) and action space (A) and design a reward function (R) in combination with the vehicle dynamics model.

(a) **State space variable description**

The parameters of the state space are the environmental observation data S_t received by the controller at each time step. Many sensors are carried by driverless cars, including cameras, light detection units, ranging units, IMU, and GPS units. However, this paper focuses on path tracking control, where the control of vehicle position and pose is the key issue; therefore, the IMU and GPS output data are selected, together with the vehicle dynamic constraints, and we can obtain the state space variable S_t. Figure 3b demonstrates a desired driven path and the related error variables, which are the lateral track error, e, its time derivative, $\dot{e}$, the heading angle error, $\Delta\varphi$, and its time derivative, $\Delta\dot{\varphi}$. We use the parameters mentioned above to describe the state of the vehicle in a specific traffic scene, as given by $S_t = \{e, \dot{e}, \Delta\varphi, \Delta\dot{\varphi}\}$.

(b) Action space variable description

As mentioned above, the dynamic characteristics of the system will be affected by the operating speed and environment, especially for unmanned vehicles running at high speeds. To allow the system to automatically adapt to changes in the environment and parameters, we designed a self-optimizing PID controller based on an RL framework, in which control parameters could be adjusted automatically online, based on real-time performance requirements. The calculation can be expressed as follows:

$$K(t) = K_0 + \Delta K \quad (17)$$

In the above, K_0 is a constant vector, determined by expert experience, and ΔK is the self-learning gain vector. Thus, the traditional PID control (Equation (16)) can be rewritten, as follows:

$$u(t) = (K_{p1} + \Delta K_{p1})e(t) + (K_{d1} + \Delta K_{d1})\dot{e}(t) - (K_{p2} + \Delta K_{p2})\Delta\varphi(t) - (K_{d2} + \Delta K_{d2})\Delta\dot{\varphi}(t) \quad (18)$$

The control parameters are adjusted to realize the dynamic compensation of the system. We use the parameters mentioned above to describe the action space, which is given by $A_t = \{\Delta K_{p1}, \Delta K_{d1}, \Delta K_{p2}, \Delta K_{p2}\}$.

(c) Reward function description

As a key element of the RL framework, the reward signal drives the agent to reach the goal by rewarding good actions and penalizing poor actions. In a path tracking control task, the goal of the reward function design is to find the optimal control strategy for making the vehicle follow the reference trajectory as closely as possible while reducing the tracking error. To optimize the path tracking performance, in this paper we adopt a piecewise linear error reward function. Its design criteria are as follows:

$$R_{t1} = \begin{cases} k|y - y_D|, & |y - y_D| > e_1 \\ -c, & e_2 \leq |y - y_D| \leq e_1 \\ 0 & |y - y_D| \leq e_2 \end{cases} \quad (19)$$

Here, k, c, e_1, and e_2 are preset constants; $e_2 \leq e_1$, $k \leq 0$ is a proportional coefficient; and the lateral deviation is $e = |y - y_D|$, as shown in Figure 3b. The design goal of the above reward function is to make the vehicle's lateral deviation as close as possible to the given reference trajectory, which exhibits exponential convergence. In addition, by combining the constraints of the vehicle dynamics model to design the reward function, R_{t2}, such that the vehicle's heading deviation is parallel to the road curvature as much as possible (as shown in the figure), the reward function expression of R_{t2} can be expressed as follows:

$$R_{t2} = V_x \cos(\Delta\varphi) - V_y \sin(\Delta\varphi) - V_x|y - y_D| \quad (20)$$

As shown in Figure 4, the vehicle needs to drive along the centerline of the lane. In an ideal state, the lateral deviation, e, and the heading angle deviation, $\Delta\varphi$, between the center axis of the vehicle and the centerline of the lane, are close to zero in value. The objective of the controller is to minimize its lateral deviation, e, and heading angle deviation, $\Delta\varphi$, from the lane centerline. In the above, $\Delta\varphi$ is the heading angle deviation. The design principle of the reward function is based on maximizing the axial speed of the vehicle (V_x) and minimizing the lateral speed of the vehicle (V_y). We add a penalty term if the control object continues to deviate significantly from the center of the road (the third term);

this will greatly improve the stability of the control system. The final reward function is $R_t = R_{t1} + R_{t2}$. The optimization goal of the RL controller is to maximize the total reward, as follows:

$$J = \sum_{t=0}^{T} \gamma * R_t \tag{21}$$

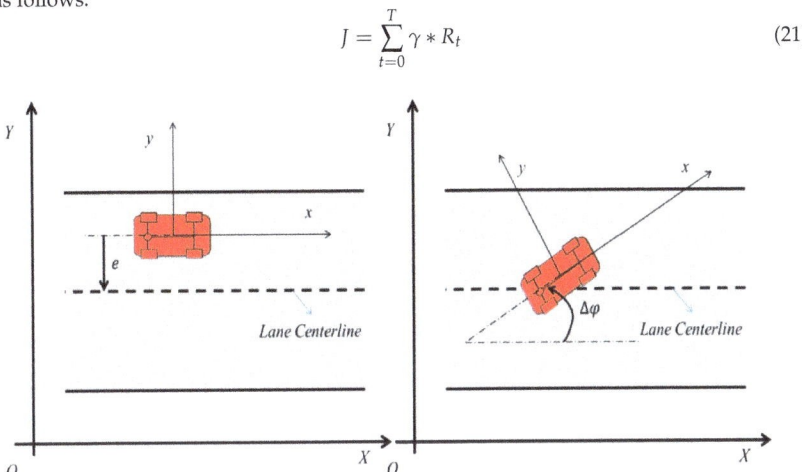

Figure 4. Schematic diagram of the vehicle lateral error deviation and heading angle deviation.

Here, γ is a discount factor and is usually a constant close to 1; in this paper, $\gamma = 0.95$. The objective of the controller is to maximize the total reward, J, and to minimize its lateral deviation (e) and heading angle deviation ($\Delta\varphi$) from the original lane. By optimizing the performance indicators, the state of the controlled system can be made to follow the reference state.

3. Self-Optimizing Path Tracking Controller Based on a Reinforcement Learning (RL) Framework

We aimed to find a control policy that minimizes the distance to the center line of the track for a given physical model and road trajectory, as well as for different vehicle speeds. In contrast to previous approaches relying on classical trajectory control, our approach leverages RL to train an actor–critic network that directly maps from observations and then provides an input to the adaptive PID controller, to calculate the vehicle control commands. To achieve this goal, we first introduced a physical model and defined a reward function for formulating the path tracking problem; these were used to perform the online adaptive tuning of the PID parameters so as to improve the path tracking effects of autonomous vehicles under complex road trajectories. In this paper, we show that, in a self-optimizing path tracking controller structure, based on reinforcement learning, the design of the controller has three advantages. Firstly, it introduces an online self-learning mechanism into the traditional controller, with the environment interactive learning mechanism, based on reinforcement learning, which can realize the optimization of PID control parameters. Secondly, it reduces the exploration space of the RL to find the optimal control parameters, which will greatly improve the learning efficiency. Thirdly, it breaks through the limitations of RL, in regard to only being used in simulation and game scenarios. To the best of our knowledge, this is the first demonstration of a deep RL agent driving on real autobus vehicle. In this section, we first present an overview of our proposed framework for the self-optimization controller and then describe each module. Our architecture consists of four modules, as follows: the operating environment, the data bridge, the RL framework, and the vehicle control module. Figure 5 shows the structure of the self-optimizing PID controller based on the RL framework.

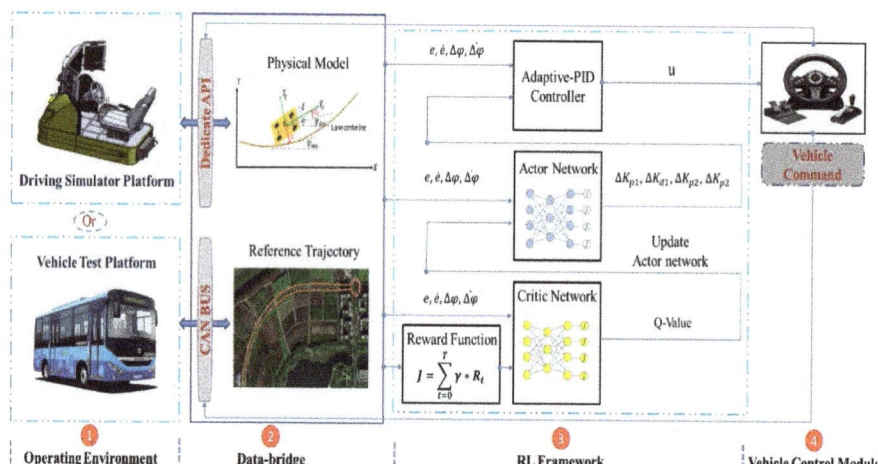

Figure 5. Structure of a self-optimizing proportional–integral–derivative (PID) controller based on a reinforcement learning (RL) framework.

The operating environment receives a series of actions from the vehicle control module, evaluates the quality of these actions, and converts them into a scalar reward, J, to be fed back to the RL framework using a data bridge.

The data bridge (or data buffer) allows for the interactions between the operating environment and the RL framework. Based on the physical model and reference trajectory, the current state values $S_t = \{e, \dot{e}, \Delta\varphi, \Delta\dot{\varphi}\}$ are extracted from the operating environment. The data bridge forwards the vehicle command (steering angle) to the environment object (driving simulator platform and vehicle test platform) for execution. After execution, the research object returns the corresponding reward value and the next state: S_{t+1}.

The RL framework consists of two parts: an actor network and a critic network. The actor network comprises a policy function, responsible for generating the actions, $A_t = \{\Delta K_{p1}, \Delta K_{d1}, \Delta K_{p2}, \Delta K_{p2}\}$. The critic network comprises a value function used to calculate the Q-value, which is responsible for evaluating the performance of the actor network, based on the DDPG algorithm, and for guiding the actor network to generate the appropriate actions, A_{t+1}, for the next state to maximize the future expected cumulative reward.

The vehicle control module receives the output, $u(t)$, from the self-optimizing PID controller and then forwards it to the environment object for execution, using the data bridge. To obtain the equations of motion for the self-optimizing controller, the expression of u is defined as Formula (18).

In the above, K_p, K_d are fixed gain constants, determined based on the developer's experience, while ΔK_p and ΔK_d are the output values of the actuator network and are used to adjust the fixed gain constant. The self-optimizing controller generates a time series control quantity $u(t)$ and acts on the steering wheel control command, for the vehicle to realize the adaptive ability in the path tracking control. Compared with traditional PID controllers (Equation (9)), our self-optimizing RL-based controller increases the system's ability to compensate for dynamic errors.

Summarizing the process in Figure 3, the self-optimizing PID controller, based on RL, is mainly composed of two parts, as follows: an actor network and a critic network. The actor network is a strategy function responsible for generating actions and interacting with the environment. The critic network is a value function responsible for evaluating the performance of the actor and guiding the output of the actor network in the next stage. Based on the content discussed in Section 2, the design of the reward function needs to consider the tracking performance of the system with regard to the reference trajectory and the constraints of the dynamic model. The calculation process and workflow architecture of the self-optimizing PID controller, based on RL, are as follows:

(1) Initialize the state of the controlled object, including the initial position and heading angle of the vehicle.
(2) Pre-set the parameters for the optimizing controller, including the weight of the actor–critic network, the learning rate, the discount factor, and the selection of the activation function.
(3) Adopt the DDPG algorithm to train the model, where the actor network outputs the PID gain, and the critic network maximizes the total reward value.
(4) According to the calculation formula for the self-optimizing PID controller, calculate the control commands.
(5) Use the time series control commands to act on the controlled object, while simultaneously observing the state of the environment at the next moment and calculating the reward function value.
(6) The actor network uses the DDPG algorithm to update its own weights. The critic network updates its weight, based on the mean squared error (MSE) loss function.
(7) If the system performance indicators meet the given requirements, or the maximum number of run episodes is reached, the training is terminated, the execution process is exited, and the experiment state is reset.

An overview of the workflow and architecture for the efficient training of the algorithm is shown in Figure 6.

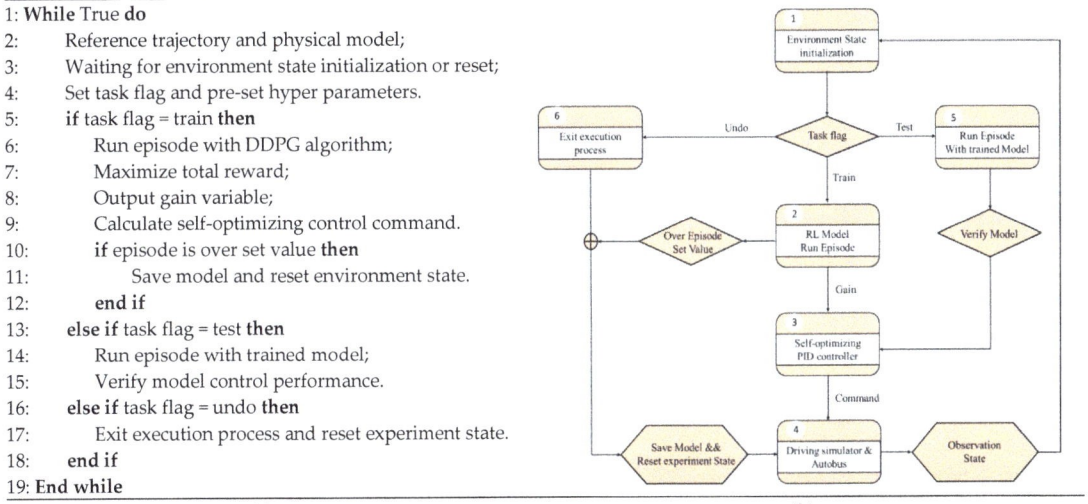

```
1: While True do
2:     Reference trajectory and physical model;
3:     Waiting for environment state initialization or reset;
4:     Set task flag and pre-set hyper parameters.
5:     if task flag = train then
6:         Run episode with DDPG algorithm;
7:         Maximize total reward;
8:         Output gain variable;
9:         Calculate self-optimizing control command.
10:        if episode is over set value then
11:            Save model and reset environment state.
12:        end if
13:    else if task flag = test then
14:        Run episode with trained model;
15:        Verify model control performance.
16:    else if task flag = undo then
17:        Exit execution process and reset experiment state.
18:    end if
19: End while
```
(a)   (b)

Figure 6. Outline of the workflow and the architecture used for efficiently training the algorithm. (a) Workflow for self-optimizing PID controller based on reinforcement learning. (b) Software execution architecture run episodes during model training or testing.

a. **Actor–critic network architecture design**

The objective of this research was to consider the path-following control problem as an optimal control problem for minimizing the lateral position deviation and lateral angle deviation of the controlled object from the reference trajectory. Summarizing the process in Figure 1, the self-optimizing PID controller in this study, based on the RL framework, mainly comprises two parts: an actor network and a critic network. The focus of the DDPG algorithm is on the design and optimization of the actor–critic network structure, with the aim of finding the optimal control strategy. Through the method of RL, the control policy of the agent is updated to maximize the value of the reward function. The actor network is a strategy function that is responsible for generating actions and interacting with the environment. The critic network is a value function that is responsible for evaluating the performance of the actor and guiding the output of the actor network in the next stage. Theoretically, a neural network with only one hidden layer is sufficient to achieve a global approximation and a description of the arbitrary nonlinear functions. In the process of training the model, a fully connected actor neural network and critic neural network are initiated to approximate the optimal control policy and true value function. Figure 7 presents the architectures of the actor and critic networks [41]. Both consist of three layers: an input layer, an output layer, and a hidden layer, with 600 neurons.

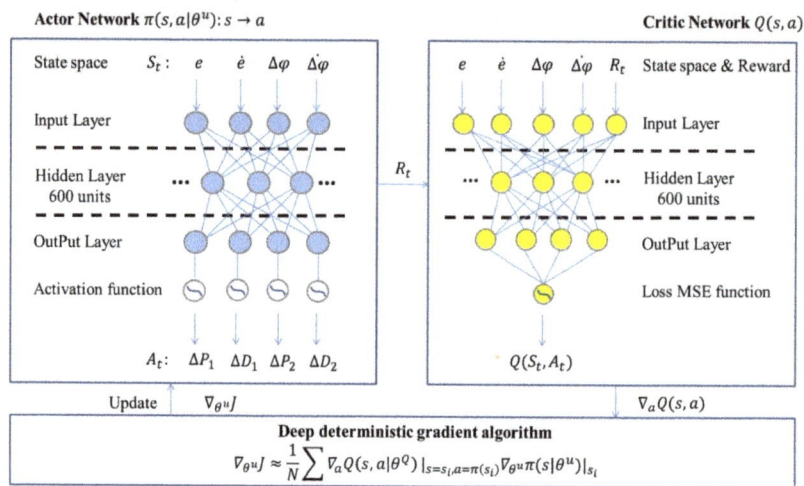

Figure 7. Architectures of the actor and critic networks.

The real-time environment state space data, $S_t = \{e, \dot{e}, \Delta\varphi, \dot{\Delta\varphi}\}$, from a virtual simulator and real-world autobus, are used as the original inputs to the deep RL, to solve the path tracking problem for autonomous vehicles. The actor network takes the preprocessed data as the input and connects with the fully connected layer; the sigmoid activation function is used to map the action directly to the range of $[-1, 1]$. The final output of the actor network represents the action space $A_t = \{\Delta K_{p1}, \Delta K_{d1}, \Delta K_{p2}, \Delta K_{p2}\}$. The critic network combines the reward value with the environment state as the input, connects through the fully connected layer, and finally outputs the Q-value. In this paper, the parameters of the networks were updated, based on the Adam [42] optimization algorithm. The DDPG algorithm [43] was employed to iteratively update the actor network weights, θ^u; the critic network weights, θ^Q, were updated to minimize the MSE loss function.

The input to the actor network is the number of features in the state space, whereas the input to the critic network is the sum of the state features and rewards. Both networks have only one fully connected layer between the input and output layers, with 600 neural units. The adopted hyper-parameters (parameters set prior to the training process) are presented in Table 2.

Table 2. Actor–critic network structure hyper-parameters.

Hyper-Parameter	Pre-Set Value
Actor network learning rate	0.001
Critic network learning rate	0.01
State space dimension	4
Action space dimension	4
Discount factor	0.95
Run max episode	200,000

The real-time environment state space data is $S_t = \{e, \dot{e}, \Delta\varphi, \Delta\dot{\varphi}\}$, so that state space dimension's pre-set value is 4; the final output of the actor network represents the action space, $A_t = \{\Delta K_{p1}, \Delta K_{d1}, \Delta K_{p2}, \Delta K_{p2}\}$, so that action space dimension's pre-set value is 4. Here, γ is a discount factor, and is usually a constant close to 1; in this paper, the discount factor's pre-set value is 0.95. In fact, with a larger γ, the agent considers more steps forward, but the difficulty of training is higher; whereas, with a smaller γ, the agent pays more attention to the immediate benefits, and the training is less difficult. In short, the principle of the value of the discount factor is to be as large as possible on the premise that the algorithm can converge. The learning rate of the actor–critic network in this article adopts the same default value as in Reference [43], where the pre-set values are 0.001 and 0.01, respectively.

b. RL deep deterministic policy gradient (DDPG) algorithm

The main research objective of this paper was to design an actor–critic network with a DDPG algorithm to control the path tracking behaviors of autonomous vehicles and characterize the adaptive ability, through considering different reference road paths and designing the reward function. The process of automatic driving path tracking control requires an autonomous agent system to address the current environmental situation and vehicle status and then implement comprehensive lateral and longitudinal control; the adaptive ability of the controller is especially important under variable speeds and complex reference trajectories. Therefore, in order to address more complex scenarios, a self-optimizing PID path tracking method for intelligent vehicles, based on RL, is presented. This is a typical data-driven and self-learning method that enables an agent to find an optimal control strategy to complete tasks through continuous "trial and error", while interacting with the environment and changes the action(s), based on a feedback reward system, based on the environment. The RL framework is used to solve practical engineering problems and can be described as an MDP [44–46].

In this paper, the environment state space and action space are continuous variables, so we define the tracking control problem as an MDP of the sequence data, which comprises a 5-tuple (S, A, R(s_t,a_t), P($s_{t+1}|s_t, a_t$), γ). As shown in Figure 8, S_t is the state space set and A_t is the action space set. At time step, t, the agent selects the action $a_t \in A_t$ by following policy π. After executing a_t, the agent is transferred to the next state, s_{t+1}, with the probability P($s_{t+1}|s_t, a_t$). Additionally, a reward signal, R(s_t,a_t), is received to describe whether the underlying action, a_t, is beneficial for reaching the goal. By repeating this process, the agent interacts with the environment and obtains a sequence of trajectories, $\tau = s_1, a_1, r_1, \ldots, s_T, a_T, r_T$, at the terminal time step, T. The discounted cumulative reward from each time step, t, can be formulated as $R_t = \sum_{t=1}^{T} \gamma^{t-1} r_t$, where $\gamma \in (0, 1)$ is a discount rate for determining the importance of future rewards. The goal is to learn an optimal policy, π^*, that maximizes the expected overall discounted reward under this strategy, which is defined as follows:

$$J = E_{s,a\sim\pi,r}\left[\sum_{t=1}^{T} \gamma^{t-1} r_t\right] \tag{22}$$

$$\pi^* = \underset{\pi}{\arg\max} E_{s,a\sim\pi,r}[R_t] \quad (23)$$

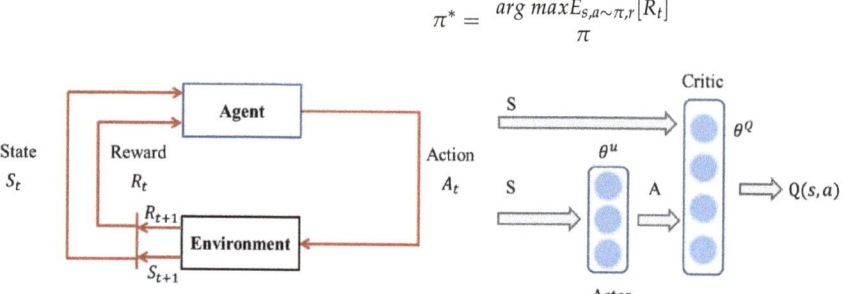

Figure 8. RL framework workflow diagram.

The framework of the actor–critic algorithm is based on the concept of the DDPG algorithm, which is widely used [47,48] and integrates the policy search and value function approximation theories. As illustrated in Figure 3b, the actor is used to adjust the network parameter, θ^u, and output determination action, A, based on the optimal control strategy, $\pi(s, a|\theta^u)$. The critic approximates the value function, $Q(s, a)$, and updates the network parameter, θ^Q. To iteratively update these neural network parameters until convergence in a near-optimal control policy, we employed the DDPG algorithm to iteratively update the actor network weights, θ^u. Additionally, the critic network weightings, θ^Q, were updated so as to minimize the MSE loss function. The updated calculations are as follows:

$$\nabla_{\theta^u} J \approx \frac{1}{N} \sum \nabla_a Q\left(s, a\big|\theta^Q\right)\bigg|_{s=s_i, a=\pi(s_i)} \nabla_{\theta^u} \pi\left(s\big|\theta^u\right)\bigg|_{s=s_i} \quad (24)$$

$$L\left(\theta^Q\right) = \frac{1}{N} \sum_i (y_i - Q(s_i, a_i|\theta^Q))^2 \quad (25)$$

$$y_i = r_i + \gamma Q'(s_{i+1}, \pi'(s_{i+1}|\theta^{u'})|\theta^{Q'}) \quad (26)$$

For the sake of achieving a more stable training process, a target actor neural network weighting parameter, $\theta^{u'}$, and target critic neural network parameter, $\theta^{Q'}$, were also initialized, and these were updated as follows:

$$\theta^{u'} \leftarrow \tau\theta^u + (1-\tau)\theta^{u'} \quad (27)$$

$$\theta^{Q'} \leftarrow \tau\theta^Q + (1-\tau)\theta^{Q'} \quad (28)$$

Here, τ is a hyperparameter that is pre-set to prevent the overfitting of these neural networks and to maintain the training stability. The pseudo-code programming process for the DDPG algorithm is presented in Algorithm 1.

The entire procedure is repeated until the optimal control policy is learned, and we use the same framework for both simulation and real-world experiments; the controller system learns basic path tracking skills to adapt to different reference trajectories and dynamic model parameters.

Algorithm 1. Pseudo-code programming process of the deterministic policy gradient (DDPG) algorithm

Actor uses a gradient algorithm to update the network parameters;
Critic uses the mean squared error (MSE) loss function to update the network parameters.
Algorithm input: Episode number, T; state dimension, n; action set, A; learning rate, α, β; discount, γ; exploration rate, τ; actor–critic network structure; randomly initialize the weighting parameter.
Algorithm output: Actor network parameters, θ^u, critic network parameters, θ^Q.
1: **for Episode from 1 to (Max Episode -1) do**
2:    Receive initial observation state, obtain environment state vector s_t.
3:    Initialize buffer replay data-buff.
3:    **for t from 1 to T do**
4:        Select action $a_t = \pi(s_t|\theta^u) + \mathcal{N}_t$.
5:        Execute action a_t and observe new state s_{t+1}. Calculate instant reward feedback. r_t
6:        Store transition $\langle s_t, a_t, s_{t+1}, r_t \rangle$ in data-buff.
7:        Random mini-batch of N transitions $\langle s_i, a_i, s_{i+1}, r_i \rangle$ from data-buff.
8:        Set $y_i = r_i + \gamma \theta^{Q'}(s_{i+1}, \pi'(s_{i+1}|\theta^{u'})|\theta^{Q'})$.
9:        Update critic by minimizing MSE loss function:
10:       $$L(\theta^Q) = \frac{1}{N} \sum_i (y_i - Q(s_i, a_i|\theta^Q))^2.$$
11:       Update the actor policy using the policy gradient function:
12:       $$\nabla_{\theta^u} J \approx \frac{1}{N} \sum \nabla_a Q(s, a|\theta^Q)\big|_{s=s_i, a=\pi(s_i)} \nabla_{\theta^u} \pi(s|\theta^u)\big|_{s=s_i}.$$
13:       Update the target networks:
14:       $\theta^{u'} \leftarrow \tau\theta^u + (1-\tau)\theta^{u'}$,
15:       $\theta^{Q'} \leftarrow \tau\theta^Q + (1-\tau)\theta^{Q'}$.
16:    **End for time step**
17: **End for Episode**

4. Experiment and Analysis of Results

Thisection describes the simulation environment, the path tracking controller training process, and the employment of the physical autonomous system, with a controller performance evaluation and a generalization ability verification. In the following, we describe each step in detail.

4.1. Experimental Setting

a. **Simulation experiment platform**

We conducted a hardware-in-the-loop test on a driving simulator to analyze the effectiveness of the proposed self-optimizing controller, based on RL. A schematic of the simulation experiment platform is shown in Figure 9.

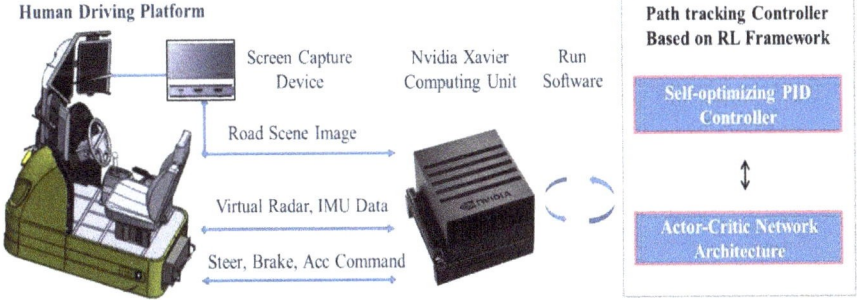

Figure 9. Hardware-in-the-loop simulation platform based on driving simulator.

To follow the desired driven path, we projected a set of trajectories onto our environment map to examine the performance of the presented controller. We selected the candidate that best minimized the lateral position deviation and lateral angle deviation of the controlled object from the reference trajectory. Thus, five urban road maps (Figure 10) with various levels of difficulty were designed for the self-optimizing path tracking controller, with reference to the tracks of the car racing games TORCS [19] and GT Sport [20]. These road maps were generated using the SCANeR™ studio engine (OKTAL, France, see: www.oktal.fr, 13 December 2019), a road and environment creation software for automotive simulation. This software was responsible for delivering the raw sensor data to the control interface and for transferring the control commands (steer, brake, acceleration) to the simulator engine for execution through a dedicated application program interface function. The driving performance data were recorded at a frequency of 20 Hz.

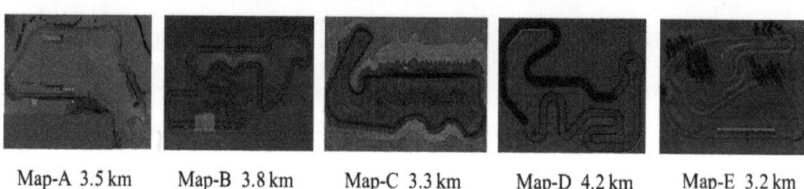

Map-A 3.5 km   Map-B 3.8 km   Map-C 3.3 km   Map-D 4.2 km   Map-E 3.2 km

Figure 10. Trajectory virtual scene road maps.

For a specific traffic environment, we aimed to provide the path tracking controller with a reference trajectory to follow. We invited an experienced driver to operate a car with a steering wheel and pedals on the different urban road maps to generate the corresponding reference trajectories. The collected data included the vehicle world location, heading angles, and velocities in the x-direction, thereby providing environmental states for training and test evaluations, based on the vehicle sensor IMU information and GPS data. At every time step, the path tracking controller calculated the reference error based on the simplified vehicle models. The vehicle's location, relative to the specific reference coordinate system, was denoted as (x, y, φ), where x and y were the coordinates of the midpoint of the vehicle's center of gravity and φ was the orientation angle of the vehicle's body.

b. **Realistic autobus experiment platform**

The realistic autobus experiment platform provided radar, GPS, and IMU data, and we could parse out obstacle distance and vehicle attitude information as well as genuine road indicator values. The autobus platform could also execute control commands (steer, brake, and acceleration) received from the path tracking controller through the vehicle's controller area network bus. The self-optimizing controller, based on the RL framework, ran on NVIDIA's computing unit Xavier and comprised two submodules. First, the actor–critic network architecture mode obtained the proportional and derivative gain values by training the network using the DDPG algorithm. Second, the self-optimizing PID controller module received the gain values and calculated the real-time control commands for acting on the vehicle steering wheel. A schematic diagram of the realistic autobus experiment platform is shown in Figure 11, and the function description and precision of each sensor are shown in Table 3.

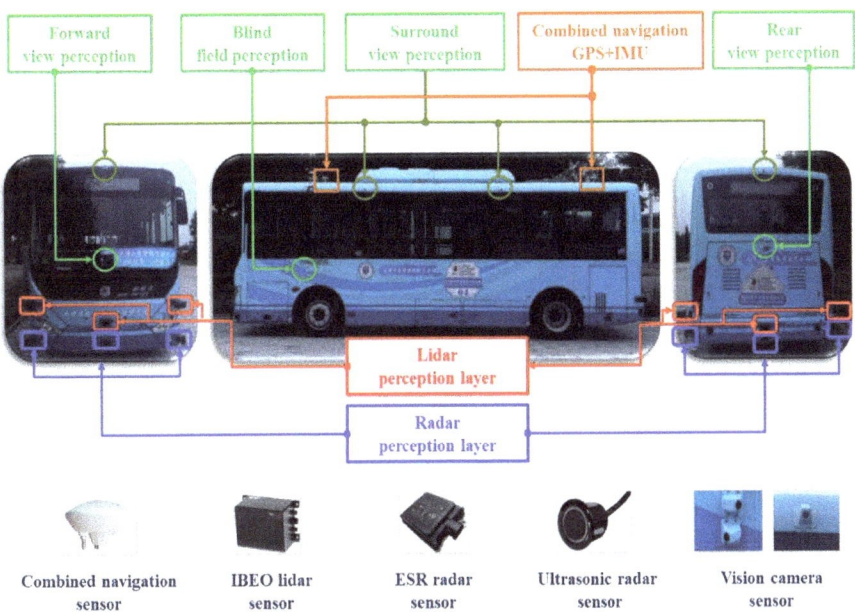

Figure 11. Schematic diagram of the realistic autobus experiment platform.

Table 3. Vehicle sensor configuration scheme. (* indicates the number of sensors).

Sensors	Position	Function Description	Precision
GPS+IMU *1	Top	Precise location of the vehicle.	Positioning accuracy: 5 cm
IBEO Lidar *6	Front, Rear	1. Vehicle, pedestrian detection. 2. Relative distance, speed, angle	Detection accuracy: 90% Effective distance: 80 m
ESR Radar *6	Front, Rear	1. Long-distance obstacle detection. 2. Road edge detection.	Detection accuracy: 90% Effective distance: 120 m
Vision Camera *12	Front, Rear Top sides	1. Traffic light status detection. 2. Lane line detection.	Detection accuracy: 95% Effective angle: 178°
Ultrasonic radar *8	Front, Rear, Both sides	1. Short-distance obstacle detection. 2. Blind field detection.	Detection accuracy: 90% 360° coverage

Our real-world driving experiment mimicked those conducted in simulations in many ways. However, executing this experiment in the real world was significantly more challenging, as the system could not automatically reset the starting state. In addition, the RL agent evaluates and improves its control policy in a trial-and-error manner; thus, it would have been dangerous and costly to train an agent on a real vehicle; moreover, particularly with dynamic balancing systems, such an approach would be complicated and expensive. We were motivated by the steady ability of the traditional PID controller and learning mechanisms that interacted with the environment. As noted above, in this paper, a self-optimizing PID path tracking controller, based on an RL framework, was proposed for use with a realistic autonomous platform. The design of the controller had three advantages, as mentioned above (reducing the exploration space of the RL, introducing an online self-learning mechanism into the traditional controller design, and using RL for practical engineering control). To the best of our knowledge, this was the first demonstration of a deep RL agent driving a real autobus. We conducted our experiment using a wire-controlled autobus ("New Energy Electric Bus") (see Table 4 for the specific vehicle parameters).

Table 4. Specific parameter information of the wire-controlled autobus.

Vehicle Information Parameters					
Length (mm)	8010	Maximum Total Mass (kg)			13000
Width (mm)	2390	Front Suspension/Rear Suspension (mm)			1820/1690
Height (mm)	3090	Approach Angle/Departure Angle (°)			8/12
Wheelbase (mm)	4500	Maximum Speed (km/h)			69
Turning Radius (mm)	9000	Tire Size × Number			245/70R19.5 × 4

c. **Software version and hardware computing platform**

In this project, we used NVIDIA's Jetson AGX Xavier computing module to run software algorithms on virtual and realistic autonomous platforms. Thus, it was possible to implement an autonomous machine domain controller using artificial intelligence (AI) technology, which was sufficient for completing the following tasks: sensor fusion, high-precision positioning, path planning, and executing tracking algorithms. The kit benefited from NVIDIA's rich set of AI tools and workflows, which can be used to quickly train and deploy neural networks. Table 5 presents the path tracking controller software and computing hardware environments that the agents relied on in the training and testing processes.

Table 5. Software and hardware technical parameters.

Software and Hardware Technical Parameters of the On-Board Computing Unit		
	GPU	512-core Volta GPU with Tensor Core
	CPU	8-core ARM 64-bit CPU
	RAM	32 GB
	Compute DL-TOPs	30 TOPs
	Operating system	Ubuntu 18.04
	RL framework	Tensorflow-1.14

4.2. Performance Verification and Results Analysis

a. **Simulation experiment setup and performance during training process**

We trained our path tracking controller on four maps (Figure 10 Map-A~Map-D). Map-A was relatively simple and was used for the first stage of training, in which the vehicle learned a basic reference trajectory-tracking task, such as on long straight roads and/or some simple corners. Map-B, Map-C, and Map-D had different levels of difficulty, with diverse corner shapes. Map-E had the most complicated trajectory and was used for testing based on the pre-trained weights from Map-A to Map-D to evaluate the control performance and generalization ability of the controller. The training rewards of the different tracks, based on the RL controller, are illustrated in Figure 12.

In the path tracking control experiments, we trained an optimal policy to achieve continuous action control in the simulation platform. During the entire training process, the ego vehicle (also referred to as host vehicle) was driven at a fixed speed of 30 km/h and the experimental frequency was 20 Hz. If the vehicle was driven out of the lane or collided and/or the vehicle speed dropped to 0, we penalized the model, and the current episode was terminated. In Figure 12, which illustrates the total rewards against the number of episodes, we can see that, as the training continues, the total reward in one episode increases, because the model gradually finds the optimal control policy. In addition, the complexity of the reference trajectory also directly affects the training time and number of episodes. With the goal of completing a lap driving task, we recorded the number of episodes, iteration steps, driving distances, and training times, and the results are shown in Table 6.

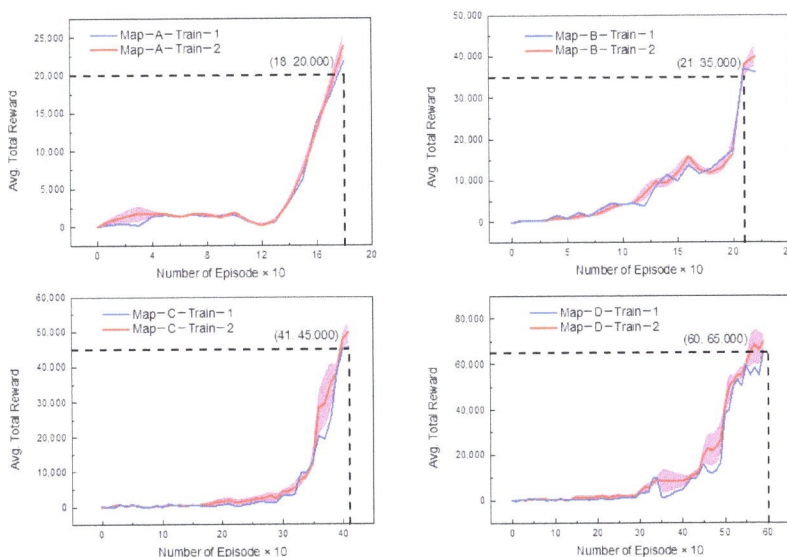

Figure 12. Average total reward value with the RL training episode.

Table 6. Reinforcement learning (RL) training result statistics.

	Number Episode	Iteration Step	Drive Distance	Training Time
Map-A	180	8858	2387.64	0.75 h
Map-B	210	16,139	3242.83	1.2 h
Map-C	410	38,926	2935.72	2.3 h
Map-D	600	61,538	6470.38	3.6 h

During this study, although the RL agent learned the optimal control strategy, the training process took a very long time; the training time reached 3.6 h during the training process of Map-D, and the numbers of episodes and iteration steps reached 600 and 61,538, respectively. The actor–critic neural network sometimes did not converge (overfitting), causing the reward to drop sharply; the pink band represents the standard deviation of the total reward, which fluctuated greatly during the training process on the roads of Map-C and Map-D. For the training result of MSE, the loss value on the road of Map-D illustrates that, at the 140th iteration step, the value converged to 4500, as shown in Figure 13.

The possible reasons for these results include the fact that the essence of the DDPG algorithm is a trial-and-error method, which is based on random sampling during the training process; thus, it can easily encounter excessive training time and overfitting problems. The key is to properly balance exploration and utilization. In this paper, the design of the controller reduces the exploration space of the RL to find the optimal control parameters, which will greatly improve the learning efficiency. The training rewards for the self-optimizing path tracking controller, based on the RL framework, are illustrated in Figure 14.

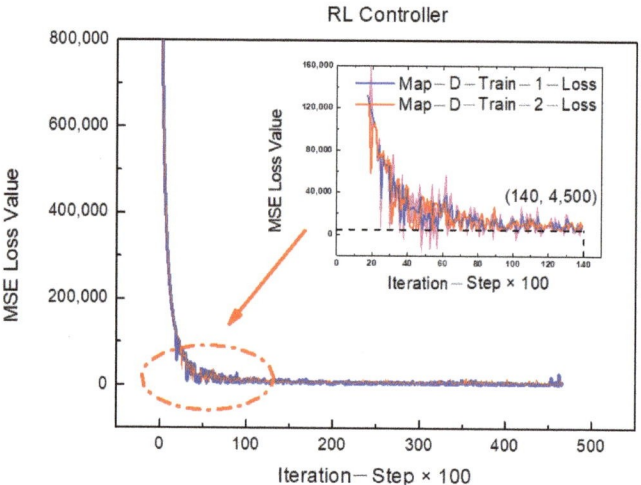

Figure 13. Mean squared error (MSE) loss value with the RL training step number.

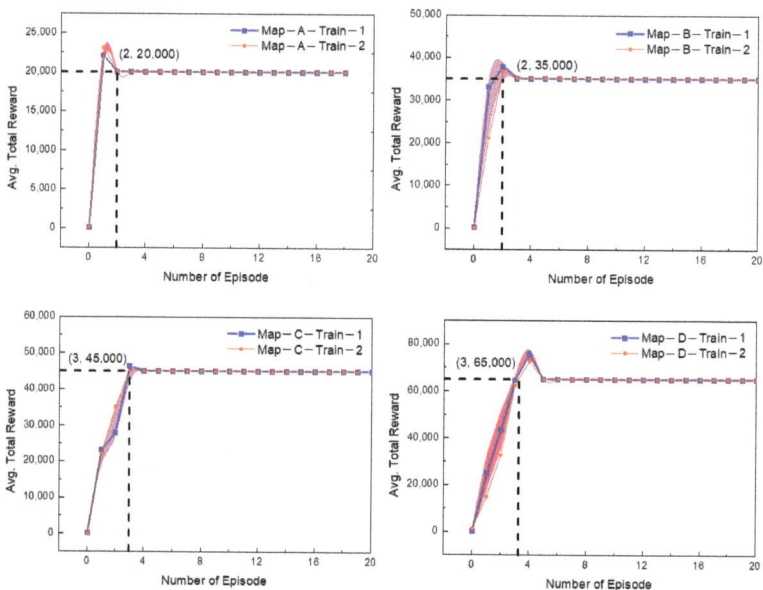

Figure 14. Average total reward value with the PID–RL training episode.

As training continues, the total reward in one episode increases linearly. Owing to the introduction of the traditional PID control parameters (as constrained by experience knowledge), the exploration space for the RL is greatly reduced, meaning that the optimal control policy can be learned quickly. Based on the goal of completing a lap driving task, the results for the number of episodes, iteration steps, driving distances, and training times are shown in Table 7.

Table 7. RL proportional–integral–derivative (PID–RL) training result statistics.

	Number Episode	Iteration Step	Drive Distance	Training Time
Map-A	2	3858	2987.4	9.8 min
Map-B	2	5139	3642.3	11.2 min
Map-C	3	6926	4732.8	13.1 min
Map-D	3	8738	6870.2	18.3 min

We can see that the self-optimizing PID path controller, based on RL (online framework), enables us to obtain an acceptable control policy quickly. The ego vehicle can pass Map-A and Map-B at the 2nd episode and Map-C and Map-D at the 3rd episode, respectively. Simultaneously, it effectively solves the problem of network overfitting, allowing for stable convergence (as shown in Figure 15). With regard to the training result for the loss value in Map-D, the result illustrates that, at the 130th iteration step, the network converges to 200. After 130 iterations, a highly effective path tracking control policy will have been learned.

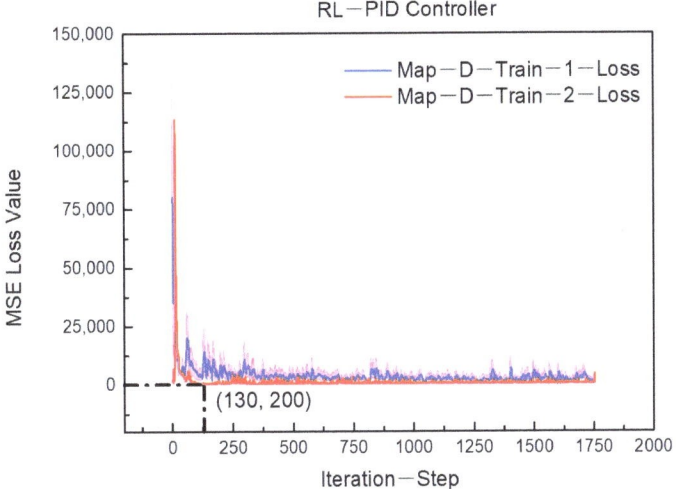

Figure 15. MSE loss value with the PID–RL training step number.

Based on a comparative analysis of the above results (Figure 12 vs. Figure 14, Figure 13 vs. Figure 15, Table 6 vs. Table 7), we can verify that the control policy, as constrained by prior experience, can help the RL agent learn relatively quickly.

b. **Evaluating the performance of self-optimizing proportional–integral–derivative (PID) controller, based on RL framework**

The purpose of the evaluation is to verify the adaptive ability of the proposed controller algorithm under complex reference trajectories and various driving speeds, as well as different dynamic models. Additionally, for the further analysis of the proposed controller, reference results from an experienced driver are presented for comparison in order to verify whether the self-optimizing controller can learn a better control policy. This paper adopted five indicators for measuring the performance of the self-optimizing path tracking controller:

- **The smoothness** indicator represents the comfort resulting from the path-following control. In this paper, the vibration amplitude of the steering wheel was used to represent the smoothness indicator.
- **The lateral track error**, e, and **heading angle error**, $\Delta \varphi$, evaluate the effects of the path tracking.

- **The maximum speed** and **average speed** indicators characterize the driving efficiency.

A traditional PID controller uses a more intuitive steering control law, where RL is a more advanced self-optimal learning controller. Hence, in this study, the self-optimizing path tracking controller proposed is based on the RL framework and combines traditional PID control algorithms and RL mechanisms. The figure below shows a performance comparison between a fixed-parameter PID controller, an RL controller, and the proposed PID–RL self-optimizing controller, in a path-following control process at 30 km/h. It can be observed that the self-optimizing controller learns a better control policy.

From Figure 16 and Table 8, it can be seen that the amplitude (min–max), mean, and standard deviation are all reduced with the self-optimizing path controller, which can quickly realize stable control and overcome the overshoots caused by PID control and the unstable characteristics of the RL controller. In particular, the standard deviation value is significantly reduced, indicating the smoothness of the steering wheel rotation and the driving comfort.

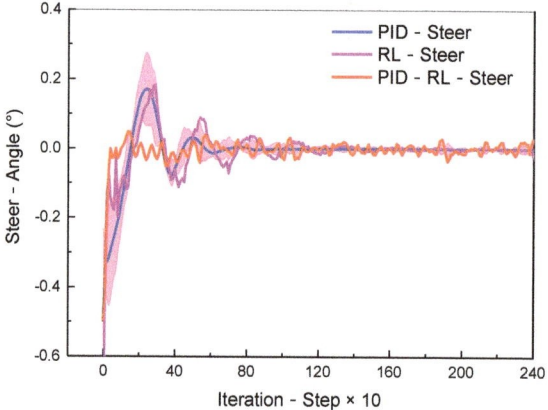

Figure 16. Steer angle of the path tracking controller with the iteration step.

Table 8. Mathematical statistics of steering wheel angles.

	Standard Deviation	Minimum	Maximum
PID−Steer	0.11785	−0.5	0.17068
RL−Steer	0.13907	−0.96124	0.18131
PID−RL−Steer	0.04705 ↓	−0.49881 ↓	0.07665 ↓

From Figure 17 and Table 9, it can be seen that the standard deviations of the lateral error for the two controllers are almost identical, whereas the amplitude of the self-optimizing path controller is the lowest, indicating that its control performance is more stable than that of the other two controllers.

Table 9. Mathematical statistics of lateral errors.

	Standard Deviation	Minimum	Maximum
PID−cross−track error (CTE)	0.1616	−0.12305	0.33338
RL−CTE	0.1220	−0.17023	0.34481
PID−RL−CTE	0.0915 ↓	−0.0092 ↓	0.29207 ↓

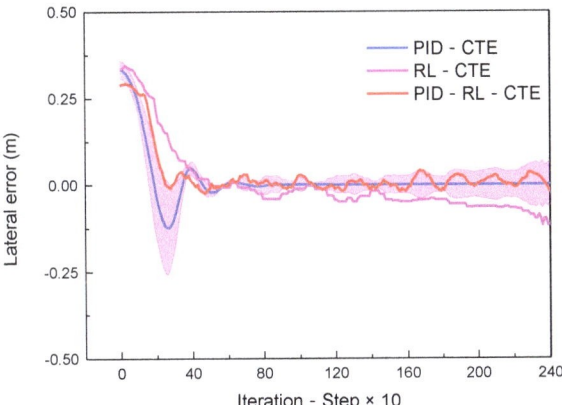

Figure 17. Lateral error of path tracking controller with the iteration step.

Another important evaluation indicator for path tracking is the heading angle error; from Figure 18 and Table 10, it can be seen that the standard deviation value is significantly reduced with the self-optimizing path controller. Considering the smoothness indicator, the lateral track error, e, and the heading angle error, $\Delta\varphi$, the controller performance can be expressed as follows.

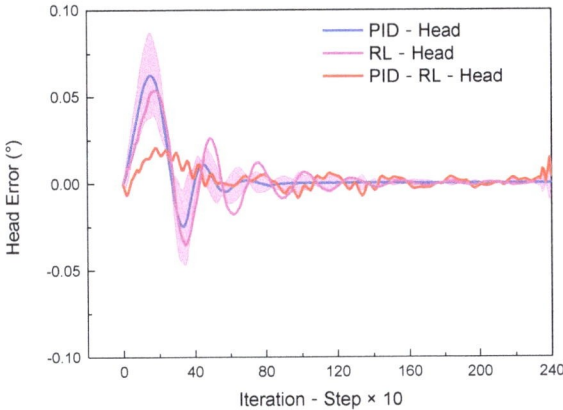

Figure 18. Heading error of path tracking controller with the iteration step.

Table 10. Mathematical statistics of heading errors.

	Standard Deviation	Minimum	Maximum
PID-Head	0.0343	−0.0247	0.0625
RL-Head	0.0349	−0.0353	0.0534
PID–RL-Head	0.0073 ↓	−0.0061 ↓	0.0208 ↓

Another important evaluation indicator for path tracking is the heading angle error; from Figure 18 and Table 10, it can be seen that the standard deviation value is significantly reduced with the self-optimizing path controller. Considering the smoothness indicator, the lateral track error, e, and the heading angle error, $\Delta\varphi$, the controller performance can be expressed as follows:

$$\text{self-optimizing controller} > \text{PID controller} > \text{RL controller}$$

The self-optimizing PID controller based on the RL framework can automatically adjust the control parameters to realize the dynamic compensation of the control system online and ultimately obtain a better path tracking control performance. The box chart distribution and mathematical statistics of the four control parameters are shown in Figure 19 and Table 11, respectively.

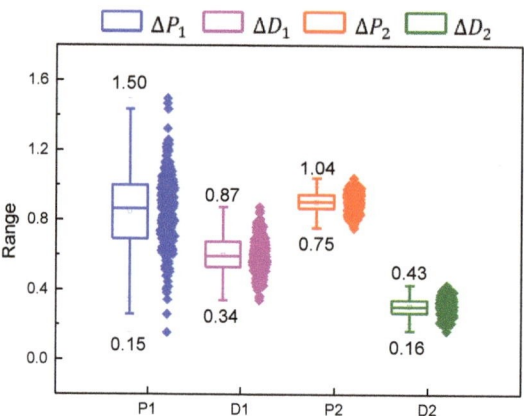

Figure 19. Data distribution of path tracking control parameters.

Table 11. Mathematical statistics of path tracking control parameters.

	Mean	Standard Deviation	Sum	Minimum	Median	Maximum
ΔP_1	0.84623	0.21836	206.48024	0.15364	0.86328	1.49518
ΔD_1	0.59826	0.10214	145.97583	0.33797	0.59185	0.87246
ΔP_2	0.90078	0.05179	219.78983	0.75222	0.90156	1.0384
ΔD_2	0.30479	0.05151	74.36867	0.16412	0.30233	0.42815

According to the fluctuation results for the standard deviation, the lateral deviation and its rate of change reached 0.2183 and 0.10214, respectively. It can be seen that when the actual trajectory is far away from the reference trajectory, the proportional adjustment of the lateral control parameters is the main factor. When approaching the reference trajectory, the heading angle deviation and its rate of change have a greater impact, with average values of 0.90078 and 0.30479, respectively. The controller can realize the self-optimization tuning of the PID control parameters based on the RL algorithm, which can then be used for online learning and the optimization of complex path tracking control.

It can be seen from the experimental results that RL can automatically optimize the PID control parameters according to the objective reward function and offer real-time online learning capabilities, providing a new solution to controller optimization problems of complex and uncertain systems.

To further verify the dynamic compensation performance of the self-optimizing controller, based on the RL framework, its performance is compared with that of an active disturbance rejection controller (ADRC). As described in References [49–51], the ADRC controller effectively alleviates the problem of vehicle jitter caused by road curvature changes under the conditions of a complex trajectory by observing internal and external disturbances of the system. This paper compared the lateral track error, e, of the two controllers on Map-E, and the speed conditions were set to 50 km/h and 60 km/h, respectively. The comparison results for the two controllers on the four corner types are shown in Figures 20 and 21, and the statistical analysis results are shown in Table 12.

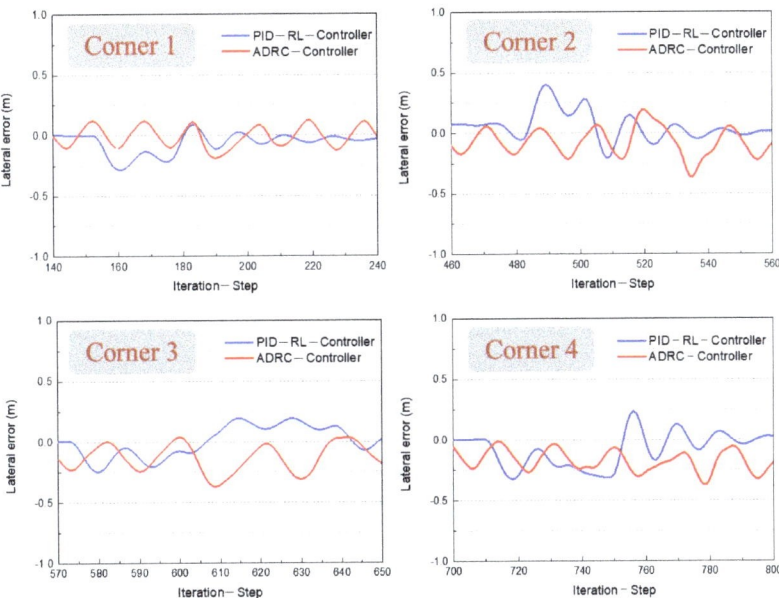

Figure 20. Self-optimizing controller and ADRC testing on road of Map-E under 50 km/h driving conditions.

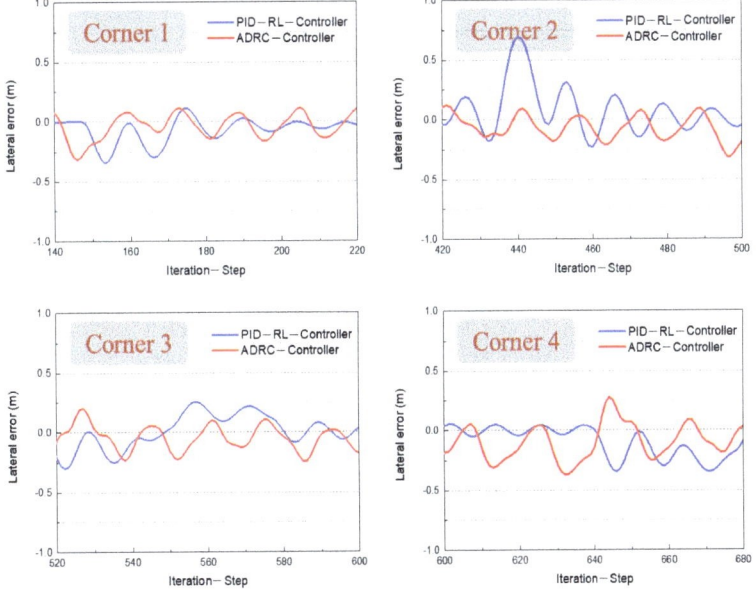

Figure 21. Self-optimizing controller and ADRC testing on road of Map-E under 60 km/h driving conditions.

Table 12. Mathematical statistics of lateral error for self-optimizing controller and ADRC controller on the road of Map-E.

	50 km/h Driving Condition on the Road of Map-E			
	Mean	Standard Deviation	Minimum	Maximum
PID–RL Controller	−0.01017 ↓	0.09325	−0.32759	0.39932 ↑
ADRC-Controller	−0.06622	0.10941	−0.37658	0.18714
	60 km/h Driving Condition on Road of Map-E			
	Mean	Standard Deviation	Minimum	Maximum
PID–RL Controller	−0.00823 ↓	0.10994	−0.35013	0.6918 ↑
ADRC-Controller	−0.04492	0.10508	−0.37490	0.27655

From the results, we can conclude that the path tracking performances of the self-optimizing controller and ADRC controller are almost unanimous. As shown in Table 12, both controllers can achieve a stable control performance under 50 km/h and 60 km/h driving conditions in terms of the standard deviation value of the lateral error. The ADRC controller observes the disturbances during the operation of the vehicle (see Figure 22), whereas the controller proposed in this study uses real-time online adjustment of controller parameters to achieve dynamic compensation during the path tracking control process (see Figure 23).

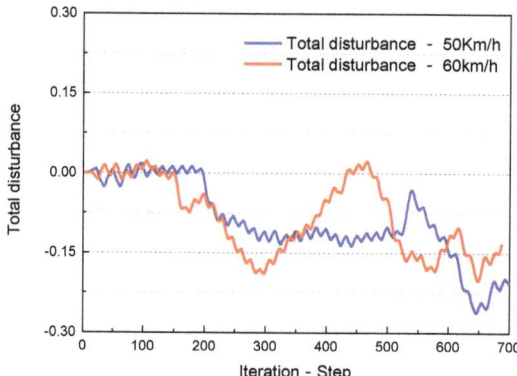

Figure 22. Total disturbance observed by ADRC.

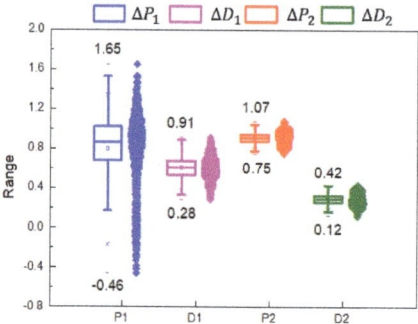

Figure 23. Distribution of control parameter.

c. **Generalization of self-optimizing PID controller based on the RL framework**

To test the generalization ability of the proposed self-optimizing PID controller, based on the RL framework, we evaluated it with complex trajectories and variable speed conditions on the road in Map-E. The different corner track types are shown in Figure 24 and include an arc curve track, a right-angle curve track, an S-curve track, and a U-turn track.

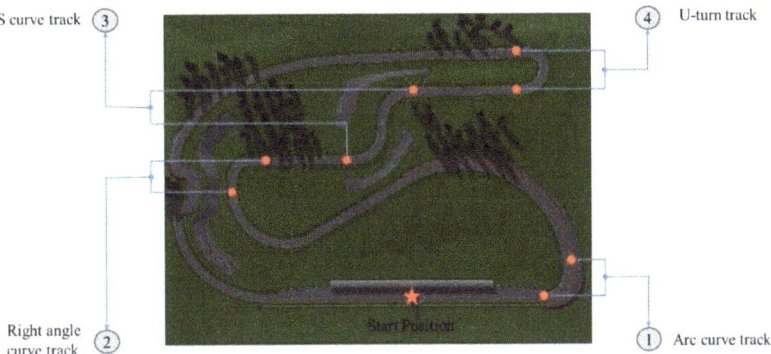

Figure 24. Complex corner track types of the road of Map-E.

The self-optimizing path tracking controller is further tested under variable speed conditions on the road of Map-E to evaluate whether the proposed controller can be implemented in a complex corner scenario at a high speed, based on using the behavioral data of professional drivers as a baseline for comparative analysis.

From Figures 25–27, and the analysis of the statistical results in Table 13, it can be seen that the max absolute value of the PID controller's lateral error reached 1.11 m, the max driving speed was 54 km/h, and the average cornering speed was concentrated in the range of 36–42 km/h (as shown in Figure 25). The analysis results show that the controller with constant control parameters found it difficult to adapt to speed changes and large curvature road trajectories. As for the self-optimizing controller, the above problems can be overcome; the max absolute value of the PID–RL Controller's lateral error was 0.66m, the max driving speed was more than 100 km/h, and the average cornering speed was concentrated in the range of 63–76 km/h (as shown in Figure 26). Furthermore, we conducted a comparative analysis with the human driver's behavior data, the max absolute value of the human driver's lateral error was 0.61 m, the lateral path track error of the method proposed in this paper is almost consistent with it. The maximum driving speed was 71 km/h; to avoid leaving the curve track, the drivers were forced to brake early before entering the corner, and the average cornering speed was concentrated in the range of 44–53 km/h (as shown in Figure 27), while the average cornering speed of the self-optimizing controller was better than that of the human driver.

Table 13. Statistical results of the generalization ability test of the self-optimizing controller.

	Indicators	Mean	Standard Deviation	Minimum	Maximum
PID Controller	Speed	41.0455	8.4158	0	55
	Lateral error	−0.1030	0.3573	−1.1125	0.9966
PID–RL Controller	Speed	84.6887	16.9462	0	101
	Lateral error	−0.0137	0.1089	−0.3844	0.6640
Human Driver	Speed	51.5378	11.8857	0	71
	Lateral error	−0.0014	0.1135	−0.6068	0.5521

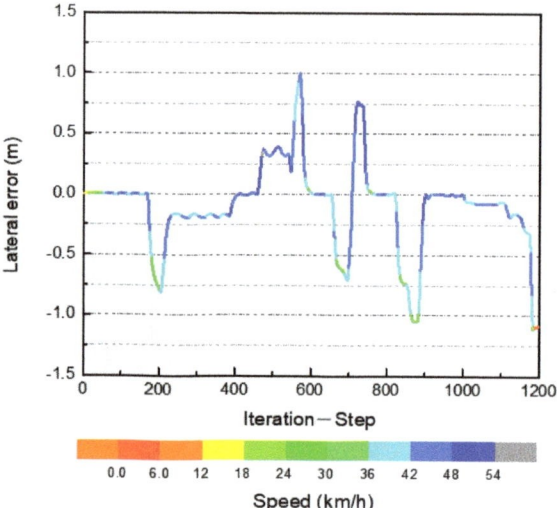

Figure 25. Lateral error of the traditional PID controller on the road of Map-E.

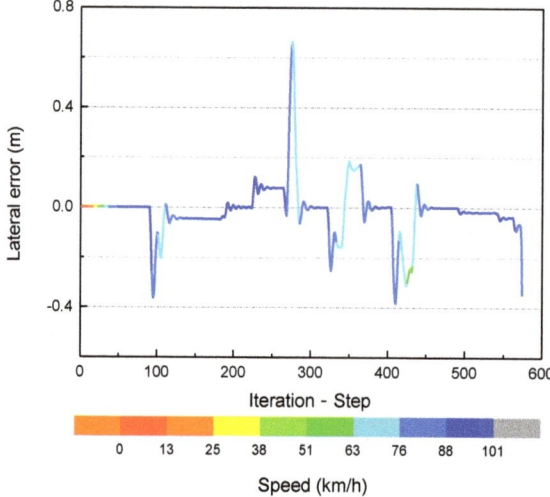

Figure 26. Lateral error of PID–RL Controller on the road of Map-E.

In summary, we can draw the conclusion that our proposed path tracking approach has the adaptability to cope with complex trajectory conditions and variation of speed by optimizing the PID controller parameters in real time.

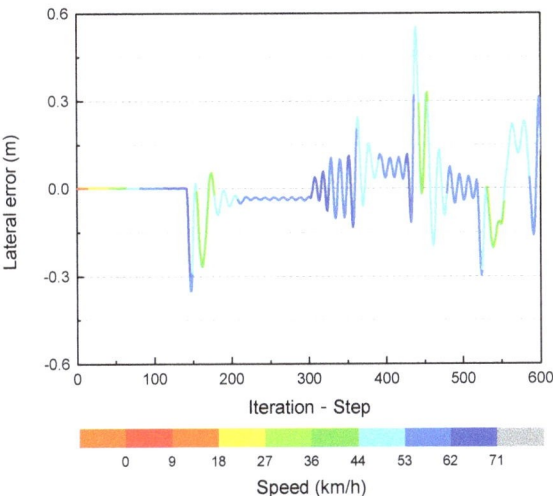

Figure 27. Lateral error of human-driver control on the road of Map-E.

d. **Steering of a realistic autobus platform, based on the self-optimizing PID controller**

Considering the achievements of self-optimizing controllers, based on the RL framework in the simulation environment, a natural question is whether these learned control policies can be deployed in real physical systems. The essence of the RL algorithm is a trial-and-error method, based on random sampling during the training process; thus, it would be dangerous to train an agent on a real vehicle. Furthermore, unlike the training process of a control policy in a simulated environment, the initial state of the controlled object cannot reset the state automatically between episodes in a real environment. The authors of [25] required a human driver to reset the vehicle to a valid starting position and initial state when the training episode terminated; however, this requires significant human labor costs. In summary, the simulation-to-reality transfer is hindered by the reality gap, in terms of how to effectively reset the initial state to ensure the stability of the control system, and how to reduce the time spent during the training process. To solve the above-mentioned problems, our real-world driving experiments imitated (in many aspects) those conducted in simulations and in steering realistic autobuses, based on a self-optimizing PID controller. This section describes in detail the deployment of the physically realistic autobus system and training process. An overview of our training method is presented in Figure 28.

For both the simulations and the real-world experiments, we realized the symmetric migration from a virtual simulation scene to a real vehicle platform, which resolved the limitation that reinforcement learning can only be used in simulation scene. We used the same actor–critic architecture and the same hyper-parameters that were found to be effective in the simulation. The common training procedures required adjustments in order to be deployed for a RL algorithm on a physical vehicle, running in a real-world environment. To account for both effectively resetting the initial state to ensure the stability of the control system and reducing the time spent during the training process, we created an architecture for the training procedures, comprising a simple state machine, as presented in Figure 28. It included five sub-modules: state initialization, model training, state automatic reset, driver takeover, and training task termination.

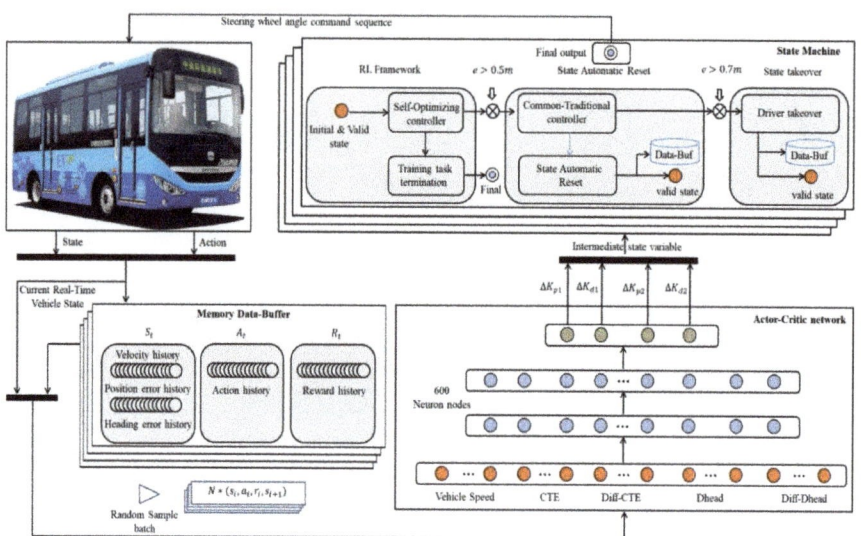

Figure 28. Architecture diagram of self-optimizing path tracking controller on a realistic autobus platform.

In fact, many environmental factors affect the training process; therefore, real-time safety and state machine monitoring mechanisms must be implemented in a physical vehicle control system. For these experiments, the vehicle was initialized at the starting position of the road during preparation for training. However, when the distance of the car from the center of the lane reached 0.5 m, the training episode was terminated and the process entered the state automatic reset module; simultaneously, the common traditional controller was used to control the vehicle, to revert to a valid state. At this point, the training process was executed. When the autobus deviated from the center line of the lane over a pre-set value ($e > 0.7$ m) and entered an unrecoverable state, a safety driver took over and steered the vehicle to return to the center of the lane—that is, to the valid state. Then, the next episode of training was begun. The introduction of the state machine effectively reset the initial state to ensure the stability of the control system.

In addition, we built a cache buffer of driver's behavior data. During the driver's driving process, the controller symmetrically learned the controllability of the human driver, in order to obtain the optimal control parameters. The memory data buffer was used to record the historical state and the action information of the vehicle. During the training process, random batches of N historical data were sampled for the online training of the network, and the actor–critic network mapped the vehicle state history to the intermediate state variable, which was used to calculate the increment of the steering wheel control sequence. Notably, if the data buffer stored positive sample data—that is, experience data from excellent human drivers—then it would contribute to the actor–critic network by quickly learning effective control policies, thus reducing the time spent on network training.

In general, the proposed self-optimizing controller learns the control policy by directly interacting with a realistic vehicle operating environment. The observation state space used by our method should be directly observable on a real vehicle equipped with sensors. The GPS allows for the determination of its relative coordinates, based on the current track of the road, and calculates the current lateral deviation error of the autobus from the given track. The heading angle deviation is obtained using the IMU sensor, which measures the difference in the change in the yaw angle with respect to the road track curvature. The generated intermediate quantity is the gain parameter of the self-optimizing controller, and its final output is the steering wheel angle control sequence data expanded over time, which directly acts on the autonomous platform. It should be emphasized that the final output calculation result depends on the working mode selected by the state machine, as discussed in the second section of this paper. The calculation method used for the self-optimizing controller, based on the RL framework, is shown in Equation (18); whereas, the calculation method for the common traditional controller, based on the PID paradigm, is shown in Equation (16).

The path tracking task description follows a given reference trajectory by controlling the steering angle of the steering wheel. The sensory inputs are the pose information of the autobus (provided by the GPS and IMU systems) and the vehicle's speed. The path tracking controller output is the desired angle of the steering wheel in the range of $\pm 620°$. The controller acts at 20 Hz, corresponding to a control interval of 50 ms. The autobus' drive-by-wire system will automatically disengage if the safety driver takes over, either by lightly stepping on the accelerator or brake pedal or by turning the steering wheel.

The path tracking controller of the vehicle system was tested on an autobus with different types of trajectories. Figure 29 is a screenshot from Google Maps, showing the curve case, the straight case, the round island case, the corner angle case, and the lane change case, etc. These were driven at speeds of 8 km/h and 10 km/h, with step speeds of 0–20 km/h. The desired trajectory was reconstructed from the data points with a 0.5 m spacing, as recorded from the GPS+IMU sensor. The 2-DOF bicycle model in vehicle dynamics was used to describe the basic motion law of the intelligent autonomous system, and the desired steering angle was determined by calculating the lateral error and the heading angle error, according to Equations (16) and (18).

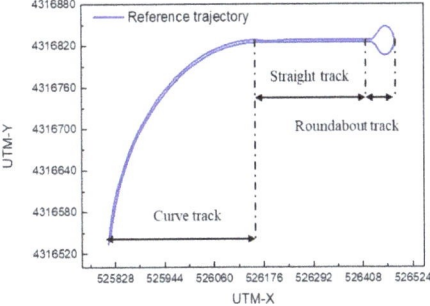

Figure 29. Schematic diagram of the test road map in the real world.

The evaluation indicators were the same as those tested on the simulation platform, to verify the path tracking control performance of the self-optimizing controller on a realistic physical vehicle platform. The resulting self-optimizing controller, based on the RL framework, showed much better behavior than the traditional controller—e.g., with respect to smoother steering wheel control sequence data, as illustrated in Figure 30.

From the experimental results in Figure 30 and Table 14, it can clearly be concluded that the human driver can complete the lateral motion control of the vehicle with a lower vibration amplitude (69.0577) in terms of the performance of the smoothness of the steering wheel control. Compared with the PID controller, the self-optimized RL controller can obtain better control stability: the vibration amplitudes of the steering wheels were 88.8032 and 80.6986, respectively. The above results verify the effectiveness of the self-optimizing controller, based on reinforcement learning, in real vehicles.

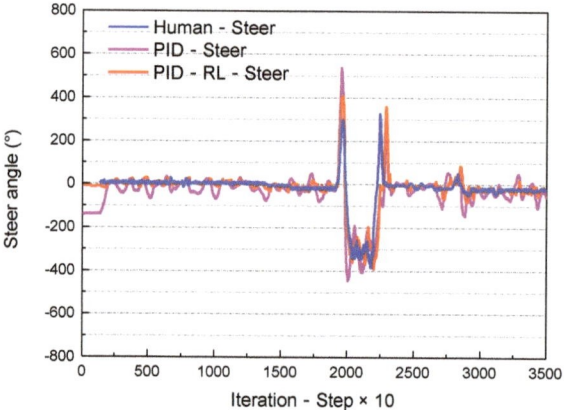

Figure 30. Steer angle of the path tracking controller with the iteration step.

Table 14. Mathematical statistics of steering wheel angles.

	Mean	Standard Deviation	Minimum	Maximum
Human−steer	−22.15445	69.05777	−386	325
PID−Steer	−42.81777	88.80323	−447	536
PID−RL−Steer	−22.06958 ↓	80.69866 ↓	−390.8 ↓	403.2 ↓

With respect to both the path tracking accuracy and efficiency, the self-optimizing controller can control the steering wheel angle with small lateral distance and heading angle deviations, to keep the vehicle driving in the center of the lane. As shown in Figures 31 and 32, the vehicle follows the reference trajectory quite satisfactorily with the self-optimizing controller on the curved track, the straight track, and the roundabout track, and its control performance was better than that of the traditional control method.

The memory data buffer stores the driver's experience behavior data, including the vehicle status information and operating sequences. Therefore, during the training process, the amount of positive sample data required for network training increases, meaning that the reward value of the controller shows an increasing trend (see Figure 33). The test results prove that after 35,000 iteration steps, the actor–critic network has learned an excellent control policy.

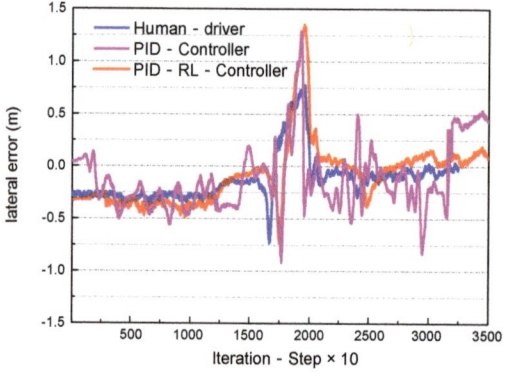

Figure 31. Lateral error of path tracking controller on a test road map.

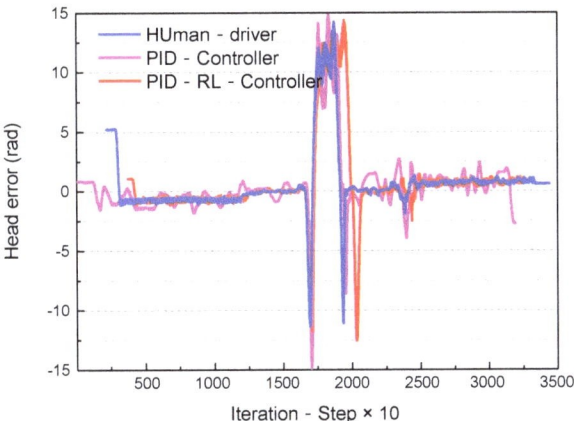

Figure 32. Heading error of path tracking controller on a test road map.

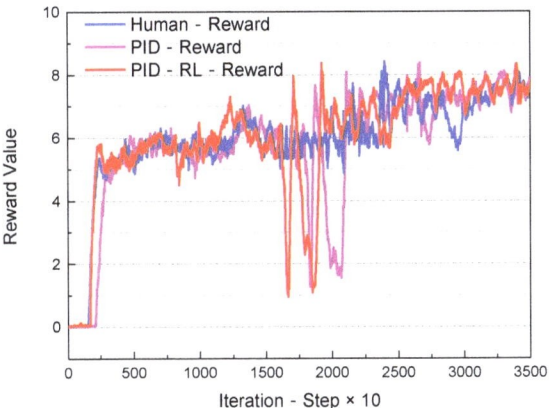

Figure 33. Single-step reward value of path tracking controller on the test road map.

The intermediate state variables generated during the training process are the gain parameters of the controller, which are used to compensate for the dynamic error of the system to keep the vehicle always driving along the center of the lane, under different types of road trajectories. The data distribution and statistical results are shown in Figure 34 and Table 15, respectively.

Table 15. Mathematical statistics of path tracking control parameters.

	Mean	Standard Deviation	Minimum	Median	Maximum
ΔP_1	53.84405	10.34426	16.2258	56.0301	79.3932
ΔD_1	92.10457	2.05332	85.6766	92.0764	98.2066
ΔP_2	39.07703	0.49852	37.5222	39.0849	40.747
ΔD_2	6.46417	0.24382	5.6081	6.46435	7.1453

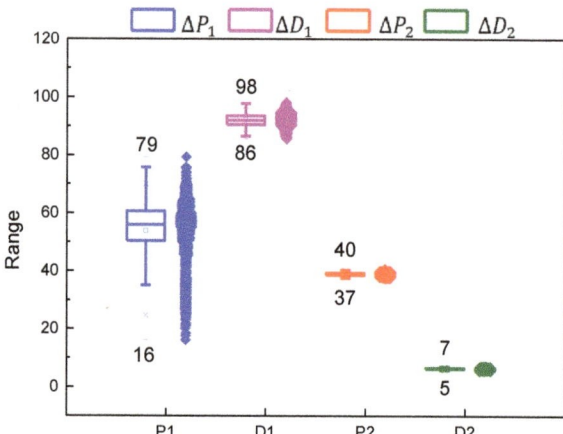

Figure 34. Data distribution of path tracking control parameters.

It can be seen that, when the actual trajectory is far away from the reference trajectory—such as on the curve and the roundabout tracks—the percentage gain, ΔP_1, increases with the curvature of the reference track. The maximum value can reach 79; when the vehicle is travelling in a straight line, the minimum value reaches 16. Therefore, the standard deviation reaches a value of 10.34426. Thus, the controller responds faster to a decrease in the lateral deviation. When approaching the reference trajectory, the heading angle deviation and its rate of change have a greater impact, with average values reaching 39.07703 and 6.46417, respectively.

We can conclude that, in the absence of prior knowledge of the dynamic characteristics of the vehicle's physical model, the optimization problem of the path tracking controller can be solved based on real-time interactive learning with the operating environment of a real vehicle; moreover, the controller can realize the self-optimized tuning of the PID control parameters, based on the RL algorithm, which can be used for online learning and the optimization of complex path tracking control.

5. Conclusions

In this paper, we propose a self-optimized path tracking controller to simultaneously track a predefined path with high accuracy and a well ride comfort experience. For the lateral control of the vehicle, a steering method, based on the fusion of the reinforcement learning with traditional PID controller, is designed to adapt to various tracking scenarios. According to the pre-defined path geometry and the real-time status of the vehicle, combined with the environment interactive learning mechanism, based on the RL framework, the optimization of the PID control parameters can be realized. The adaptive performance of velocity changes was also considered in the tracking process. Both the driving simulator and the on-site vehicle experiments have verified the effects of our proposed self-optimization controller. Nevertheless, there remains a gap between simulation and real scenes; a transfer learning (sim-to-real) strategy can better adapt to controllers to real vehicles, which should be emphasized in our further research.

6. Discussion of Limitations and Future Work

One challenge for the self-optimizing path tracking controller, based on RL, is the question of how to design an accurate reward function and effectively balance exploration and utilization, in order to avoid the network training falling into local optimality. In addition, although the simulations can provide large amounts of cheap data for the training and testing of the RL agent, the gap between simulation and reality is also the main reason that these approaches are difficult to popularize and apply in real-word engineering problems. In future research, we will focus on the application of transfer learning in the sim-to-real domain. The full name of sim-to-real is simulation to reality, which is a branch of reinforcement learning and a kind of transfer learning [52]. In the field of robotics or autonomous driving, the main problem that transfer learning solves is that of how to directly allow the autonomous systems or agents to interact with the virtual environment and the real environment [53,54]. Reinforcement learning is considered as a promising direction for driving policy learning. However, training autonomous driving vehicle with reinforcement learning in real environment involves non-affordable trial-and-error research methods [55]. It is more desirable to first train in a virtual environment and then transfer to the real environment.

Author Contributions: Data curation, J.M.; formal analysis, J.M.; funding acquisition, H.X.; investigation, J.M.; project administration, H.X.; funding acquisition, H.X. and K.S.; software, J.M.; supervision, H.X.; validatiown, H.L.; visualization, H.L.; writing—original draft, J.M.; Writing—review and editing, K.S. All authors have read and agreed to the published version of the manuscript.

Funding: This work was supported by the Tianjin Science and Technology Planning Project (2019): Research and Application of Deep Reinforcement Learning Control Algorithm for Intelligent Unmanned System (award number: 19ZXZNGX00050).

Conflicts of Interest: There are no conflict of interest to declare.

References

1. Visioli, A. *Practical PID Control*; Springer: Berlin/Heidelberg, Germany, 2006.
2. Jeffrey, S.; Wit, J.; Crane, C.D., III; Armstrong, D. *Autonomous Ground Vehicle Path Tracking*; University of Florida: Gainesville, FL, USA, 2000.
3. Johary, N.M. Path Tracking Algorithm for An Autonomous Ground Robot. Ph.D. Thesis, Universiti Tun Hussein Onn Malaysia, Batu Pahat, Malaysia, 2014.
4. Goh, J.Y.; Goel, T.; Gerdes, J.C. A controller for automated drifting along complex trajectories. In Proceedings of the 14th International Symposium on Advanced Vehicle Control (AVEC 2018), Beijing, China, 16–20 July 2018.
5. Goh, J.Y.; Gerdes, J.C. Simultaneous stabilization and tracking of basic automobile drifting trajectories. In Proceedings of the 2016 IEEE Intelligent Vehicles Symposium (IV), Los Angeles, CA, USA, 11–14 June 2017; pp. 597–602.
6. Hindiyeh, R.Y.; Gerdes, J.C. A controller framework for autonomous drifting: Design, stability, and experimental validation. *J. Dyn. Syst. Meas. Control.* **2014**, *136*, 051015. [CrossRef]
7. Kim, D.; Yi, K. Design of a Path for Collision Avoidance and Path Tracking Scheme for Autonomous Vehicles. *IFAC Proc. Vol.* **2009**, *42*, 391–398. [CrossRef]
8. Chen, S.-P.; Xiong, G.-M.; Chen, H.-Y.; Negrut, D. MPC-based path tracking with PID speed control for high-speed autonomous vehicles considering time-optimal travel. *J. Central South Univ.* **2020**, *27*, 3702–3720. [CrossRef]
9. Wang, H.; Liu, B.; Ping, X.; An, Q. Path Tracking Control for Autonomous Vehicles Based on an Improved MPC. *IEEE Access* **2019**, *7*, 161064–161073. [CrossRef]
10. Kim, D.; Kang, J.; Yi, K. Control strategy for high-speed autonomous driving in structured road. In Proceedings of the 2011 14th International IEEE Conference on Intelligent Transportation Systems (ITSC), Washington, DC, USA, 5–7 October 2011.
11. Vivek, K.; Sheta, M.A.; Gumtapure, V. A Comparative Study of Stanley, LQR and MPC Controllers for Path Tracking Application (ADAS/AD). In Proceedings of the 2019 IEEE International Conference on Intelligent Systems and Green Technology (ICISGT), Visakhapatnam, India, 29–30 June 2019.
12. Tiep, D.K.; Lee, K.; Im, D.-Y.; Kwak, B.; Ryoo, Y.-J. Design of Fuzzy-PID Controller for Path Tracking of Mobile Robot with Differential Drive. *Int. J. Fuzzy Log. Intell. Syst.* **2018**, *18*, 220–228. [CrossRef]
13. El Hamidi, K.; Mjahed, M.; El Kari, A.; Ayad, H. Neural Network and Fuzzy-logic-based Self-tuning PID Control for Quadcopter Path Tracking. *Stud. Inform. Control* **2019**, *28*, 401–412. [CrossRef]
14. Liang, X.; Zhang, W.; Wu, Y. Automatic Collimation of Optical Path Based on BP-PID Control. In Proceedings of the 2017 10th International Conference on Intelligent Computation Technology and Automation (ICICTA), Changsha, China, 9–10 October 2017.
15. Ma, L.; Yao, Y.; Wang, M. The Optimizing Design of Wheeled Robot Tracking System by PID Control Algorithm Based on BP Neural Network. In Proceedings of the 2016 International Conference on Industrial Informatics-Computing Technology, Wuhan, China, 3–4 December 2016.
16. El Sallab, A.; Abdou, M.; Perot, E.; Yogamani, S. Deep Reinforcement Learning framework for Autonomous Driving. *Electron. Imaging* **2017**, *2017*, 70–76. [CrossRef]
17. Wang, S.; Jia, D.; Weng, X. Deep Reinforcement Learning for Autonomous Driving. *arXiv* **2018**, arXiv:1811.11329.
18. Dong, L.; Zhao, D.; Zhang, Q.; Chen, Y. Reinforcement Learning and Deep Learning based Lateral Control for Autonomous Driving. *arXiv* **2018**, arXiv:1810.12778.

19. Wymann, B.; Espié, E.; Guionneau, C.; Dimitrakakis, C.; Coulom, R.; Sumner, A. TORCS, The Open Racing Car Simulator, v1.3.5. 2013. Available online: http://torcs.sourceforge.net/ (accessed on 10 December 2019).
20. Ingram, A. Gran Turismo Sport—Exploring Its Impact on Real-World Racing with Kazunori. 2019. Available online: Yamauchi. evo.co.uk (accessed on 1 June 2020).
21. Fuchs, F.; Song, Y.; Kaufmann, E.; Scaramuzza, D.; Dürr, P. Super-Human Performance in Gran Turismo Sport Using Deep Reinforcement Learning. *arXiv* **2020**, arXiv:2008.07971. [CrossRef]
22. Cai, P.; Mei, X.; Tai, L.; Sun, Y.; Liu, M. High-Speed Autonomous Drifting With Deep Reinforcement Learning. *IEEE Robot. Autom. Lett.* **2020**, *5*, 1247–1254. [CrossRef]
23. Dosovitskiy, A.; Ros, G.; Codevilla, F.; Lopez, A.; Koltun, V. Carla: An open urban driving simulator. *arXiv* **2017**, arXiv:1711.03938.
24. Gao, X.; Gao, R.; Liang, P.; Zhang, Q.; Deng, R.; Zhu, W. A Hybrid Tracking Control Strategy for Nonholonomic Wheeled Mobile Robot Incorporating Deep Reinforcement Learning Approach. *IEEE Access* **2021**, *9*, 15592–15602. [CrossRef]
25. Zhang, Y.; Zhang, Y.; Yu, Z. Path Following Control for UAV Using Deep Reinforcement Learning Approach. *Guid. Navig. Control* **2021**, *1*, 2150005. [CrossRef]
26. Duan, K.; Fong, S.; Chen, C.P. Reinforcement Learning Based Model-free Optimized Trajectory Tracking Strategy Design for an AUV. *Neurocomputing* **2022**, *469*, 289–297. [CrossRef]
27. Li, B.; Wu, Y. Path Planning for UAV Ground Target Tracking via Deep Reinforcement Learning. *IEEE Access* **2020**, *8*, 29064–29074. [CrossRef]
28. Wang, S.; Yin, X.; Li, P.; Zhang, M.; Wang, X. Trajectory Tracking Control for Mobile Robots Using Reinforcement Learning and PID. *Iran. J. Sci. Technol. Trans. Electr. Eng.* **2020**, *44*, 1059–1068. [CrossRef]
29. Xiao, J.; Li, L.; Zou, Y.; Zhang, T. Reinforcement Learning for Robotic Time-optimal Path Tracking Using Prior Knowledge. *arXiv* **2019**, arXiv:1907.00388.
30. Zhang, S.; Wang, W. Tracking Control for Mobile Robot Based on Deep Reinforcement Learning. In Proceedings of the 2019 2nd International Conference on Intelligent Autonomous Systems (ICoIAS), Singapore, 28 February–2 March 2019.
31. Arroyo, M.A.; Giraldo, L.F. Data-driven Outer-Loop Control Using Deep Reinforcement Learning for Trajectory Tracking. *arXiv* **2020**, arXiv:2008.13732.
32. Shan, Y.; Zheng, B.; Chen, L.; Chen, L.; Chen, D. A Reinforcement Learning-Based Adaptive Path Tracking Approach for Autonomous Driving. *IEEE Trans. Veh. Technol.* **2020**, *69*, 10581–10595. [CrossRef]
33. Puccetti, L.; Köpf, F.; Rathgeber, C.; Hohmann, S. Speed Tracking Control using Online Reinforcement Learning in a Real Car. In Proceedings of the 6th IEEE International Conference on Control, Automation and Robotics (ICCAR), Singapore, 20–23 April 2020.
34. Wang, N.; Gao, Y.; Yang, C.; Zhang, X. Reinforcement Learning-based Finite-time Tracking Control of an Unknown Unmanned Surface Vehicle with Input Constraints. *Neurocomputing* **2021**. Available online: https://www.sciencedirect.com/science/article/abs/pii/S0925231221015733 (accessed on 10 June 2021). [CrossRef]
35. Jiang, L.; Wang, Y.; Wang, L.; Wu, J. Path tracking control based on Deep reinforcement learning in Autonomous driving. In Proceedings of the 2019 3rd Conference on Vehicle Control and Intelligence (CVCI), Hefei, China, 21–22 September 2019.
36. Kamran, D.; Zhu, J.; Lauer, M. Learning Path Tracking for Real Car-like Mobile Robots From Simulation. In Proceedings of the 2019 European Conference on Mobile Robots (ECMR), Prague, Czech Republic, 4–6 September 2019.
37. Riedmiller, M.; Montemerlo, M.; Dahlkamp, H. Learning to Drive a Real Car in 20 Minutes. In Proceedings of the Frontiers in the Convergence of Bioscience & Information Technologies IEEE Computer Society, Jeju City, Korea, 11–13 October 2007.
38. Kendall, A.; Hawke, J.; Janz, D.; Mazur, P.; Reda, D.; Allen, J.-M.; Lam, V.-D.; Bewley, A.; Shah, A. Learning to Drive in a Day. *arXiv* **2018**, arXiv:1807.00412.
39. Rajamani, R. *Vehicle Dynamics and Control*; Springer Science & Business Media: Berlin/Heidelberg, Germany, 2011.
40. Kong, J.; Pfeiffer, M.; Schildbach, G.; Borrelli, F. Kinematic and dynamic vehicle models for autonomous driving control design. In Proceedings of the 2015 IEEE Intelligent Vehicles Symposium (IV), Seoul, Korea, 29 June–1 July 2015.
41. Zhu, M.; Wang, X.; Wang, Y. Human-like autonomous car-following model with deep reinforcement learning. *Transp. Res. Part C Emerg. Technol.* **2018**, *97*, 348–368. [CrossRef]
42. Kingma, D.P.; Ba, J. Adam: A method for stochastic optimization. *arXiv* **2014**, arXiv:1412.6980.
43. Lillicrap, T.P.; Hunt, J.J.; Pritzel, A.; Heess, N.; Erez, T.; Tassa, Y.; Silver, D.; Wierstra, D. Continuous control with deep reinforcement learning. *arXiv* **2015**, arXiv:1509.02971.
44. Yu, A.; Palefsky-Smith, R.; Bedi, R. Course Project Reports: Deep Reinforcement Learning for Simulated Autonomous Vehicle Control. *Course Proj. Rep. Winter* **2016**. Available online: http://cs231n.stanford.edu/reports/2016/pdfs/112_Report.pdf (accessed on 10 June 2021).
45. Yu, R.; Shi, Z.; Huang, C.; Li, T.; Ma, Q. Deep reinforcement learning based optimal trajectory tracking control of autonomous underwater vehicle. In Proceedings of the 2017 36th Chinese Control Conference (CCC), Dalian, China, 26–28 July 2017.
46. Monahan, G.E. A Survey of Partially Observable Markov Decision Processes: Theory, Models, and Algorithms. *Manag. Sci.* **1982**, *28*, 1–16. [CrossRef]
47. Sutton, R.S.; Barto, A.G. *Reinforcement Learning: An Introduction*; MIT Press: Cambridge, MA, USA, 2018.
48. Konda, V.R.; Tsitsiklis, J.N. Actor-critic algorithms. *SIAM J. Control Optim.* **2002**, *42*, 1143–1166. [CrossRef]

49. Yan, Z.; Zhuang, J. Active Disturbance Rejection Algorithm Applied to Path Tracking in Autonomous Vehicles. *J. Chongqing Univ. Technol. Nat. Sci.* **2020**, 1–10. (In Chinese). Available online: http://kns.cnki.net/kcms/detail/50.1205.T.20200522.1459.004.html (accessed on 10 June 2021).
50. Chao, C.; Gao, H.; Ding, L.; Li, W.; Yu, H.; Deng, Z. Trajectory tracking control of wmrs with lateral and longitudinal slippage based on active disturbance rejection control. *Robot. Auton. Syst.* **2018**, *107*, 236–245.
51. Gao, Y.; Xia, Y. Lateral path tracking control of autonomous land vehicle based on active disturbance rejection control. In Proceedings of the 32nd Chinese Control Conference, Xian, China, 26–28 July 2013.
52. Pan, X.; You, Y.; Wang, Z.; Lu, C. Virtual to Real Reinforcement Learning for Autonomous Driving. In Proceedings of the 2017 British Machine Vision Conference, London, UK, 4–7 September 2017.
53. Hu, H.; Zhang, K.; Tan, A.H.; Ruan, M.; Agia, C.; Nejat, G. A Sim-to-Real Pipeline for Deep Reinforcement Learning for Autonomous Robot Navigation in Cluttered Rough Terrain. *IEEE Robot. Autom. Lett.* **2021**, *6*, 6569–6576. [CrossRef]
54. Chaffre, T.; Moras, J.; Chan-Hon-Tong, A.; Marzat, J. Sim-to-Real Transfer with Incremental Environment Complexity for Reinforcement Learning of Depth-based Robot Navigation. In Proceedings of the 17th International Conference on Informatics in Control, Automation and Robotics, Paris, France, 7–9 July 2020.
55. Suenaga, R.; Morioka, K. Development of a Web-Based Education System for Deep Reinforcement Learning-Based Autonomous Mobile Robot Navigation in Real World. In Proceedings of the 2020 IEEE/SICE International Symposium on System Integration (SII), Honolulu, HA, USA, 12–15 January 2020.

Article

Key Validity Using the Multiple-Parameter Fractional Fourier Transform for Image Encryption

Tieyu Zhao *[ ] and Yingying Chi

Information Science Teaching and Research Section, School of Mathematics and Statistics, Northeastern University at Qinhuangdao, Qinhuangdao 066004, China; chiyingying@neuq.edu.cn
* Correspondence: zhaotieyu@neuq.edu.cn

Abstract: As a symmetric encryption algorithm, multiple-parameter fractional Fourier transform (MPFRFT) is proposed and applied to image encryption. The MPFRFT with two vector parameters has better security, which becomes the main technical means to protect information security. However, our study found that many keys of the MPFRFT are invalid, which greatly reduces its security. In this paper, we propose a new reformulation of MPFRFT and analyze it using eigen-decomposition-type fractional Fourier transform (FRFT) and weighted-type FRFT as basis functions, respectively. The results show that the effective keys are extremely limited. Furthermore, we analyze the extended encryption methods based on MPFRFT, which also have the security risk of key invalidation. Theoretical analysis and numerical simulation verify our point of view. Our discovery has important reference value for a class of generalized FRFT image encryption methods.

Keywords: multiple-parameter fractional Fourier transform; image encryption; weighted fractional Fourier transform; information security

Citation: Zhao, T.; Chi, Y. Key Validity Using the Multiple-Parameter Fractional Fourier Transform for Image Encryption. *Symmetry* **2021**, *13*, 1803. https://doi.org/10.3390/sym13101803

Academic Editors: Rudolf Kawalla, Beloglazov Ilya and Jan Awrejcewicz

Received: 2 September 2021
Accepted: 26 September 2021
Published: 28 September 2021

Publisher's Note: MDPI stays neutral with regard to jurisdictional claims in published maps and institutional affiliations.

Copyright: © 2021 by the authors. Licensee MDPI, Basel, Switzerland. This article is an open access article distributed under the terms and conditions of the Creative Commons Attribution (CC BY) license (https://creativecommons.org/licenses/by/4.0/).

1. Introduction

With the rapid development of information technology, image transmission has become an important means of communication. Traditional symmetric encryption algorithms (such as DES, AES, etc.) are very time-consuming and costly when applied to image encryption. The development of new image encryption algorithms has become the focus of research. Therefore, many image encryption methods have been proposed [1,2]. These include image encryption methods based on multiple-parameter fractional Fourier transform (MPFRFT) [3]. In 2008, Tao et al. proposed an image encryption method based on multiple-parameter fractional Fourier transform (MPFRFT) [3]. In the encryption process, multiple keys are used to expand the key space of the system and thus have better security. Since then, the MPFRFT has become an important means to protect information security, and many research results have been proposed [4–18]. The MPFRFT is an extended definition of multifractional Fourier transform [19]. Compared with previous encryption schemes [19,20], the MPFRFT not only uses the period and the transformation order as the keys, but also introduces two vector parameters, and vector parameters increase with the increase of the period, so it has better security. The existing encryption schemes mainly focus on two aspects: One is to use the MPFRFT combined with other encryption methods to ensure security [4–9]. For example, its combination with chaos is currently the most used encryption strategy [4–7], and its combination with other scrambling techniques [8,9], and so on. The second is the improvement of the algorithm. The two vector parameters introduced by the MPFRFT are integers, which will face security risks in applications [10,11]. Therefore, some improved schemes have been proposed [10–18]. For example, Ran et al. proposed a modified MPFRFT (m-MPFRFT), which overcomes the security risk of parameter redundancy [10], Zhao et al. proposed the vector power MPFRFT (VPMPFRFT) to overcome the security risk of parameter translation [16], and Kang et al. presented a unified framework for the MPFRFT and proposed new types of transforms in signal processing and information security [17]. These new encryption methods improve the security of image encryption to a certain extent [10,15–17]. However, it is not difficult to find that such definitions have the same basis functions as MPFRFT. Whether the security risk of MPFRFT for image encryption affects these encryption methods is also the focus of this paper.

In this paper, we propose a new reformulation of MPFRFT. With the help of the proposed reformulation, the definition of MPFRFT is demonstrated to use eigen-decomposition-type FRFT and weighted-type FRFT as basis functions, respectively. However, our research shows that many parameter keys of either the MPFRFT or its modified schemes are invalid, and it cannot obtain a larger key space with the increase of the weighting term. This is determined by the periodicity of the basis function itself, and we will present a detailed analysis.

2. Reformulation of the MPFRFT

In order to demonstrate our point of view, we propose a new reformulation of the MPFRFT. Firstly, Tao et al. proposed the MPFRFT [3], which is defined as:

$$F_M^\alpha(\mathfrak{M},\mathfrak{N})[f(t)] = \sum_{l=0}^{M-1} A_l^\alpha(\mathfrak{M},\mathfrak{N}) f_l(t), \tag{1}$$

where the basic functions can be expressed as $f_l(t) = F^{4l/M}[f(t)]; l = 0, 1, 2, \cdots, M-1$. The weighting coefficient, $A_l^\alpha(\mathfrak{M},\mathfrak{N})$, is expressed as:

$$A_l^\alpha(\mathfrak{M},\mathfrak{N}) = \frac{1}{M} \sum_{k=0}^{M-1} \exp\left\{\frac{2\pi i}{M}[(m_k M + 1)\alpha(k + n_k M) - lk]\right\}, \tag{2}$$

where $\mathfrak{M} = (m_0, m_1, \cdots, m_{M-1}) \in \mathbb{Z}^M$, $\mathfrak{N} = (n_0, n_1, \cdots, n_{M-1}) \in \mathbb{Z}^M$. According to Shih's definition [21], the weighting coefficient, A_l^α, can also be expressed as:

$$\begin{pmatrix} A_0^\alpha \\ A_1^\alpha \\ \vdots \\ A_{M-1}^\alpha \end{pmatrix} = \frac{1}{M} \begin{pmatrix} u^{0\times 0} & u^{0\times 1} & \cdots & u^{0\times(M-1)} \\ u^{1\times 0} & u^{1\times 1} & \cdots & u^{1\times(M-1)} \\ \vdots & \vdots & \ddots & \vdots \\ u^{(M-1)\times 0} & u^{(M-1)\times 1} & \cdots & u^{(M-1)\times(M-1)} \end{pmatrix} \begin{pmatrix} B_0^\alpha \\ B_1^\alpha \\ \vdots \\ B_{M-1}^\alpha \end{pmatrix}, \tag{3}$$

where $u = \exp(-2\pi i/M)$, and

$$B_k^\alpha = \exp\left[\frac{2\pi i \alpha (m_k M + 1)(n_k M + k)}{M}\right], \tag{4}$$

where $k = 0, 1, 2, \cdots, M-1$, $m_k \in \mathfrak{M}$ and $n_k \in \mathfrak{N}$.

Next, we will present a new reformulation of the MPFRFT, and Equation (1) can be re-expressed as:

$$\begin{aligned} F_M^\alpha(\mathfrak{M},\mathfrak{N})[f(t)] &= A_0^\alpha(\mathfrak{M},\mathfrak{N}) f_0(t) + A_1^\alpha(\mathfrak{M},\mathfrak{N}) f_1(t) + \cdots + A_{M-1}^\alpha(\mathfrak{M},\mathfrak{N}) f_{M-1}(t) \\ &= A_0^\alpha F^{\frac{0}{M}}[f(t)] + A_1^\alpha F^{\frac{4}{M}}[f(t)] + \cdots + A_{M-1}^\alpha F^{\frac{4(M-1)}{M}}[f(t)] \\ &= \left(A_0^\alpha I + A_1^\alpha F^{\frac{4}{M}} + \cdots + A_{M-1}^\alpha F^{\frac{4(M-1)}{M}}\right) f(t) \\ &= \left(I, F^{\frac{4}{M}}, \cdots, F^{\frac{4(M-1)}{M}}\right) \begin{pmatrix} A_0^\alpha \\ A_1^\alpha \\ \vdots \\ A_{M-1}^\alpha \end{pmatrix} f(t). \end{aligned} \tag{5}$$

From Equations (3) and (5), we can obtain:

$$F_M^\alpha(\mathfrak{M},\mathfrak{N})[f(t)] = \frac{1}{M}\left(I, F^{\frac{4}{M}}, \cdots, F^{\frac{4(M-1)}{M}}\right)\begin{pmatrix} u^{0\times 0} & u^{0\times 1} & \cdots & u^{0\times(M-1)} \\ u^{1\times 0} & u^{1\times 1} & \cdots & u^{1\times(M-1)} \\ \vdots & \vdots & \ddots & \vdots \\ u^{(M-1)\times 0} & u^{(M-1)\times 1} & \cdots & u^{(M-1)\times(M-1)} \end{pmatrix}\begin{pmatrix} B_0^\alpha \\ B_1^\alpha \\ \vdots \\ B_{M-1}^\alpha \end{pmatrix} f(t), \quad (6)$$

where $u = \exp(-2\pi i/M)$ and B_k^α is Equation (4). Here, we let:

$$\begin{cases} Y_0 = u^{0\times 0} I + u^{1\times 0} F^{\frac{4}{M}} + \cdots + u^{(M-1)\times 0} F^{\frac{4(M-1)}{M}} \\ Y_1 = u^{0\times 1} I + u^{1\times 1} F^{\frac{4}{M}} + \cdots + u^{(M-1)\times 1} F^{\frac{4(M-1)}{M}} \\ Y_2 = u^{0\times 2} I + u^{1\times 2} F^{\frac{4}{M}} + \cdots + u^{(M-1)\times 2} F^{\frac{4(M-1)}{M}} \\ \vdots \\ Y_{M-1} = u^{0\times(M-1)} I + u^{1\times(M-1)} F^{\frac{4}{M}} + \cdots + u^{(M-1)\times(M-1)} F^{\frac{4(M-1)}{M}} \end{cases} \quad (7)$$

Therefore, a new reformulation of the MPFRFT is obtained, as:

$$\begin{aligned} F_M^\alpha(\mathfrak{M},\mathfrak{N})[f(t)] &= \frac{1}{M}(Y_0, Y_1, \cdots, Y_{M-1})\begin{pmatrix} B_0^\alpha \\ B_1^\alpha \\ \vdots \\ B_{M-1}^\alpha \end{pmatrix} f(t) \\ &= \frac{1}{M}\sum_{k=0}^{M-1} Y_k B_k^\alpha f(t). \end{aligned} \quad (8)$$

where B_k^α is Equation (4).

3. Security Analysis

We know that the MPFRFT and the multifractional Fourier transform have the same basis function, $F^{4l/M}$; $l = 0, 1, \cdots, M-1$. Fractional Fourier transform (FRFT) has diversity, so we will discuss the eigen-decomposition-type FRFT and linear weighted-type FRFT as basis functions, respectively.

3.1. Eigen-Decomposition-Type FRFT as a Basis Function

In [3], the basis function involved in the MPFRFT is defined as:

$$F^\alpha[f(t)] = \int_{-\infty}^{\infty} K_\alpha(u,t) f(t) dt, \quad (9)$$

where the transform kernel is given by:

$$K_\alpha(u,t) = \begin{cases} A_\alpha e^{i\frac{u^2+t^2}{2}\cot\phi - iut\csc\phi}, & \alpha \neq k\pi \\ \delta(u-t), & \alpha = 2k\pi \\ \delta(u+t), & \alpha = (2k+1)\pi. \end{cases} \quad (10)$$

where $\phi = \alpha\pi/2$ is interpreted as a rotation angle in the phase plane and $A_\alpha = \sqrt{(1-i\cot\alpha)/2\pi}$.

As we know, Equation (9) is a continuous FRFT, and a discrete FRFT is used for numerical simulation. At present, the discrete definition [22] closest to the continuous FRFT is:

$$F^\alpha(m,n) = \sum_{k=0}^{N-1} v_k(m) e^{-i\frac{\pi}{2}k\alpha} v_k(n), \quad (11)$$

where $v_k(n)$ is an arbitrary orthonormal eigenvectors set of the $N \times N$ discrete Fourier transform (DFT). Equation (11) can be written as:

$$F^\alpha = VD^\alpha V^H, \tag{12}$$

where $V = (v_0, v_1, \cdots, v_{N-1})$, v_k is the kth order DFT Hermite eigenvector, and D^α is a diagonal matrix defined as:

$$D^\alpha = \text{diag}\left(1, e^{-i\frac{\pi}{2}\alpha}, \cdots, e^{-i\frac{\pi}{2}(N-2)\alpha}, e^{-i\frac{\pi}{2}(N-1)\alpha}\right), \text{ for } N \text{ odd}, \tag{13}$$

and

$$D^\alpha = \text{diag}\left(1, e^{-i\frac{\pi}{2}\alpha}, \cdots, e^{-i\frac{\pi}{2}(N-2)\alpha}, e^{-i\frac{\pi}{2}(N)\alpha}\right), \text{ for } N \text{ even}. \tag{14}$$

We only prove that N is odd (when N is even, the proof process is the same). In [23,24], the eigenvalues of the DFT can be expressed as $\lambda_n = e^{n\pi i/2}$. Then, the possible values of the eigenvalue are $\lambda_n = \{1, -1, i, -i\}$. Therefore, there is:

$$D^\alpha = \text{diag}((1)^\alpha, (-i)^\alpha, (-1)^\alpha, (i)^\alpha, (1)^\alpha, (-i)^\alpha, (-1)^\alpha, (i)^\alpha, \cdots, (1 \text{ or } -1)^\alpha). \tag{15}$$

Thus, Equation (7) can be written as:

$$Y_k = u^{0 \times k} \times I + u^{1 \times k} \times F^{\frac{4}{M}} + \cdots + u^{(M-1) \times k} \times F^{\frac{4(M-1)}{M}}, \tag{16}$$

where $u = \exp(-2\pi i/M)$ and $k = 0, 1, \cdots, M-1$. The eigen-decomposition-type FRFT is used as the basis function, and Equation (17) is obtained as:

$$\begin{aligned}
Y_k &= u^{0 \times k} \times F^0 + u^{1 \times k} \times F^{\frac{4}{M}} + \cdots + u^{(M-1) \times k} \times F^{\frac{4(M-1)}{M}} \\
&= u^{0 \times k} VD^0 V^H + u^{1 \times k} VD^{\frac{4}{M}} V^H + \cdots + u^{(M-1) \times k} VD^{\frac{4(M-1)}{M}} V^H \\
&= u^{0 \times k} V \begin{pmatrix} 1 & 0 & \cdots & 0 \\ 0 & (-i)^0 & \cdots & 0 \\ \vdots & \vdots & \ddots & \vdots \\ 0 & 0 & \cdots & (1 \text{ or } -1)^0 \end{pmatrix} V^H + u^{1 \times k} V \begin{pmatrix} 1 & 0 & \cdots & 0 \\ 0 & (-i)^{\frac{4}{M}} & \cdots & 0 \\ \vdots & \vdots & \ddots & \vdots \\ 0 & 0 & \cdots & (1 \text{ or } -1)^{\frac{4}{M}} \end{pmatrix} V^H + \\
&\quad \cdots + u^{(M-1) \times k} V \begin{pmatrix} 1 & 0 & \cdots & 0 \\ 0 & (-i)^{\frac{4(M-1)}{M}} & \cdots & 0 \\ \vdots & \vdots & \ddots & \vdots \\ 0 & 0 & \cdots & (1 \text{ or } -1)^{\frac{4(M-1)}{M}} \end{pmatrix} V^H.
\end{aligned} \tag{17}$$

Therefore, we obtain Equation (18) as:

$$Y_k = V \begin{pmatrix} S^{(1)}(k) & 0 & \cdots & 0 \\ 0 & S^{(-i)}(k) & \cdots & 0 \\ \vdots & \vdots & \ddots & \vdots \\ 0 & 0 & \cdots & S^{(1 \text{ or } -1)}(k) \end{pmatrix} V^H. \tag{18}$$

From Equation (18), the diagonal matrix only contains $S^{(1)}(k)$, $S^{(i)}(k)$, $S^{(-1)}(k)$, and $S^{(-i)}(k)$.

When the eigenvalue is 1, $S^{(1)}(k)$ can be expressed as:

$$\begin{aligned} S^{(1)}(k) &= u^{0\times k}1^0 + u^{1\times k}1^{4/M} + \cdots + u^{(M-1)\times k}1^{4(M-1)/M} \\ &= 1 + e^{-2\pi i 1 k/M} + e^{-2\pi i 2k/M} + \cdots + e^{-2\pi i (M-1)k/M} \\ &= \frac{1-\left(e^{-2\pi i k/M}\right)^M}{1-e^{-2\pi i(k-0)/M}}. \end{aligned} \qquad (19)$$

Therefore, we obtain:

$$S^{(1)}(k) = \begin{cases} 0 & k \not\equiv 0 \bmod M \\ M & k \equiv 0 \bmod M. \end{cases} \qquad (20)$$

When the eigenvalue is i, $S^{(i)}(k)$ can be expressed as:

$$\begin{aligned} S^{(i)}(k) &= u^{0\times k}(i)^0 + u^{1\times k}(i)^{4/M} + \cdots + u^{(M-1)\times k}(i)^{4(M-1)/M} \\ &= 1 + e^{-2\pi i 1(k-1)/M} + e^{-2\pi i 2(k-1)/M} + \cdots + e^{-2\pi i (M-1)(k-1)/M} \\ &= \frac{1-\left(e^{-2\pi i(k-1)/M}\right)^M}{1-e^{-2\pi i(k-1)/M}}. \end{aligned} \qquad (21)$$

Therefore, there is:

$$S^{(i)}(k) = \begin{cases} 0 & k \not\equiv 1 \bmod M \\ M & k \equiv 1 \bmod M. \end{cases} \qquad (22)$$

When the eigenvalue is -1, $S^{(-1)}(k)$ can be expressed as:

$$\begin{aligned} S^{(-1)}(k) &= u^{0\times k}(-1)^0 + u^{1\times k}(-1)^{4/M} + \cdots + u^{(M-1)\times k}(-1)^{4(M-1)/M} \\ &= 1 + e^{-2\pi i 1(k-2)/M} + e^{-2\pi i 2(k-2)/M} + \cdots + e^{-2\pi i (M-1)(k-2)/M} \\ &= \frac{1-\left(e^{-2\pi i(k-2)/M}\right)^M}{1-e^{-2\pi i(k-2)/M}}. \end{aligned} \qquad (23)$$

Then, we can obtain:

$$S^{(-1)}(k) = \begin{cases} 0 & k \not\equiv 2 \bmod M \\ M & k \equiv 2 \bmod M. \end{cases} \qquad (24)$$

When the eigenvalue is $-i$, $S^{(-i)}(k)$ can be expressed as:

$$\begin{aligned} S^{(-i)}(k) &= u^{0\times k}(-i)^0 + u^{1\times k}(-i)^{4/M} + \cdots + u^{(M-1)\times k}(-i)^{4(M-1)/M} \\ &= 1 + e^{-2\pi i 1(k-3)/M} + e^{-2\pi i 2(k-3)/M} + \cdots + e^{-2\pi i (M-1)(k-3)/M} \\ &= \frac{1-\left(e^{-2\pi i(k-3)/M}\right)^M}{1-e^{-2\pi i(k-3)/M}}. \end{aligned} \qquad (25)$$

Therefore, there is:

$$S^{(-i)}(k) = \begin{cases} 0 & k \not\equiv 3 \bmod M \\ M & k \equiv 3 \bmod M. \end{cases} \qquad (26)$$

From Equations (20), (22), (24), and (26), then, Equation (18) can be written as:

$$Y_k = \begin{cases} Y_k & k = 0,1,2,3 \\ 0 & k = 4,5,\cdots, M-1. \end{cases} \qquad (27)$$

Thus, for Equation (8), the MPFRFT is expressed as:

$$F_M^\alpha(\mathfrak{M}, \mathfrak{N})[f(t)] = \frac{1}{M}(Y_0, Y_1, \cdots, Y_{M-1}) \begin{pmatrix} B_0^\alpha \\ B_1^\alpha \\ \vdots \\ B_{M-1}^\alpha \end{pmatrix} f(t)$$

$$= \frac{1}{M}(Y_0, Y_1, Y_2, Y_3, 0, \cdots, 0) \begin{pmatrix} B_0^\alpha \\ B_1^\alpha \\ \vdots \\ B_{M-1}^\alpha \end{pmatrix} f(t) \quad (28)$$

$$= \frac{1}{M}(Y_0 B_0^\alpha + Y_1 B_1^\alpha + Y_2 B_2^\alpha + Y_3 B_3^\alpha) f(t).$$

From Equation (28), we find that there are only four effective weighted terms. That is, for the vector parameters $(\mathfrak{M}, \mathfrak{N})$ of the MPFRFT, only $(m_0, m_1, m_2, m_3; n_0, n_1, n_2, n_3)$ can be used as valid encryption keys, and the other keys $(m_4, m_5, \cdots, m_{M-1}; n_4, n_5, \cdots, n_{M-1})$ are invalid. This leads to the security of the MPFRFT being impaired.

3.2. Weighted-Type FRFT as a Basis Function

The MPFRFT is a generalized multifractional Fourier transform, which has the same basis function, $F^{4l/M}$. The multifractional Fourier transform is a generalized definition of the weighted fractional Fourier transform (WFRFT) [21]. The basis functions of the WFRFT are I, F, F^2, and F^3. Therefore, we can determine the time-frequency representation of the basis function, as shown in Figure 1. We consider using the WFRFT as the basis function of the MPFRFT.

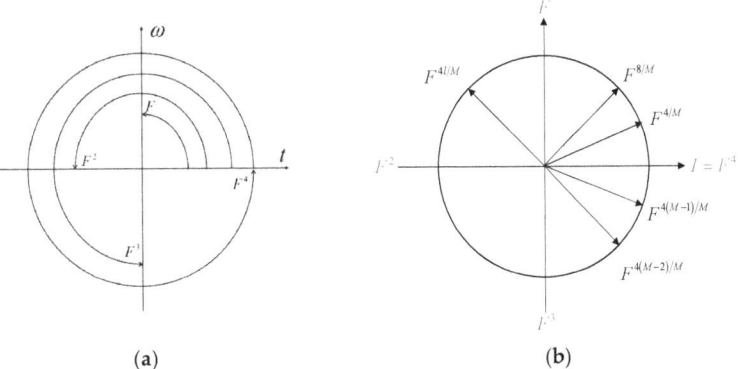

(a)   (b)

Figure 1. (a) Time-frequency representation of Fourier transform, and (b) time-frequency representation of fractional Fourier transform.

Shih proposed the WFRFT [21], which is defined as:

$$F^\alpha[f(t)] = \sum_{l=0}^{3} A_l^\alpha f_l(t), \quad (29)$$

with

$$A_l^\alpha = \cos\left(\frac{(\alpha-l)\pi}{4}\right) \cos\left(\frac{2(\alpha-l)\pi}{4}\right) \exp\left(\frac{3(\alpha-l)i\pi}{4}\right), \quad (30)$$

where $f_l(t) = F^l[f(t)]; l = 0, 1, 2, 3$ (F denotes Fourier transform). Shih's WFRFT with period 4 is also called the 4-weighted-type fractional Fourier transform (4-WFRFT). Equation (29) can also be expressed as:

$$\begin{aligned} F^\alpha[f(t)] &= (A_0^\alpha \cdot I + A_1^\alpha \cdot F + A_2^\alpha \cdot F^2 + A_3^\alpha \cdot F^3) f(t) \\ &= (I, F, F^2, F^3) \begin{pmatrix} A_0^\alpha \\ A_1^\alpha \\ A_2^\alpha \\ A_3^\alpha \end{pmatrix} f(t). \end{aligned} \quad (31)$$

According to the definition of the weighting coefficient, A_l^α [21], then, Equation (31) can be expressed as:

$$F^\alpha[f(t)] = \frac{1}{4}(I, F, F^2, F^3) \begin{pmatrix} 1 & 1 & 1 & 1 \\ 1 & -i & -1 & i \\ 1 & -1 & 1 & -1 \\ 1 & i & -1 & -i \end{pmatrix} \begin{pmatrix} B_0^\alpha \\ B_1^\alpha \\ B_2^\alpha \\ B_3^\alpha \end{pmatrix} f(t), \quad (32)$$

where $B_k^\alpha = \exp\left(\frac{2\pi i k \alpha}{4}\right), k = 0, 1, 2, 3$. Here, we let:

$$\begin{cases} P_0 = I + F + F^2 + F^3 \\ P_1 = I - F * i - F^2 + F^3 * i \\ P_2 = I - F + F^2 - F^3 \\ P_3 = I + F * i - F^2 - F^3 * i. \end{cases} \quad (33)$$

Therefore, the WFRFT can be represented as:

$$F^\alpha[f(t)] = \frac{1}{4}(P_0, P_1, P_2, P_3) \begin{pmatrix} B_0^\alpha \\ B_1^\alpha \\ B_2^\alpha \\ B_3^\alpha \end{pmatrix} f(t). \quad (34)$$

From Equations (7) and (34), we can obtain:

$$\begin{aligned} Y_k &= u^{0 \times k} \times F^0 + u^{1 \times k} \times F^{\frac{4}{M}} + \cdots + u^{(M-1) \times k} \times F^{\frac{4(M-1)}{M}} \\ &= \frac{1}{4}(P_0, P_1, P_2, P_3) \left(u^{0 \times k} \times \begin{pmatrix} B_0^0 \\ B_1^0 \\ B_2^0 \\ B_3^0 \end{pmatrix} + u^{1 \times k} \times \begin{pmatrix} B_0^{\frac{4}{M}} \\ B_1^{\frac{4}{M}} \\ B_2^{\frac{4}{M}} \\ B_3^{\frac{4}{M}} \end{pmatrix} + \cdots + u^{(M-1) \times k} \times \begin{pmatrix} B_0^{\frac{4(M-1)}{M}} \\ B_1^{\frac{4(M-1)}{M}} \\ B_2^{\frac{4(M-1)}{M}} \\ B_3^{\frac{4(M-1)}{M}} \end{pmatrix} \right) \\ &= \frac{1}{4}(P_0, P_1, P_2, P_3) \begin{pmatrix} u^{0 \times k} \times B_0^0 + u^{1 \times k} \times B_0^{\frac{4}{M}} + \cdots + u^{(M-1) \times k} \times B_0^{\frac{4(M-1)}{M}} \\ u^{0 \times k} \times B_1^0 + u^{1 \times k} \times B_1^{\frac{4}{M}} + \cdots + u^{(M-1) \times k} \times B_1^{\frac{4(M-1)}{M}} \\ u^{0 \times k} \times B_2^0 + u^{1 \times k} \times B_2^{\frac{4}{M}} + \cdots + u^{(M-1) \times k} \times B_2^{\frac{4(M-1)}{M}} \\ u^{0 \times k} \times B_3^0 + u^{1 \times k} \times B_3^{\frac{4}{M}} + \cdots + u^{(M-1) \times k} \times B_3^{\frac{4(M-1)}{M}} \end{pmatrix}, \end{aligned} \quad (35)$$

where $k = 0, 1, \cdots, M-1$, $u = \exp(-2\pi i/M)$, and $B_k^\alpha = \exp\left(\frac{2\pi i k \alpha}{4}\right)$. Therefore,

Equation (36) is obtained as:

$$Y_k = \frac{1}{4}(P_0, P_1, P_2, P_3) \begin{pmatrix} 1 + \exp\left(\frac{-2\pi i 1 k}{M}\right) + \exp\left(\frac{-2\pi i 2 k}{M}\right) + \cdots + \exp\left(\frac{-2\pi i (M-1) k}{M}\right) \\ 1 + \exp\left(\frac{-2\pi i 1 (k-1)}{M}\right) + \exp\left(\frac{-2\pi i 2 (k-1)}{M}\right) + \cdots + \exp\left(\frac{-2\pi i (M-1)(k-1)}{M}\right) \\ 1 + \exp\left(\frac{-2\pi i 1 (k-2)}{M}\right) + \exp\left(\frac{-2\pi i 2 (k-2)}{M}\right) + \cdots + \exp\left(\frac{-2\pi i (M-1)(k-2)}{M}\right) \\ 1 + \exp\left(\frac{-2\pi i 1 (k-3)}{M}\right) + \exp\left(\frac{-2\pi i 2 (k-3)}{M}\right) + \cdots + \exp\left(\frac{-2\pi i (M-1)(k-3)}{M}\right) \end{pmatrix}$$

$$= \frac{1}{4}(P_0, P_1, P_2, P_3) \begin{pmatrix} Q_0(k) \\ Q_1(k) \\ Q_2(k) \\ Q_3(k) \end{pmatrix}. \qquad (36)$$

According to Equations (19), (21), (23), and (25), we can easily determine:

$$Q_0(k) = \begin{cases} M & k \equiv 0 \bmod M \\ 0 & k \not\equiv 0 \bmod M, \end{cases} \qquad (37)$$

$$Q_1(k) = \begin{cases} M & k \equiv 1 \bmod M \\ 0 & k \not\equiv 1 \bmod M, \end{cases} \qquad (38)$$

$$Q_2(k) = \begin{cases} M & k \equiv 2 \bmod M \\ 0 & k \not\equiv 2 \bmod M, \end{cases} \qquad (39)$$

and

$$Q_3(k) = \begin{cases} M & k \equiv 3 \bmod M \\ 0 & k \not\equiv 3 \bmod M. \end{cases} \qquad (40)$$

Thus, Equation (36) is simplified as:

$$Y_k = \begin{cases} \frac{M}{4} P_k & k = 0, 1, 2, 3 \\ 0 & k = 4, 5, \cdots, M-1. \end{cases} \qquad (41)$$

From Equation (8), the MPFRFT can be expressed as:

$$\begin{aligned} F_M^\alpha(\mathfrak{M}, \mathfrak{N})[f(t)] &= \frac{1}{M}(Y_0, Y_1, \cdots, Y_{M-1}) \begin{pmatrix} B_0^\alpha \\ B_1^\alpha \\ \vdots \\ B_{M-1}^\alpha \end{pmatrix} f(t) \\ &= \frac{1}{4}(P_0, P_1, P_2, P_3, 0, \cdots, 0) \begin{pmatrix} B_0^\alpha \\ B_1^\alpha \\ \vdots \\ B_{M-1}^\alpha \end{pmatrix} f(t) \\ &= \frac{1}{4}\left(P_0 B_0^\alpha + P_1 B_1^\alpha + P_2 B_2^\alpha + P_3 B_3^\alpha\right) f(t). \end{aligned} \qquad (42)$$

At present, the MPFRFT has only four weighted terms, so the effective parameter keys are $(m_0, m_1, m_2, m_3; n_0, n_1, n_2, n_3)$. This is consistent with our previous analysis.

4. Simulation Verification

In Equation (8), the MPFRFT encryption keys are $(M, \alpha, \mathfrak{M}, \mathfrak{N})$. Here, M is a positive integer to determine the number of weighted terms $(M > 4)$, α is the transformation order

$\alpha \in \mathbb{R}$, and $\mathfrak{M}$ and $\mathfrak{N}$ are vector parameters, where $\mathfrak{M} = (m_0, m_1, \cdots, m_{M-1}) \in \mathbb{Z}^M$ and $\mathfrak{N} = (n_0, n_1, \cdots, n_{M-1}) \in \mathbb{Z}^M$. We set the keys to:

$$\begin{cases} M = 7 \\ \alpha = \sqrt{5} \\ \mathfrak{M} = (m_0, m_1, m_2, m_3, m_4, m_5, m_6) = (45, 8, 20, 76, 657, 211, 7) \\ \mathfrak{N} = (n_0, n_1, n_2, n_3, n_4, n_5, n_6) = (3, 234, 54, 687, 763, 5, 365) \end{cases}$$

Therefore, the encryption keys can be represented as:

$$(M; \alpha; \mathfrak{M}; \mathfrak{N}) = \left(7; \sqrt{5}; \; 45, 8, 20, 76, 657, 211, 7; 3, 234, 54, 687, 763, 5, 365\right)$$

and the decryption keys can be represented as:

$$(M; \alpha; \mathfrak{M}; \mathfrak{N}) = \left(7; -\sqrt{5}; \; 45, 8, 20, 76, 657, 211, 7; 3, 234, 54, 687, 763, 5, 365\right)$$

The simulation results are shown in Figure 2. Figure 2a is the original image, the encrypted image (ciphertext) is shown in Figure 2b, and Figure 2c is the decrypted image. Next, we select a set of wrong keys to decrypt the ciphertext. The selected wrong keys are:

$$(M; \alpha; \mathfrak{M}; \mathfrak{N}) = \left(7; -\sqrt{5}; \; 45, 8, 20, 76, 98, 321, 65; 3, 234, 54, 687, 73, 425, 5\right)$$

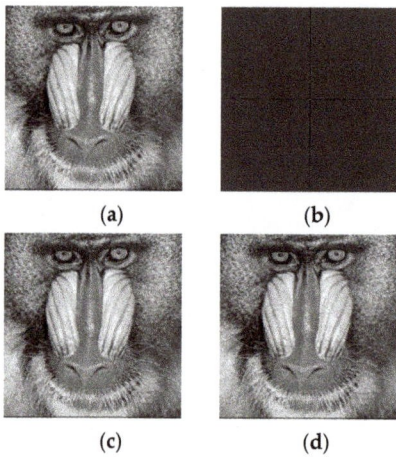

Figure 2. Image encryption based on MPFRFT: (**a**) original image, (**b**) encrypted image, (**c**) decrypted image with correct keys, and (**d**) decrypted image with wrong keys.

The wrong keys are used to decrypt the ciphertext, and the result is that the original image is well-recovered, as shown in Figure 2d.

Our theoretical analysis was verified by numerical simulation. In Appendix A, the Matlab code of the MPFRFT is presented, and interested researchers can verify it by themselves.

5. Discussion

The m-MPFRFT and VPMPFRFT are generalized definitions based on MPFRFT and are widely used in image encryption. Such image encryption methods will also have security risks of key invalidation.

In 2009, Ran et al. proposed a m-MPFRFT [10]. If B_k^α in Equation (4) becomes:

$$B_k^\alpha(r_k) = \exp\left[\frac{2\pi i \alpha (r_k M + k)}{M}\right], \qquad (43)$$

then the weighting coefficient A_l^α becomes:

$$A_l^\alpha(\Re) = \frac{1}{M}\sum_{k=0}^{M-1}\exp\left\{\frac{2\pi i}{M}[\alpha(k+r_kM)-lk]\right\}, \quad (44)$$

where $\Re = (r_0, r_1, \cdots, r_{M-1}) \in \mathbb{R}^M$. Thus, the m-MPFRFT is obtained by:

$$F_M^\alpha(\Re)[f(x)] = \sum_{l=0}^{M-1} A_l^\alpha(\Re) f_l(x). \quad (45)$$

Recently, Zhao et al. proposed the definition of VPMPFRFT [15,16]. If B_k^α in Equation (4) becomes:

$$B_k^{\bar{\alpha}}(r_k) = \exp\left[\frac{2\pi i\alpha_k(r_kM+k)}{M}\right], \quad (46)$$

then the weighting coefficient A_l^α becomes:

$$A_l^{\bar{\alpha}}(\Re) = \frac{1}{M}\sum_{k=0}^{M-1}\exp\left\{\frac{2\pi i}{M}[\alpha_k(k+r_kM)-lk]\right\}, \quad (47)$$

where $\bar{\alpha} = (\alpha_0, \alpha_1, \cdots, \alpha_{M-1}) \in \mathbb{R}^M$, $\Re = (r_0, r_1, \cdots, r_{M-1}) \in \mathbb{R}^M$. Then, the definition of the VPMPFRFT can be expressed as:

$$F_M^{\bar{\alpha}}(\Re)[f(x)] = \sum_{l=0}^{M-1} A_l^{\bar{\alpha}}(\Re) f_l(x). \quad (48)$$

In the above definition, when B_k^α is given a different form, the corresponding weighting coefficient is A_l^α, and various definition forms are obtained. The common features of these definitions have the same basis function, $f_l(t) = F^{4l/M}[f(t)]$.

According to the analysis in Section 2, when Equation (43) replaces B_k^α of Equation (8), thus, the reformulation of m-MPFRFT can be obtained as:

$$F_M^\alpha(\Re)[f(t)] = \frac{1}{M}\sum_{k=0}^{M-1} Y_k B_k^\alpha(r_k) f(t). \quad (49)$$

Therefore, when Equation (46) replaces B_k^α of Equation (8), the reformulation of m-MPFRFT can be obtained as:

$$F_M^{\bar{\alpha}}(\Re)[f(t)] = \frac{1}{M}\sum_{k=0}^{M-1} Y_k B_k^{\bar{\alpha}}(r_k) f(t). \quad (50)$$

Compared with the definition of MPFRFT, m-WFRFT and VPMPFRFT are only different in the selection of B_k^α, while other basis functions are the same. That is, the effective weighting terms of Equations (49) and (50) are only 4. Such image encryption methods also have the security risk of key invalidation.

The m-MPFRFT is now applied to image encryption, and its keys are $(M, \alpha, \Re)$. Here, M is a positive integer to determine the number of weighted terms, α is the transformation order $\alpha \in \mathbb{R}$, and $\Re$ is the vector parameters, $\Re = (r_0, r_1, \cdots, r_{M-1}) \in \mathbb{R}^M$. In the numerical simulation, we take the keys as:

$$\begin{cases} M = 8 \\ \alpha = \sqrt{5} \\ \Re = (r_0, r_1, r_2, r_3, r_4, r_5, r_6, r_7) = \left(\sqrt{6}, \sqrt{51}, \sqrt{43}, 30, 38/3, \sqrt{19}, 11, \sqrt{62}\right) \end{cases}$$

Thus, the encryption keys are:

$$(M; \alpha; \Re) = \left(8; \sqrt{5}; \sqrt{6}, \sqrt{51}, \sqrt{43}, 30, 38/3, \sqrt{19}, 11, \sqrt{62}\right)$$

The original image and the encrypted image are shown in Figure 3a,b, respectively.

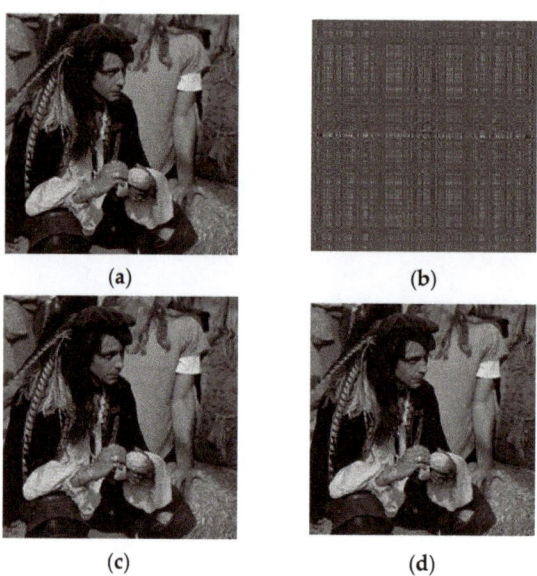

Figure 3. Image encryption based on m-MPFRFT: (**a**) original image, (**b**) encrypted image, (**c**) decrypted image with correct keys, and (**d**) decrypted image with wrong keys.

The correct decryption keys are:

$$(M; -\alpha; \Re) = \left(8; -\sqrt{5}; \sqrt{6}, \sqrt{51}, \sqrt{43}, 30, 38/3, \sqrt{19}, 11, \sqrt{62}\right)$$

The decrypted image is shown in Figure 3c.

According to our analysis, the vector parameters (r_4, r_5, r_6, r_7) are invalid. Therefore, when we use the wrong decryption keys as follows:

$$(M; -\alpha; \Re) = \left(8; -\sqrt{5}; \sqrt{6}, \sqrt{51}, \sqrt{43}, 30, 45, \sqrt{38}, \sqrt{3}, 91\right)$$

we obtain the decrypted image shown in Figure 3d, and the original image can still be recovered intact.

The keys for an image encryption method based on VPMPFRFT are $(M, \bar{\alpha}, \Re)$, where M is a positive integer, $\bar{\alpha}$ and $\Re$ are vector parameters, $\bar{\alpha} = (\alpha_0, \alpha_1, \cdots, \alpha_{M-1}) \in \mathbb{R}^M$, and $\Re = (r_0, r_1, \cdots, r_{M-1}) \in \mathbb{R}^M$. In the numerical simulation, we take the keys as:

$$\begin{cases} M = 9 \\ \bar{\alpha} = (\alpha_0, \alpha_1, \alpha_2, \alpha_3, \alpha_4, \alpha_5, \alpha_6, \alpha_7, \alpha_8) = \left(\sqrt{6}, 17, \sqrt{19}, 30, 41/3, \sqrt{52}, 63, \sqrt{65}, 76\right) \\ \Re = (r_0, r_1, r_2, r_3, r_4, r_5, r_6, r_7, r_8) = \left(37/2, \sqrt{48}, \sqrt{59}, 70/3, 81, \sqrt{2}, 13/3, 24, \sqrt{35}\right) \end{cases}$$

Thus, the encryption keys are:

$$(M; \bar{\alpha}; \Re) = \left(9; \sqrt{6}, 17, \sqrt{19}, 30, 41/3, \sqrt{52}, 63, \sqrt{65}, 76; 37/2, \sqrt{48}, \sqrt{59}, 70/3, 81, \sqrt{2}, 13/3, 24, \sqrt{35}\right)$$

The original image is shown in Figure 4a, and Figure 4b shows the encrypted image.

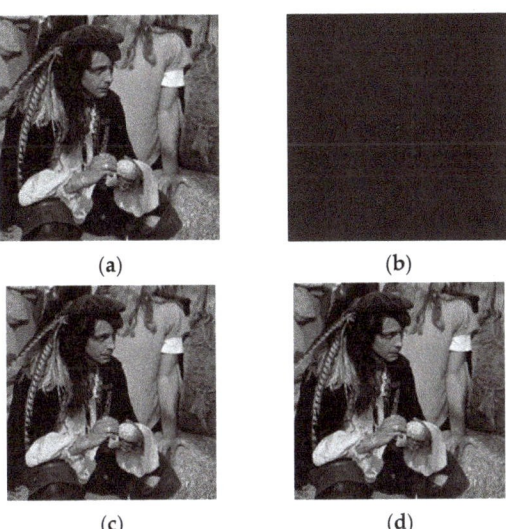

Figure 4. Image encryption based on VPMPFRFT: (**a**) original image, (**b**) encrypted image, (**c**) decrypted image with correct keys, and (**d**) decrypted image with wrong keys.

The correct decryption keys are:

$$(M; -\overline{\alpha}, \Re) = \left(9; -\sqrt{6}, -17, -\sqrt{19}, -30, -41/3, -\sqrt{52}, -63, -\sqrt{65}, -76; \right.$$
$$\left. 37/2, \sqrt{48}, \sqrt{59}, 70/3, 81, \sqrt{2}, 13/3, 24, \sqrt{35}\right)$$

The decrypted image is shown in Figure 4c.

According to our analysis, the vector parameter keys $(\alpha_4, \alpha_5, \alpha_6, \alpha_7, \alpha_8)$ and $(r_4, r_5, r_6, r_7, r_8)$ are invalid. Therefore, when we use the following wrong decryption keys:

$$(M; -\overline{\alpha}, \Re) = \left(9; -\sqrt{6}, -17, -\sqrt{19}, -30, -3, -\sqrt{5}, -\sqrt{6}, -19, -\sqrt{7}; \right.$$
$$\left. 37/2, \sqrt{48}, \sqrt{59}, 70/3, \sqrt{8}, \sqrt{73}, 9, 56, \sqrt{58}\right)$$

we obtain the decrypted image shown in Figure 4d, and the original image can still be recovered intact.

Both the image encryption method based on MPFRFT and the improved image encryption methods (m-MPFRFT, VPMPFRFT) have the security risk of key invalidation. The fundamental reason for this is caused by the period of the basis function. Since the basis function has a period of 4, there are only 4 valid weighting terms for the definitions (MPFRFT, m-MPFRFT, and VPMPFRFT). In practical application, the first parameter key is also invalid due to $B_k^\alpha(k=0)$.

6. Conclusions

MPFRFT is widely used in information security, and its security mainly depends on parameter keys. However, our study found that many parameter keys are invalid. The MPFRFT is a generalized definition of the WFRFT. Its basis function is extended from the Fourier transform with period 4 to period M ($M > 4$). Our theoretical analysis shows that the weighted terms of the MPFRFT do not increase with the increase of the period, and there are only four weighted terms. Therefore, the keys of the system are limited, and the proponent cannot obtain a larger key space with the increase of the period. In this way, the security of the MPFRFT cannot be guaranteed. Moreover, we analyzed the generalized definitions (m-MPFRFT and VPMPFRFT) of MPFRFT and proposed the reformulation of the definitions, which also have the security risk of key invalidation. Finally, numerical simulation verified our point of view.

Author Contributions: Methodology, T.Z.; software, T.Z.; validation, T.Z. and Y.C.; investigation, Y.C.; writing—original draft preparation, T.Z.; writing—review and editing, T.Z.; supervision, T.Z.; funding acquisition, T.Z. All authors have read and agreed to the published version of the manuscript.

Funding: This study was supported by the Fundamental Research Funds for the Central Universities (N2123016), and the Scientific Research Projects of Hebei colleges and universities (QN2020511).

Institutional Review Board Statement: Not applicable.

Informed Consent Statement: Not applicable.

Data Availability Statement: Not applicable.

Acknowledgments: The authors would like to express our great appreciation to the editor and reviewers.

Conflicts of Interest: The authors declare no conflict of interest.

Appendix A

Algorithm A1. MPFRFT_code

```
%% Multiple-parameter Fractional Fourier Transform (MPFRFT);
%Shih's fractional Fourier transform as basis function.
function F = MPFRFT(alpha,M,ml,nl,N)
%This code is written by Tieyu Zhao,E-mail:zhaotieyu@neuq.edu.cn;
% alpha is the transform order;
% M is the resulting weighting term (period);
% ml and nl are parameters;
% N is the length of the signal;
for l=0:M-1
yy=wfrft(N,4*l/M); % WFRFT
y{l+1}=yy;
end
Al=zeros(1,M);
for l=0:M-1
for k=0:M-1
Al(l+1)=Al(l+1)+exp(2*pi*i*((alpha*(M*ml(k+1)+1)*(M*nl(k+1)+k))-l*k)/M)/M;
end
end
F=zeros(N);
for k=1:M
F=F+Al(k)*y{k};
end

function F = wfrft(N,beta)
% Shih's fractional Fourier transform (WFRFT)
Y=eye(N);
y1=fftshift(fft(Y))/(sqrt(N));
y2=y1*y1;
y3=conj(y1);
pl=zeros(1,4);
for k=0:3
pl(k+1)=pl(k+1)+exp(i*3*pi*(beta-k)/4)*cos(pi*(beta-k)/2)*cos(pi*(beta-k)/4);
end
F=pl(1)*Y+pl(2)*y1+pl(3)*y2+pl(4)*y3;
```

References

1. Chen, W.; Javidi, B.; Chen, X. Advances in optical security systems. *Adv. Opt. Photon* **2014**, *6*, 120–155. [CrossRef]
2. Javidi, B.; Carnicer, A.; Yamaguchi, M.; Nomura, T.; Cabre, E.P.; Millan, M.; Nishchal, N.K.; Torroba, R.; Barrera, J.F.; He, W.; et al. Roadmap on optical security. *J. Opt.* **2016**, *18*, 083001. [CrossRef]
3. Tao, R.; Lang, J.; Wang, Y. Optical image encryption based on the multiple-parameter fractional Fourier transform. *Opt. Lett.* **2008**, *33*, 581–583. [CrossRef]
4. Shan, M.; Chang, J.; Zhong, Z.; Hao, B. Double image encryption based on discrete multiple-parameter fractional Fourier transform and chaotic maps. *Opt. Commun.* **2012**, *285*, 4227–4234. [CrossRef]
5. Lang, J. Image encryption based on the reality-preserving multiple-parameter fractional Fourier transform and chaos permutation. *Opt. Lasers Eng.* **2012**, *50*, 929–937. [CrossRef]
6. Lang, J. Color image encryption based on color blend and chaos permutation in the reality-preserving multiple-parameter fractional Fourier transform domain. *Opt. Commun.* **2015**, *338*, 181–192. [CrossRef]
7. Sui, L.; Duan, K.; Liang, J. Double-image encryption based on discrete multiple-parameter fractional angular transform and two-coupled logistic maps. *Opt. Commun.* **2015**, *343*, 140–149. [CrossRef]
8. Keshari, S.; Salim, M.; Modani, S.G. Single channel modified multiple-parameter fractional Fourier transform and scrambling technique. *Optik* **2015**, *126*, 5845–5849. [CrossRef]
9. Li, H.; Bai, X.; Shan, M.; Zhong, Z.; Liu, L.; Liu, B. Optical encryption of hyperspectral images using improved binary tree structure and phase-truncated discrete multiple-parameter fractional Fourier transform. *J. Opt.* **2020**, *22*, 055701. [CrossRef]
10. Ran, Q.W.; Zhang, H.Y.; Zhang, J.; Tan, L.Y.; Ma, J. Deficiencies of the cryptography based on multiple-parameter fractional Fourier transform. *Opt. Lett.* **2009**, *34*, 1729–1731. [CrossRef]
11. Zhao, T.; Ran, Q. The Weighted Fractional Fourier Transform and Its Application in Image Encryption. *Math. Probl. Eng.* **2019**, *2019*, 4789194. [CrossRef]
12. Zhou, N.; Dong, T.; Wu, J. Novel image encryption algorithm based on multiple-parameter discrete fractional random transform. *Opt. Commun.* **2010**, *283*, 3037–3042. [CrossRef]
13. Lang, J. Image encryption based on the reality-preserving multiple-parameter fractional Fourier transform. *Opt. Commun.* **2012**, *285*, 2584–2590. [CrossRef]
14. Lang, J. A no-key-exchange secure image sharing scheme based on Shamir's three-pass cryptography protocol and the multiple-parameter fractional Fourier transform. *Opt. Express* **2012**, *20*, 2386–2398. [CrossRef]
15. Ran, Q.; Zhao, T.; Yuan, L.; Wang, J.; Xu, L. Vector power multiple-parameter fractional Fourier transform of image encryption algorithm. *Opt. Lasers Eng.* **2014**, *62*, 80–86. [CrossRef]
16. Zhao, T.; Ran, Q.; Yuan, L.; Chi, Y.; Ma, J. Security of image encryption scheme based on multi-parameter fractional Fourier transform. *Opt. Commun.* **2016**, *376*, 47–51. [CrossRef]
17. Kang, X.; Tao, R.; Zhang, F. Multiple-Parameter Discrete Fractional Transform and its Applications. *IEEE Trans. Signal Process.* **2016**, *64*, 3402–3417. [CrossRef]
18. Chen, B.; Yu, M.; Tian, Y.; Li, L.; Wang, D.; Sun, X. Multiple-parameter fractional quaternion Fourier transform and its application in colour image encryption. *IET Image Process.* **2018**, *12*, 2238–2249. [CrossRef]
19. Zhu, B.; Liu, S.; Ran, Q. Optical image encryption based on multifractional Fourier transforms. *Opt. Lett.* **2000**, *25*, 1159–1161. [CrossRef]
20. Zhu, B.; Liu, S. Optical image encryption based on the generalized fractional convolution operation. *Opt. Commun.* **2001**, *195*, 371–381. [CrossRef]
21. Shih, C.C. Fractionalization of Fourier-Transform. *Opt. Commun.* **1995**, *118*, 495–498. [CrossRef]
22. Candan, C.; Kutay, M.A.; Ozaktas, H.M. The discrete fractional Fourier transform. *IEEE Trans. Signal Process.* **2000**, *48*, 1329–1337. [CrossRef]
23. McClellan, J.; Parks, T. Eigenvalue and eigenvector decomposition of the discrete Fourier transform. *IEEE Trans. Audio Electroacoust.* **1972**, *20*, 66–74. [CrossRef]
24. Dickinson, B.; Steiglitz, K. Eigenvectors and functions of the discrete Fourier transform. *IEEE Trans. Acoust. Speech Signal Process.* **1982**, *30*, 25–31. [CrossRef]

MDPI AG
Grosspeteranlage 5
4052 Basel
Switzerland
Tel.: +41 61 683 77 34

Symmetry Editorial Office
E-mail: symmetry@mdpi.com
www.mdpi.com/journal/symmetry

Disclaimer/Publisher's Note: The title and front matter of this reprint are at the discretion of the . The publisher is not responsible for their content or any associated concerns. The statements, opinions and data contained in all individual articles are solely those of the individual Editors and contributors and not of MDPI. MDPI disclaims responsibility for any injury to people or property resulting from any ideas, methods, instructions or products referred to in the content.

www.ingramcontent.com/pod-product-compliance
Lightning Source LLC
LaVergne TN
LVHW070736100526
838202LV00013B/1245